THE GREAT TRADITION OF HOPI KATSINA CARVERS

1880 TO PRESENT

BARRY WALSH

PRIMARY PHOTOGRAPHER
ANNA KIM WALSH

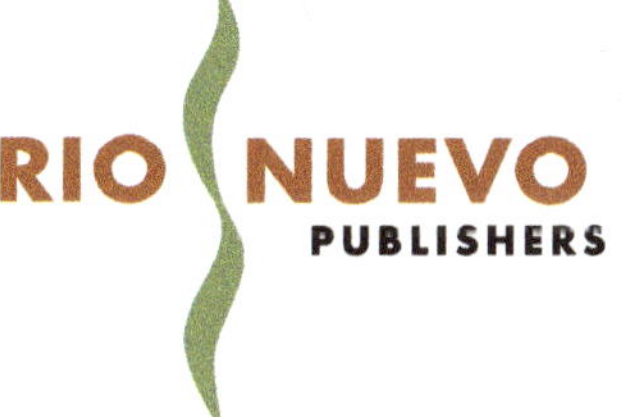

Rio Nuevo Publishers®
P. O. Box 5250
Tucson, AZ 85703-0250
(520) 623-9558, www.rionuevo.com

Managing Editor: Aaron Downey
Book Design: David Jenney Design

10 9 8 7 6 5 4 3 2 1

Library of Congress Cataloging-in-Publication Data

Names: Walsh, Barent W., author. | Walsh, Anna Kim, photographer.
Title: The great tradition of Hopi katsina carvers : 1880 to the present / by Barry Walsh, PhD ; photography by Anna Kim Walsh.
Description: Tucson : Rio Nuevo Publishers, [2018] | Includes bibliographical references.
Identifiers: LCCN 2018042261| ISBN 9781940322353 (pbk.) | ISBN 1940322359 (pbk.)
Subjects: LCSH: Hopi wood-carvers—Biography. | Hopi wood-carving—History. | Kachinas—History. | LCGFT: Biographies.
Classification: LCC E99.H7 W28 2018 | DDC 745.592/21089974—dc23
LC record available at https://lccn.loc.gov/2018042261

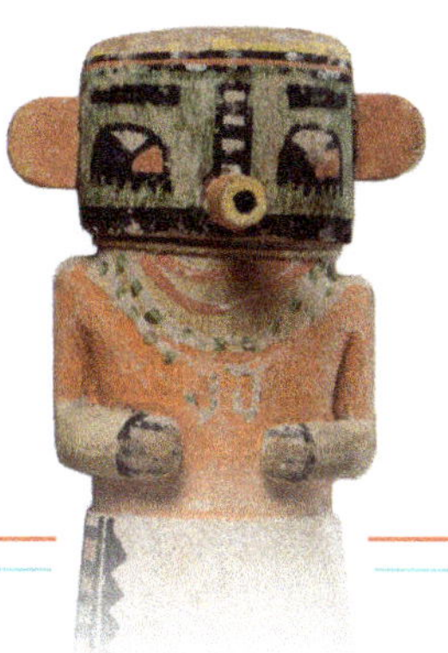

To

Mom and Dad

and

All Who Went Before

Anna and Ben

Valerie

Declan and Ariel

All the Dogs . . .

Goldfinches, Cedar Waxwings,

and

Red-Tailed Hawks

To Every Hopi Carver

CONTENTS

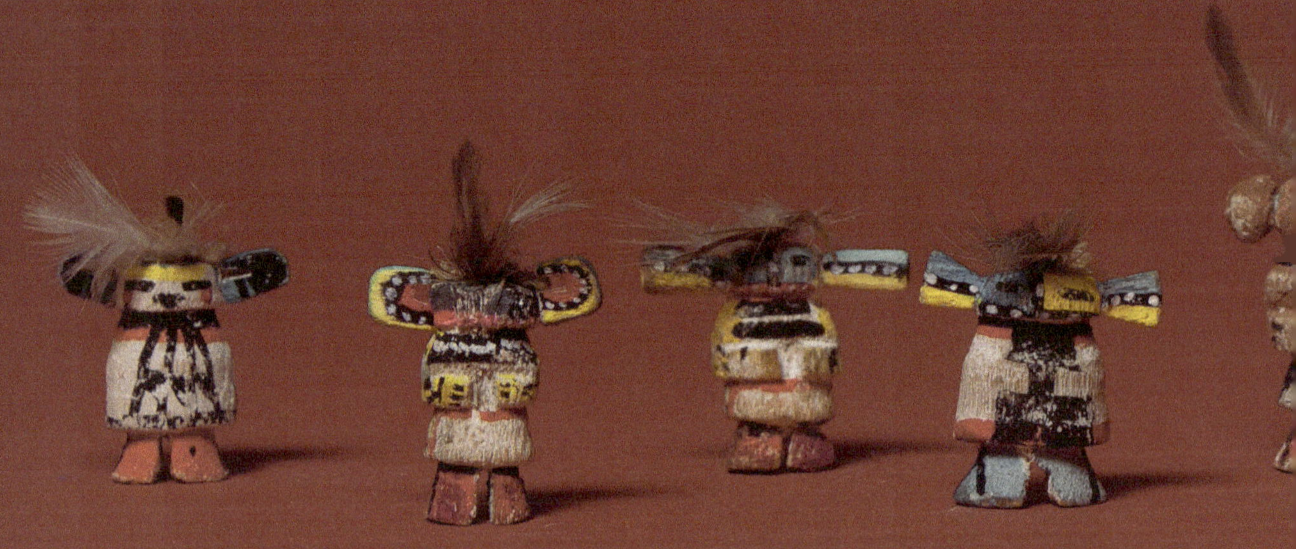

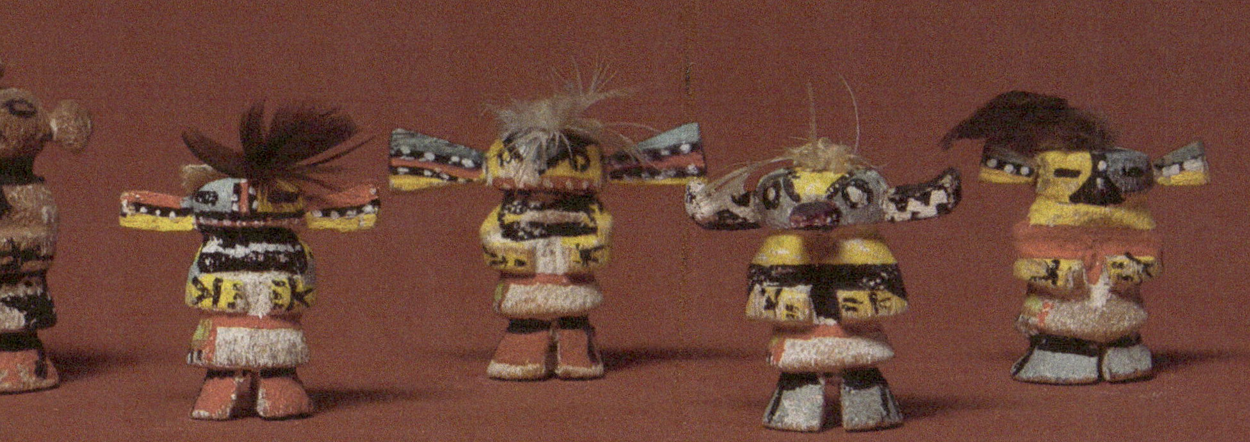

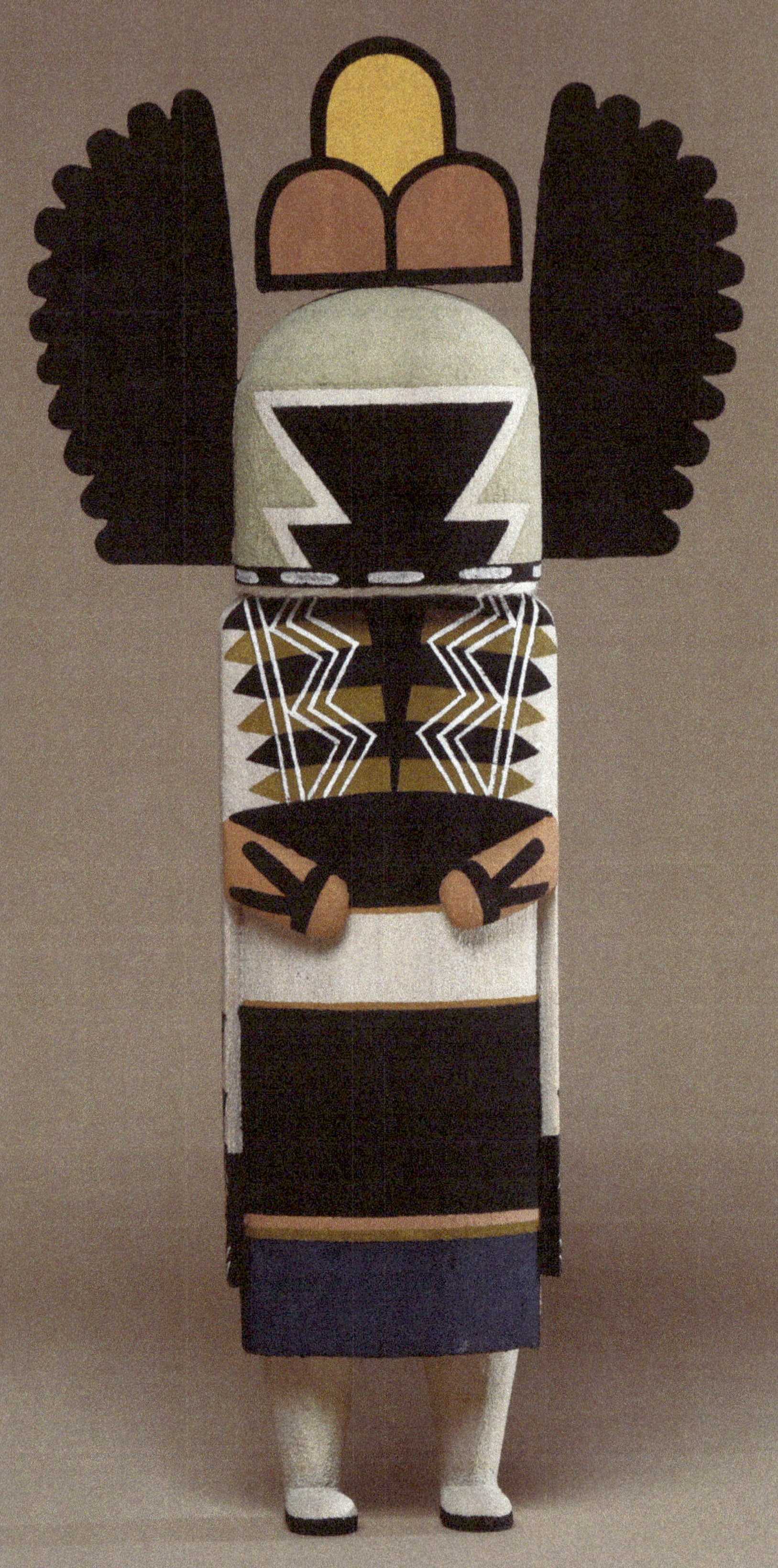

INTRODUCTION

"Art is a wonderful world, but a hard and cruel life."
—Clark Tenakhongva

Let me begin with a note on the Hopi language used in this book. All Hopi spellings come from the *Hopi Dictionary* (1998) with recent assistance from local Hopi consultants using the standard Hopi orthography. I have striven for maximum accuracy and currency in using Hopi words for the katsina figures, village names, and other details in this book.

In the language of the Hopi Indians of North Central Arizona, the word *katsina* has three distinct but inter-related meanings. First are the *Katsina* spirits, the ineffable beings who support, sponsor, and sometimes chastise the Hopi people (and all humankind). These generally benevolent spirit beings are said to visit Hopiland from January through July each year, bringing with them blessings, fertility, life-giving rain, good health, long life, and other forms of sponsorship. For the remainder of each year, they reside at Nuvatukya'ovi, also called the San Francisco Peaks near Flagstaff, Arizona.

The second meaning of *Katsinam* (plural) is that of "dancers"—perhaps better referred to as participants in the sacred ceremonies of the Katsina religion. These Katsina rituals occur during the cold winter months in the underground kivas and as the weather warms in the outdoor plazas on the reservation. The Katsina participants are sacred figures who embody, personify, and represent the ineffable Katsina spirits of the first meaning.

The third connotation of *katsina* is the subject of this book. This meaning refers to wood carvings. In the Hopi language, the terms are *katsintihu* (singular) and *katsintithu* (plural). These carvings are intended to embody and represent the Katsina "dancers" in wood. Thus, it is a three-tiered system of language regarding the word *Katsina*:

- The ineffable, sponsoring Katsina Spirit Beings
- The Katsina dancers who embody, personify, and represent the Spirit Beings at Hopi ceremonies
- The katsina wood carvings that represent the Katsina dancers or participants

Please note that in this book, I use the capitalized "Katsina" to refer to the first two meanings and the lower case "katsina" to refer to the wood carvings. As noted by Hopi artist, musician, lecturer, and writer, Alph Secakuku,

> We do not perceive the katsina dolls simply as carved figurines or bright decorated objects. They have important meaning to us, the Hopi people. We believe they are personifications of the katsina spirits, originally created by the spirits in their physical embodiment. (Secakuku 1995, 4)

Although writing about katsintithu inevitably involves some reference to the Katsina religion, this book is about *human beings*, not *spirit beings*. This work focuses on the great tradition of Hopi katsina carvers. I will not refer to Hopi Katsina religion at any length. Hopi friends have trained me to view Hopi ceremonies and religion from a respectful distance. Describing the lives and artistry of katsina carvers requires less distance. Accordingly, this book attempts to review some of the major carvers from 1880 to the present.

The format of this book is simple: katsina carvers are discussed in chronological order. For each carver, I provide a biography and photographs of his work. These biographical sketches are based on my interviews with the carvers themselves or in the case of deceased artists, with information from surviving family members, friends, or previous publications known to be reliable. I shared my notes and transcriptions of all interviews with the carvers and their families. They provided feedback, made corrections, and approved final versions. Some people declined to participate. The artists and family members were in control.

Most early makers of katsinam (1880–1920) are unnamed and unidentifiable; carving styles will be reviewed for these important artists. From the 1920s onward, the work of several katsina makers can be attributed by name. These seminal figures will receive considerable emphasis. They include Wilson Tawaquaptewa, Otto Pentewa, Jimmie Kewanwytewa, and James Kootshongsie.

Jimmie Kewanwytewa, better known as Jimmie K, was the first to place his initials on his carvings starting in the 1940s. Following his lead, more and more artists began signing their work. As a result, identifying the work of specific artists since that decade is often not difficult.

Any time one attempts a compendium of "great" artists, the topic of criteria must be addressed. How does one justify referring to one artist as great while excluding another? My goal in this book is to be *representative rather than all-inclusive*. No pretense is made that I am providing an exhaustive and definitive list of "the best" carvers. To develop the list of artists employed here I have solicited suggestions and feedback from knowledgeable Hopi friends, academic scholars, art dealers, gallery owners, serious collectors, and most important, from Hopi carvers themselves. All these people helped greatly in developing the following criteria for selection. In this book, I have selected:

- Carvers who represent some of the *finest* work across the major eras of Hopi katsina carving, from 1880 to the present
- Artists whose work is unique, *distinctive*, and easily identifiable without needing to refer to artists' signatures or hallmarks
- Artists whose work has been *innovative* as to carving style, subject matter, mood, use of wood, paints, body postures, details, and accoutrements

In short, the goal has been to feature those who have created the finest, most distinctive, and innovative work across the decades.

If you are a relative who is pleased to have your loved one recognized posthumously in this book, I am honored to be part of that process. If you are an artist who was willing to be included, I am grateful to have gotten to know you and include your work. If on the other hand, you are a carver not featured, I assure you I meant no harm. I hope I will be able to recognize your artistry in some other forum down the line.

Barry Walsh
January, 2019

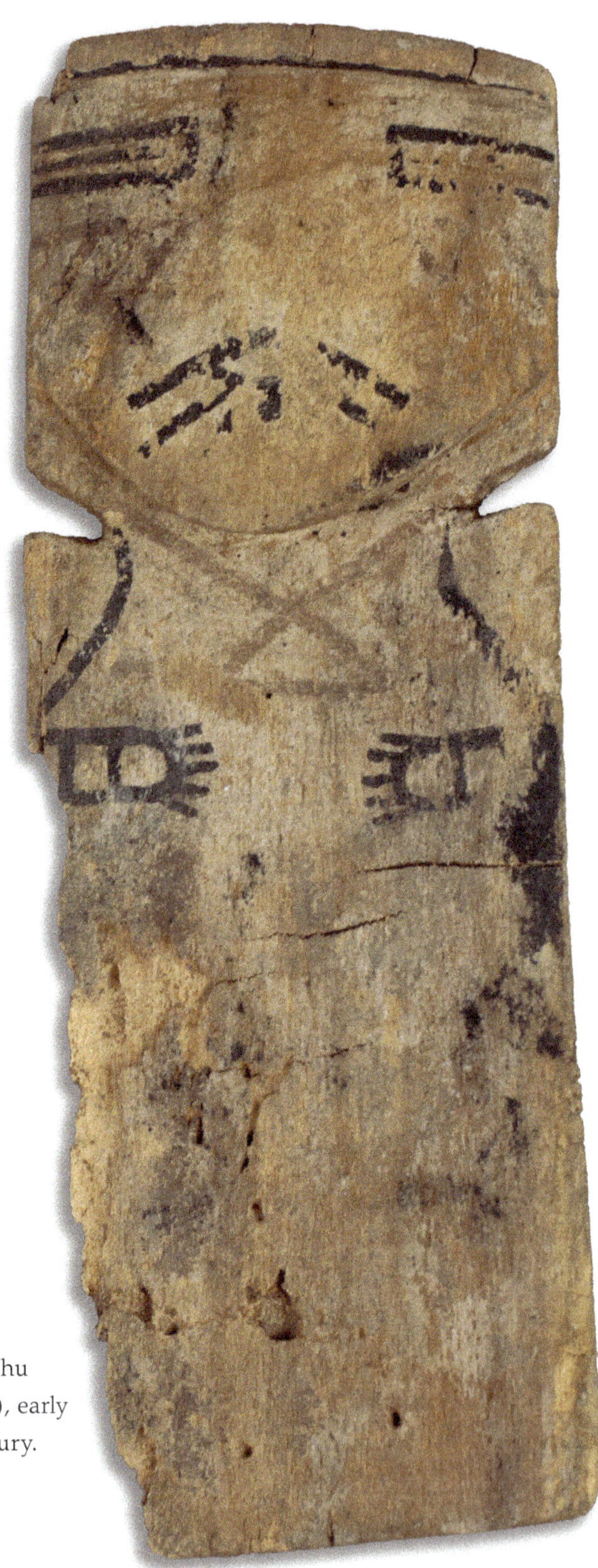

Figure 1.
FIRST PHASE.
Sa'lako Putsqatihu (Cradle Katsina), early nineteenth century.

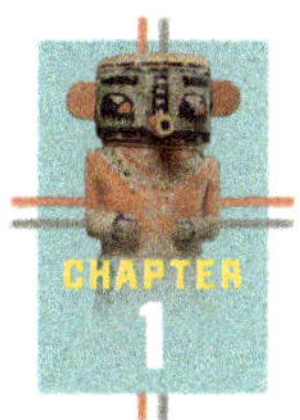

EARLY KATSINA CARVINGS

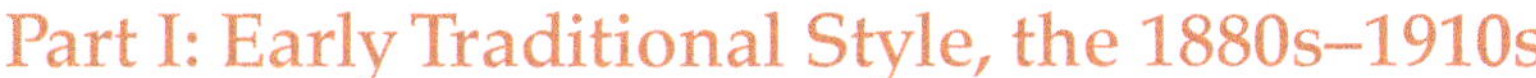

Part I: Early Traditional Style, the 1880s–1910s

While Katsina prototypes have been identified on prehistoric petroglyphs, pictographs, pottery, and kiva walls, the earliest examples of katsina wood carvings date to the nineteenth century. Not surprisingly, Hopi insiders and Anglo outsiders have described the development and evolution of the katsina *tihu* differently. (Note: *tihu* is singular; *tithu* is plural).

The first meaning in the *Hopi Dictionary* for the word "tihu" is "child, son, daughter, offspring," and the second is "katsina doll" (1998, 591). Thus, the relationship between the cottonwood tihu and Hopi children is inextricably linked, both linguistically and culturally. More specifically, the cottonwood carvings given out by the Katsinam at ceremonies are said to be their children (Sekaquaptewa in Teiwes 1991). Adding to the multiplicity of meanings is that these "children" are given to Hopi children. Children to children.

Emory Sekaquaptewa (1928–2007), a noted Hopi scholar and cultural editor for *Hopi Dictionary Project*, described four historical forms of tithu that represent four phases of development (Teiwes 1991, 38–40). These are:

- *putsqatihu*: The earliest phase, usually given to both male and female newborns. These are flat "cradle katsinam" (usually Hahay'iwuuti, the female katsina who represents the ideal characteristics of womanhood) that are essentially thin, rectangular boards with painted faces, slight vestiges of arms and hands, and three red stripes painted beneath the head. For examples of this simplest of forms, see Figures 1 and 2.
- *putstihu taywa'yta*: The second phase of development, given to Hopi female toddlers. This form is very similar to the previous phase, putsqatihu, except the face is raised and three-dimensional. An example of this type is shown in Figure 3.
- *muringputihu*: The third phase of development, given to young Hopi girls, around ages two to three. These are cylindrical carvings with an extended body and some suggestion of arms and feet. An example of this type is provided in Figure 4.

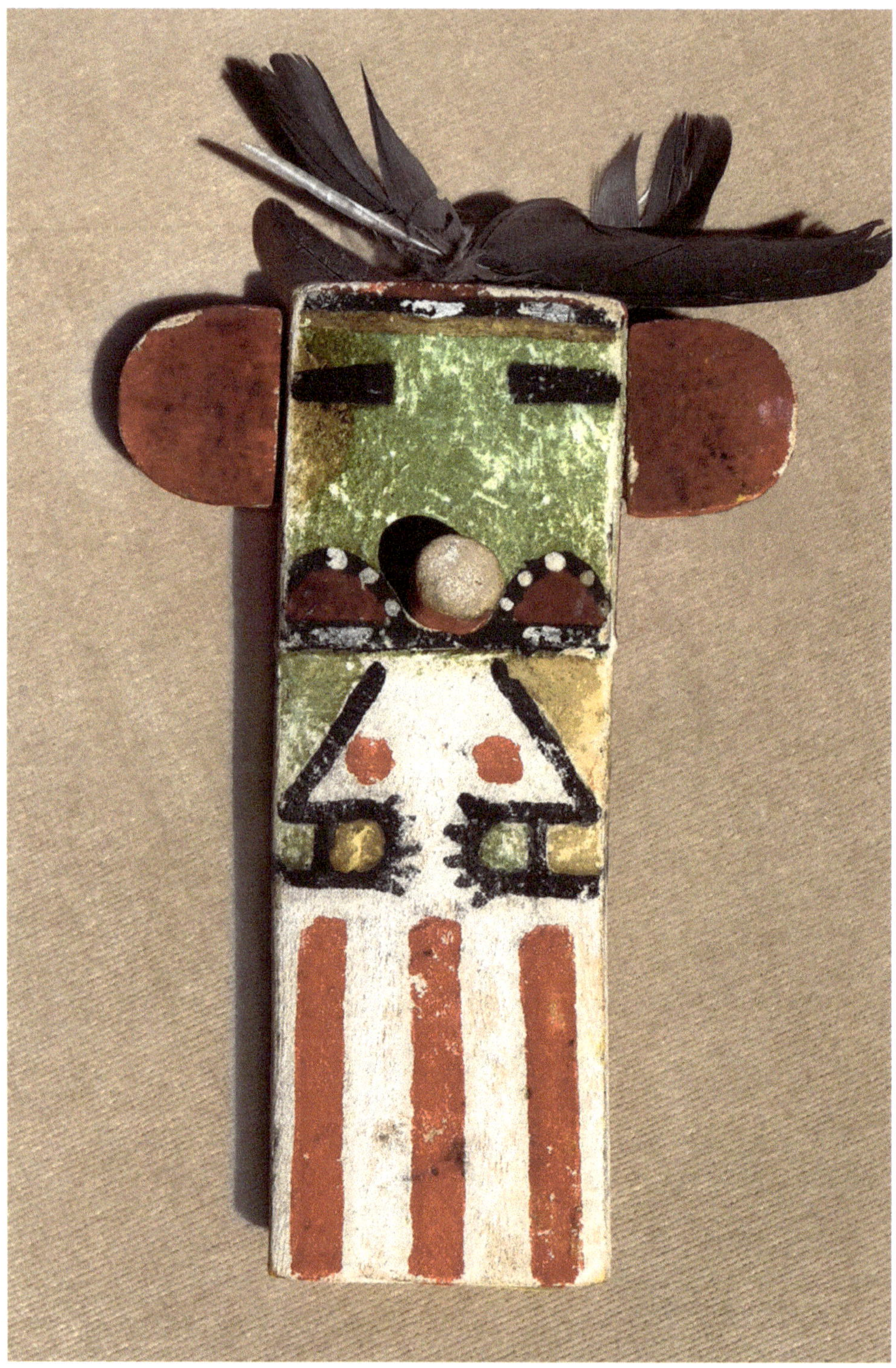

Figure 2. FIRST PHASE. Putsqatihu, 1890.

- *tihu*: The final phase in development, given to Hopi girls around the age of four and until they undergo their katsina initiation. This form is full-figured and has more elaborate details such as arms, feet, and some aspects of costume or accoutrements. Examples are provided in Figures 5 and 6. Most of the katsinam throughout this book are of this tihu type.

Anglo experts are fond of categorization and have proposed different phases or styles to describe the evolution of katsina carvings, 1850 to present. Erickson (1977) and Barton Wright (in Teiwes 1991) have presented similar but distinct versions. For example, Erickson organizes katsina-carving history by time periods, these being:

- Pre-1870
- 1870–1910
- 1910–1945
- 1945 to present (Erickson's book was published in 1977)

Wright (in Teiwes 1991), organized types by date and style consisting of:

- 1850–1910, Early Traditional
- 1910–1930, Late Traditional
- 1930–1945, Early Action
- 1945–Present, Late Action (Teiwes's book was published in 1991)

As one can see from above, the two authors selected somewhat differing time periods. I've chosen to follow Wright's schema with some modifications, including updating categories to the present era (2018 as of this writing). The general framework I will refer to in this book consists of:

- Category 1: 1880–1910: Early Traditional
- Category 2: 1910–Late 1920s: Late Traditional
- Category 3: 1930–Mid-1940s: Early Action
- Category 4: Mid-1940s–1960s: Late Action
- Category 5: Mid-1960s–Present: Ultra-Realistic
- Category 6: 1970s–Present: Traditional Style Revival or Traditional
- Category 7: Mid-1980s–Present: Sculptural

Let me say that I don't take these categories too seriously. They are meant only to be general guidelines and tools for summarizing trends. What matters are

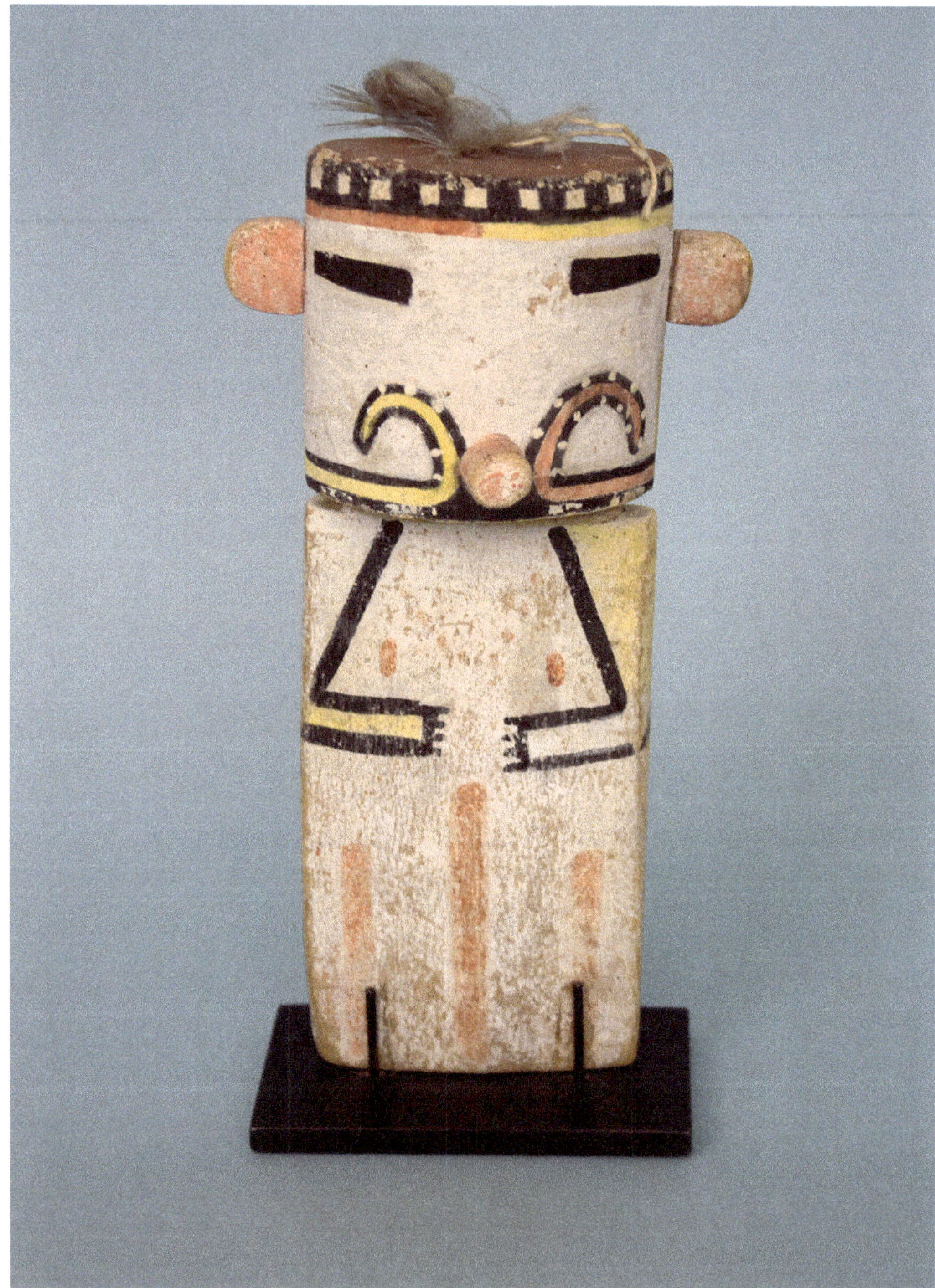

Figure 3. SECOND PHASE. Putstihu Taywa'yta. Morivosi (Bean).

the individual carvings themselves, not reductionist categories. Above all, these katsinam, regardless of period or style, represent Spirit Beings. Those that evoke the spiritual dimension of the figure portrayed are generally the most authentic, and the most effective, art.

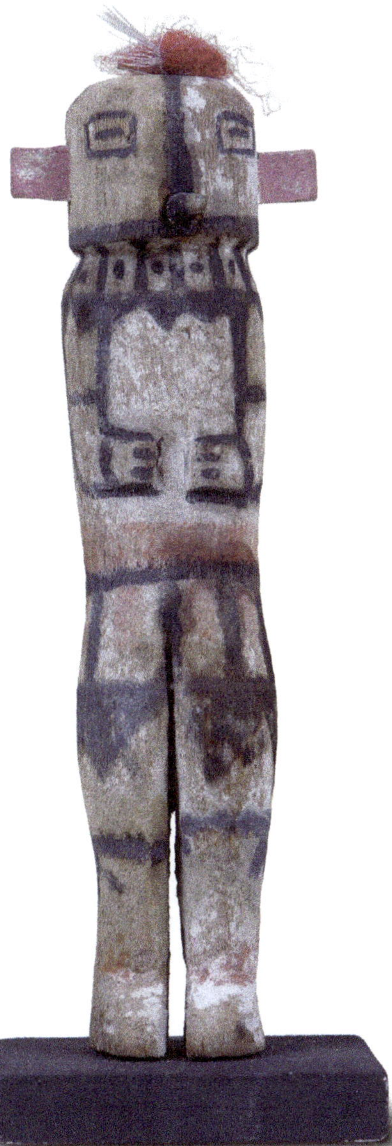

Figure 4. THIRD PHASE.
Muringputihu. Kookopölö.

Category 1: 1880–1910, Early Traditional

Katsina carvings prior to 1880 are hard to identify reliably. Museum records are spotty and dates for creation are often nonexistent. This section of the book provides several examples that can be dated with some reliability from 1880 to the 1910s.

An especially early example is the first to be discussed. Figure 1 is a Sa'lako putsqatihu (cradle katsina) from the collection of the Museum of Northern Arizona (MNA). Collection data indicate that this carving was found by Bernard Dawahoya as he was renovating his house in Songoopavi in the 1970s. His renovation involved breaking through a floor into a much earlier, sealed-off floor. The estimate at the time of the excavation was that the older floor goes back 100 to 150 or more years. While precise dating is not possible without scientific analysis, the MNA has dated this putsqatihu to the 1850s or earlier. Note that this example has the features of Sekaquaptewa's earliest form. It is a cradle katsina with a flat face. This is also true for the katsina in Figure 2.

Figure 3 shows a Morivosi (Bean) katsina, in what Sekaquaptewa calls the putstihu taywa'yta form. The only change stylistically is that the face is now raised above the simple, flat body. This carving appears to be from the nineteenth century as well. One common feature of nineteenth-century cradle katsinam is the splayed, spindly fingers shown in Figures 2 and 3.

Figure 4 is an example of Sekaquaptewa's muringputihu, or third phase form. The carving of a Kookopölö is now cylindrical, not flat, with arms and legs suggested but not fully painted or carved.

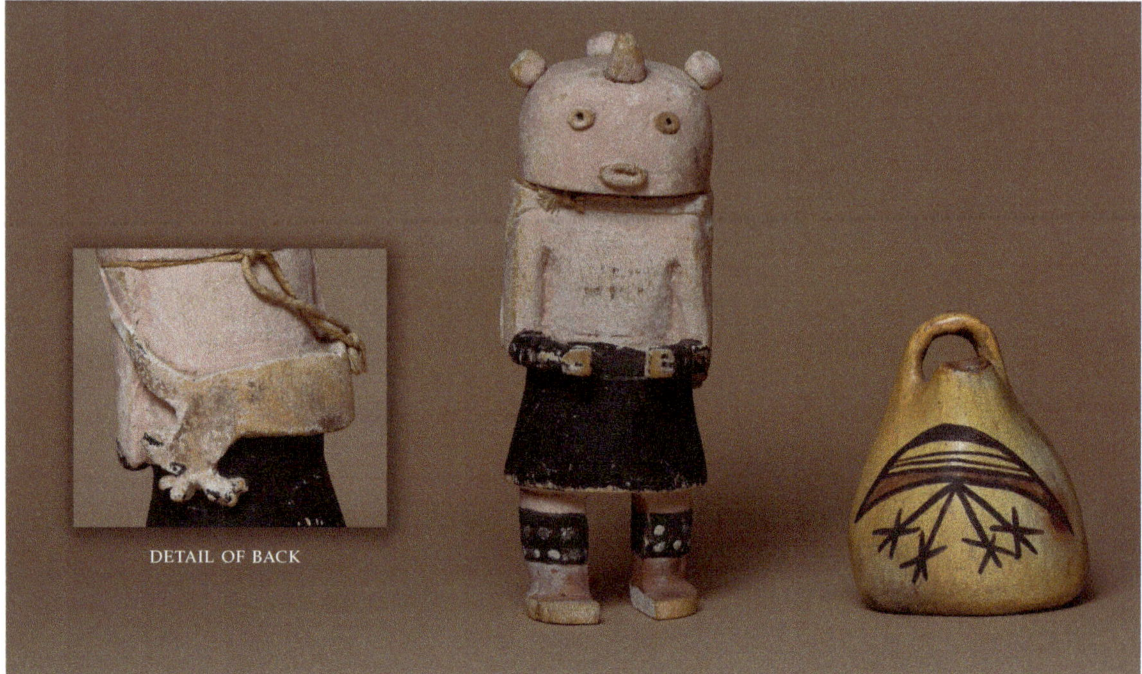

Figure 5. FOURTH PHASE. Tihu. Kooyemsi and canteen, 1890.

The simplicity of the carving and paint suggests nineteenth- or early twentieth-century origin.

Figures 5 and 6 are early examples of Sekaquaptewa's full-sized tihu, the fourth and final phase of development. The patina and simplicity of the Kooyemsi indicate nineteenth-century origin. Note the especially appealing detail of the deer carved in bas-relief on the back of the katsina. Figure 6 is another nineteenth-century example of a full-figured tihu. She is Angwusnasomtaqa or "the one with raven wings attached to the side of the head," commonly referred to as Crow Mother.

Another distinguishing characteristic as to nineteenth-century origin is the occasional presence of genitals. These features seem to have disappeared by about 1900, probably due to squeamishness from and condemnation by zealous Christian missionaries. One example of such genitalia is found in Figure 7, an exceptional Leenangwkatsina (Flute) katsina, with elaborate headdress. With this katsina, there is a bump suggesting a penis. See also, the stacked Kooyemsi and Hehey'a (no English translation) in Figure 8. The Hehey'a on the bottom has a very visible extended penis. Genitalia is generally good evidence of nineteenth-century origin on older carvings.

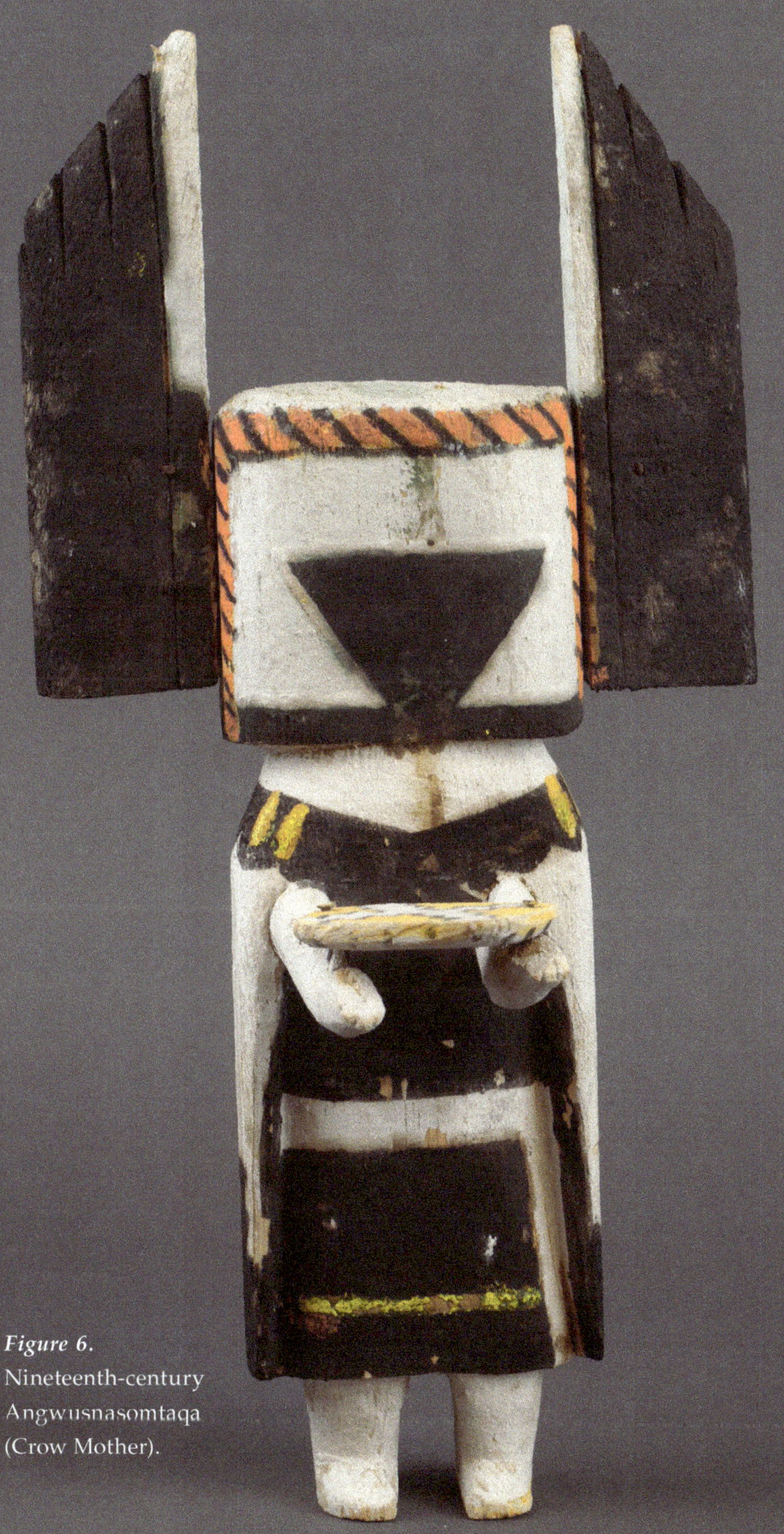

Figure 6.
Nineteenth-century
Angwusnasomtaqa
(Crow Mother).

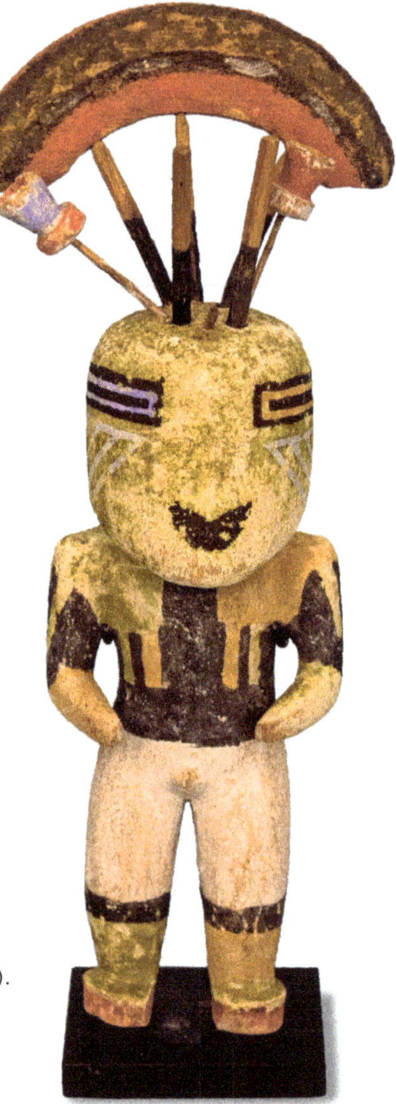

Figure 7.
Leenangwkatsina (Flute).

Speaking of stacked katsinam, these are quite rare and often suggestive of late nineteenth-century or early twentieth-century dating. Another example of such a carving is shown in Figure 9, with two Kooyemsis. This is probably from about 1910.

Another key detail as to dating early katsinam concerns paints. For those made in the nineteenth century, paints were almost exclusively mineral and vegetal from local Hopi sources. Erickson (1977) noted that most katsina carvings after 1910 had at least some commercial paints on them. He said the one exception was the continued use of copper carbonate because Hopi were not able to obtain satisfactory blue-green pigments commercially. Three examples of early katsinam

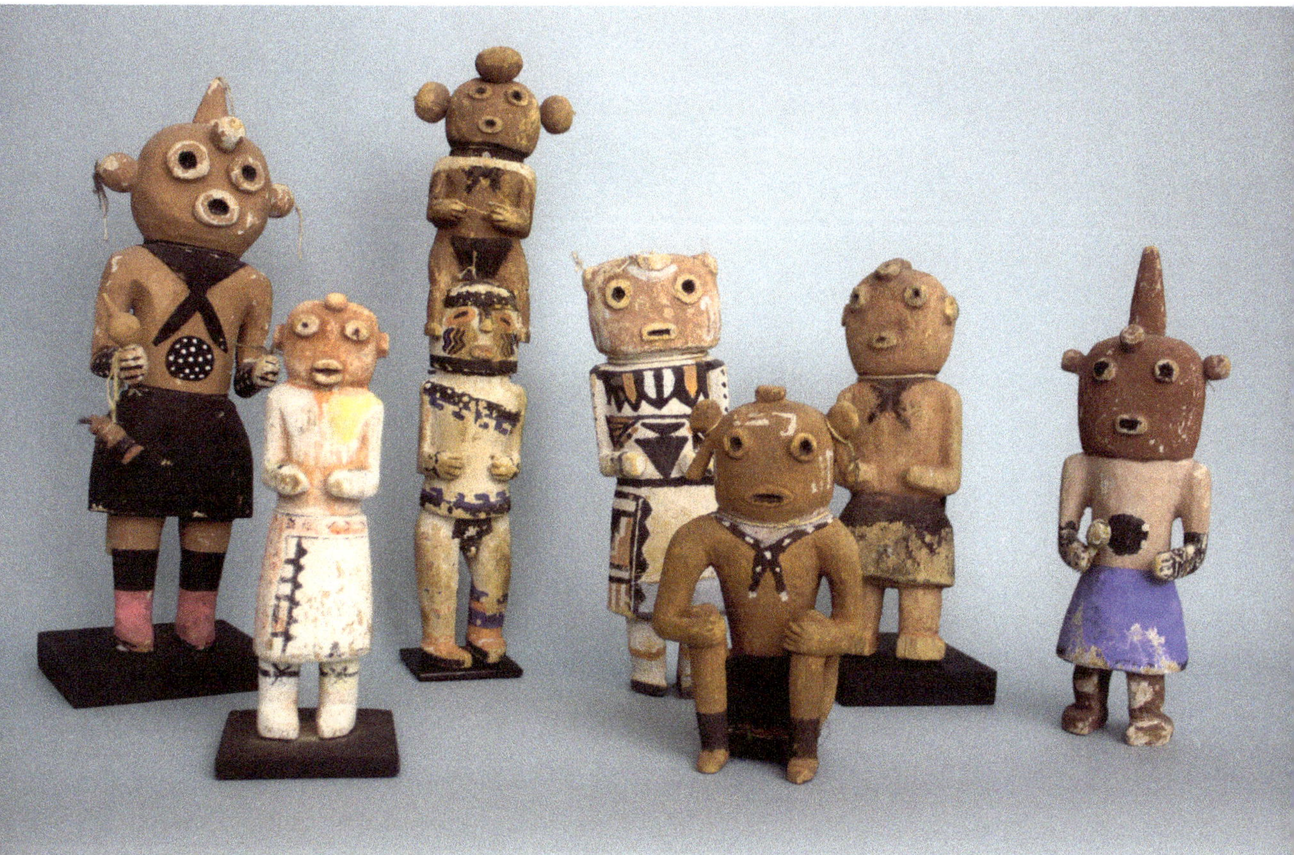

Figure 8. Diverse Kooyemsi, 1890–1920.

that show a preponderance of copper carbonate paint are Figures 2, 7, and 10. Copper carbonate starts out a vibrant blue-green and over time oxidizes to a darker olive or murky green color as shown on these three katsinam. Figure 10 is a minimally carved Tsöpkatsina (Pronghorn) katsina. The simple, cylindrical carving style and early paints again suggest nineteenth-century origin.

One aspect that I believe must be emphasized regarding nineteenth-century carvings is that *there were no rules*. Katsina carving had not fallen into predictable forms and shapes and was not yet heavily influenced by an outside Anglo market. Examples of the experimentation during the 1880s and 90s include a wide range in body types from static and simple (e.g., Figures 4 and 10) to dynamic and complex (Figure 7). The zany stacked katsinam (Figures 8 and 9) are two other examples of an unfettered creative spirit. Some katsinam from this era were oversized and elaborate. Others were simple and tiny. The period from 1880–1900 was a period of freedom and experimentation for carvers, which in some ways was about to change.

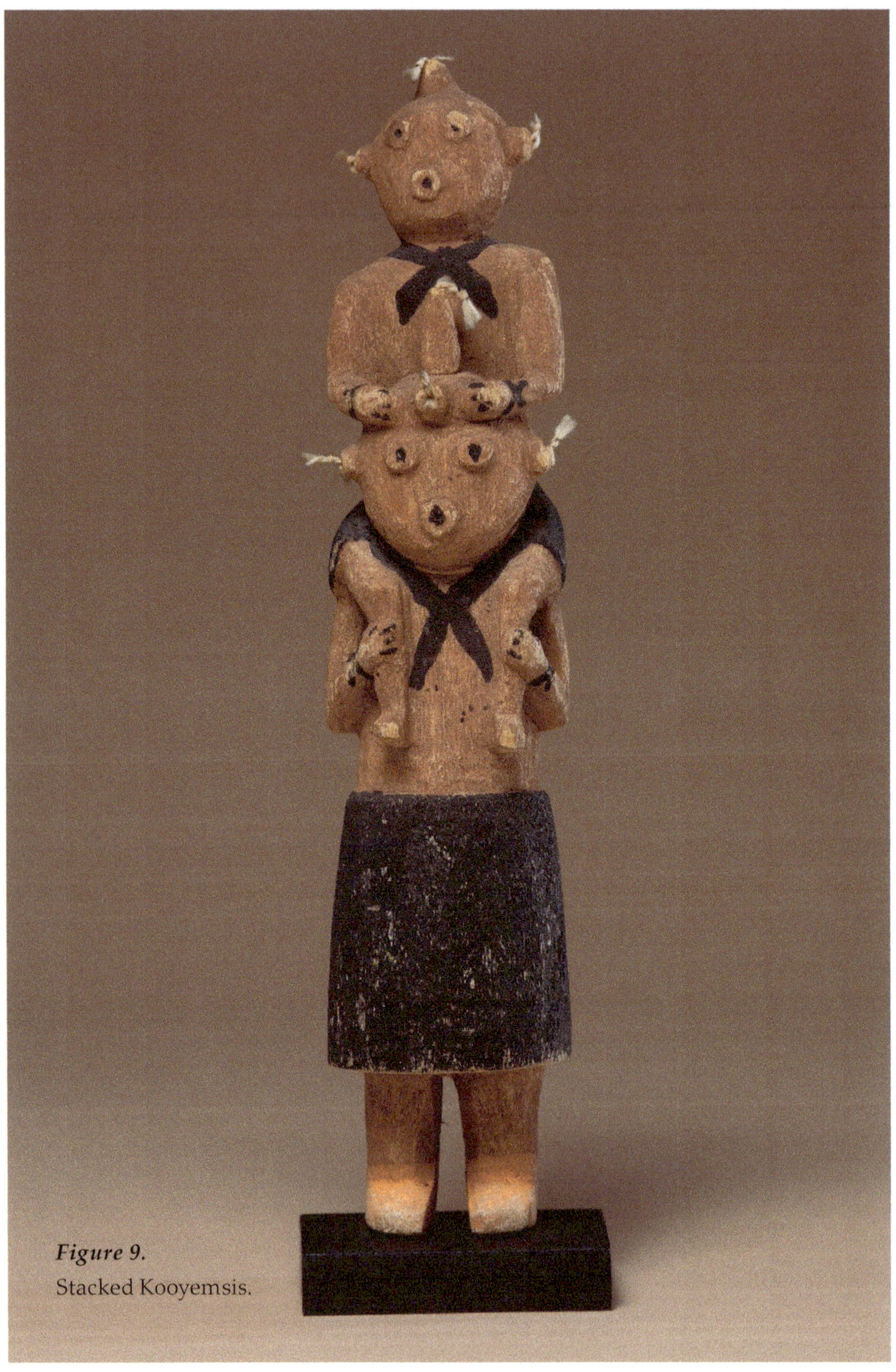

Figure 9.
Stacked Kooyemsis.

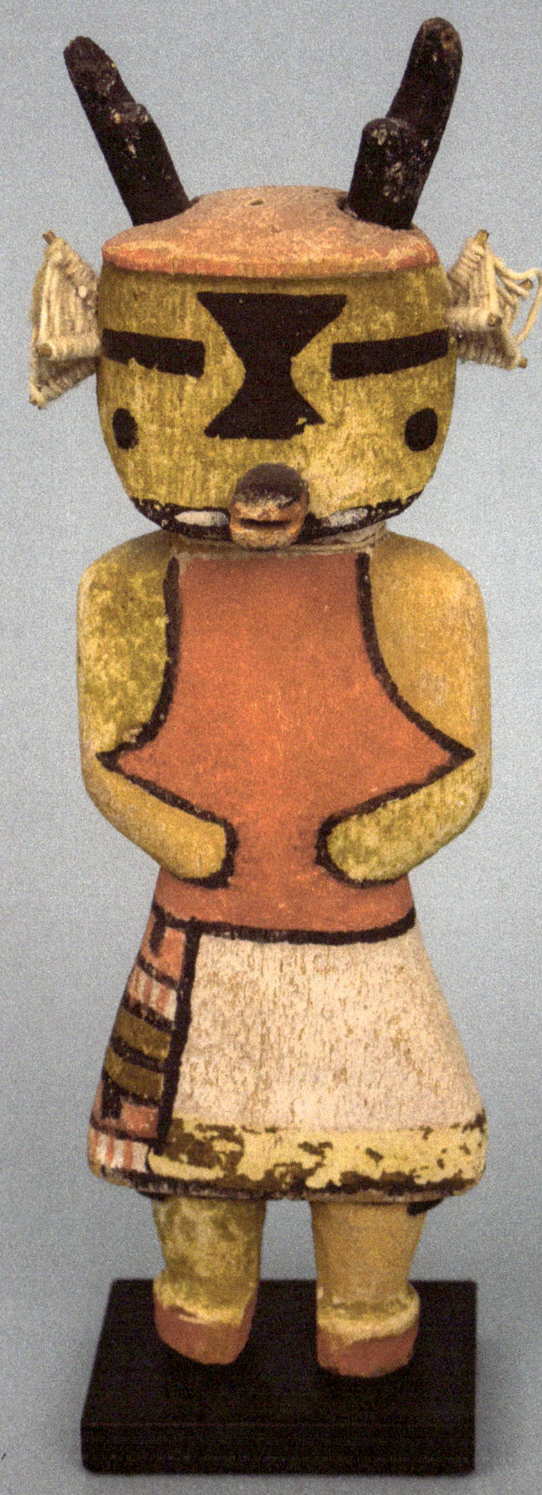

Figure 10.
Tsöpkatsina
(Pronghorn),
circa 1900.

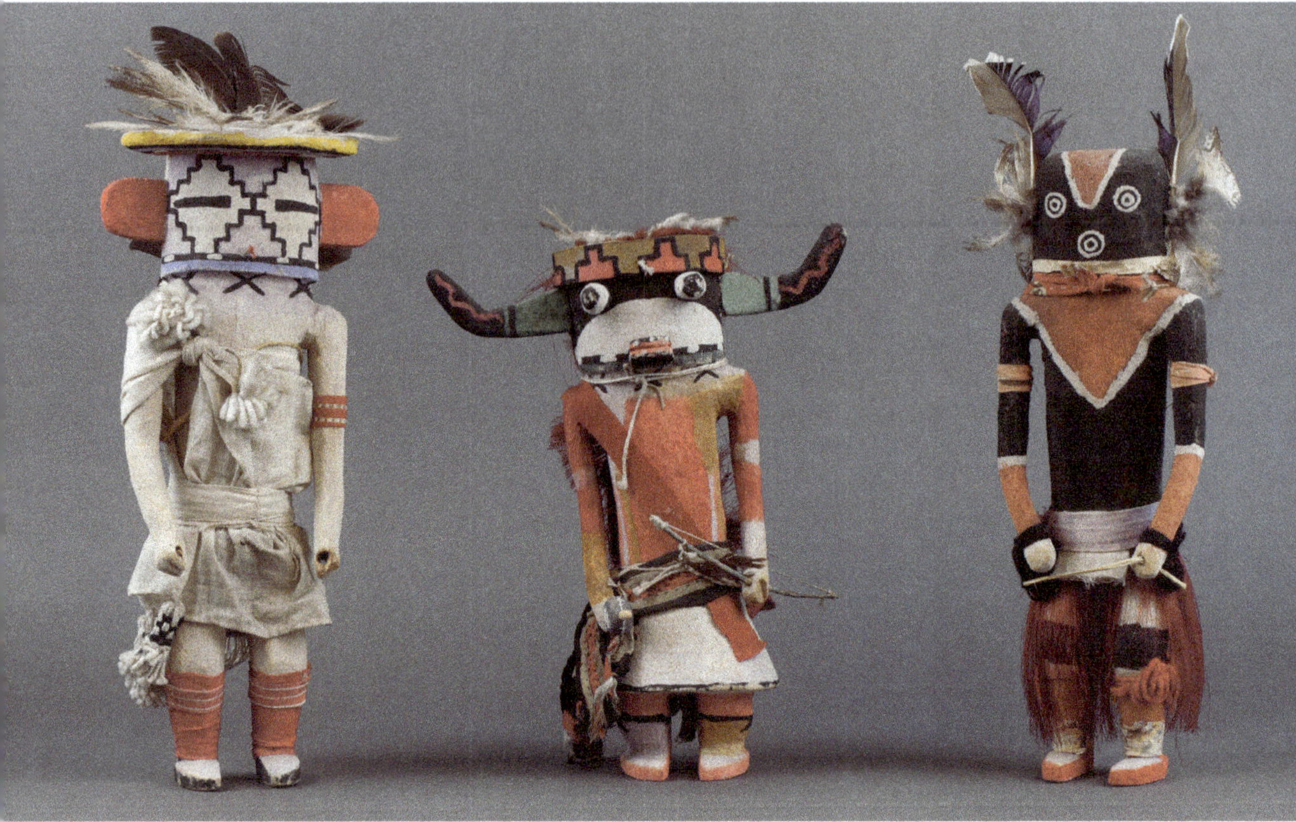

Figure 11.
Volz Katsinam: Nuvakatsina (Snow), Mosayru (Bison), and Wiktsinhoya (Grease).

1900, Volz Carvings

Frederick Volz (1856–1913) was born in Germany and emigrated to the United States at age 20. He was to become a noted entrepreneur in the Southwest with trading posts in Canyon Diablo, Ganado, Orayvi (formerly Oraibi), and other locations. For a full biography of Volz, see Loscher's article, "The Volz Collection of Hopi Katsina Dolls at the Heard Museum" (2005). In 1901, Volz sold about four hundred katsina carvings and other Native items to the Fred Harvey Company. This is a remarkable number of katsinam! These items were to be displayed and sold at the new Alvarado Hotel in Albuquerque, New Mexico, which was part of the Fred Harvey circuit for Southwestern tours.

The dolls sold by Volz were Hopi-made and are utterly distinctive. Today, many are in museum collections, including the Heard and the MNA. They are important examples in the history of Hopi katsina carvings for several reasons.

Loscher has proposed that the Anglo tourist marketplace affected the creation of these katsinam. She indicated that these carvings were deliberately modified in multiple ways to appeal to the Anglo tourist. More specifically, the carvings were simplified as to katsina details, employed brighter "more attractive colors," and added clothing as accents. (Keep in mind that early twentieth-century Anglo dolls almost always wore clothes.) However, some have suggested that the use of clothing on the dolls was a Zuni influence (Erickson 1977; Kessler 1988).

Many of the Volz dolls seem to be of a common length (about 13 to 14 inches) as if they were produced in something resembling an assembly-line fashion. Loscher noted that many were carved more simply than those made for Hopi use. Streamlining makes sense, as producing four hundred carvings must have required some effort toward standardization. One could argue that the Volz dolls may have been among the first katsinam to be markedly influenced by an outside marketplace.

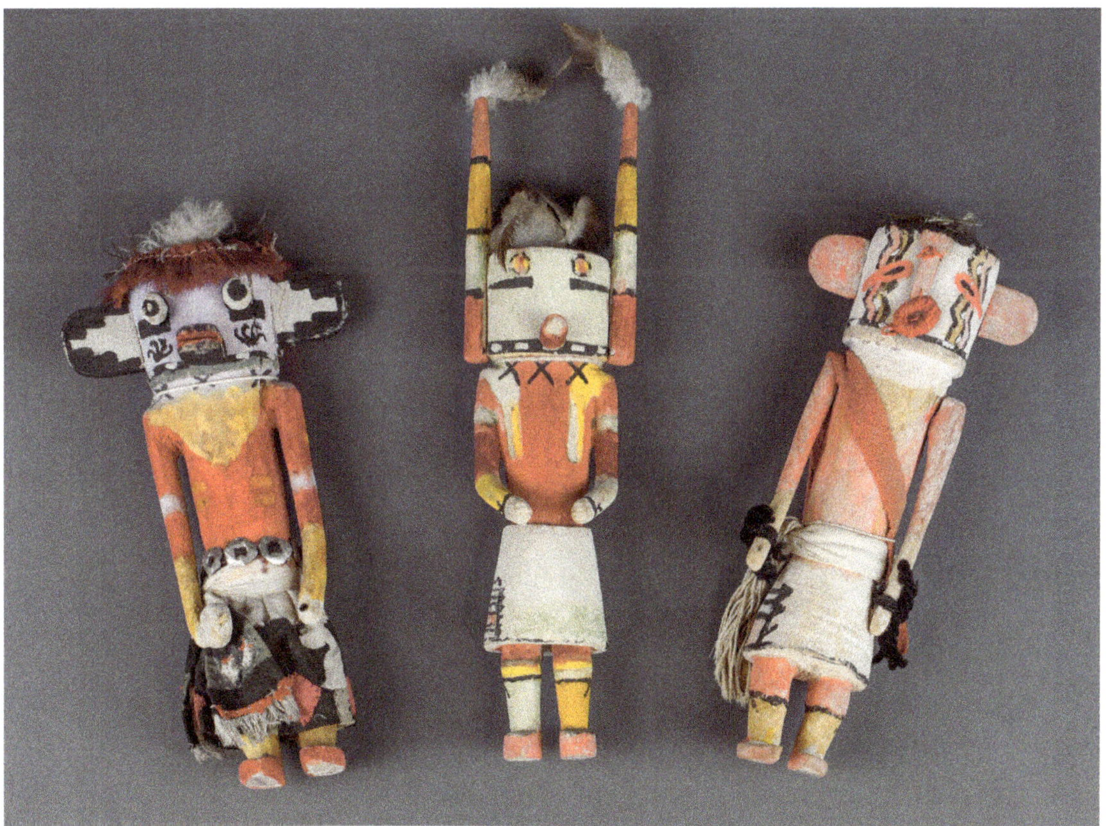

Figure 12. Volz Katsinam: Honan (Badger), possibly a Taatangaya (Hornet), and Hehey'a.

There were probably three different makers working in three distinctive styles who produced the Volz dolls (2005). The most common examples, which Loscher refers to as created by Artist 1, are characterized by single, long, narrow blocks of straight wood, with arms smoothly carved out from and parallel to the body. The arms are very elongated and usually have simple, ball-shaped hands which may carry bows, rattles, or yucca whips. Figures by Artist 1 are usually adorned with hand-sewn clothing more typically found on Zuni katsinam. All these described features are found on the katsinam in Figure 11, which consist of left to right: a Nuvakatsina, or Snow katsina, a Mosayru (Bison) katsina, and a Wiktsinhoya (Grease) katsina. Note they all share small, ding-toed feet, which generally do not allow them to stand. On the left in Figure 12 is an additional carving in the style of Artist 1. This is a Honan (Badger) katsina.

The artist identified as number 2 by Loscher produced very different arms. The arms generally are bent at the elbows, not straight. An example of work by Artist 2 is found in the middle of Figure 12. It may be a Taatangaya (Hornet) katsina or it may have been so "simplified" as to defy identification. Note that the katsina in Figure 12 is not clothed. It may be that katsinam by Artist 2 have either simpler clothing or no clothes at all.

Far fewer examples of work by Artist 3 are included in Loscher's article. This maker may have been less prolific. The features for this type include a turned body with arms attached at the shoulders with nails. A distinctive example of this type is shown in Figure 13, which is a Wiharu (White Ogre). The katsina on the right in Figure 12, a Hehey'a, also appears to be by Artist 3 given that the arms are attached with nails.

Not all Volz dolls fit cleanly into Loscher's attempts at discrete categories for Artists 1 to 3. Nonetheless, they represent an important chapter in the history of Hopi katsinam. It won't be the last time the Anglo marketplace affects the style and content of the Hopi katsina.

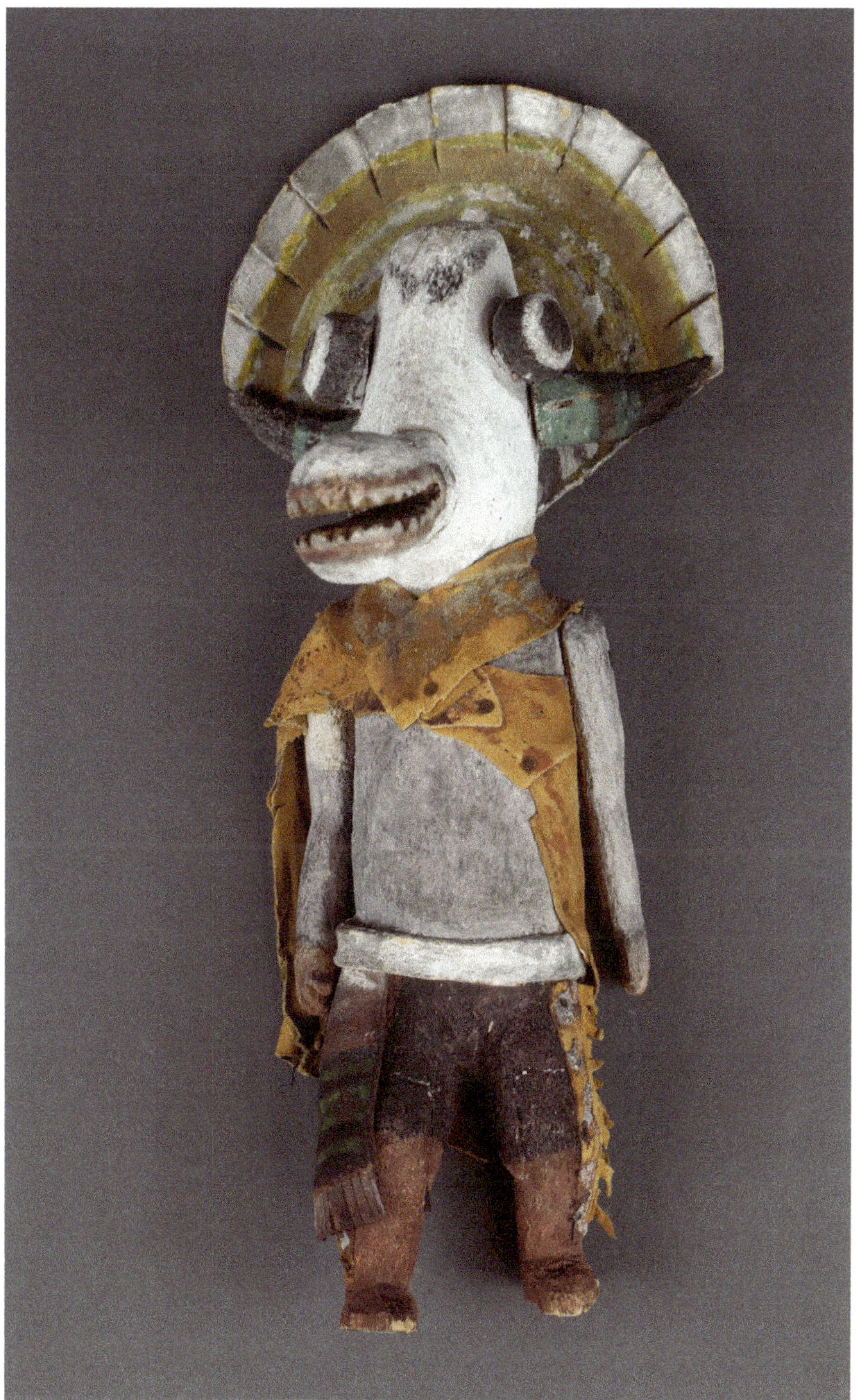

Figure 13. Volz Katsina: Wiharu (White Ogre).

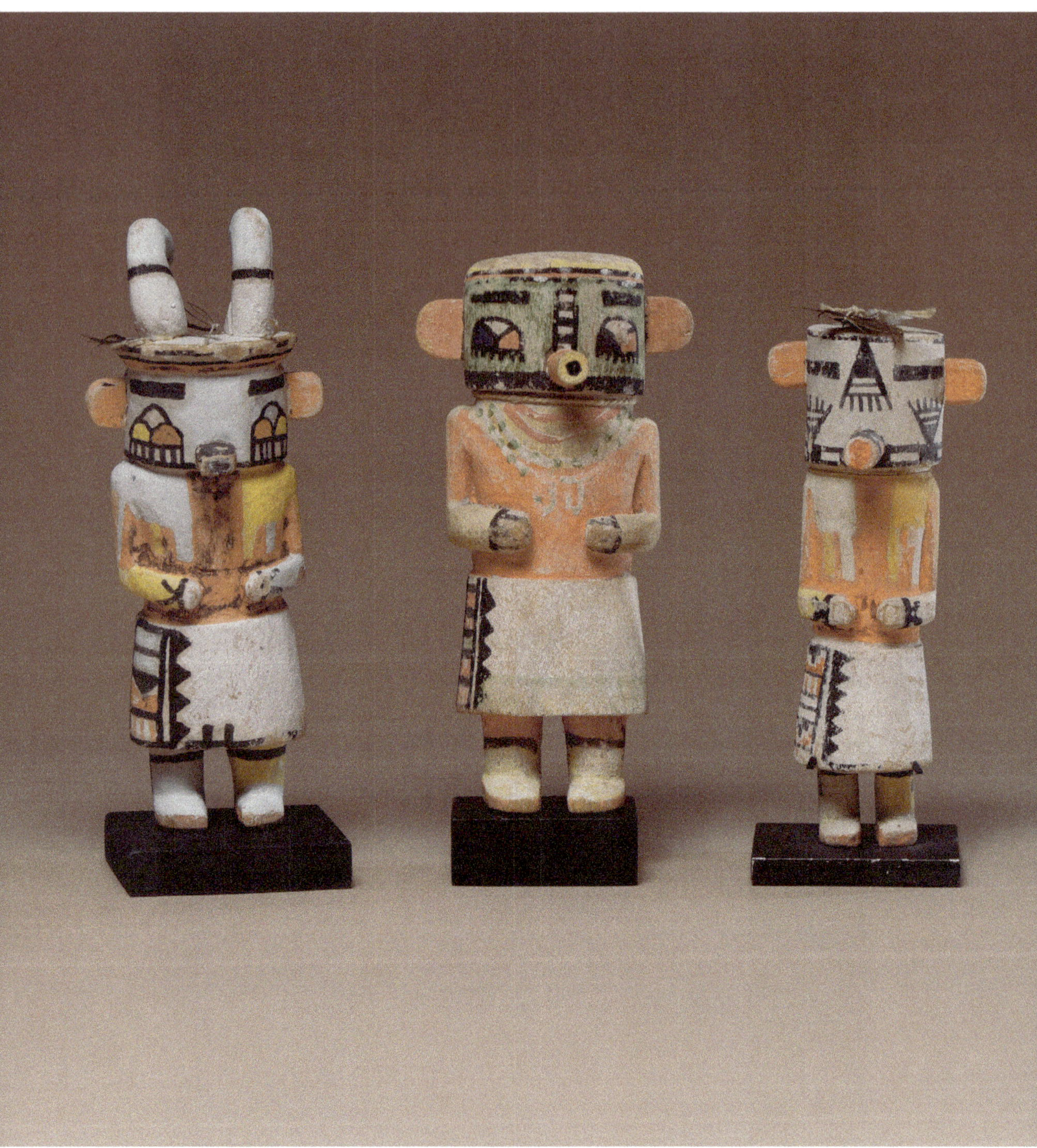

Figure 1. Aaloosaka (a deity), Talavaykatsina (Morning Katsina), and unknown.

EARLY KATSINA CARVINGS

Part II: Late Traditional, the 1910s–1920s and Early Action, 1930s

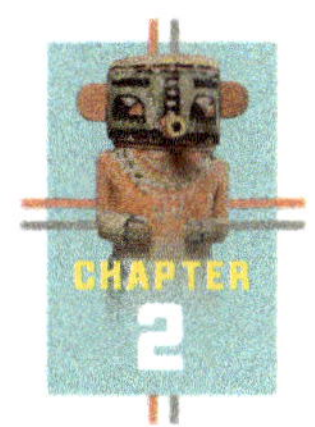

By the 1920s, Hopi katsina carvings had become somewhat uniform. This era can be referred to as Late Traditional. The most typical examples from this period include the following features:

- Full-figured katsinam with heads clearly differentiated from bodies. Legs and feet were carved out below the kilts of the katsinam.
- Hands were generally placed in the so-called "bellyache position." The Hopi call such carvings *"ponotutuyqa"* (one with a stomachache) (Breunig & Lomatuway'ma 1992). Hands in this position were not carved separately from the bodies but appeared in bas-relief over the lower chest or abdomen.
- Aspects of the katsinams' costumes were depicted, including body paint, kilt, and sash.
- Some carvings were freestanding due to larger feet.
- Paints were often a combination of mineral and vegetal pigments and commercial poster or tempera paints.

Examples that demonstrate these characteristics are shown in Figure 1. Note that all three katsinam in the photo have roughly one-third devoted to the head, one-third apportioned to the chest, and one-third expended on the kilt and feet. All three have simply carved arms and hands positioned on the lower chest or abdomen. Each has a somewhat detailed rendering of a kilt and sash, and the feet are distinctly carved out below the kilt. As for paints, these three share a *douma* (Hopi clay base). The carvings on the left (Aaloosaka, a deity) and in the center (Talavaykatsina, the Morning katsina) may have jet (coal) or vegetal paint for its black decorations. The figure on the right (unknown katsina with turkey feathers on the face) appears to have a commercial black paint. And all three have a bright orange commercial paint (tempera) on the ears and body that had become quite popular on Hopiland by the 1920s.

To demonstrate that these features were common in general, consider Figure 2. Here we have left to right: a Kooninkatsina (Havasupai), Mosayru Mana

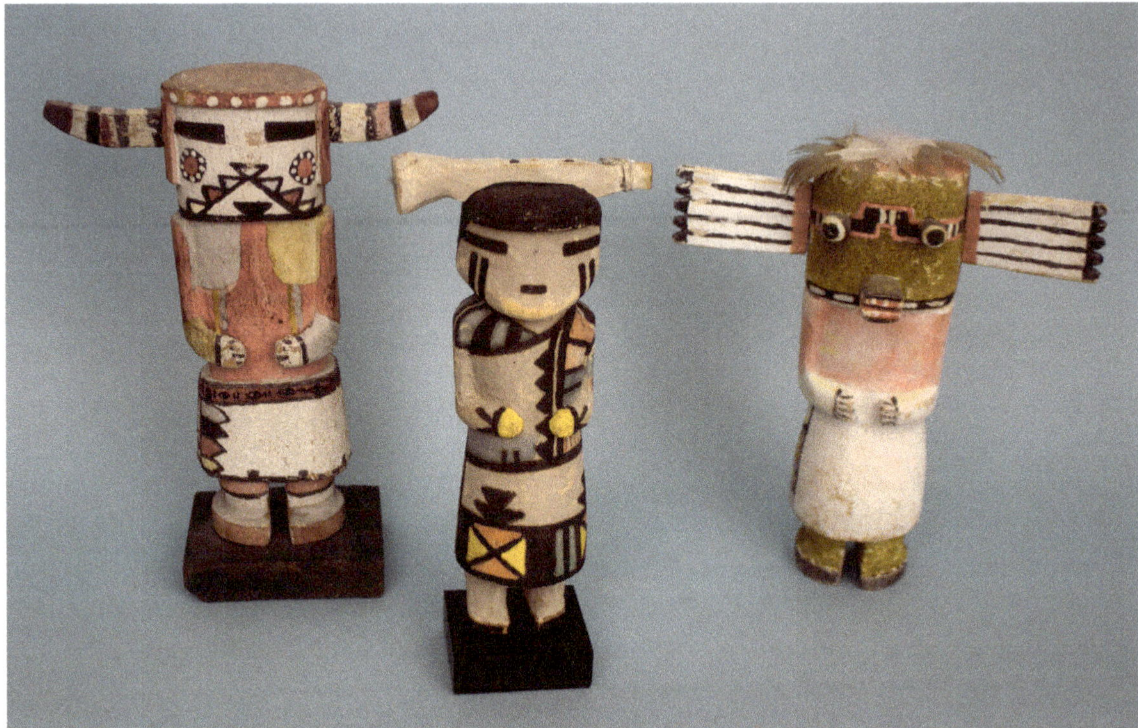

Figure 2. Kooninkatsina (Havasupai), Mosayru Mana (Bison Maiden), and Hooli.

(Bison Maiden), and a Hooli (no translation, named for the sound he makes). The patina and feet of these katsinam suggest that they may have come from 1910–1920. The spool feet found on the Koonin and Hooli are somewhat earlier manifestations. Also, the very oxidized copper carbonate paint on the Hooli also suggests an early twentieth-century lineage. The bellyache position for all three points to how common this posture was on carvings from 1910–1920s.

The katsinam in Figures 1 and 2 are all about 8 to 10 inches tall, but there are larger examples from this time period. Consider the Siohemiskatsina (Zuni Jemez) katsina in Figure 3. This stately katsina is 16 inches tall. A similar large-scale carving from the 1920s is shown in Figure 4. This is an Angakatsina (Longhair) katsina. Both share the characteristics provided in the list above.

Figure 5 shows two additional exceptionally large katsinam in the 1920s style. These are from the left, a Poliimana, the Butterfly Maiden, and on the right, Palhikwmana, the Water Drinking Maiden. The Poliimana is 19½ inches tall and the Palhikwmana, 17½ inches tall and 11 inches wide. The small Hopi female figure in the middle is included for scale.

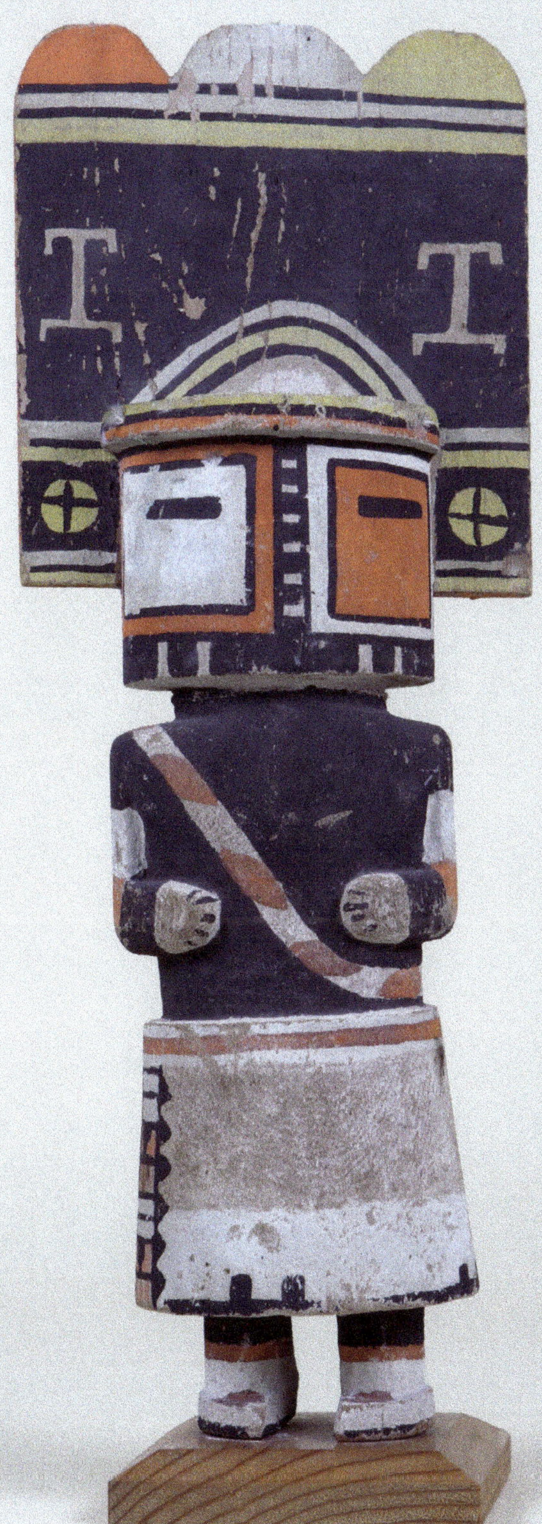

Figure 3.
Siohemiskatsina
(Zuni Jemez).

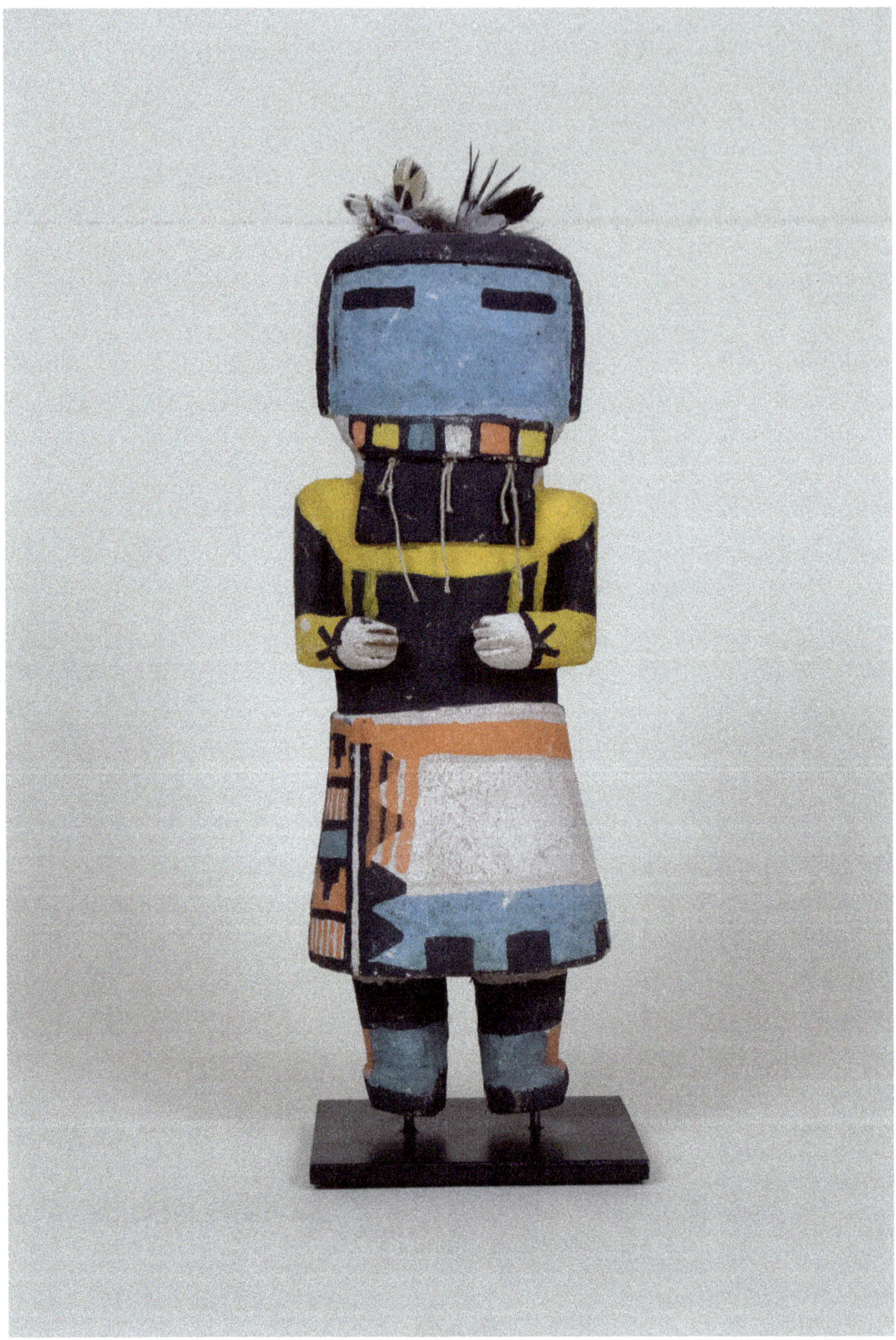

Figure 4. Angakatsina (Longhair).

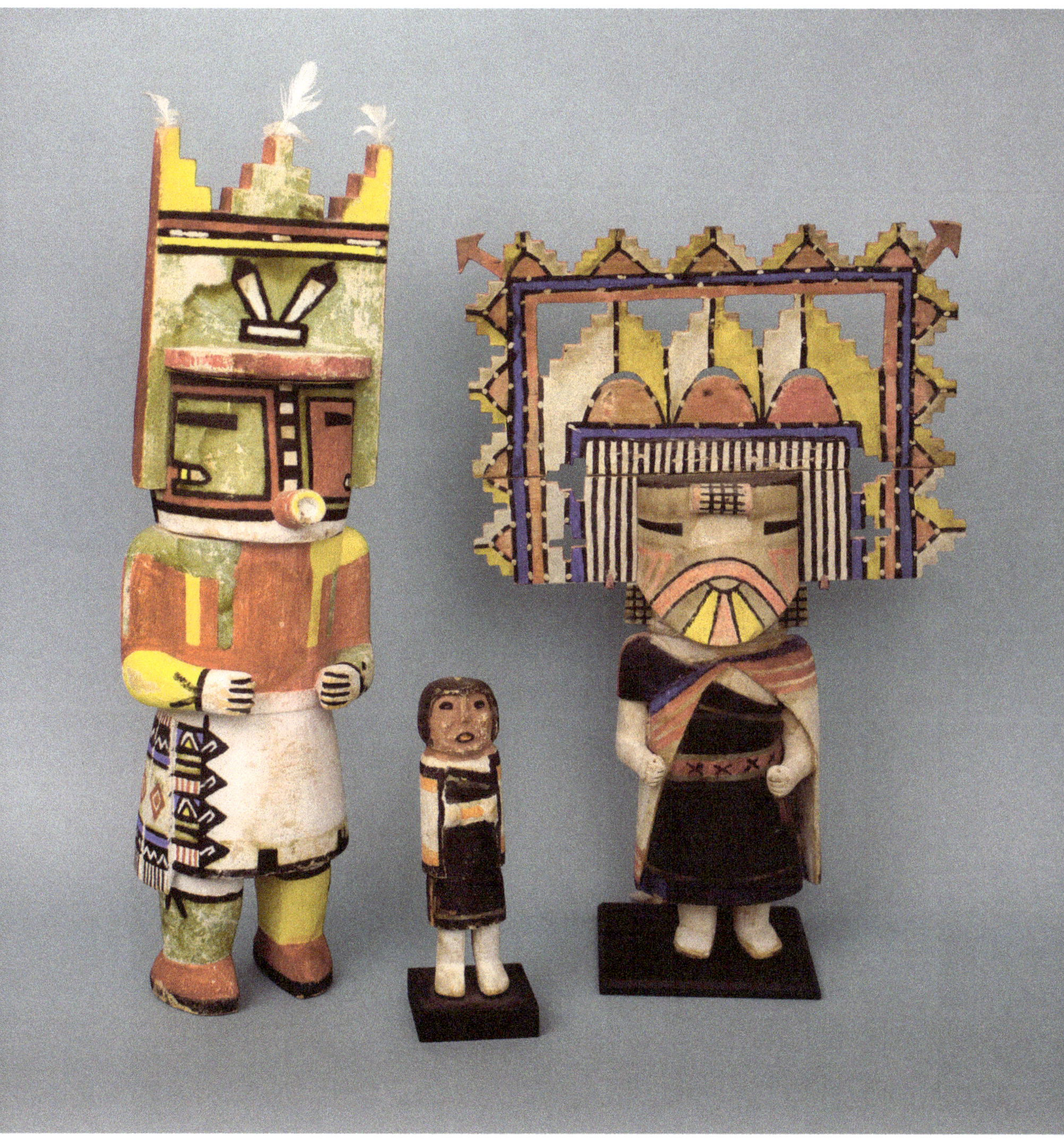

Figure 5.
Poliimana (Butterfly Maiden), Hopi female, Palhıkwmana (Water Drinking Maiden).

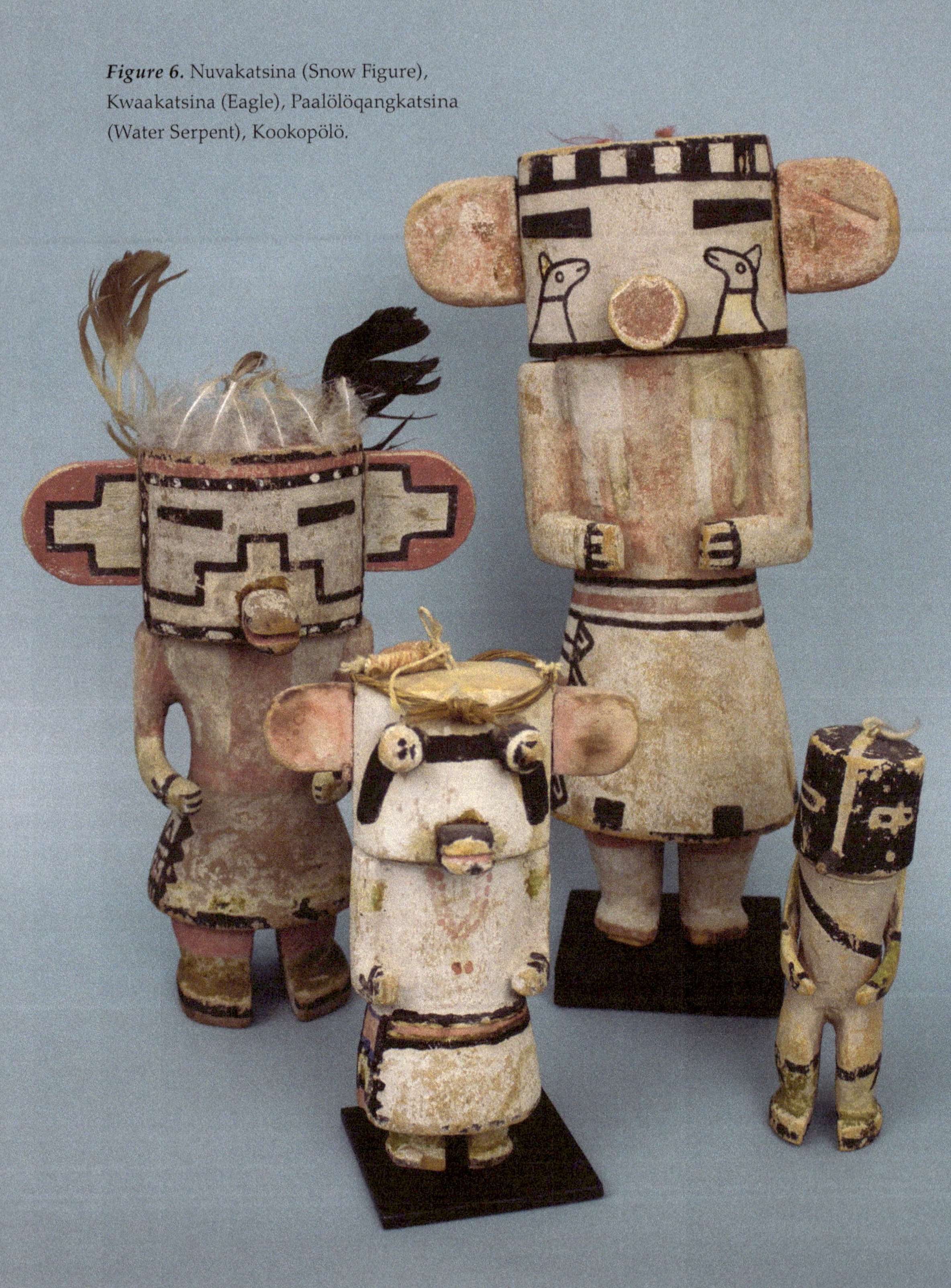

Figure 6. Nuvakatsina (Snow Figure), Kwaakatsina (Eagle), Paalölöqangkatsina (Water Serpent), Kookopölö.

1930s–1940s: Early Action Figures

By the 1930s, body types were changing on katsina carvings. Was this change due to the preferences of an increasing Anglo market, or the creativity and evolution of Hopi carvers? As with many forms of Native American art, such as Navajo rugs, Pueblo pottery, or jewelry, the answer is: probably both. A cross-fertilization appears to have been beneficial for both parties. Carvers updated their wares and had good sales; customers felt they were buying something current and exciting.

During this period, katsina carvings were beginning to show some "action." Quite commonly, arms were now extended from the bodies, depicting the beginnings of dance movement. In addition, knees were often bent, suggesting the motion of a Katsina in a line of dancers. Figure 6 shows several katsinam indicating body postures "in transition." The white-faced Kwaakatsina (Eagle) in the foreground is a prototypical 1920s doll with arms tucked in. However, the terrace-faced Nuvakatsina (Snow figure) on the left has cut-out arms that are beginning to suggest action and dance movement. The Paalölöqangkatsina (Water Serpent) katsina's arms are more cut out than a typical 1920s doll, as are those of the small Kookopölö. While the exact dates of these carvings are unknown, the photo does suggest the evolution of body types.

Figures 7a and 7b provide more definitive examples of the Early Action type of carving. The dynamic Tsu'sona (Snake Dancer, Figure 7a) is an exceptional piece. The arms are extended and clenched and the legs are firmly planted. The snake is writhing yet firmly held in the mouth of the Tsu'sona. And there is provenance that this figure was collected in the 1930s. This eerie and charismatic figure certainly has plenty of "action" to recommend it.

The Pangwkatsina (Bighorn Sheep) in Figure 7b is another fine example of a 1930s Early Action figure. Note the extended arms, bent knees, and the dance stick that symbolizes the Sheep's front legs. This katsina is on the move.

By the mid-1930s, several carvers were becoming well known and their work clearly identified. These were Wilson Tawaquaptewa, Otto Pentewa, and Jimmie Kewanwytewa. For more than forty years, Tawaquaptewa worked primarily in the Late Traditional/Early Action style (see the next chapter). Also for the next four decades, Otto Pentewa and Jimmie Kewanwytewa would create katsinam in the Early Action mode.

At this point in the book, the narrative moves from the trends of early anonymous carvers to the discussion of specific artists and their work.

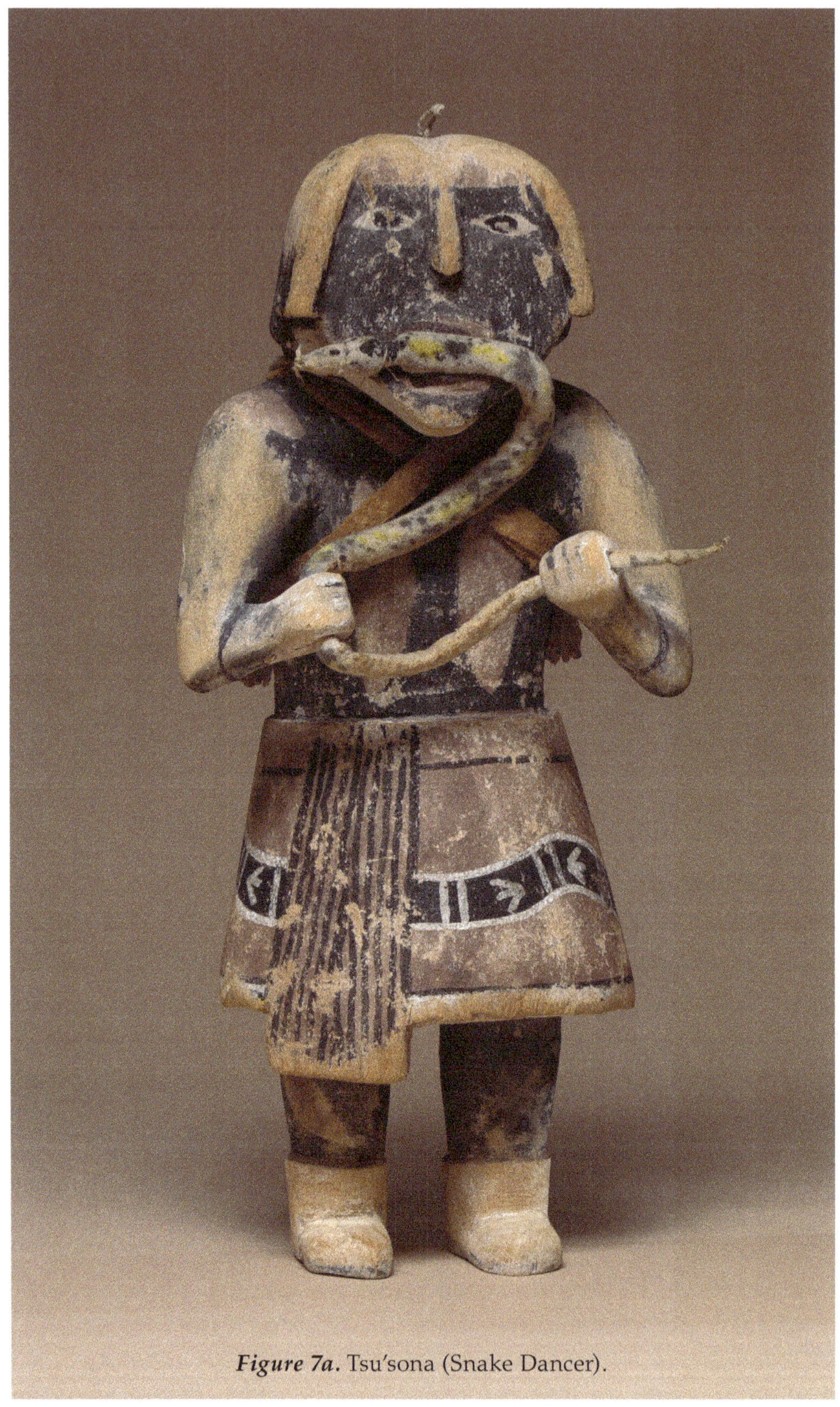

Figure 7a. Tsu'sona (Snake Dancer).

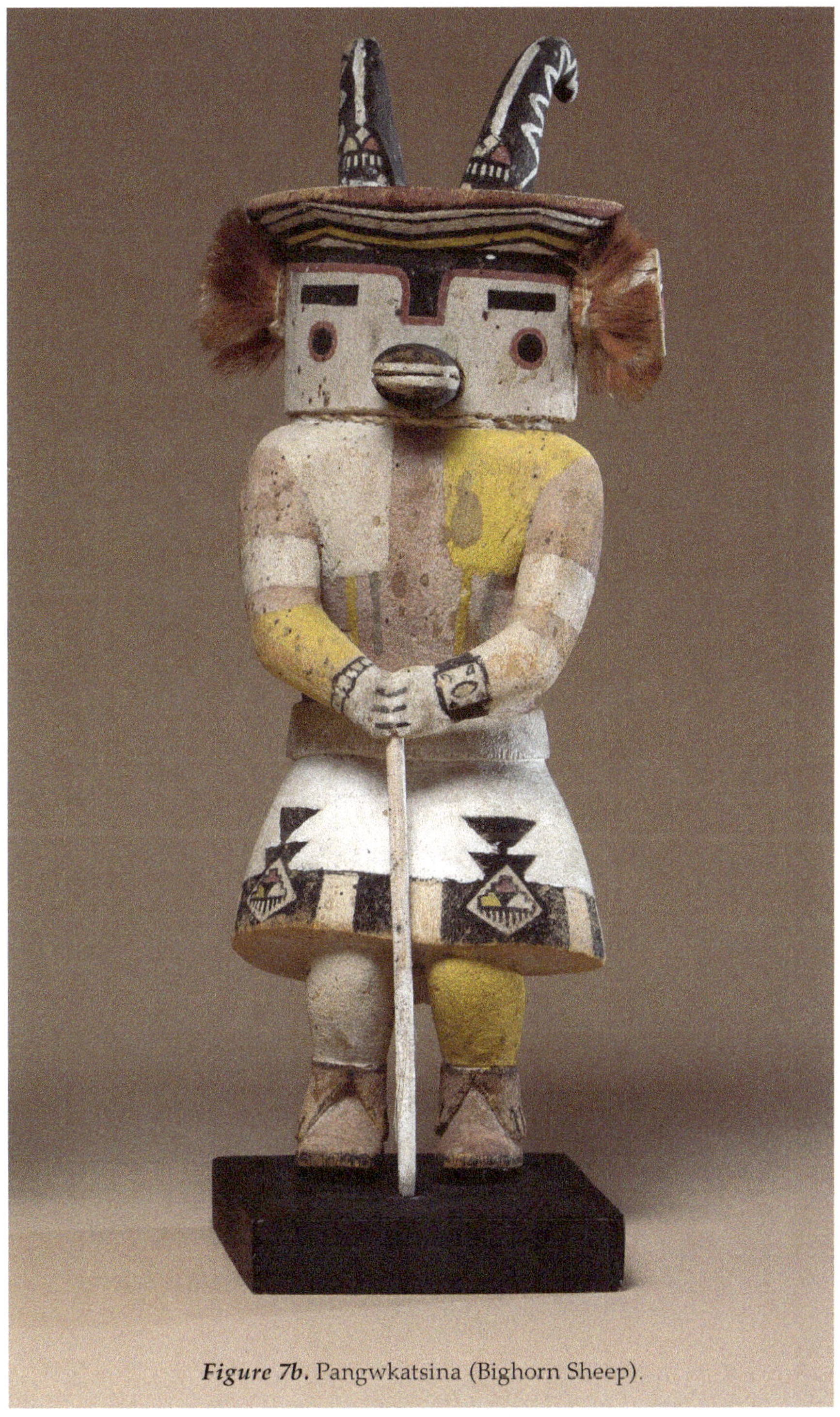

Figure 7b. Pangwkatsina (Bighorn Sheep).

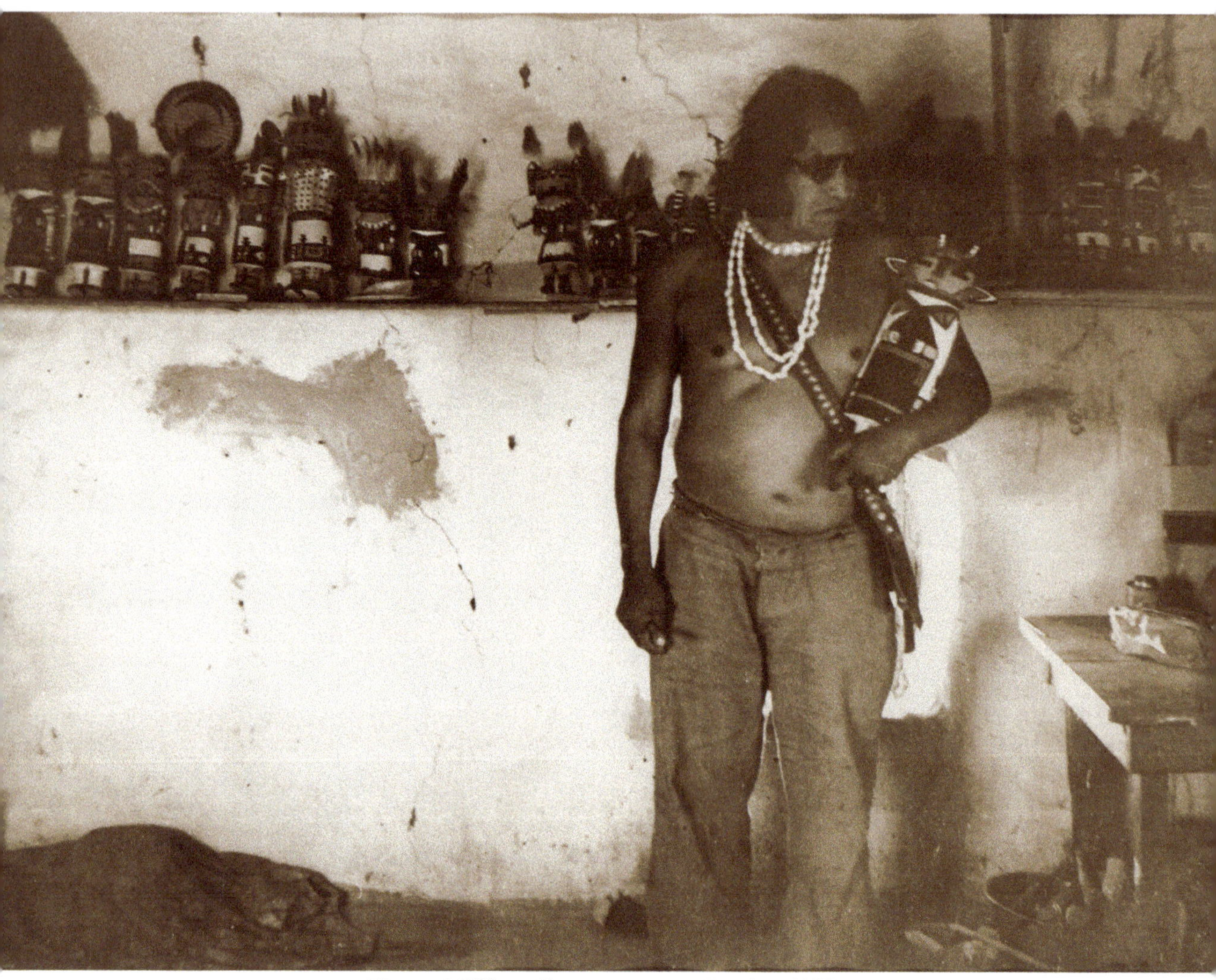

Figure 1. Wilson Tawaquaptewa, October 1935.

WILSON TAWAQUAPTEWA

"Turning the Power"

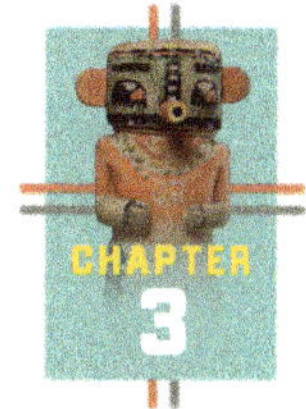

DURING THE FIRST FORTY YEARS that outsiders collected Hopi katsina dolls with some frequency (1880–1920), the creators of the carvings were essentially anonymous. Collectors were unlikely to know the identity of carvers unless they purchased the dolls directly because katsina carvings were usually not signed. Also, early museum records rarely attributed dolls to specific individuals. As a result, the identity of the makers of katsina dolls passed into oblivion as soon as the relationship between purchaser and creator faded due to memory loss or death.

This all changed in the 1920s when the Orayvi Bear Clan chief, Wilson Tawaquaptewa (1873–1960), began carving katsina dolls (see Figure 1). The attribution of his dolls was not likely to be forgotten because of three factors: 1) Tawaquaptewa's political prominence and visibility in the village of Orayvi, 2) the sheer volume he produced, and 3) the uniqueness of his dolls.

The story of the life of Wilson Tawaquaptewa is familiar to many ardent katsina collectors but foreign to many others. This version will emphasize a different theme in his life, that of "turning the power" (Gilbert 2010).

Tawaquaptewa was born in 1873 in the ancient village of Orayvi (Oraibi). At the time of Tawaquaptewa's birth, Orayvi was the largest and most important Hopi village. Tawaquaptewa was born into his mother's Bear Clan, a religiously significant group. After a childhood immersed in traditional Hopi culture and religion, in 1904 Tawaquaptewa assumed the most prominent religious and political position in the village, *Kikmongwi* (Village Chief). He remained in this position until his death in 1960, with a few interruptions related to political imprisonment and health challenges, which are described below (Whiteley 1988).

In assuming the position of Kikmongwi, Wilson Tawaquaptewa entered center stage in a major controversy. The conflict involved a split between two Hopi groups, recently referred to by Hopi scholar Matthew Gilbert as "Resisters" vs. "Accommodators." (For an extended discussion of this complex conflict, see Titiev 1944; Whiteley 1988; Gilbert 2010). Tawaquaptewa was the leader of the Accommodator faction, and, as the name implies, he and his followers supported limited cooperation between the Hopi people and representatives of the United States government, primarily the Bureau of Indian Affairs (BIA). In contrast, the Resisters were adamantly opposed to any assimilation or compromise with "the White man's way of life." As one example of the conflict, the Accommodators supported the attendance of Hopi children at schools run by the BIA. The Resisters were adamantly opposed to such school attendance in part because Hopi students were required to adopt Anglo names and dress, and speak only English while in school.

Tawaquaptewa's position as an Accommodator was that the influence of Anglo culture was inevitable and, in some cases, advantageous (e.g., literacy, Western medicine, and agricultural tools), and that the wisest course was for the Hopi to pursue a strategic cooperation. In contrast, the Resister group accused Tawaquaptewa and his followers of abandoning traditional Hopi ways and selling out Hopi children and culture for the material advantages offered by the Anglos. As with most bitter conflicts, there may have been reasonable and irrational elements to the positions assumed by both sides.

Fueled by the escalating intrusiveness of the U.S. government, the conflict between the Accommodators and the Resisters reached an explosive crescendo in 1906. In September of that year, the two factions engaged in a ritualized pushing match near Orayvi, which resulted in the expulsion of the Resisters from the village. During the next several years, the Resisters established new villages at Hotvela (Hotevilla) and Paaqavi (Bacavi), which survive to this day.

Ostensibly the "winner" of the longstanding conflict, Tawaquaptewa must have been shocked and outraged when two months later, in November 1906, the U.S. government insisted on shipping seventy-one Hopis, including Tawaquaptewa and his family, to the Sherman Institute in Riverside, California (Gilbert 2010). The Sherman Institute was one of many BIA schools designed to eradicate Indian culture and transform Natives into homogenized U.S. citizens. This decision was intended to punish Tawaquaptewa for behaving in an "un-American way" by forcing the Resisters to leave Orayvi.

Remarkably, Tawaquaptewa adjusted very well to his "schooling." He was said to have learned English in less than five months and was frequently cited as a positive role model for Hopi children and other Native students (Gilbert 2010). He encouraged young Hopi students to take advantage of the positive aspects of their education, but also consistently fostered their learning about Hopi religion and culture in a remote place. For example, Tawaquaptewa organized performances of a traditional Eagle dance, which helped sustain Hopi culture in the Anglo school setting. Moreover, in 1907, he and his students performed the dance at an annual meeting of the National Education Association in Los

Angeles. As Gilbert noted, Tawaquaptewa "helped preserve the Hopi way through an institution designed to destroy it. Tawaquaptewa exerted great agency and succeeded." Tawaquaptewa was said to have "turned the power," and it was not to be the last time (Gilbert 2010).

After three years of "schooling," Tawaquaptewa was allowed to return to Orayvi. The Tawaquaptewa of 1909 was apparently a changed man. As noted by BIA Indian Agent Leo Crane,

> As his Indian agent, I tried for eight long years to make a sensible human being of him, but failed, for lack of material. After having tried him as an Indian judge, and then as an Indian policeman, in the hope of preserving his dignity and authority as hereditary (sic) chief, he was found to be the most negatively contentious savage and unreconstructed rebel remaining in the Orayvi community… (Crane 1925, 86–87)

In this racist rant, it is striking that Crane failed to refer to Tawaquaptewa's three-year incarceration as impacting his subsequent conduct and lack of cooperation with the government. Be that as it may, it is clear by 1910 that Tawaquaptewa could no longer be considered an "Accommodator" in relation to the U.S. government. This was by no means surprising given the treatment accorded him by the authorities in response to his cooperation and spirit of compromise. By consistently resisting, he had again turned the power.

On his return, Tawaquaptewa found himself presiding over an ever-shrinking number of subjects. With the departure of the Resisters, Orayvi lost its status as the most populous and religiously important of the Hopi villages. Instead, Orayvi increasingly became an underpopulated town of deteriorating sandstone structures. In Tawaquaptewa's later years, some Anglos viewed him as an embittered loner, a tragic figure who had attempted to lead his people into the twentieth century only to be abandoned by his own people and the government he had attempted to appease. But as indicated below, there is much more to the story.

Sometime after his return to Orayvi, perhaps in the 1920s, Tawaquaptewa began to carve and sell katsina dolls. This initiative became another example of Tawaquaptewa "turning the power." He became a familiar figure to the ever-increasing numbers of Anglo tourists. He offered tours of the village that culminated at his doorstep in Orayvi, where he sold his carvings for fifty cents or a dollar or two. In the past, many other Hopi had sold katsina dolls to Anglos, but Tawaquaptewa's were unique.

What made Tawaquaptewa's carvings utterly different was that he made sure each of his carvings was not an accurate portrayal of a katsina. He again "turned the power," by selling what the customers believed to be authentic Hopi katsina dolls, which, in fact, were anything but. Instead, his carvings were strange combinations of characteristics from different katsinam in addition to features from his own fertile imagination. His dolls are immediately recognizable in that they are decorated with weird, often bizarre amalgams of oversized ears, crossed eyes, jagged jailhouse stripes, stinger-like snouts, and frenetic patterns of polka dots. If one looks carefully at the photos of his carvings in this chapter, it would be hard to conclude that Tawaquaptewa became an embittered nihilist. His carvings are frequently comic, even hilarious, in their execution.

Why did Tawaquaptewa carve in this fashion? As I was preparing an earlier article on his work in 1997 (Walsh 1998), I met with Tawaquaptewa's adopted son, Stanley Bahnimptewa, in Orayvi. (Bahnimptewa was then in his seventies and is now deceased.) During our long conversation, Bahnimptewa explained that he used to sit with his father on his doorstep as he was carving his dolls. Asked if Tawaquaptewa had any favorite katsinam that he carved, Bahnimptewa replied, "Well, he didn't do them the right way, the way the Katsinas looked. He didn't think they should be made like the ones given to the girls by the Katsinas at the dances."

Barton Wright, author of thirteen books on Hopi and Zuni culture, confirmed Bahnimptewa's opinion, in saying,

> As Kikmongwi, Tawaquaptewa had a special relationship to all the Katsinas. He had a knowledge of and responsibility for the Katsinas that no one else had. . . . With that privilege went a duty and a responsibility, and a traditional proscription, that the Kikmongwi do nothing in relation to the Katsinas that would be improper or disrespectful. Therefore, to use Katsinas, or the carved representations of them, in any way that was commercially exploitive or opportunistic would be unthinkable. (Wright, personal communication, 1997)

The conclusion is that Tawaquaptewa deliberately distorted all his carvings to be consistent with his religious convictions and role as Kikmongwi, the ceremonial leader. He gave the Anglos what they wanted, but also turned the power, made a few dollars to support his family, and maintained his religious integrity.

One can classify his carvings as falling into two categories: 1) dolls that resemble actual katsinam, but which have been deliberately distorted or modified, and 2) dolls that bear little or no resemblance to any actual katsina and are the product of Tawaquaptewa's idiosyncratic imagination. I refer to these two types as "mixed-up" versus "made-up."

In turning to the carvings in this chapter, it is easy to find prominent examples

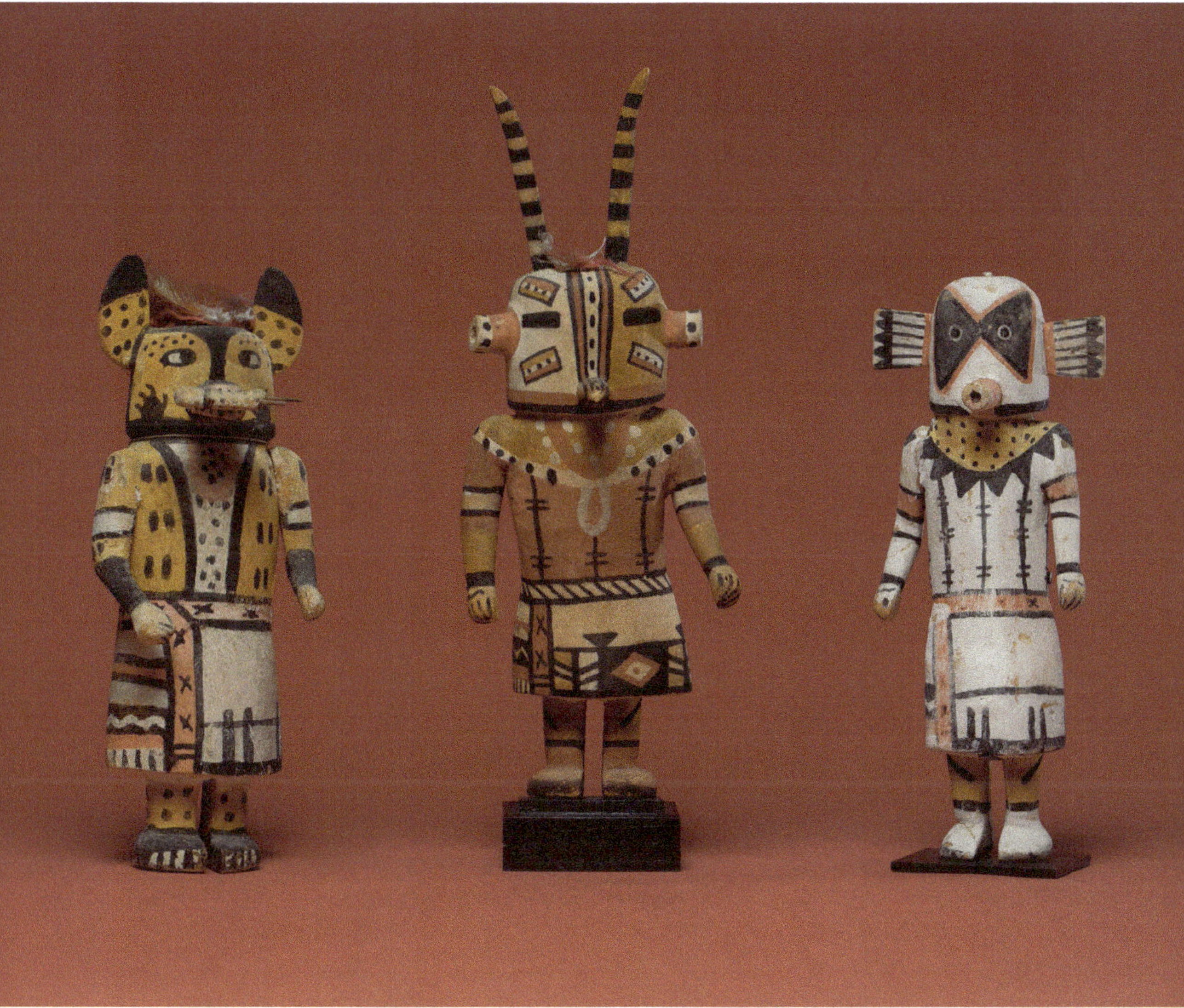

Figure 2. These resemble Chipmunk, Cicada, and Hooli (no translation).

of both types. Consider the katsinam in Figure 2. These three are excellent representatives of Tawaquaptewa's distorted or mixed-up type. On the left is a carving that resembles a Chipmunk, in the middle, an approximation of a Cicada, and on the right, "sort of" a Hooli. With all three examples, Tawaquaptewa was careful to make modifications that render the figure "not a real katsina." More specifically, he added polka dots on all three carvings that do not occur on accurate versions of the katsinam. In addition, on all three, the body paint

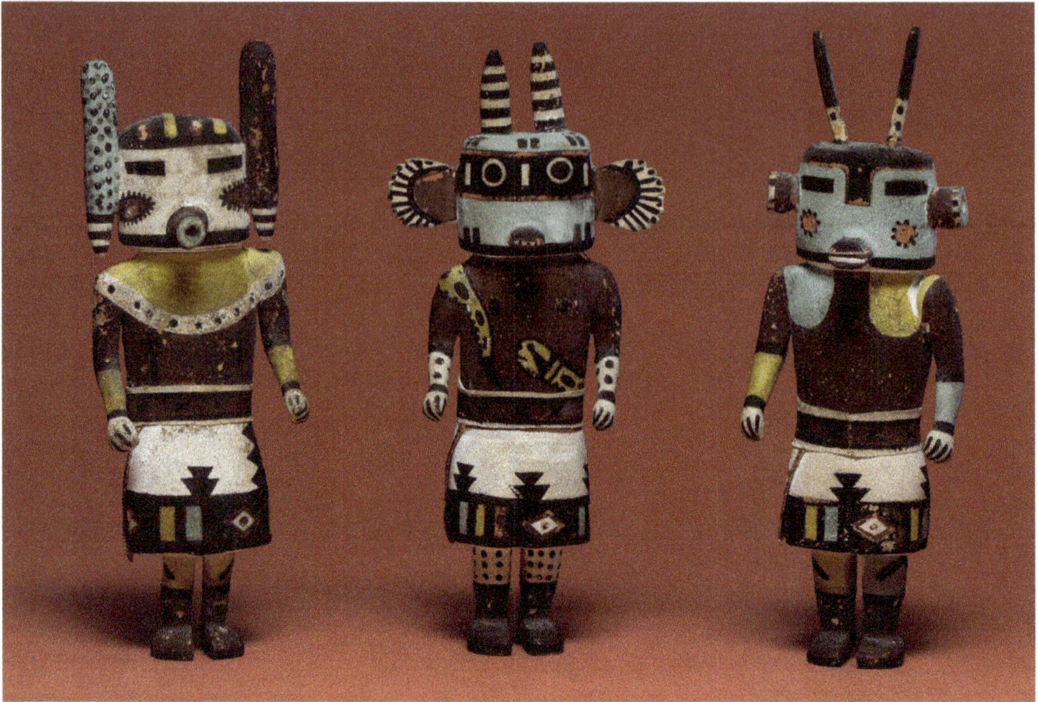

Figure 3. Made-up type katsinam.

designs do not exist on any real Hopi katsina. And as another example, it is quite nonsensical for a "Chipmunk" to have bear claws on his face! This is Tawaquaptewa being playful, maybe even sardonic.

Examples of the entirely "made-up" katsinam are well represented in Figure 3. This group is a remarkable, and probably unique, matched set from the 1930s collected by Betty Toulouse, a Santa Fe academic and expert on Pueblo pottery. On the left is a figure with multi-colored ears of corn on his head, along with amoeba-like figures on his face. No such katsina exists. The same can be said for the carving in the middle, a hilarious figure with scalloped ears and stunted koshare-like horns. He also bears an amusing undulating serpent on his chest. And on the right is a katsina with slender antennae and spools for ears. None of these figures exist in the Hopi pantheon.

A wonderful range of Tawaquaptewa's work is shown in the group shot (Figure 4). This superb collection shows his extensive reach as to size, shape, figures, mood, and coloration. His predilection for polka dots, crossed eyes, exaggerated horns, and zany stripes is much in evidence. Many of these must be seen as whimsical.

While we're on the topic of the breadth of Tawaquaptewa's work, take another look at Figure 1 at the beginning of this chapter. What struck me about this photo by Paul Coze from 1935 was the sheer number of carvings Tawaquaptewa had on hand at one time! I always assumed that he was like most other carvers: carve a few, sell a few, and move on. But as this photo indicates, at least in 1935, he had an extensive inventory to offer. This suggests he wasn't living hand-to-mouth, but rather he had enough resources to build up and hold onto a large selection.

Worth noting is that he also made diverse forms of other objects, as shown in Figure 5. The items include a katsina with a rattle-top head, a rasp, sheep scapula, dance wand, and gourd resonator. Figure 6 shows a unique "Mudhead" and "Wolf" game set by Tawaquaptewa that is truly endearing. And finally, Figure 7 shows three female figures, which were quite uncommon in Tawaquaptewa's work overall. Their gender is indicated by their mantas (or robes) and white boots.

The "katsina" carvings depicted in this chapter are entirely representative of Tawaquaptewa the artist, the man, and the historical figure. Tawaquaptewa was an individual of complex contradictions and intriguing incompatibilities. He was a traditional Hopi chief of the prestigious Bear Clan, yet he was also an assimilationist, an "accommodator." In the past, he has been viewed by some as a sellout to the United States government, and by others as a selfless, strategic protector of the Hopi way. A more current view is to recognize his strategic

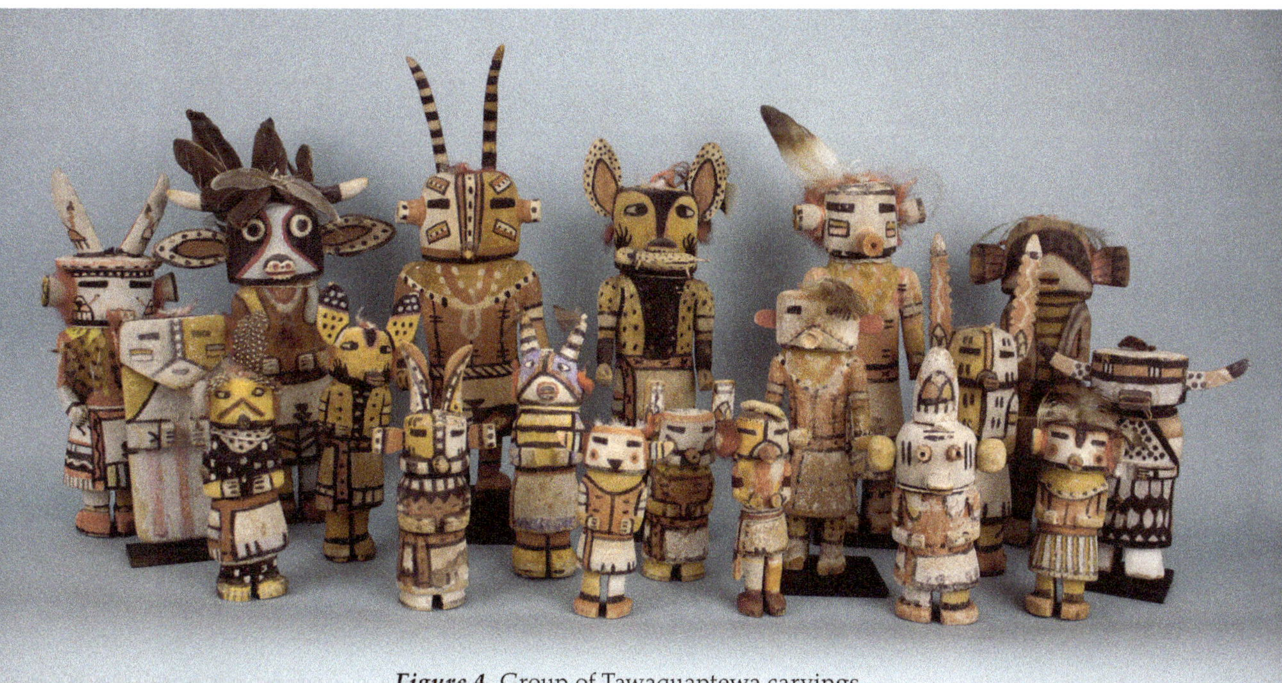

Figure 4. Group of Tawaquaptewa carvings.

acumen in "turning the power." He encountered massive challenges to Hopi culture, deflected their impact, and facilitated survival. He did this during his time at the Sherman Institute, after his return to the reservation, and via his unique katsina carvings. Tawaquaptewa's katsinam are now valued by collectors, art dealers, and museums for their distinctiveness, aesthetic humor and charisma, and symbolic meaning and significance.

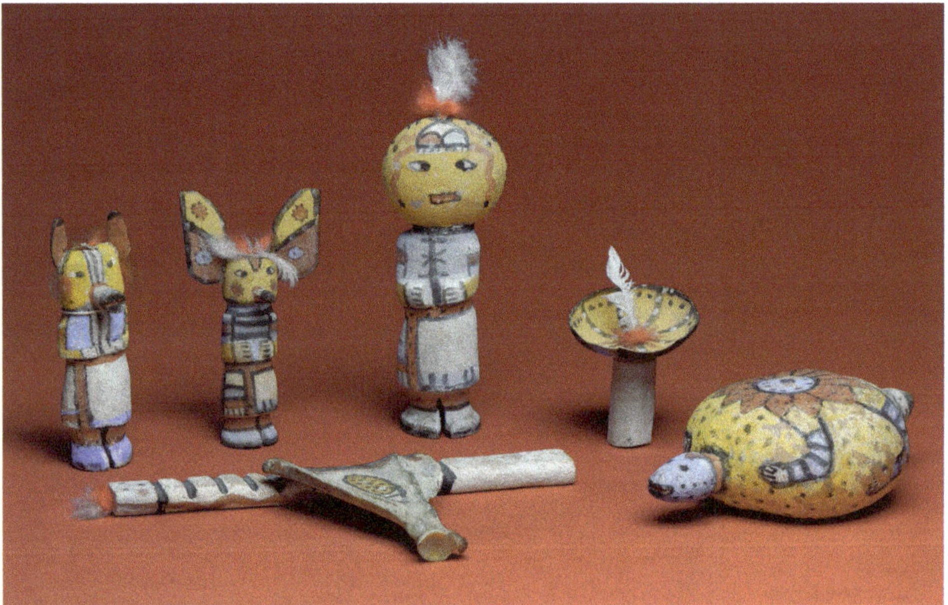

Figure 5. Diverse objects.

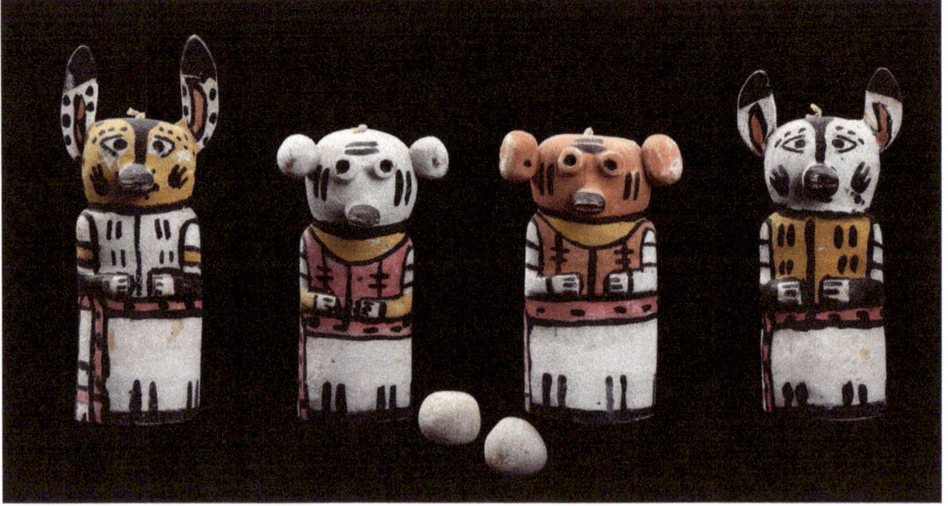

Figure 6. Mudhead and Wolf game set.

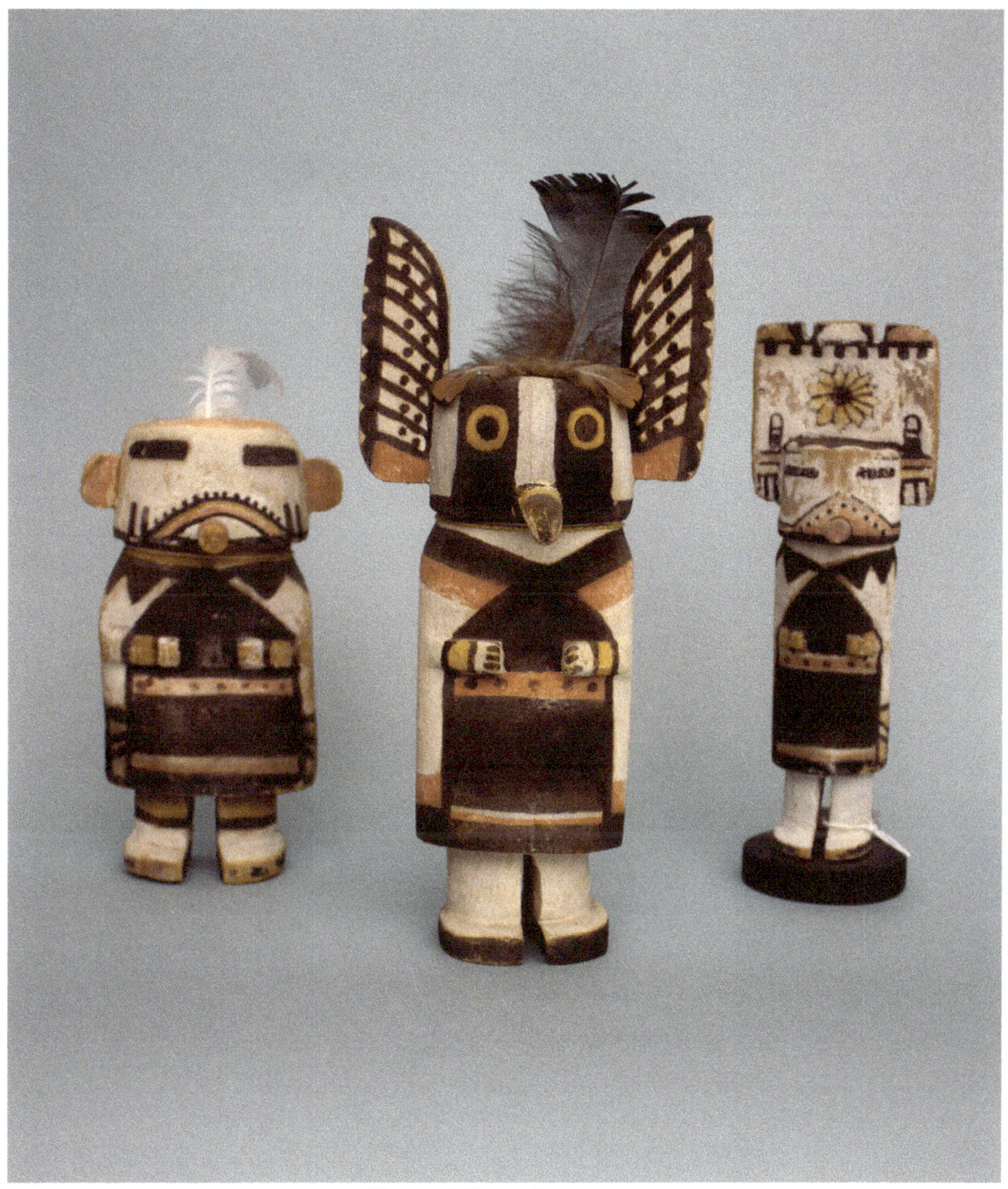

Figure 7. Three female figures.

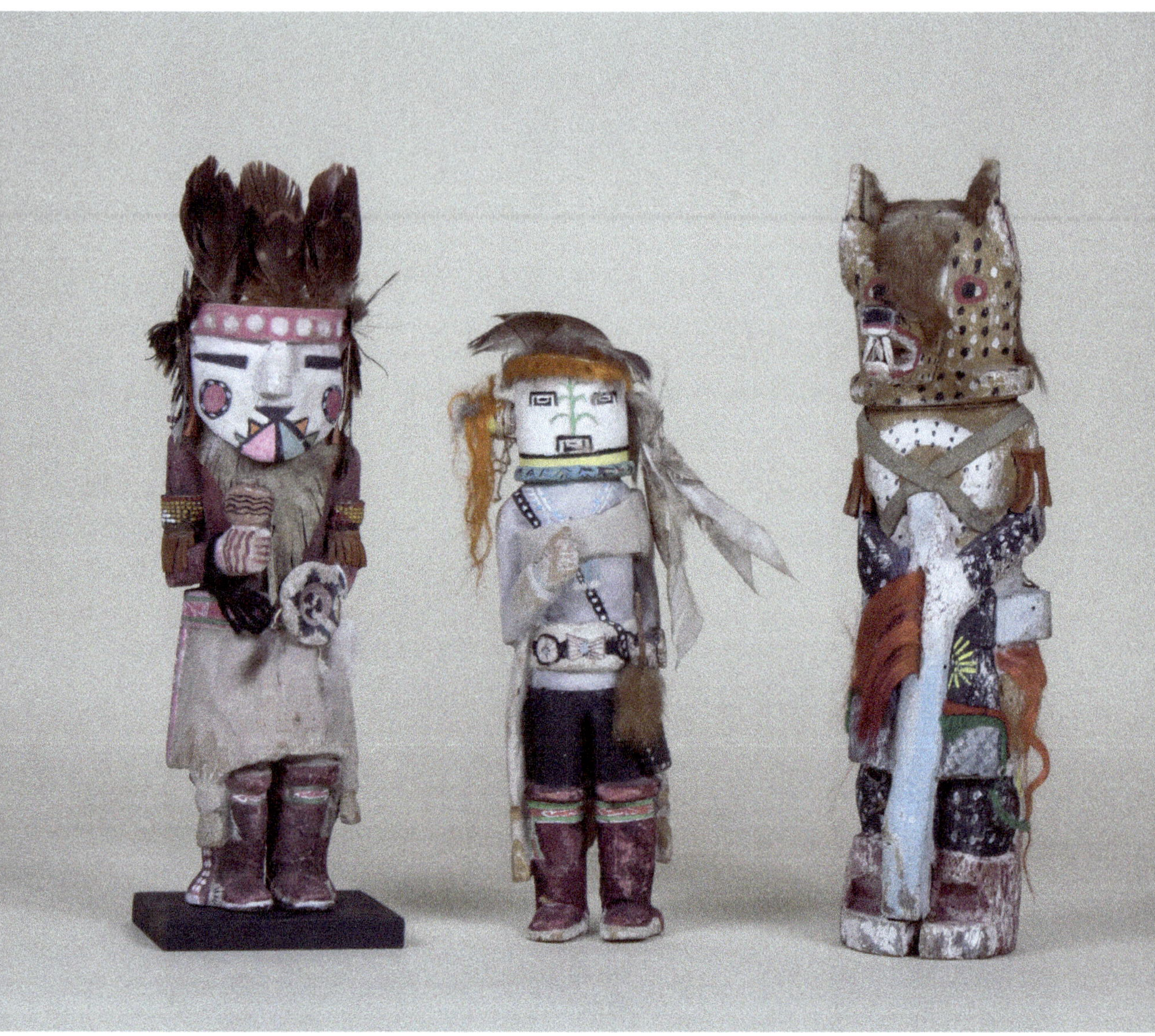

Figure 1. Kooninkatsina (Havasupai), Tasapkatsinmuykwa'am (Grandfather of the Navajo), and Kwewu (Wolf).

OTTO PENTEWA

A Quirky Creativity

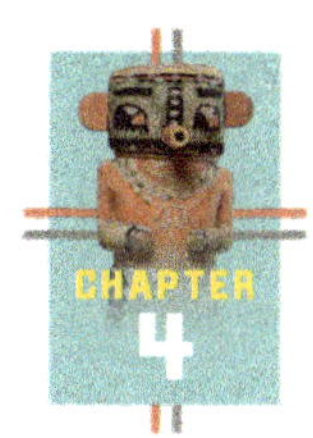

WHILE TAWAQUAPTEWA MAY HAVE BEEN THE FIRST CARVER to establish a uniquely identifiable style (see the previous chapter), not long after in the 1930s, a second carver emerged with an utterly distinctive artistry. Otto Pentewa was born in the mid-to-late 1880s in Orayvi on Third Mesa, Arizona.[1] His maternal clan was Katsina. He had a long life, dying in 1961. These biographical details, along with much of the other information regarding Otto Pentewa, were provided to me by Richard "Dick" Pentewa, Otto's son. Dick (1927–2002) shared information about his father during multiple conversations at his home in Kiqotsmovi (Kykotsmovi), Arizona, from 1998 to 2001.

I returned to see Dick after my article on his father was published in *American Indian Art Magazine* in the summer of 2001. I received $300 from the magazine for the article and, when I visited Dick, I gave him a $100 bill. He shook his head in disbelief and said, "Jeesh, I haven't had a friend like you in a lon-n-n-n-g time." I was fortunate to know Dick Pentewa.

Otto Pentewa's original family name was Tuwaventewa, which referred to a type of Hopi sandpainting. However, the name was shortened and the spelling altered, probably for the convenience of English speakers. Otto Pentewa's Hopi name, Sikovaya, was given to him by his Pumpkin Clan relatives. *Sikovaya* is a pumpkin flower that Hopi females pick to make a pudding.

While little is known of Mr. Pentewa's early life, it is well established that he moved from Orayvi to Kiqotsmovi before the notorious split in 1906 (Whiteley 1988). The details of this split are provided in the previous chapter on Tawaquaptewa.

In Kiqotsmovi, Pentewa built a small sandstone house where he resided until his death. Throughout his life, Otto Pentewa lived in a traditional Hopi manner, tending his fields, herding a few sheep, and taking an active part in the religious life of his village. Otto and his wife, Rhoda, had approximately eleven children.

---

[1] Richard Pentewa told the author that his father was born "about 1886." However, Roxie McLeod's (1994) thesis, "Dreams and Rumors," citing census data, indicated his birthdate to be 1889. Because of this discrepancy, I chose to use an approximation of his birth year.

When I interviewed Dick, he was still living in the original family home built by his father in Kiqotsmovi, more than a hundred years later.

Like Tawaquaptewa, Otto Pentewa was one of the first carvers to make a large number of dolls for sale. In fact, Oscar Branson and Mark Bahti, both long-time traders on the Hopi reservation, told me independently about a link between Pentewa and Tawaquaptewa. Each stated that the Orayvi chief and Pentewa knew each other well and that they used to sell carvings together along the roadside to tourists following Katsina dances. This is an intriguing personal connection between two of the most famous katsina carvers in history. Yet it should also be pointed out that their carvings in no way resemble each other.

Pentewa's success in selling katsinam to traders, tourists, and other outsiders was very much due to his idiosyncratic, charismatic artistic style. His dolls include the following distinctive characteristics:

- Frequent use of large semi-circular, pigeon-toed feet that enabled free-standing dolls.
- Carving on the feet that rendered moccasin flaps in a thick, bulky fashion, to make the feet appear "terraced." At times, he added leather fringe to make the feet even more terraced in appearance.
- Minimalist carving on some dolls, resulting in the cottonwood root retaining a large portion of its original shape.
- Frequent use of bent wood, which he employed to depict dance motion or other unusual postures.
- Distinctive hands minimally carved away from the trunk of the doll, producing a bas-relief effect.
- Occasional use of unusual materials such as animal pelts from moles, mice, dogs, cats, coyote, fox, bear, and buffalo.
- Lastly, many, but not all, of his katsinam, have an unmistakable comic presence. These include exaggerated facial features, distorted body postures, and odd hand positions.

Taken in combination, the above list of features makes it possible to reliably identify most carvings by Pentewa, even though he never signed his dolls. For example, several Pentewa dolls in this chapter show his unique manner of carving feet. More specifically, in Figure 1, the Kwewu (Wolf) and both katsinam in Figure 2, show the exaggerated half-moon feet that allow the dolls to stand.

Dolls in Figure 2 demonstrate examples of another Pentewa distinguishing characteristic. Both Umtoynaqa (One Who Makes Thunder) and the Angwusnasomtaqa (Crow Mother) show the minimalist, bas-relief carving of the

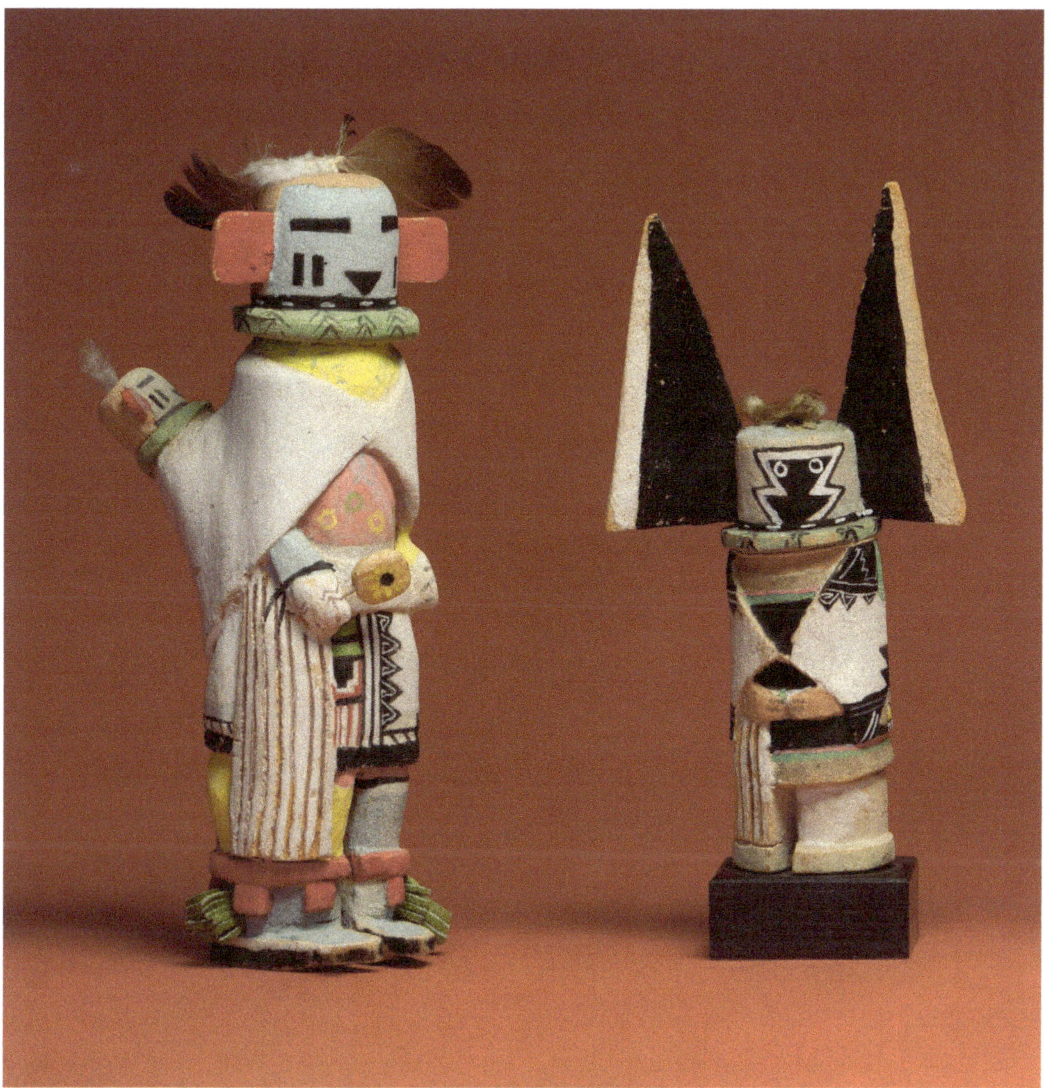

Figure 2. Umtoynaqa (One Who Makes Thunder) and Angwusnasomtaqa (Crow Mother).

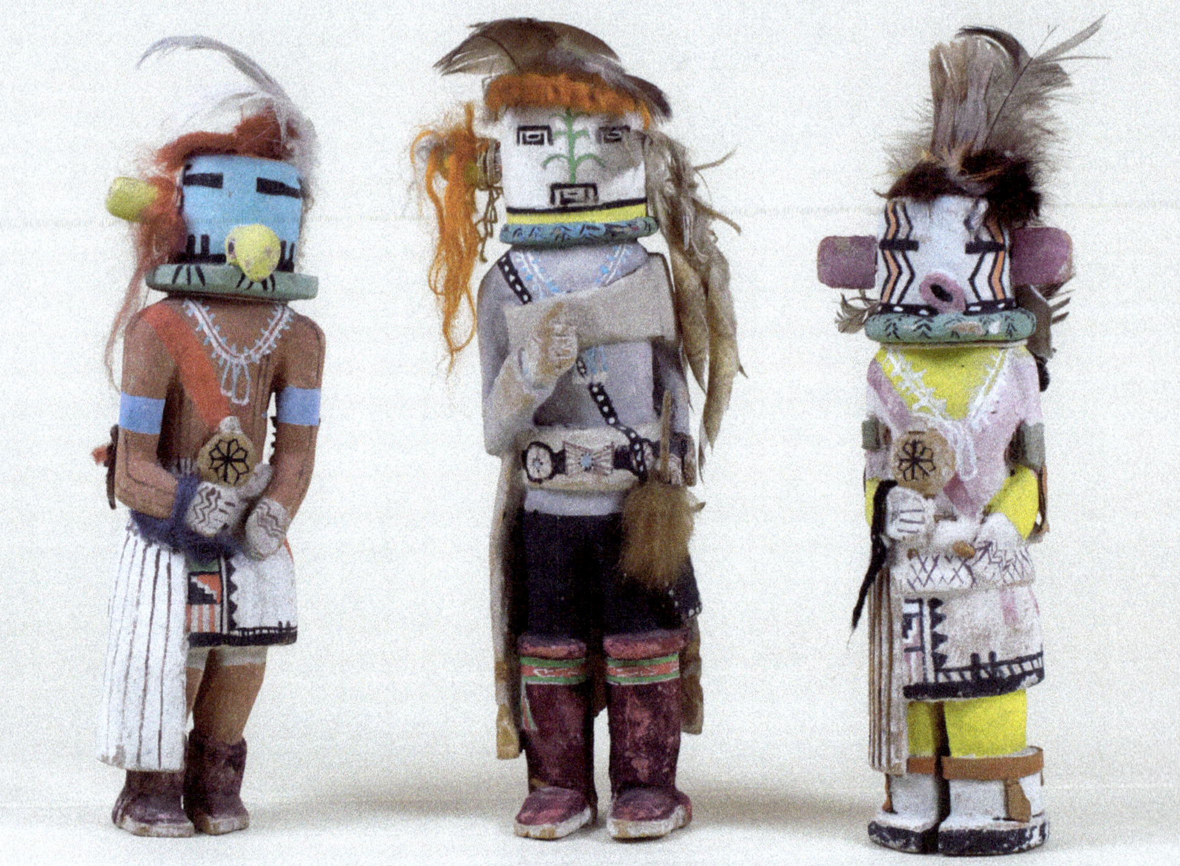

Figure 3. Tasapkatsina (Navajo), Tasapkatsinmuykwa'am (Grandfather of the Navajo), and Hehey'a.

hands and body that Pentewa often preferred. This is also true for the Hehey'a on the right in Figure 3.

Making identification somewhat more complicated is that at times Pentewa took far more care in carving some of his dolls than other examples of his work. For example, the Kooninkatsina (Havasupai) and Tasapkatsinmuykwa'am (Grandfather of the Navajo) katsinam in Figure 1 and the huge Lenwimkya (Flute Priest) in Figure 4 have been executed with meticulous attention to detail. For these katsinam, the face, arms, and legs are carved in full-figure form, and the body paint and katsina garments are portrayed with considerable finesse. More specifically, the Kooninkatsina (Havasupai) katsina in Figure 1 has beaded and fringed armbands and is carrying a miniature coiled basket. The Flute Priest has a separately carved flute and rattle and is wearing a felt bandolier, yarn necklace,

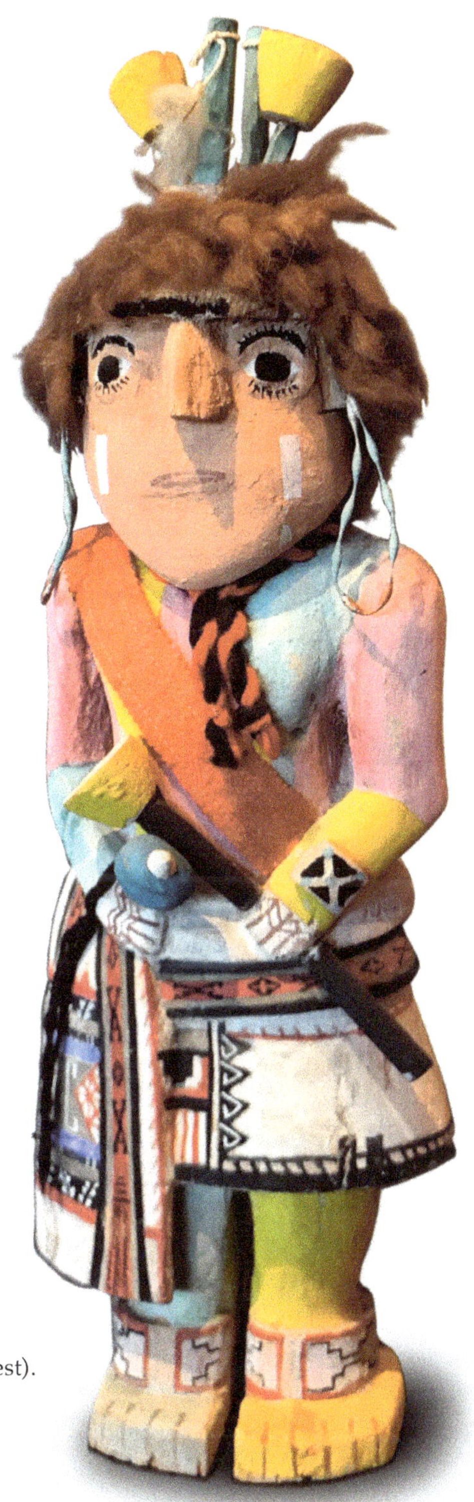

Figure 4.
Lenwimkya (Flute Priest).

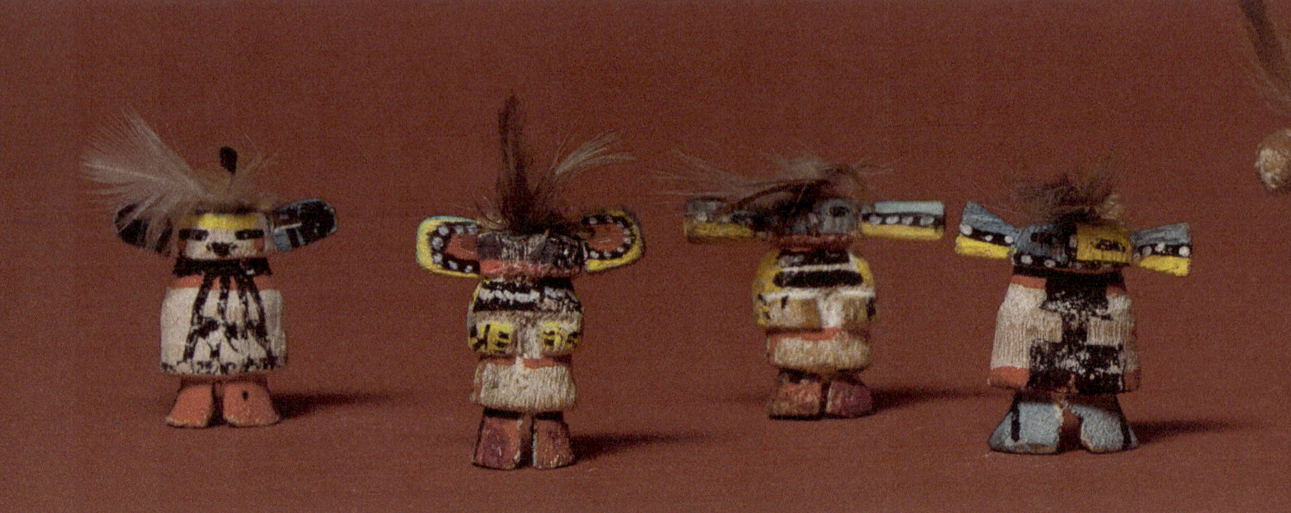

Figure 5. Nine mini katsinam.

and *jacla* earrings. The Flute Priest's kilt and sash are also painted with great care and a complex flower blossom apparatus is attached to the top of his head.

In all likelihood, the contrast between the simply carved, bas-relief carvings, and the exceptionally detailed dolls, was the result of combined factors, including customer demand, time availability, financial pressures, and artistic temperament. When requested by the customer, or Pentewa had time to invest, he produced detailed, precisely made dolls. At other times, when money was quickly needed, the customer was in a rush, or the artist was fatigued, he produced the bas-relief carvings. Whatever the explanation, Pentewa clearly had a remarkable artistic range.

His artistic diversity is also evident in the great variation in the size of the katsinam he produced. Figure 5 shows nine katsinam by Otto that range in height from one to two inches. During the 1950s, these were certainly among the smallest katsinam made by any carver. However, during the same decade, Pentewa also produced a considerable number of very large dolls, some of which were more than two feet tall. An especially interesting example is the already mentioned Flute Priest in Figure 4. This carving is 21½ inches tall by 6½ inches wide by 5 inches deep. It was made from a huge piece of cottonwood root! In addition, the Honkatsina (Bear) katsina shown in Figure 6 is 18 inches tall. In a previous article, I published on Otto (Walsh 2001), katsina figures were included that were 22 inches and 26½ inches tall. Pentewa's carvings ranged from the miniature to the gigantic.

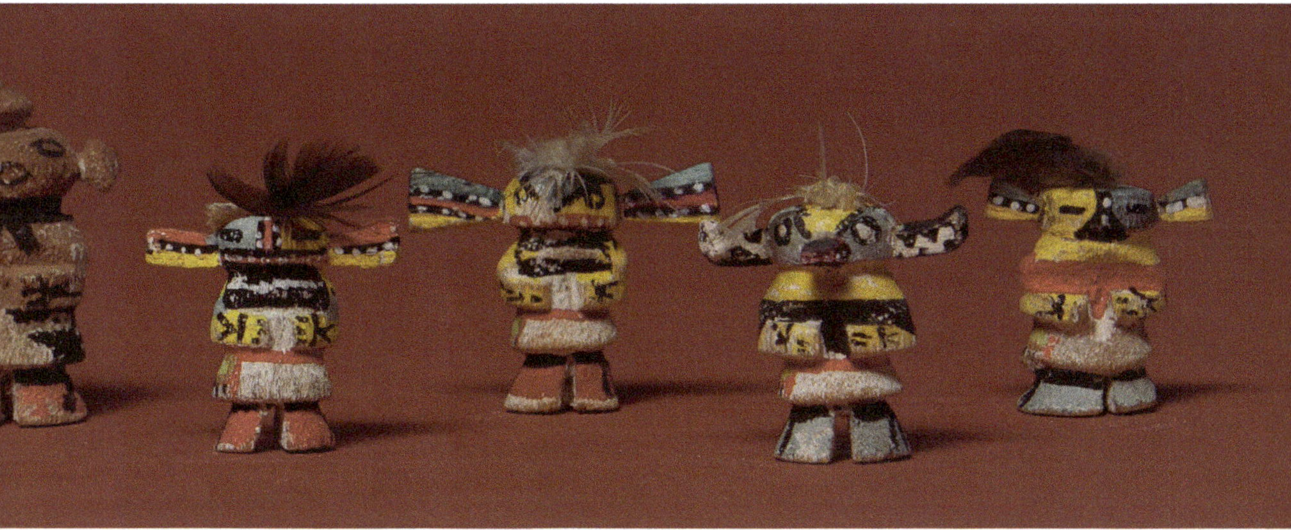

Yet another feature worth mentioning was Pentewa's seemingly unique use of animal parts and pelts on his katsina dolls. In various museums and private collections, I have seen Pentewa use mouse, mole, and dog fur, a cat and fox skull, and bear and buffalo pelts to adorn various katsinam. The Flute Priest in Figure 4 has a buffalo pelt for the hair on his head, and the Bear in Figure 6 has a bear pelt on the body and fox fur on the face.

How is it that Pentewa used these pelts and skulls in the construction of his dolls? Oscar Branson once told me how he frequently brought Pentewa skulls and pelts from deceased animals he had found in the desert. Branson explained he gave these objects to Pentewa because the carver was poor yet resourceful. He indicated that Pentewa made the most of what was at hand and didn't worry about its lineage.

Beyond these practicalities, one can easily imagine Pentewa chuckling at selling a katsina doll made from dog, mouse, mole, and cat parts to an unknowing and undoubtedly squeamish Anglo tourist. That Pentewa was a prankster toward Anglos is not just idle speculation. Both Oscar Branson and Mark Bahti spoke of Otto's sense of humor and his love of practical jokes. Bahti, a second-generation Indian trader whose father, Tom Bahti, probably bought more katsina dolls from Pentewa than anyone else, shared this story about Pentewa:

> Otto Pentewa loved to tease Anglo folks, especially first-time visitors. He would string them along with some fanciful tale. For example, one time my

father left an Anglo alone at Otto's house while he did some sort of errand. As time passed, Pentewa began to stare intensely at the man, which the visitor knew was very atypical behavior for a Hopi. As the staring and silence became increasingly uncomfortable, Pentewa finally spoke, "Long time ago Indians and white men fought." This statement was followed by more staring and another long silence. Pentewa again broke the silence, "Some of them even killed each other!" More silence. . . . Then Pentewa said quite loudly, "Sometimes we Hopi used to scalp the white man!" As the visitor's eyes widened in disbelief and alarm, Pentewa leaped out of his chair at him, yelling, "You scared now?!" After which, Pentewa broke up laughing.

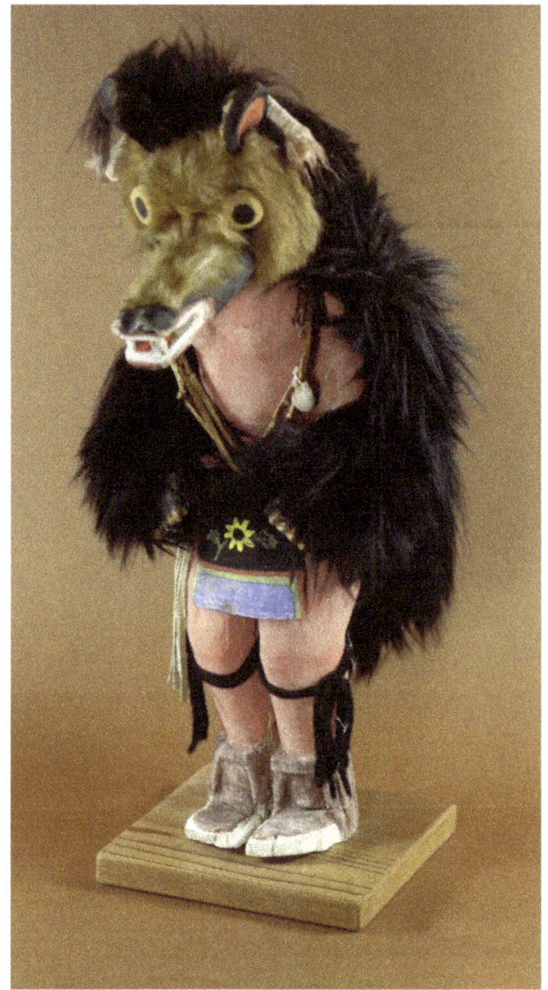

Figure 6. Honkatsina (Bear).

Given this story and others like it, it is not surprising that Pentewa inserted a comic element into many of the dolls he produced. An example of his mischievous spirit can be seen in the huge-headed, cartoon-like Kwewu (Wolf, Figure 1). Another example is the humorous yet eerie Angwusnasomtaqa (Crow Mother), with over-sized wings (Figure 2). Nonetheless, Pentewa also produced katsinam that had great dignity and solemnity. The Kooninkatsina (Havasupai) and the Tasapkatsinmuykwa'am (Navajo Grandfather) katsina (Figure 1) are prominent examples of his more serious, even stately side.

Another Pentewa innovation was his use of bent or contorted wood, sometimes suggesting the motion of the Katsina dancer. He may have used such wood in part because it is the least expensive to acquire. Examples of his using bent wood include the baby katsina on the back of the Umtoynaqa, which takes advantage of a secondary branch on the cottonwood root (Figure 2). Yet another is the bent over Honkatsina (Bear, Figure 6).

While it is now common for Native American artists to receive both personal acclaim and reasonable reimbursement for their work, such was not the case during the early to mid-twentieth century. One of those artists deserving posthumous recognition is Otto Pentewa. He was a complex, creative, eccentric, and humorous artist who helped introduce Hopi katsina carving to a much broader audience. Selling his dolls for one to three dollars, Pentewa made them as much out of love and commitment as for the minimal reimbursement he received. Like so many Native artists from the past, recognition has been late in coming to Otto Pentewa. Yet it has come nonetheless, as his unique talent is now widely recognized and affirmed.

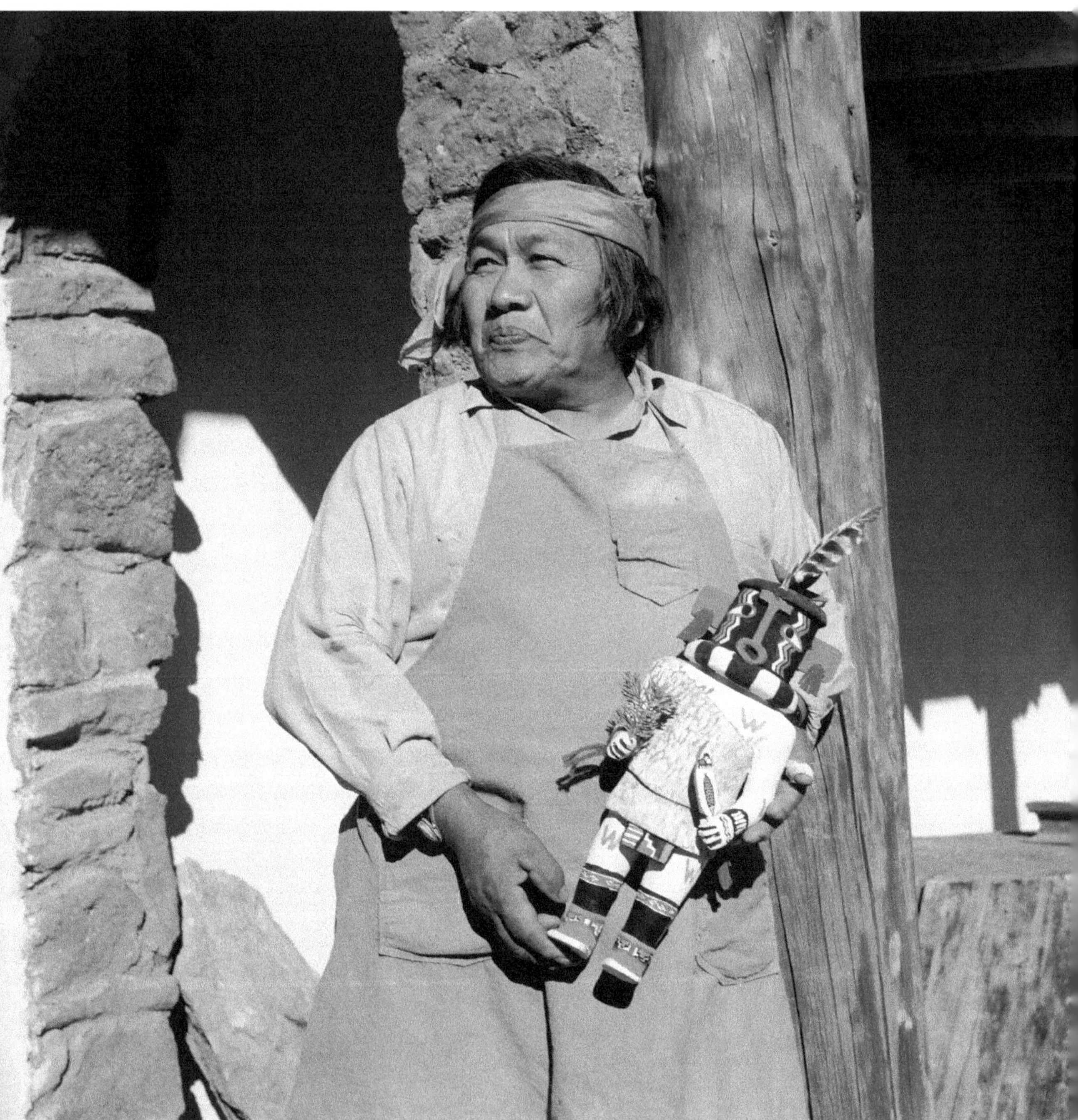

Figure 1. Jimmie Kewanwytewa holding a Hehey'a.

JIMMIE KEWANWYTEWA
Cultural Emissary

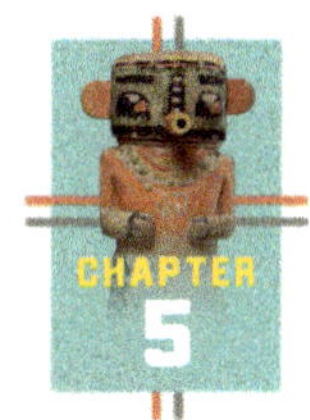

by Barry Walsh and Valerie Wedge

AFTER WILSON TAWAQUAPTEWA and Otto Pentewa, the third in the great line of identified Hopi katsina carvers was Jimmie Kewanwytewa (Figure 1). Jimmie K—as he was better known—was *Piikyas* (Young Corn) Clan. Piikyas is the name for the emerging nubs that first protrude from cornstalks and will grow into full ears. Jimmie's name, Kewanwytewa, means "running away colorful" in Hopi. The word carries the sense of a sudden flash of beauty or intricacy that quickly disappears as one might experience when a fox or coyote vanishes in an instant behind a rock (Wright, personal communication with author, 1997).

According to his widow, Agnes, Jimmie was born sometime around 1888. Jimmie K had two families. In his first marriage to Pansy, he had six children: Spencer, Flora, Willis, Orin, Louise, and Warren. Pansy died due to complications related to childbirth in the mid-1930s, and some twenty years later Jimmie K married again. He was sixty-eight years old when he married Agnes, who was forty-four. As Agnes shared with me back in 2001, her father opposed the match, thinking Jimmie was too old. When I interviewed her, Jimmie had been gone for almost forty years, and Agnes was ninety-one. But as she reminisced, a dreamy smile lit up her face, and she said, "he may have been older, but he was strong!" (See Figure 2.)

Jimmie K's early life in Orayvi (Oraibi) was traditionally Hopi. He received some unspecified schooling on the Hopi reservation. Later he spent an indefinite period at the Sherman Institute in Riverside, California, where Tawaquaptewa had been sent after the 1906 split. He was initiated and active in ceremonial life as an adult.

Around 1931, the Museum of Northern Arizona (MNA) in Flagstaff hired Jimmie to be a general handyman. At about the same time, the museum also hired Edmund Nequatewa to do similar chores. The museum's founder and director, Harold Colton, must have had a sharp eye for talent, as Jimmie K and Nequatewa became two of the most important members of the museum staff in its history. Jimmie K quickly became the museum's primary Hopi educator,

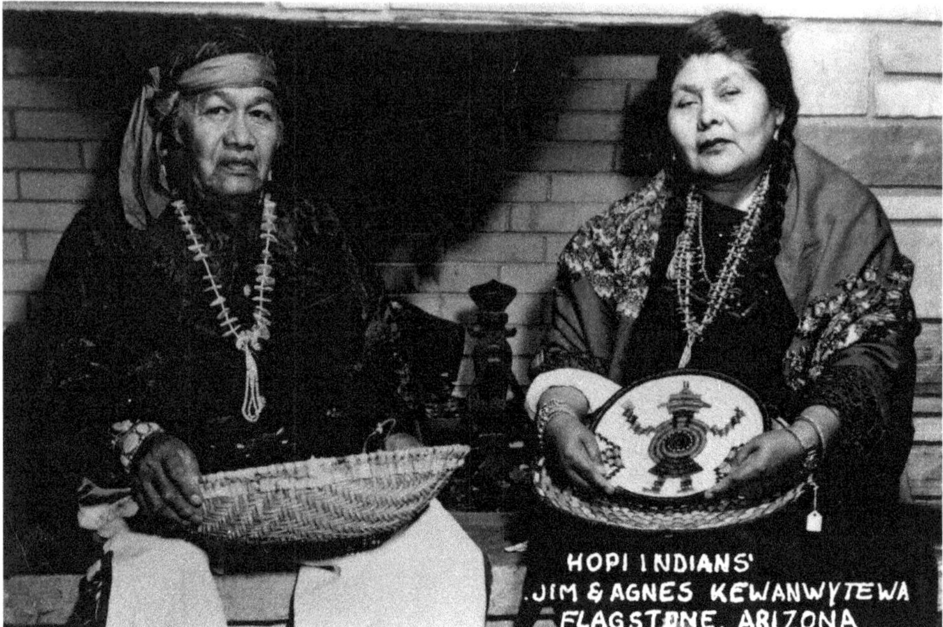

Figure 2. Jimmie and Agnes Kewanwytewa.

presenting countless demonstrations as a katsina carver, dancer, singer, and lecturer on Hopi culture. Edmund Nequatewa was accomplished in his own right. He became renowned for two influential books, *Born a Chief* (1934) and *Truth of a Hopi* (1936), both of which are still in print. However, valuable as they both were to the museum, Nequatewa and Jimmie K were apparently not easy companions with one another. This may have been because of their differing worldviews— Nequatewa was a Christian and Jimmie K was a traditional Hopi in his religious practice.

Jimmie K's effectiveness as an educator was due to more than his insider knowledge of Hopi culture. He was uniquely charismatic. Standing barely over five feet, he was nonetheless barrel-chested, immensely strong and imposing, and behind his physical presence was a force of personality. Those who knew him described him as humorous, energetic, vital, knowledgeable, entertaining, self-confident, and articulate. Barton Wright, who became curator of the museum in 1955, worked with Jimmie K through the last decade of his life. Barton and his wife, Margaret, shared stories about the carver that leave no doubt as to his exceptional personality and talent.

Jimmie K was a bridge between Hopi, the broader community, and the museum. Each year he would serve as driver and translator for Harold and Mary-Russell Ferrell Colton, and later the Wrights when they visited the Hopi

Mesas to collect material for the museum's annual Hopi Show. Driving to the Mesas with Jimmie K at the wheel was not an experience for the faint of heart. The Wrights described Jimmie's habit of singing extended Hopi songs while driving. This was not in and of itself problematic as Jimmie K had an exceptional voice; however, he liked to sing with gusto, belting out his songs with both hands in constant motion. Once, Barton Wright recalled, the museum truck made a sharp turn in Munqapi (Moenkopi) and suddenly encountered a large truck rumbling straight toward it from the opposite direction. Wright screamed, "Take the wheel!" and on this one occasion, Jimmie had to terminate his song mid-verse. There were times when he did not. On another trip to the Mesas, Jimmie K was stopped by a policeman for a missing taillight. As the officer approached the vehicle, Jimmie was still in mid-song, both hands gesticulating. Only when he finished the song did he turn to address the policeman. Learning of the taillight problem, he cheerfully removed the red bandana from his head, got out of the truck, tied the bandana onto the missing taillight, and drove off, leaving the policeman agape, citation book in hand.

While Jimmie K was both a born comic and a gifted teacher, scholars and members of the general public appreciated his knowledge and his ability to discuss Hopi religion, music, and customs. Even within a formal lecture format, his wit was apparent. Bill Breed, a former geologist at the museum, recalls the warm reception Jimmie received when he sang Hopi songs for the public. Frequently asked to perform another, Jimmie would introduce the next song as one of deep meaning to the Hopi. Only several minutes into it would the audience realize they were listening to a Hopi vocalized version of "Dixie."

Jimmie K's sphere of influence extended far beyond the Mesas and Flagstaff. Sometime in the 1950s, he met Gerald A. Smith, superintendent of schools for California's San Bernardino County. The two became friends, and Smith invited the Kewanwytewas to visit schools in California. Jimmie K and Agnes accepted, traveling to California the next winter when museum work lulled. There they gave a presentation at a school with Jimmie demonstrating katsina carving, drumming, and singing, and Agnes, the grinding of corn and making of *piki* bread. It was such a success that the Kewanwytewas were soon touring schools throughout San Bernardino County. This became an annual pattern, and for a decade or so the Hopi educators spent two to three weeks a year in California. San Bernardino schools developed an entire curriculum on Hopi culture, the core of which was based on demonstrations by the Kewanwytewas.

In the 1950s, Jimmie visited the opposite coast of the continent as well.

Segments of the movie *Oklahoma!* had been filmed in Arizona, and as the shooting neared completion, a publicist for the studio conceived the improbable idea of having Indians from Arizona and Oklahoma exchange tribal flags atop the Empire State Building to promote it. The studio approved the concept, and the publicist sought Native American representatives from the two states for the photo opportunity in New York City. Probably related to his increasing renown at the MNA, Jimmie K became the Arizona representative.

Jimmie K's trip to Manhattan was a series of adventures, tales of which he shared with amused friends. Upon arrival at the Waldorf Astoria Hotel, he could tell that it was a "pretty fancy place." Not wanting to look unsophisticated, he immediately demanded a new mattress for his room. He also managed to make the trip profitable. While strolling about the city dressed in a bright headband, velvet shirt, white pants, and a large pair of turquoise jacla earrings, he was approached by a woman of means who commented on the beauty of his earrings and asked whether he would consider selling them. Jimmie K declined, saying they were his grandfather's and therefore too precious to part with. Pressed to do so with escalating offers from the New York matron, Jimmie eventually relented for some fantastic sum. As soon as the satisfied customer disappeared, he took another pair of jaclas from his pocket and put them on. Later, as he was walking about admiring the city, another New Yorker approached him, saying, "I see you're not from around here. How do you like our city?" Jimmie replied, "I like it fine. How do you like our country?"

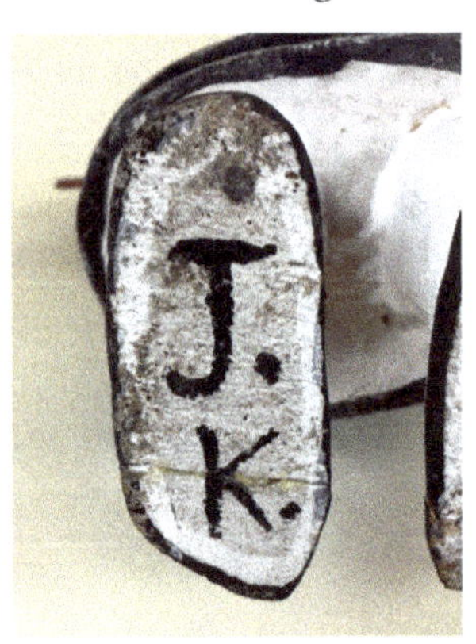

Figure 3.

Jimmie K was memorable as a person, but his legacy will also live on because of his katsina carving. He provided 120 katsina dolls to the MNA's permanent collection through gift or sale, the earliest dating to 1935 and the latest to the year of his death, 1965. Jimmie's dolls were exceptional examples of the art of katsina carving and had several distinctive features. He was the first Hopi carver to sign his katsinam, a practice that elicited considerable opposition from other Hopi at the time. As shown in Figure 3, his signature usually consisted of his initials "J. K." found on the bottom of the same foot. He did not sign consistently, however. Of the approximately 100 dolls we examined at the MNA, only about 40 percent were signed.

Where did the idea for signing his dolls originate? It appears to have come from Harold Colton's wife, Mary-Russell Ferrell Colton, who encouraged the artistic endeavors of generations of Hopi and other Native American artists

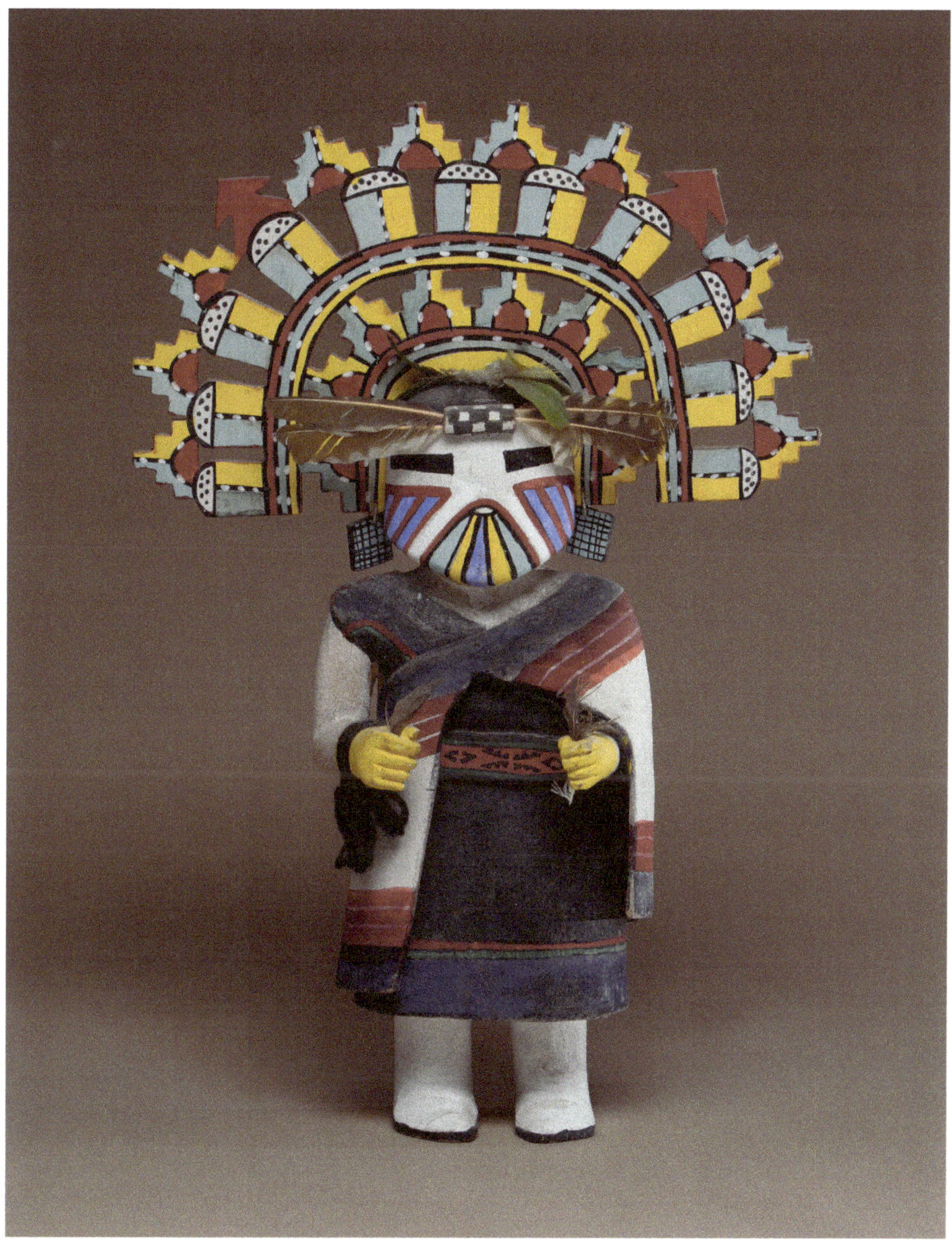

Figure 4. Palhikwmana (Water Drinking Maiden).

via her work at the MNA. She brought to her appreciation of the art an Anglo's desire for attribution, to which Jimmie K and other Native American artists begrudgingly agreed. The result is that the large majority of Hopi katsina carvers, following Jimmie K's lead, have signed their dolls since the 1950s.

Figure 4 shows a large 20-inch Palhikwmana (Water Drinking Maiden) that manifests many of Jimmie's distinguishing carving characteristics. These features can be seen in the many other examples provided in this chapter. Jimmie had a prodigious output. Figures 5 and 6 show a marvelous assemblage of his work from the Bob and Le Oehrli collection. Note the range in katsina figures, every one of which is well executed.

Also worth noting is that Jimmie carved in very different sizes. Figure 7 shows a set of Qöqlö katsinam that are less than three inches tall. In contrast, Figure 8 depicts a matched set of Hemiskatsinam (Jemez katsinam) that are 40 inches and 38 inches in height. Both sets are from the MNA.

Toward the end of his life in the early 1960s, Jimmie K's eyesight dimmed due to cataracts, and the quality of his carving and painting declined. Examples of katsinam from this period include the set of Qöqlö katsinam in Figure 7. Note the rather rough carving style and imprecise painting that were entirely uncharacteristic of his previous work. However, in about 1963 Jimmie K had cataract surgery, and the quality of his production returned.

Jimmie K died in his sleep in 1965 at his small home on the grounds of the MNA. The day before, he had been working, singing, and functioning in his normal vital manner. He was approximately 77 years old.

Jimmie Kewanwytewa is remembered fondly by everyone we encountered. He provided a unique bridge between Hopi and Anglo culture, doing so with both goodwill and a sense of collaboration, and yet never compromised his Hopi ideals and values. Jerilynn Smith, the daughter of school superintendent Gerald Smith, perhaps best summarized his character and influence: "Jimmie Kewanwytewa was a person who transcended culture, race, age, and educational background. He was a universal man in many ways." Today his katsinam are distributed throughout the world in museums and private collections, a dissemination that reflects both the cross-cultural influence and the immense talent of this "universal man" and master Hopi katsina carver.

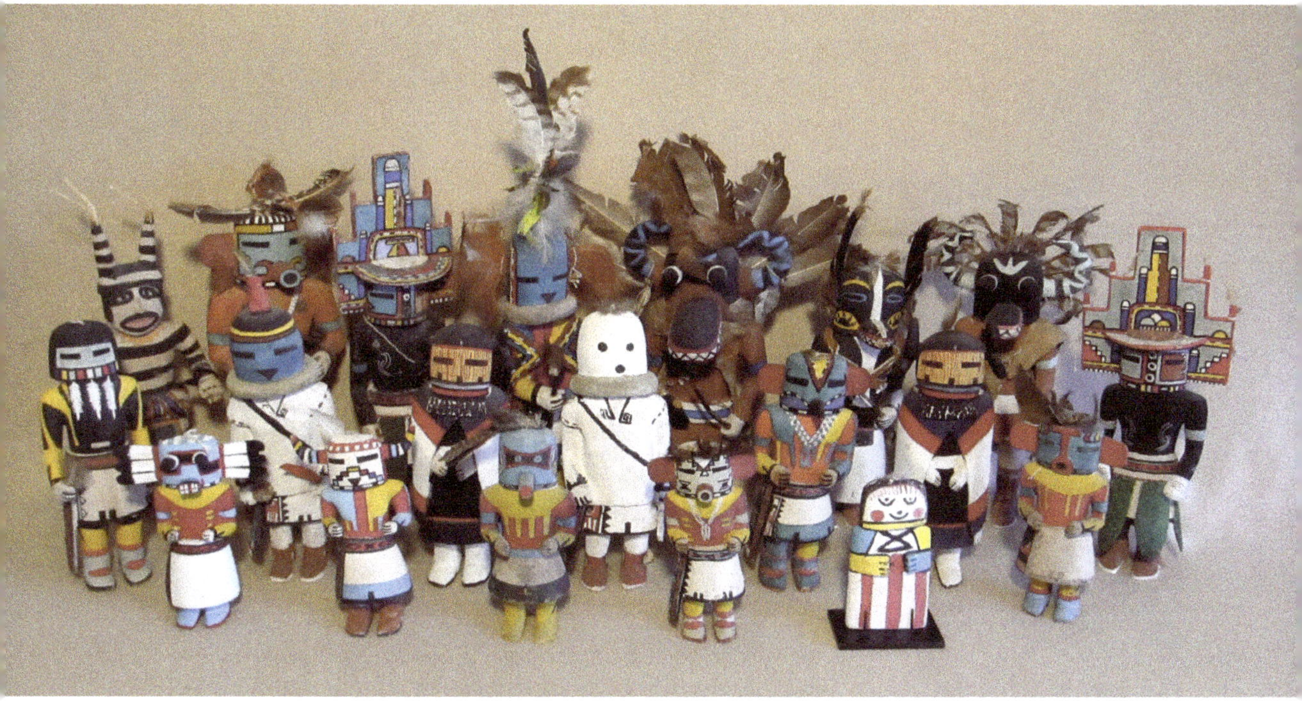

Figure 5.

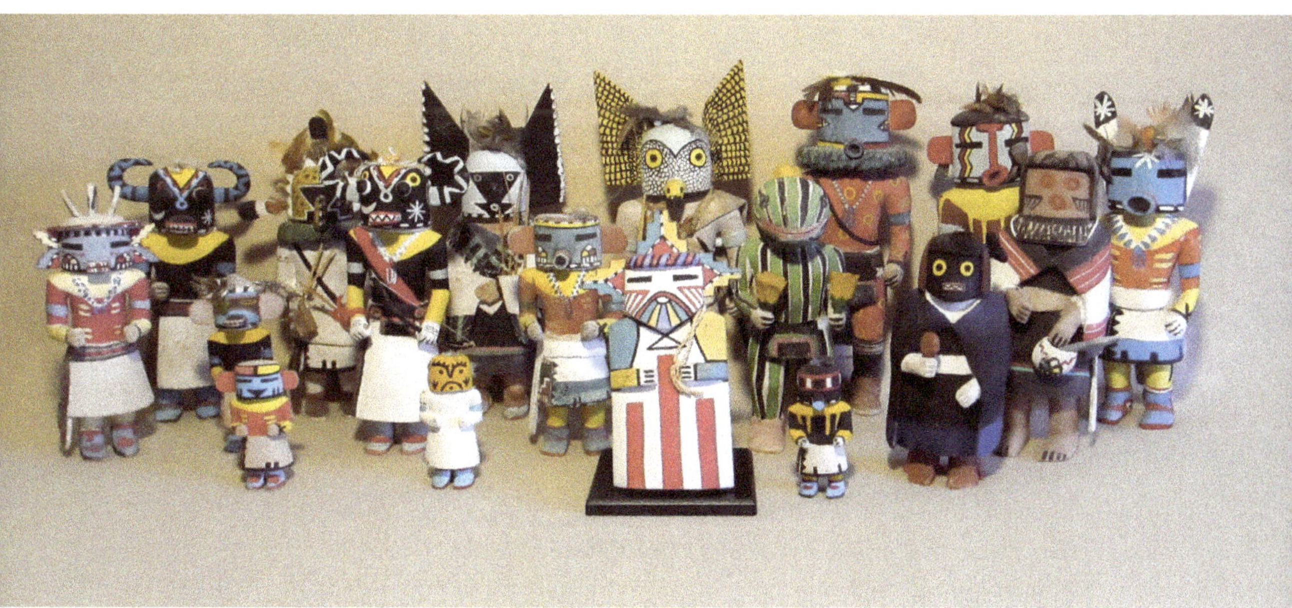

Figure 6.

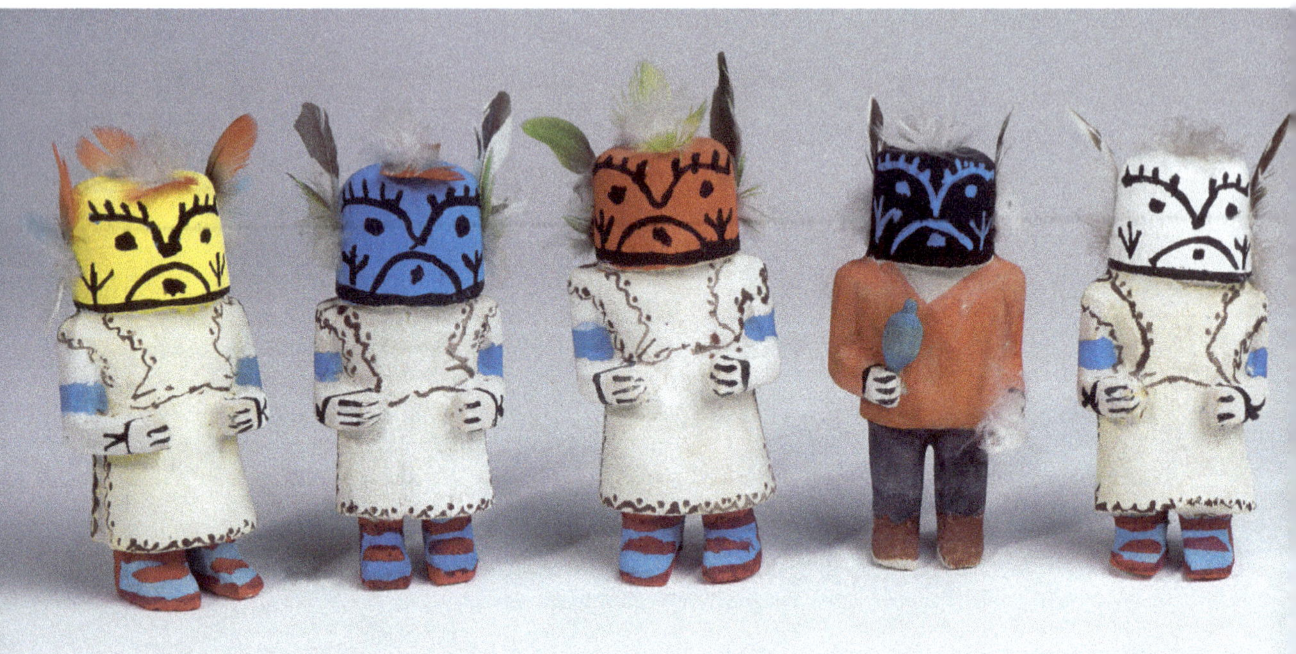

Figure 7. Set of mini Qöqlö katsinam.

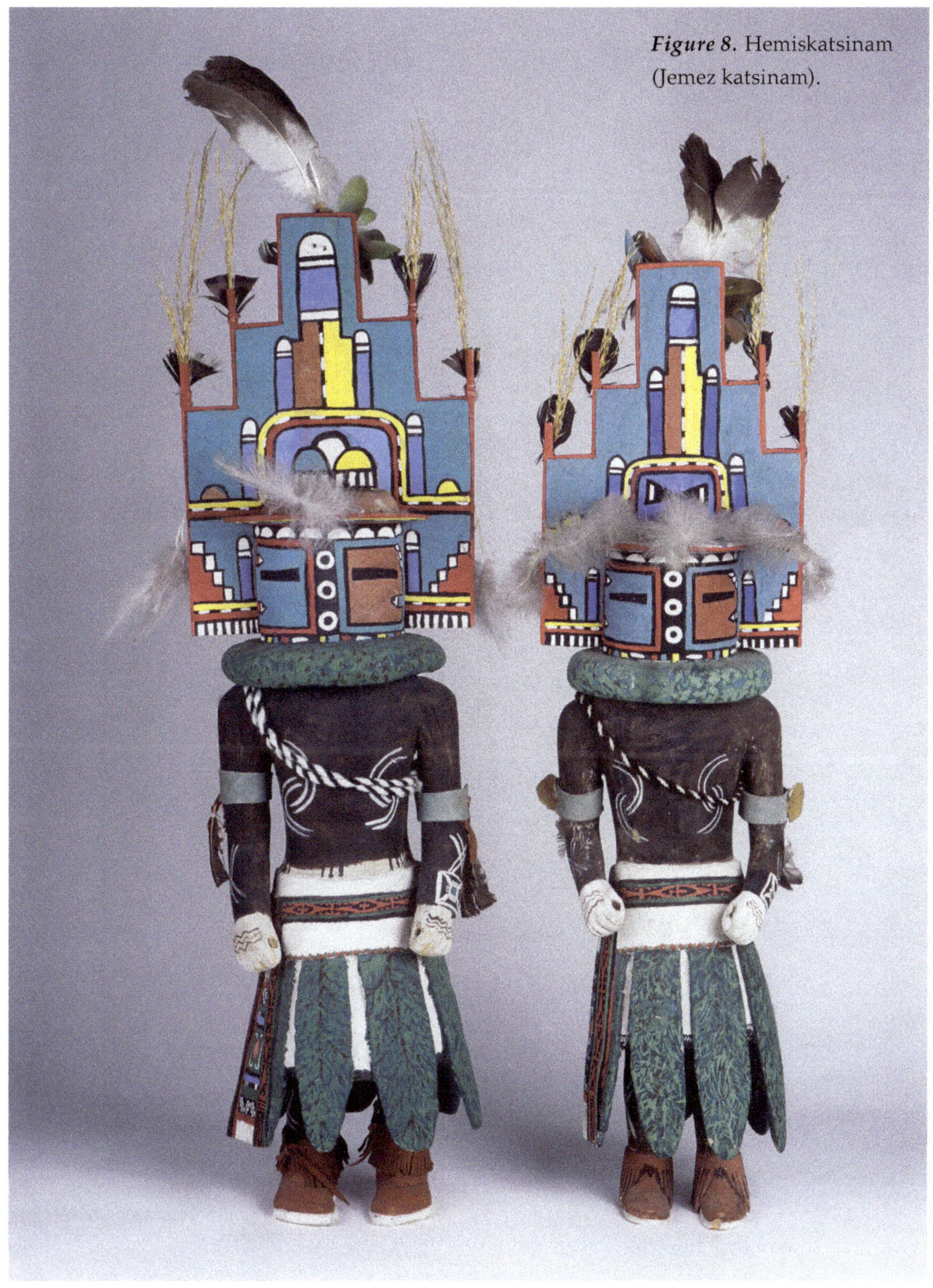

Figure 8. Hemiskatsinam (Jemez katsinam).

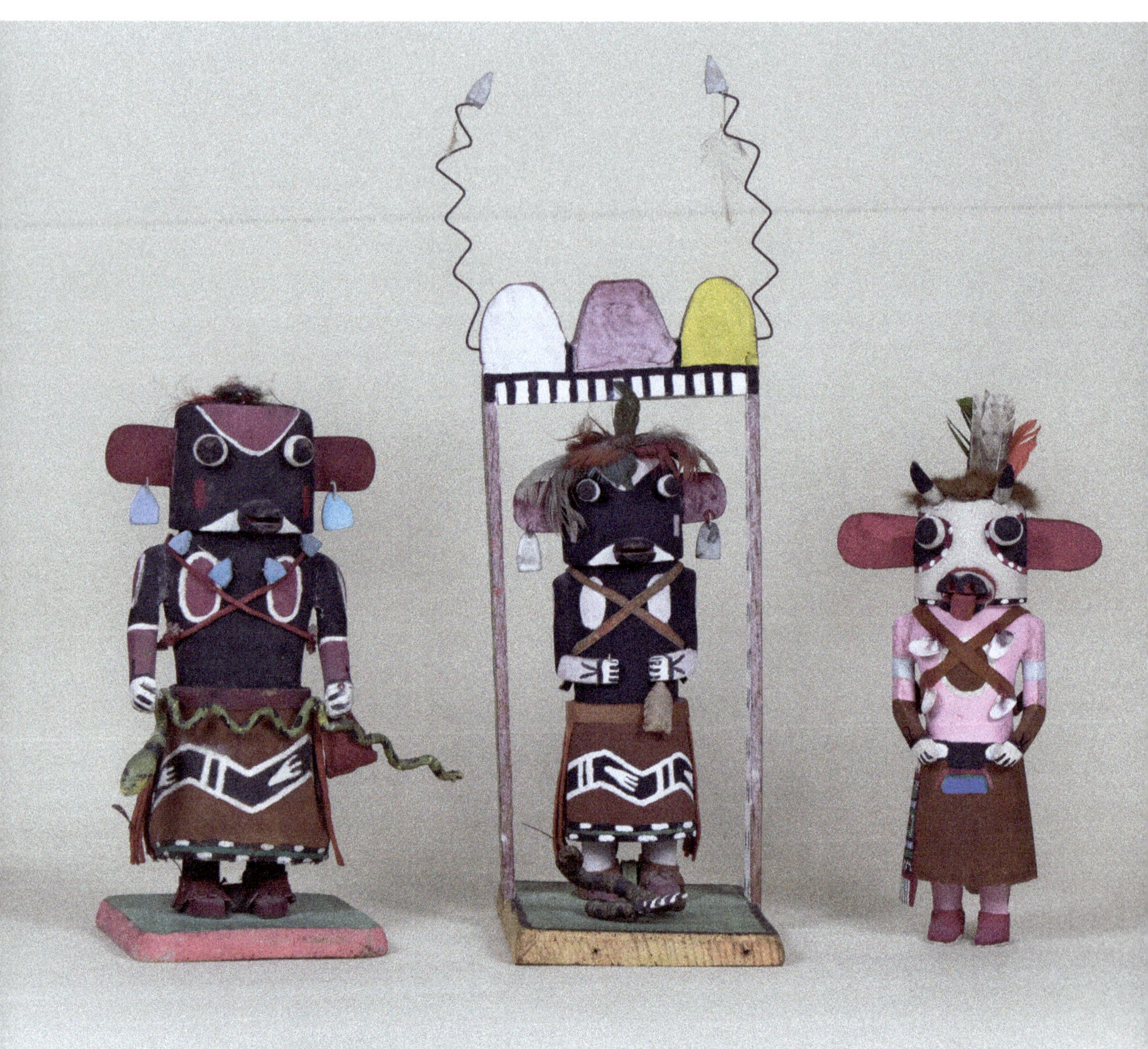

Figure 1. Two Tsukatsina (Snake) figures and a Wakaskatsina (Cow).

CHARLES FREDERICKS

A Family Tradition

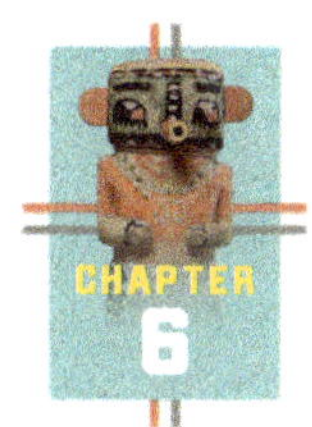

CHARLES FREDERICKS WAS an important katsina carver for three reasons: 1) he was the brother of Tawaquaptewa, 2) he was the father of Oswald "White Bear" Fredericks, and most importantly, 3) he was a fine and distinctive carver in his own right.

Due to family wishes, I am not able to provide a biography of Charles. I will only say that Charles was Bear Clan and was born in Orayvi (Oraibi) in the mid- to late-1870s. He is said to have passed about 1964.

In all likelihood, Charles began making katsinam for village matters like the majority of Hopi carvers. However, it's quite clear he eventually entered the commercial market in selling katsinam, probably in part to support his family. Evidence that he made katsinam to sell is provided in Figure 1. Two of the Tsukatsina (Rattlesnake) figures have attached bases. Katsina tithu given to children at dances never have bases attached. In addition, the Wakaskatsina (Cow) katsina in Figure 1 is signed "Charles Fredericks" in pencil on the bottom of the kilt. Only a katsina made for sale would have a signature on it.

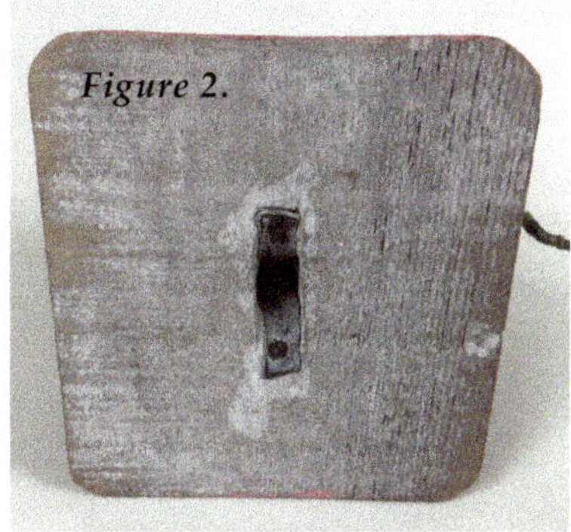
Figure 2.

The bases on the katsinam in Figure 1 require additional comment. Both Tsukatsinam katsinam are attached to their bases in a very unusual way. A metal rod is attached between the feet near the ankles. A leather thong is then looped over this rod and secured to the underside of the base with two nails (see Figure 2). The katsina is thereby loosely attached to the base. I've only seen this method of attaching katsinam to a base used by Charles.

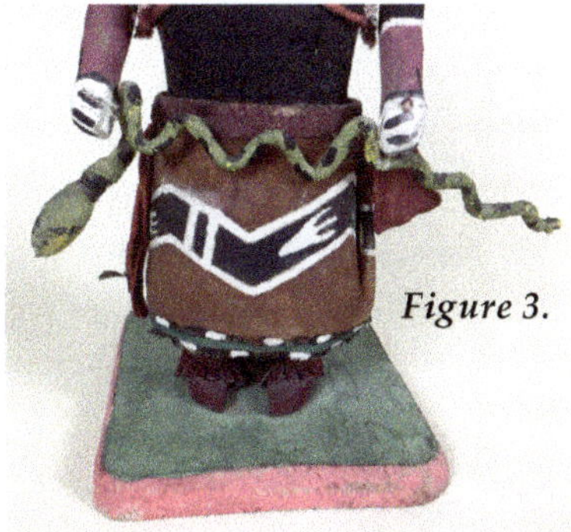
Figure 3.

Also worth noting is that Charles appeared to like to make Tsukatsinam, as shown in Figure 2 where there are two examples. See a close up in Figure 3 of the elaborate snake held by the Tsu. I've encountered several of his Tsukatsinam over the years. He seems to have made these far more often than any other katsina figure.

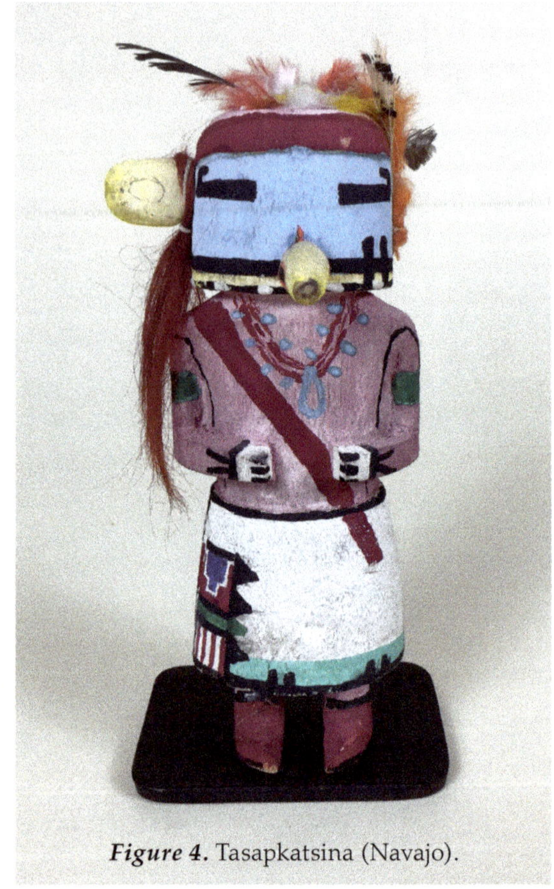
Figure 4. Tasapkatsina (Navajo).

Charles made katsinam in a rather wide range of sizes. Figure 4 shows a simple Tasapkatsina (Navajo) katsina that is a mere 6 inches tall. Figure 5 shows Charles at the peak of his powers. This is the best carving I've seen by him. It is a Siosakwahonankatsina (Zuni Blue Badger). It is unusually large at 14 inches tall and is exceptional due to the detail on the face, ears, kilt, and body paint. The tablita, a ceremonial headpiece, is also very well executed. Charles has also added a carefully made rattle and strung bow. The katsina is wearing leather armbands and a felt sash, and has a string of multi-colored piki dangling from his left hand. Charles went all-out with this carving.

On many of his katsinam, Charles had some stylistic traits that make his work easy to identify. These include arms that are sawed off at right angles to the torso and that have not been sanded. Note the sharp edges on the arms of the Tsukatsina in the middle of Figure 1 and the Tasapkatsina in Figure 4. This style for the arms resembles what appeared on many Route 66 dolls during the 1950s. However, Charles used this mode on full-figured katsinam. Another distinctive feature for Charles's work are sharply pointed feet that are curved on the outside but straight cut on the inside. Examples are shown in Figures 3, 4, and 5.

Charles's work was notable and deserves to be listed in the roster of important carvers from 1880 to the present.

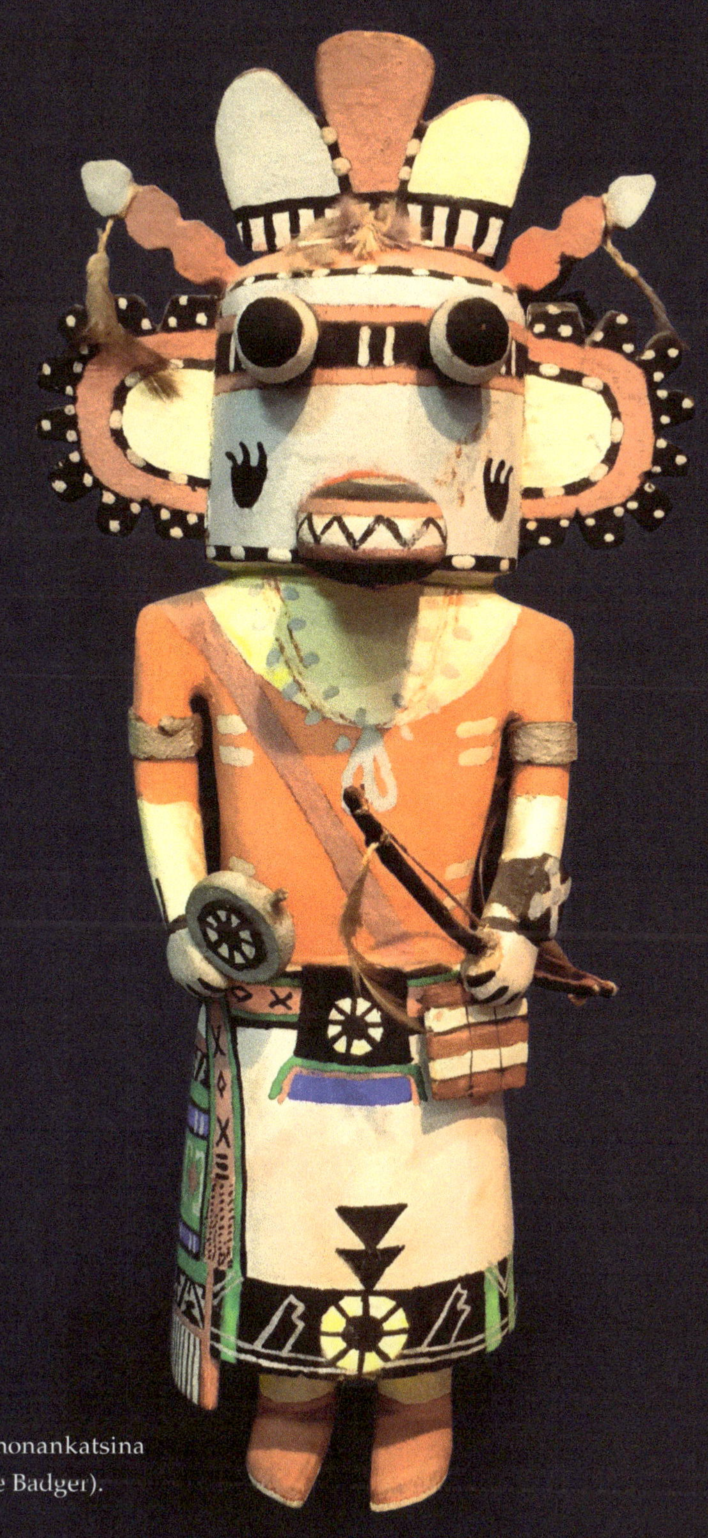

Figure 5.
Siosakwahonankatsina
(Zuni Blue Badger).

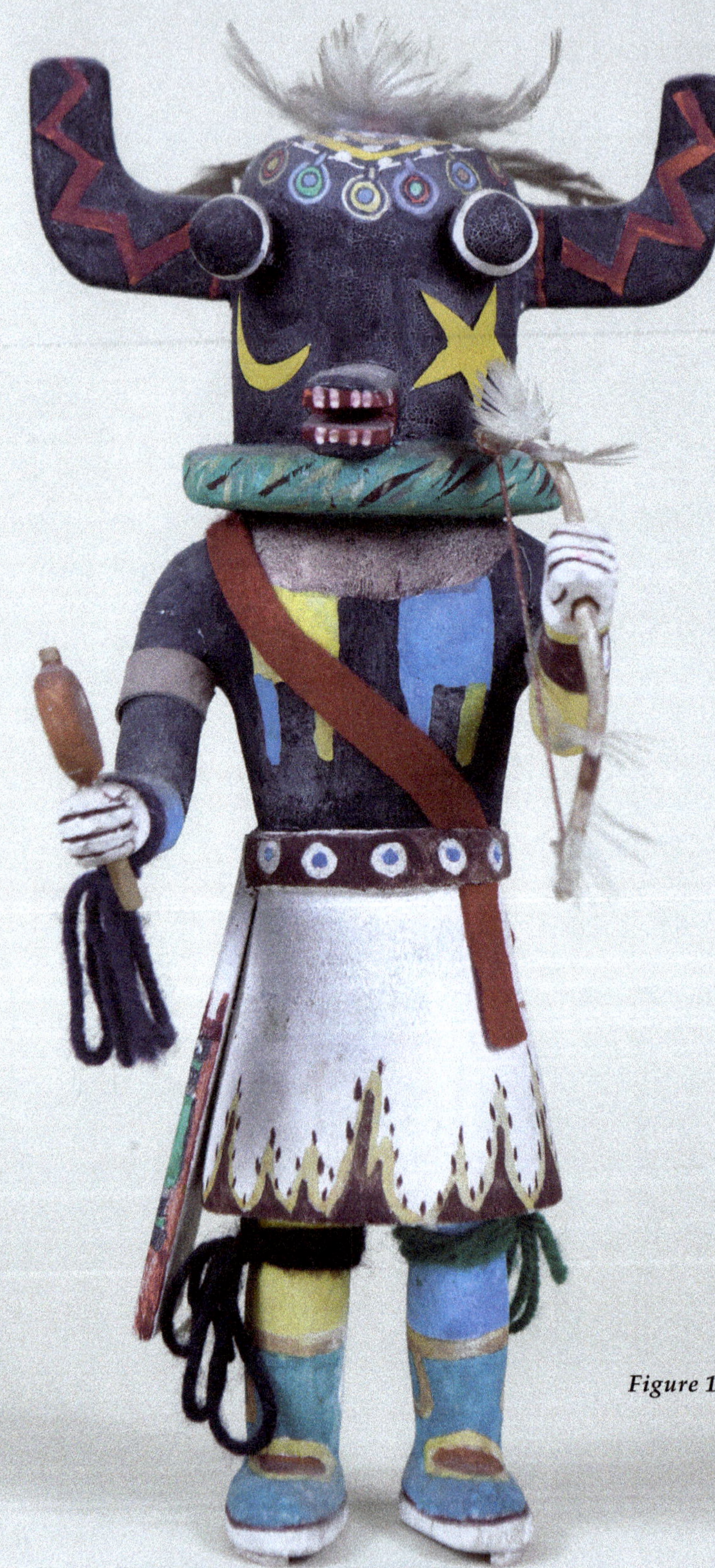

Figure 1. Hoot'e.

OSWALD "WHITE BEAR" FREDERICKS

A Man Well Traveled

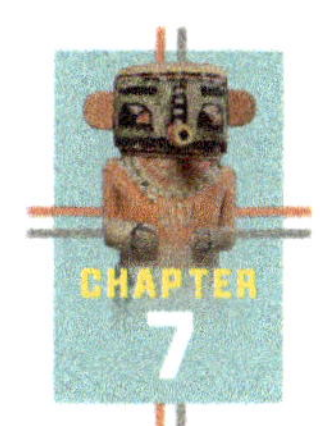

OSWALD "WHITE BEAR" FREDERICKS was the son of Charles Fredericks. His uncle was Tawaquaptewa. Both of these relatives have chapters devoted to their carvings in this book. White Bear was born in Orayvi in 1905. His mother, Anna, was Coyote Clan and his father, Charles, was Bear Clan. [2]

White Bear had a complex and interesting life. He was educated early on at the Orayvi Day School, then sent to the Phoenix Indian School, and from there to the Haskell Institute in Lawrence, Kansas. Later he attended Bacone College in Oklahoma where he became a devout Christian. After graduating from college, White Bear became an art teacher at a New Jersey YMCA. How he ended up in New Jersey is not clear, but he remained in this position for fifteen years.

Eventually, he returned to Arizona where he taught arts and crafts at the Phoenix Boys Club. At some point, his artistic talent became noticed in the Phoenix area, as his paintings of katsinam appeared in *Arizona Highways*. He is also said to have met Senator Barry Goldwater on a golf course, which led to a decades-long friendship. Goldwater was an ardent collector of katsina carvings, and White Bear provided many to the Senator's collection. Goldwater eventually donated his world-class assemblage to the Heard Museum. Many examples of White Bear's dolls from the Heard collection are featured in Alph Secakuku's book, *Following the Sun and Moon* (1995).

In the late 1950s, White Bear convinced Fredrick Howell, Director of the Charles Ulrick and Josephine Bay Foundation to underwrite a history of the Hopi people. Eventually noted Southwestern writer, Frank Waters, was selected for this project. Waters began a multi-year collaboration with White Bear that resulted in the immensely popular *Book of the Hopi* (1963). The book had the unintended consequence of attracting droves of European tourists and American hippies to Hopiland in search of Hopi mythology, prophecy, and spiritual inspiration. It eventually became a New Age bible of sorts.

[2] My primary source for this chapter is Arizona Archives Online, operated by Northern Arizona University.

The book was not without its controversy. A master's thesis by a woman named Roxie McLeod (1994) disputed the accuracy of much of *Book of the Hopi*. McLeod argued that White Bear was not a reliable source on Hopi myth, religious meaning, and prophecy because he often lived off-reservation, was Christian, and not fully initiated. Others disputed this criticism, saying that White Bear's Hopi sources were strong.

However, since the current book is about katsina carvings and not Hopi history, ethnology, or religion, I take no position as to the accuracy of *Book of the Hopi*. Accordingly, I will confine my attention to discussing White Bear's high-quality katsina carvings and other ventures. For those interested in the relationship between White Bear and Frank Waters, read the latter's *Pumpkin Seed Point* (1969).

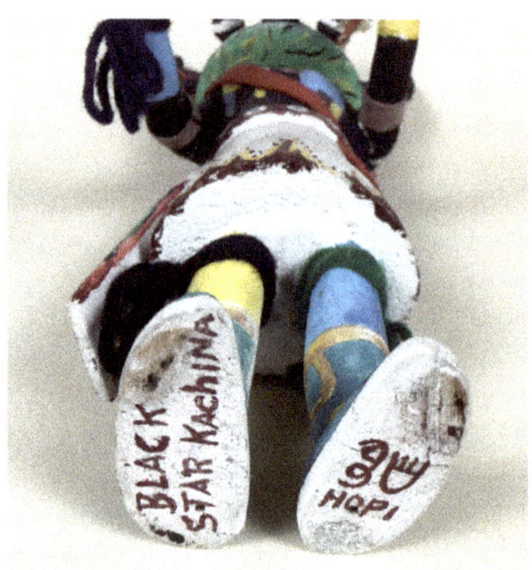

Figure 2.

Barry Goldwater had a fine eye for Hopi katsinam and would not have purchased a large number of dolls from White Bear if they were not high quality. A particularly nice example is shown in Figure 1. This is a Hoot'e katsina, named for the sound he makes. On the bottom of the right foot, White Bear has written "Black Star Kachina." On the bottom of the left foot, he has painted his usual wave and Bear Claw symbols along with the word "Hopi," (see Figure 2). The katsina is made with fine attention to detail especially as to the designs on the head and the accoutrements. It is also large at 14 inches tall.

White Bear's dolls have very distinctive feet. They are essentially oval-shaped and almost dome-like. See the feet in Figures 1 and 3. A rare exception to this type of foot is found on the Qötsahonaw (White Bear) katsina in Figure 4. Mr. Fredericks made this figure quite whimsical with small toothpick-like claws emerging from all four feet directed

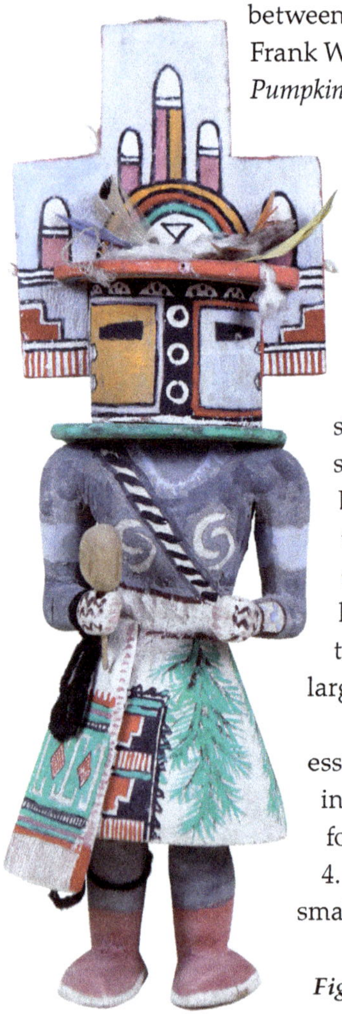

Figure 3. Hemiskatsina (Jemez katsina).

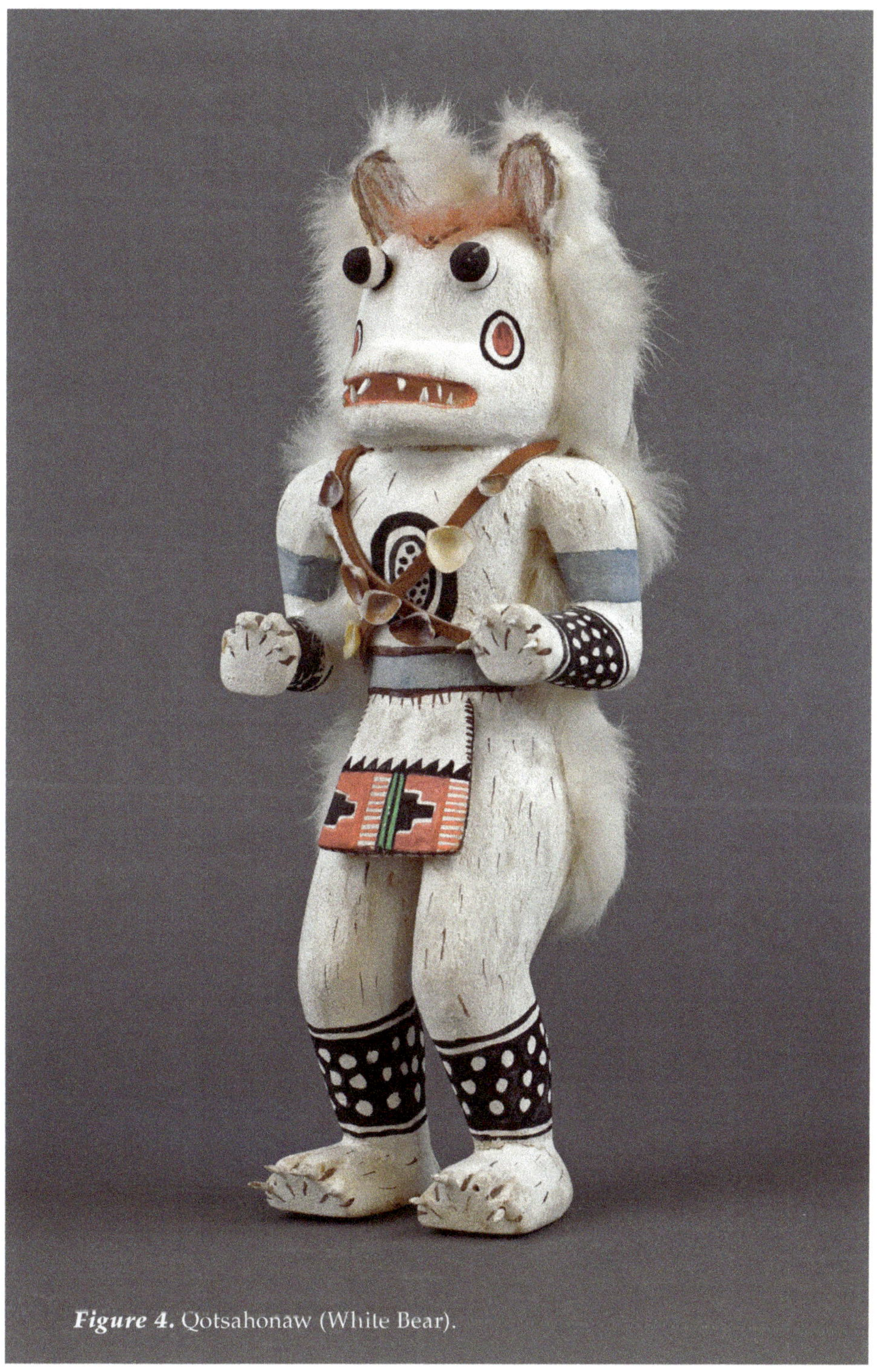

Figure 4. Qotsahonaw (White Bear).

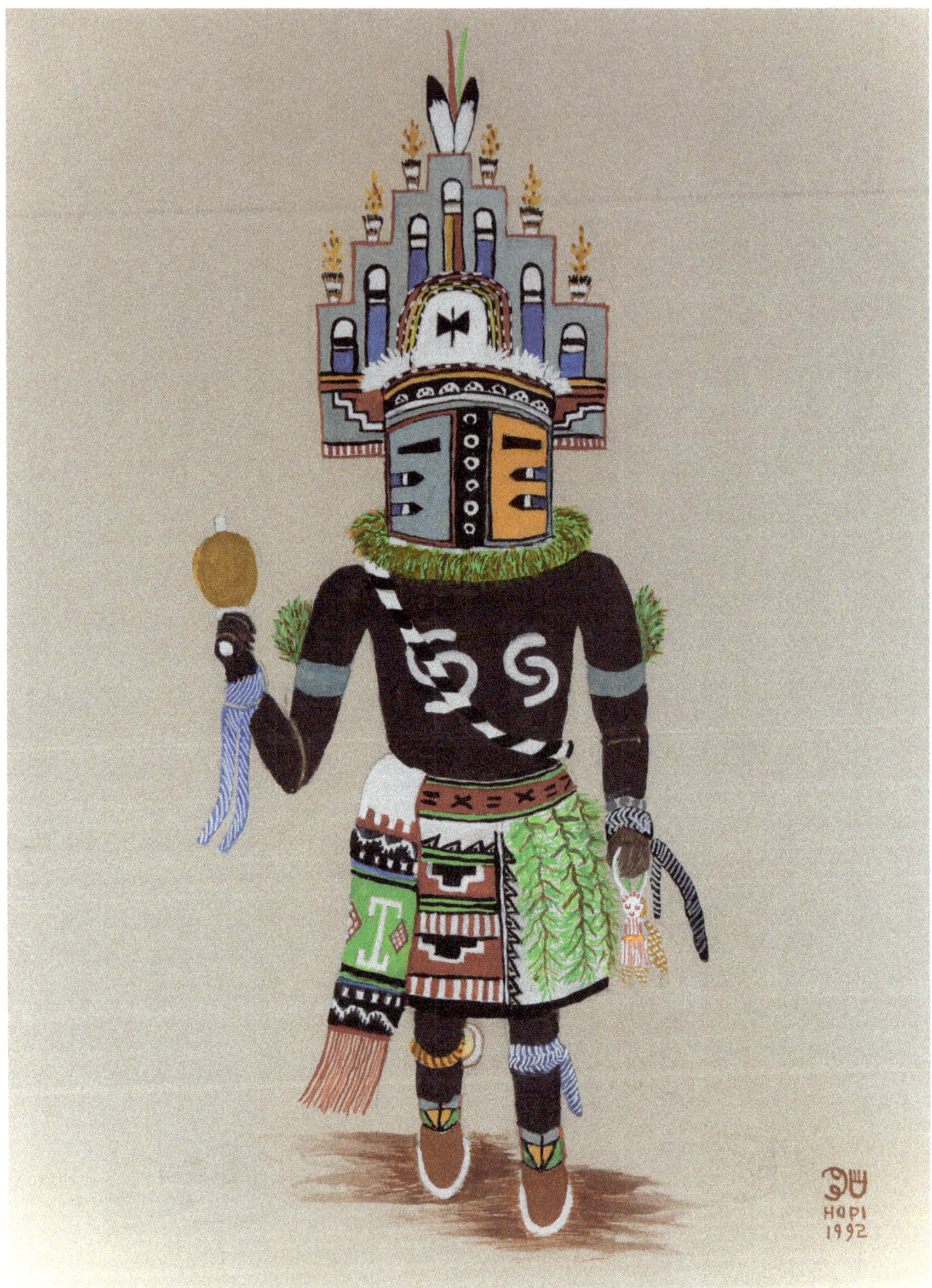

Figure 5. Painting of Hemiskatsina (Jemez katsina).

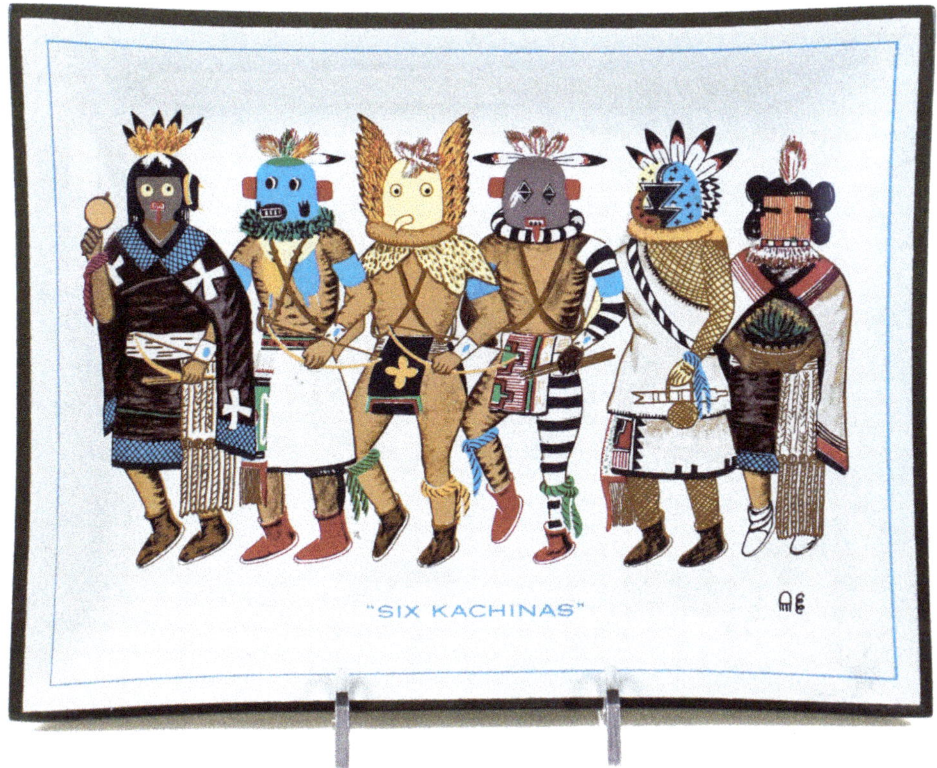

Figure 6. Dish with six katsina portraits.

toward the viewer. In addition, the cartoon-like face on this katsina makes it effectively comical.

A more serious carving is presented in Figure 3. This is the Hemiskatsina (Jemez katsina). It is carefully rendered, signed with the usual symbols, and dated 1961. Speaking of a Hemiskatsina, Figure 5 shows a very fine painting by White Bear of the Home Dance katsina. Clearly, White Bear was an artist of diverse talents.

He traveled in such wide circles within both the Anglo and Hopi worlds that he sometimes became involved in unusual projects. Figure 6 shows a mass-produced, commercially-fired dish with six katsina portraits by White Bear. I was not able to locate the origins of this venture.

White Bear's art clearly deserves to be included in this volume. His katsinam were distinctive, innovative, and high quality. An obituary for the Hopi newspaper *Tutuveni* reported that White Bear died in 1996 when he was more than 90 years old. The paper indicated that he had served as a judge at the Hopi Tribal Court and as the governor of Kiqotsmovi (Kykotsmovi). He traveled and excelled in many circles.

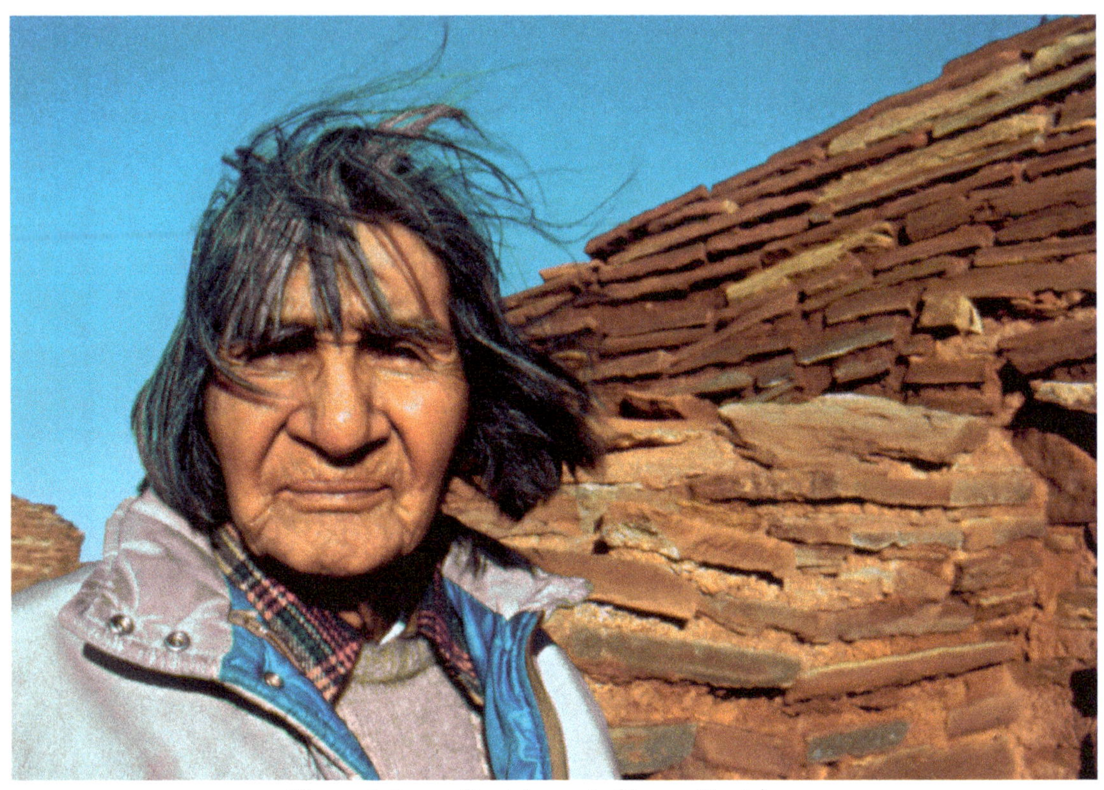

Figure 1. James Kootshongsie (Jimmy Koots).

JAMES KOOTSHONGSIE (JIMMY KOOTS)

A Complex Genius

JAMES KOOTSHONGSIE (Figure 1)—better known to avid katsina collectors as Jimmie Koots—was born in the Third Mesa village of Hotvela (Hotevilla) in 1916. He was to become one of the major advocates for Hopi traditionalism in the twentieth century, while also gaining renown as one of the finest katsina carvers of all time. Explicating this dual trajectory involves some complex twists and turns.

As his son Dennis told me, James grew up in Hotvela until about age five. At that time, he was "relocated" —some would say kidnapped—by United States government forces. At the time, the federal government had a goal of fully assimilating Native children into mainstream Anglo culture. In order to accomplish this goal, Native youth were routinely rounded up and forced to reside at such facilities as the Sherman Institute in Riverside, California. In these schools, they were required to sacrifice their native languages, dress, and religious practices. And if they failed to do so, students were often physically punished (see Gilbert 2010; Lajimodiere & Carmen 2014).

In the film *Autobiography of a Hopi* (which features James), he shares that he left home one day expecting to be back in a few hours and instead didn't return for five years. While at Sherman, James said he largely forgot how to speak his native language. For many, that would be the end of fluency in one's mother tongue, but not for James. Years later, he would return to traditional ways with a vengeance.

As James indicated in the movie cited above, he emerged from Sherman convinced that what was important was to "make money." As a young adult, he took jobs in various factories before joining the military and serving in the Philippines during WWII. After the war, he lived in Chicago for about ten years where he worked as a welder and car mechanic. During this period, he and his wife, Helen, began their family, which eventually reached five children. The first four were born in Chicago, while Dennis was born in Hotvela. Despite achieving reasonable success in Chicago, something more important than "making money" drew James back to Hotvela, where he spent the rest of his days, passing in 1996.

After returning home to Hopiland, James discovered that "the U.S. government in collusion with the big energy corporations, was trying to remove the Hopi and Navajo from their ancestral lands rich in coal, oil, gas, and uranium" (Schaaf 2008, 172). James was especially responsive to this concern since he had already experienced trauma at the hands of the United States government. So, James, along with key Hopi elders, began to oppose strip mining and other forms of abuse and disrespect for Hopi land.

As noted by historian Greg Schaaf (who knew James well), Kootshongsie "went on to become the Ben Franklin of the Hopi" (personal communication, 2016). James created, edited, and was largely the sole author for the newsletter *Techqua Ikachi* (*Land and Life*). He published this newsletter and advocacy voice regarding Hopi sovereignty from 1975–1990. (All forty-four issues are still available online). Following are two examples of James's writing.

> We see the abuse of the earth for its resources, for wealth and power and destructive purposes. By so polluting the air, water, and land, depleting the soil where once all plants grew healthy...The earth's wonderful numbers of live species are becoming extinct because of man's carelessness. (*Techqua Ikachi*, #28)

> Hopi will attend the gathering of indigenous people from different parts of the world around July in Geneva. We find that most every country has been creating problems by violating the human rights of indigenous minorities. We think the Commission on Human Rights is doing a great job. They support and believe we were born free and equal in dignity and rights. That we should be protected against genocide and discrimination. That we have the right to preserve our culture and tradition, the right to pursue our own cultural development, the right to practice our own religion, the right to protect and use traditional lands. (*Techqua Ikachi*, #43)

Somewhat astonishingly, the advocacy of James and other elders from Hopiland, such as David Monongye and Thomas Banyacya, was heard and responded to internationally. As Dennis shared with me, his father met with representatives from the United Nations (UN) on four occasions with the Assistant Secretary of the UN once staying at James and Helen's home. The UN conferred on the Hopi elders Peace Medals for their important efforts to promote Hopi sovereignty and world peace (Schaaf 2008). And perhaps most important, the efforts to control and exploit Hopi land and resources were significantly neutralized.

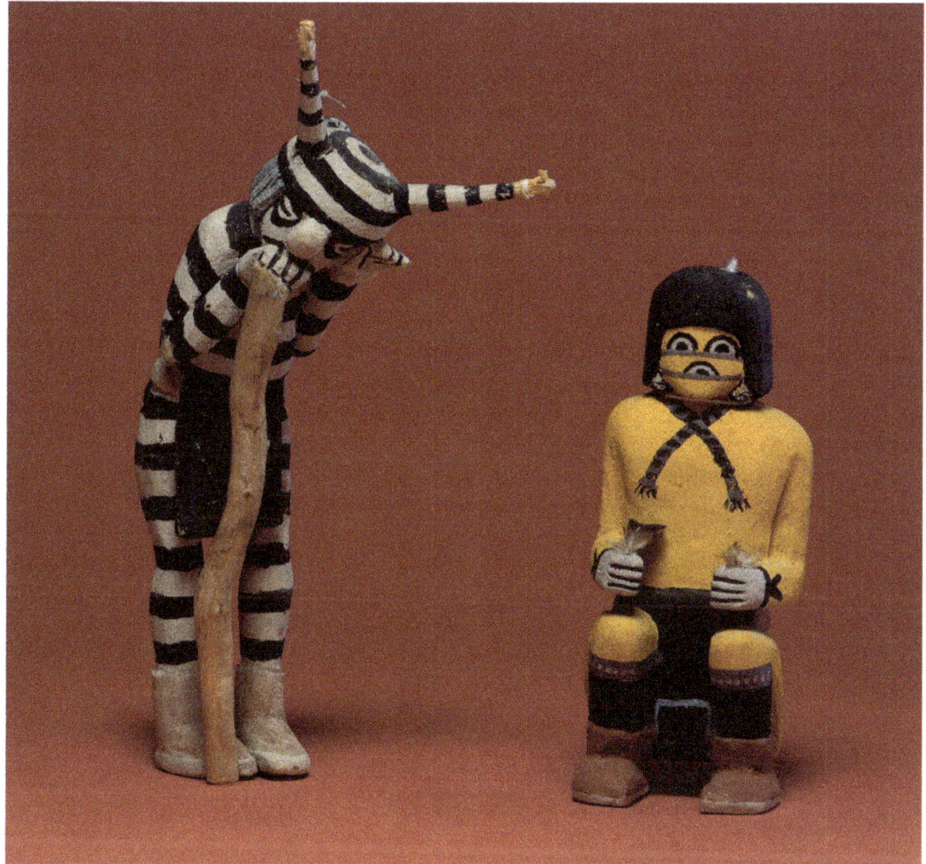

Figure 2. Eavesdropping Koyaala and squatting Sikyatsuku (Yellow Clown).

How does all this history link with Jimmie Koots, the renowned katsina carver? The answer is not simple, or certainly not directly apparent. James appears to have started carving katsinam on his return to Hotvela in the 1950s. He developed a relationship with Bill Dutton, a well-known dealer in Santa Fe, who owned a gallery called Rare Things. In Santa Fe, James was known as "Jimmie Koots," where few people knew about James's central role in advocating for traditional Hopi ways. In turn, few on Hopiland knew of Jimmie's Santa Fe success and fame as a katsina carver. It was as if James and Jimmie were two personas he chose to keep separate.

Why did Jimmie achieve such recognition as a carver? The simplest explanation is that he was perhaps the greatest comic carver of all time. Consider a few examples depicted in Figures 2, 3, and 4. In Figure 2 we have a humorous, eavesdropping Koyaala and a squatting Sikyatsuku (Yellow Clown). In Figure

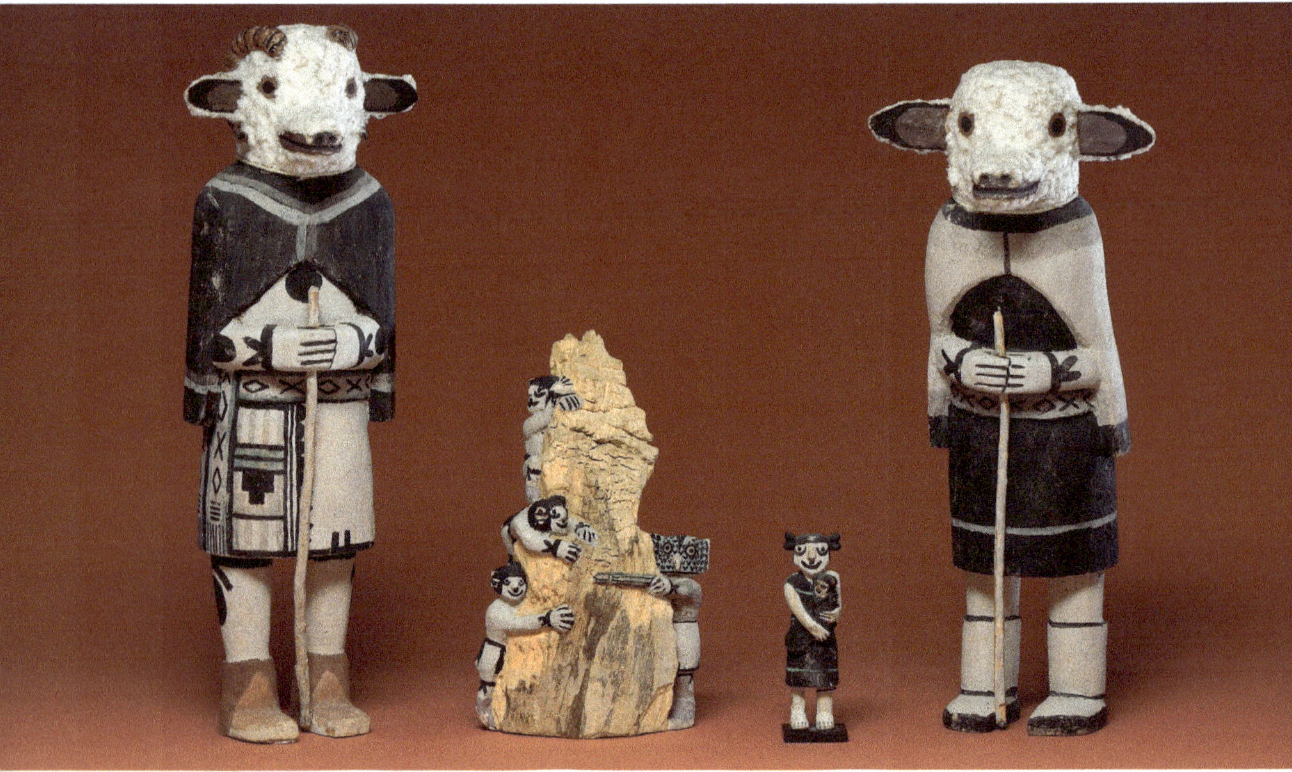

Figure 3.
Pangwkatsinam (Bighorn Sheep), Mongwu (Great Horned Owl) pursuing three Qötsatsuku (White Clowns), small Hopi maiden, and Pangwkatsinam (Bighorn Sheep).

3, second from the left, is a clown vignette where an enforcer Mongwu (Great Horned Owl) katsina is pursuing three taunting Qötsatsuku (White Clowns). On the right in Figure 4, a grumpy Koyaala is pounding a drum. What's the joke? Clowns are supposed to be happy and funny; this one is out of his role. In Figure 5 on the right are two gleeful Koyaalas in piggyback mode. In Figure 6, there are two figures that are more subtly comic: A mixed-up half Ho'e half Mosayru (Bison) katsina and a dynamic Tsaaveyo (Ogre). Both are overstated and cartoon-like. Another humorous group is found in Figure 7, left to right: a Pöqangwhoya, the katsina aspect of the older brother of the Twin Warrior Gods, two Kwikwilyaqa katsinam (Striped-Nose, Imitator katsinam) and a pair of Koyaalas. All these comic carvings bring smiles to katsina collectors due to their vivacious spirit and very atypical presentation. In the era when Jimmie carved, most katsinam were stoic and serious in style.

Jimmie's comic creativity could also take an erotic turn. Figure 4 shows an

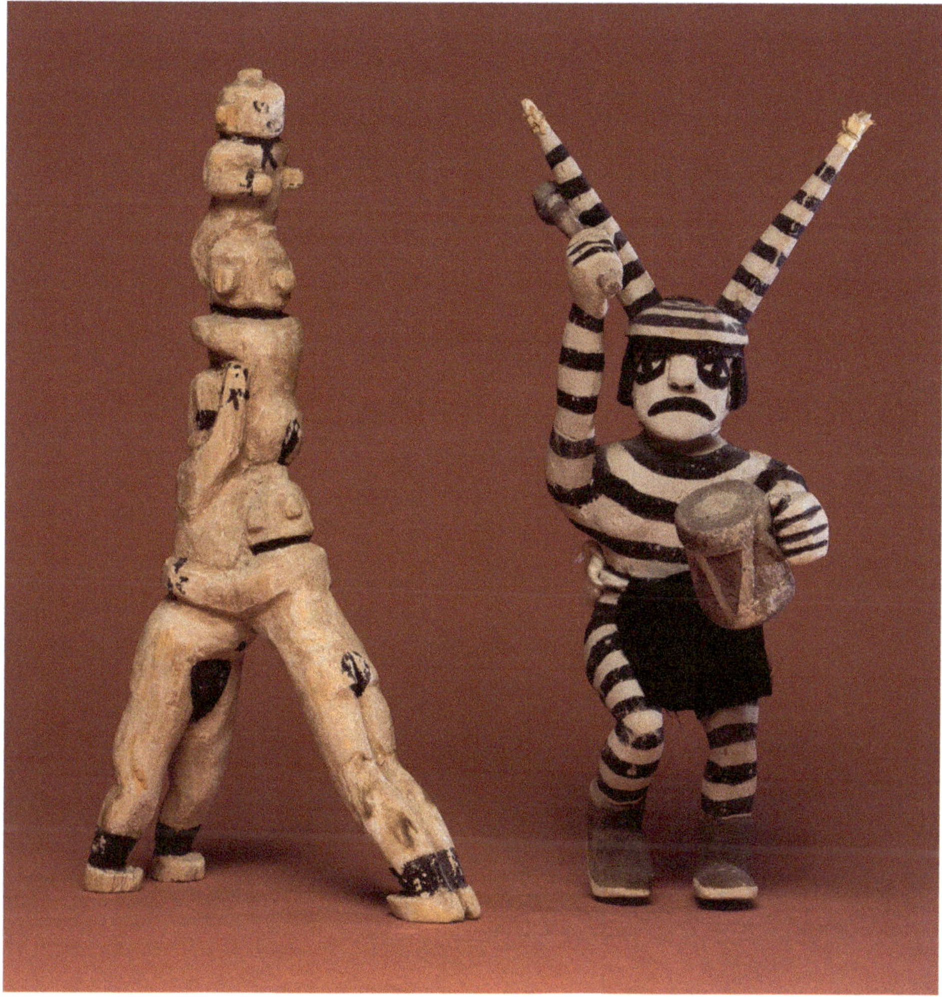

Figure 4. Stack of Kooyemsi and a grumpy Koyaala.

acrobatic stack of Kooyemsi that look innocent enough until examined carefully. On closer inspection, one can see that the mouths of some of the figures match up with the genitals of the others. This homosexual humor was puzzling to me until art appraiser Joan Caballero explained it. Joan worked for Bill Dutton at Rare Things, a shop specializing in Native American material, for years and she indicated that he "was an openly gay man who had a zest for all things unique including Jimmie's carvings." Bill enjoyed (and purchased) Jimmie's erotic carvings, so Jimmie accommodated by creating them with some frequency. Another erotic example is shown in Figure 8, in the two views of a sleeping Kookopölö—with a surprise.

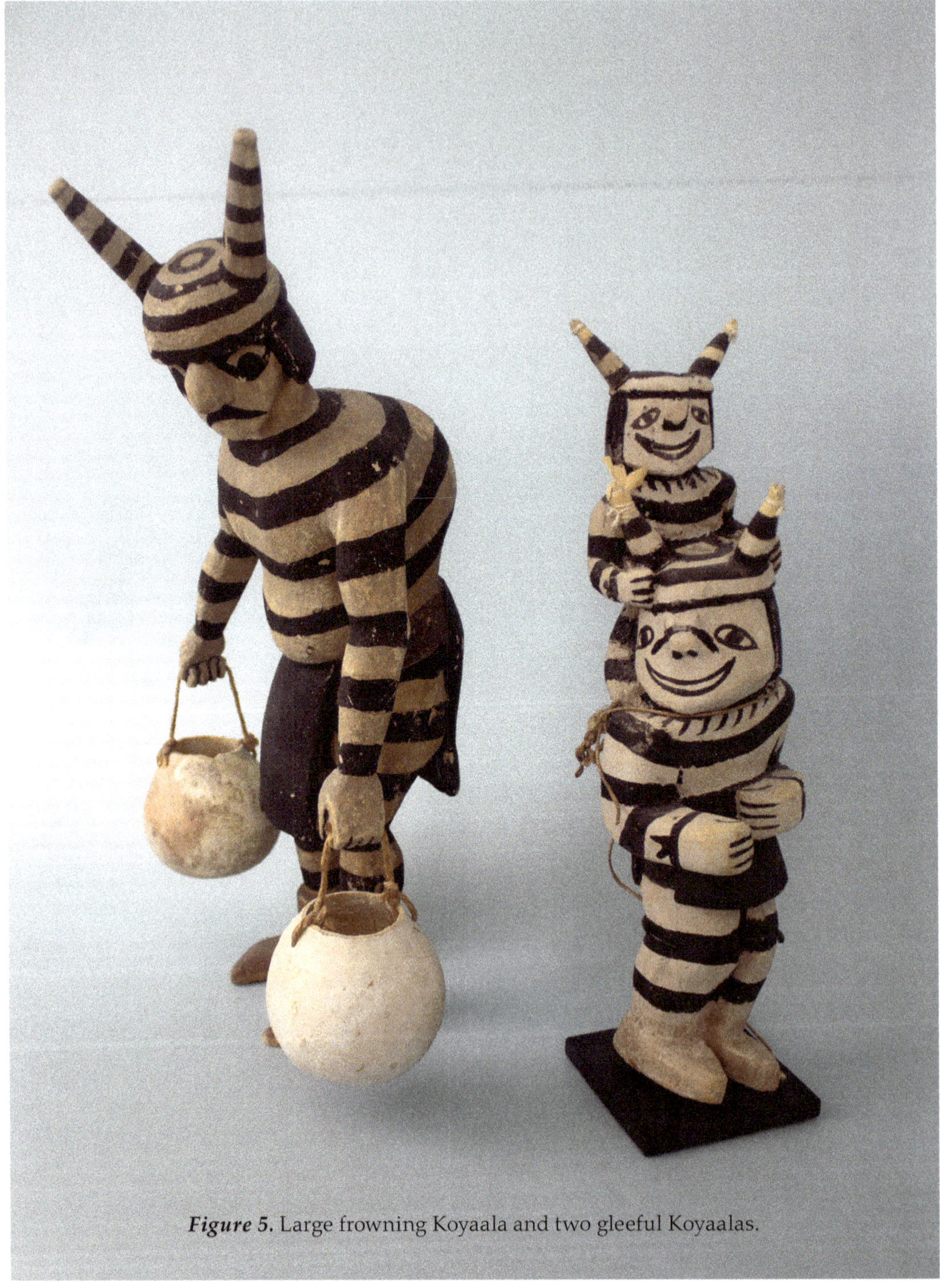

Figure 5. Large frowning Koyaala and two gleeful Koyaalas.

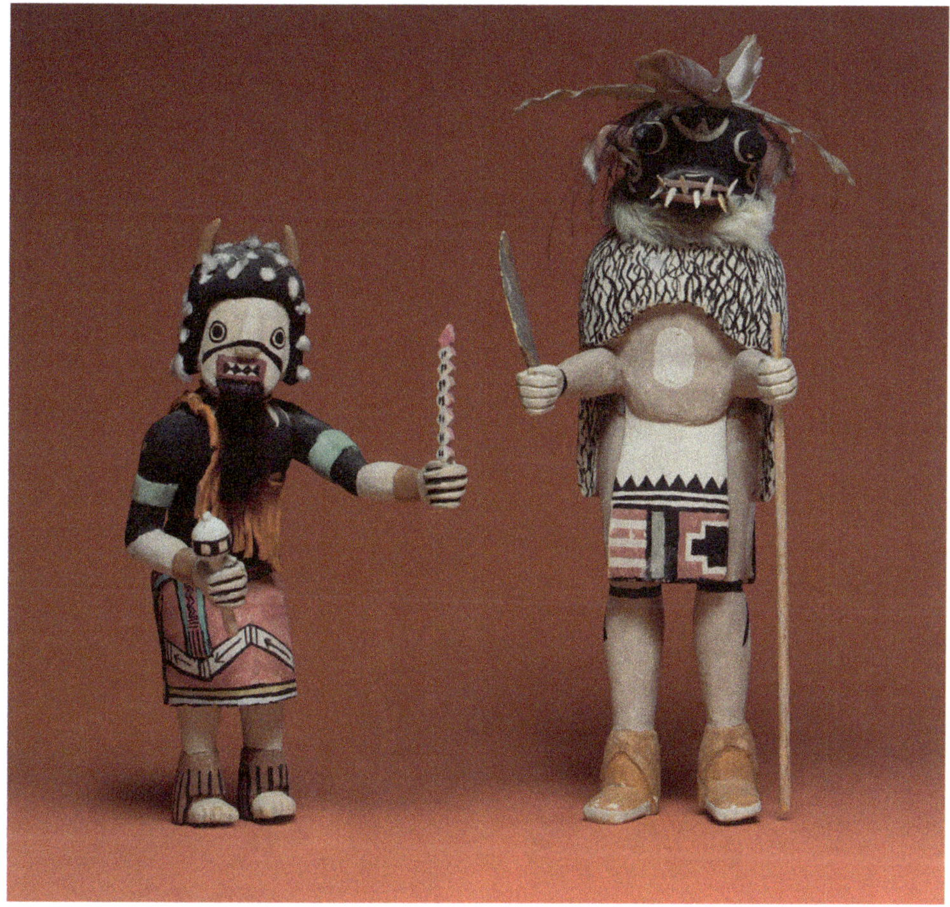

Figure 6. Mixed-up Ho'e (Mosayru) or Ho'e (Bison) and Tsaaveyo (Ogre).

While many of Jimmie's carvings were hilarious, Jimmie's work did not have a narrow emotional range. For example, the two huge Pangwkatsinam (Bighorn Sheep) katsinam, in Figure 3 are serious carvings; no humor is intended. As Joan Caballero shared, these Sheep were the unofficial mascots in Rare Things for years. They were high up on a shelf, not for sale. A different emotional tone can be found in the large Koyaala in Figure 5 on the left. His frowning mouth, downcast eyes, and the burden of the two large gourds suggest that this figure has the world on his shoulders. This sad, poignant, even grieving clown in Figure 5 is yet another example of Jimmie's creative genius. A couple of other interesting carvings are shown in Figure 9, with two putsqatihu (cradle) katsinam, consisting of a Koo'aakatsina, a katsina named for the sound he makes, and a tiny Hemiskatsina (Jemez katsina). Jimmie made very few cradle dolls.

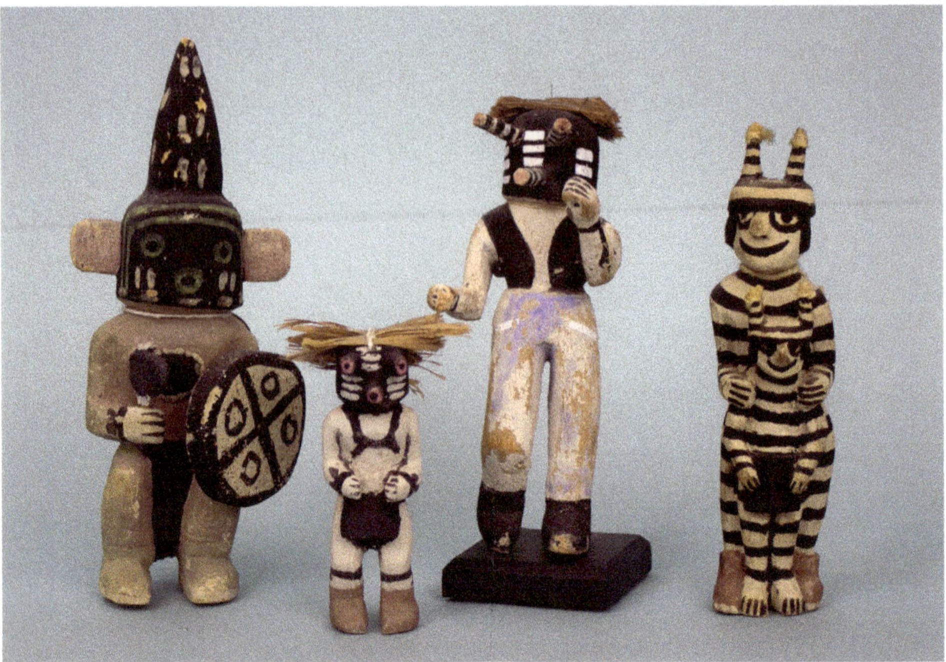

Figure 7. Pöqangwhoya, two Kwikwilyaqa (Striped-Nose), and a pair of Koyaalas.

It should also be noted that Jimmie's carvings were so varied and innovative that much of his work doesn't fall cleanly into any of the categories proposed in Chapter 1. This speaks to his immense creativity. He was not classifiable.

Ultimately, it may be possible to connect and integrate James with Jimmie. James was a strong advocate for Hopi traditional ways for many years. It was no easy task opposing massive forces such as the wealth and power of energy companies and the United States government. The process must have entailed many defeats, and one must question how James dealt with these. His son, Dennis, put it simply, saying, "He did what he could." I would speculate that carving katsinam was one way for James to escape the crush of advocacy into the mindful and exclusive focus of the carving process. As shown, many of his results were comical, and a time-honored way of dealing with oppression is through humor. The activity of carving may have helped him persist in his advocacy and provided a more traditional way to "make money."

In closing, much of the footage in the movie, *Autobiography of a Hopi,* is of James planting and harvesting corn, demonstrating the most basic and meaningful elements of a traditional Hopi life.

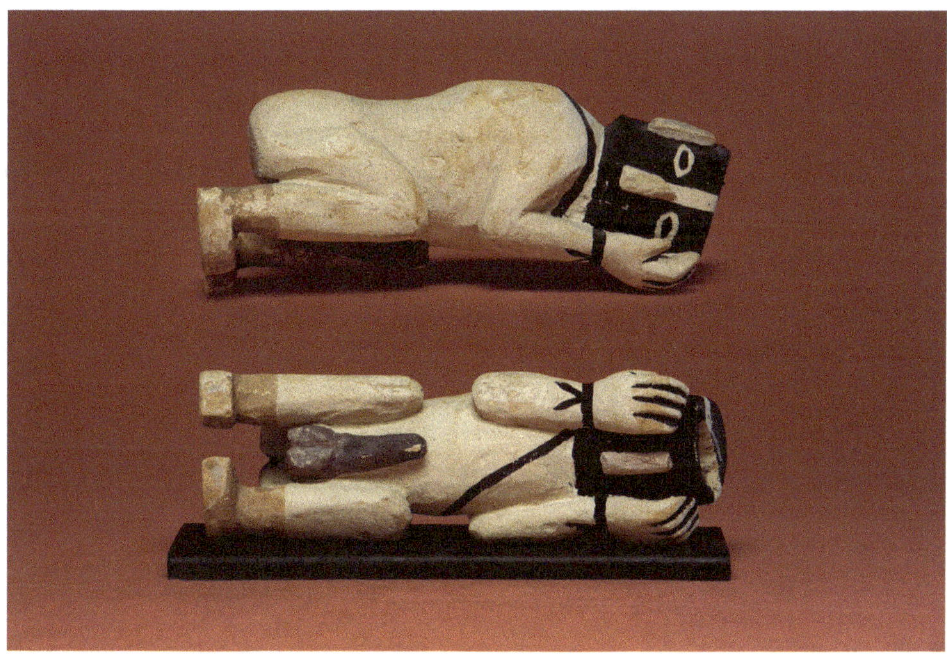

Figure 8. Two views of a sleeping Kokopölö.

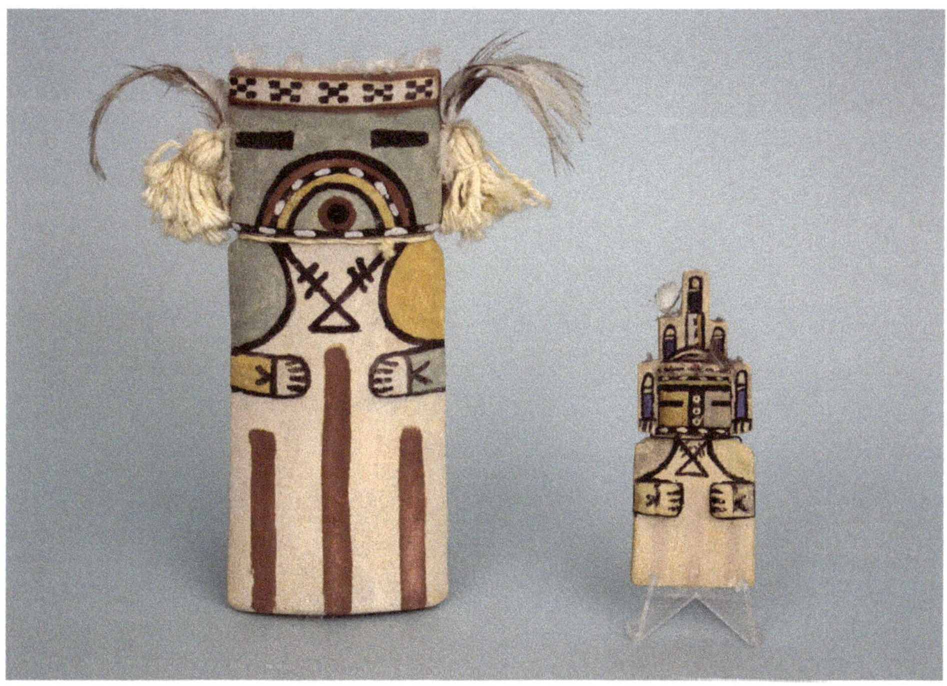

Figure 9. Koo'aakatsina and a tiny Hemiskatsina (Jemez katsina).

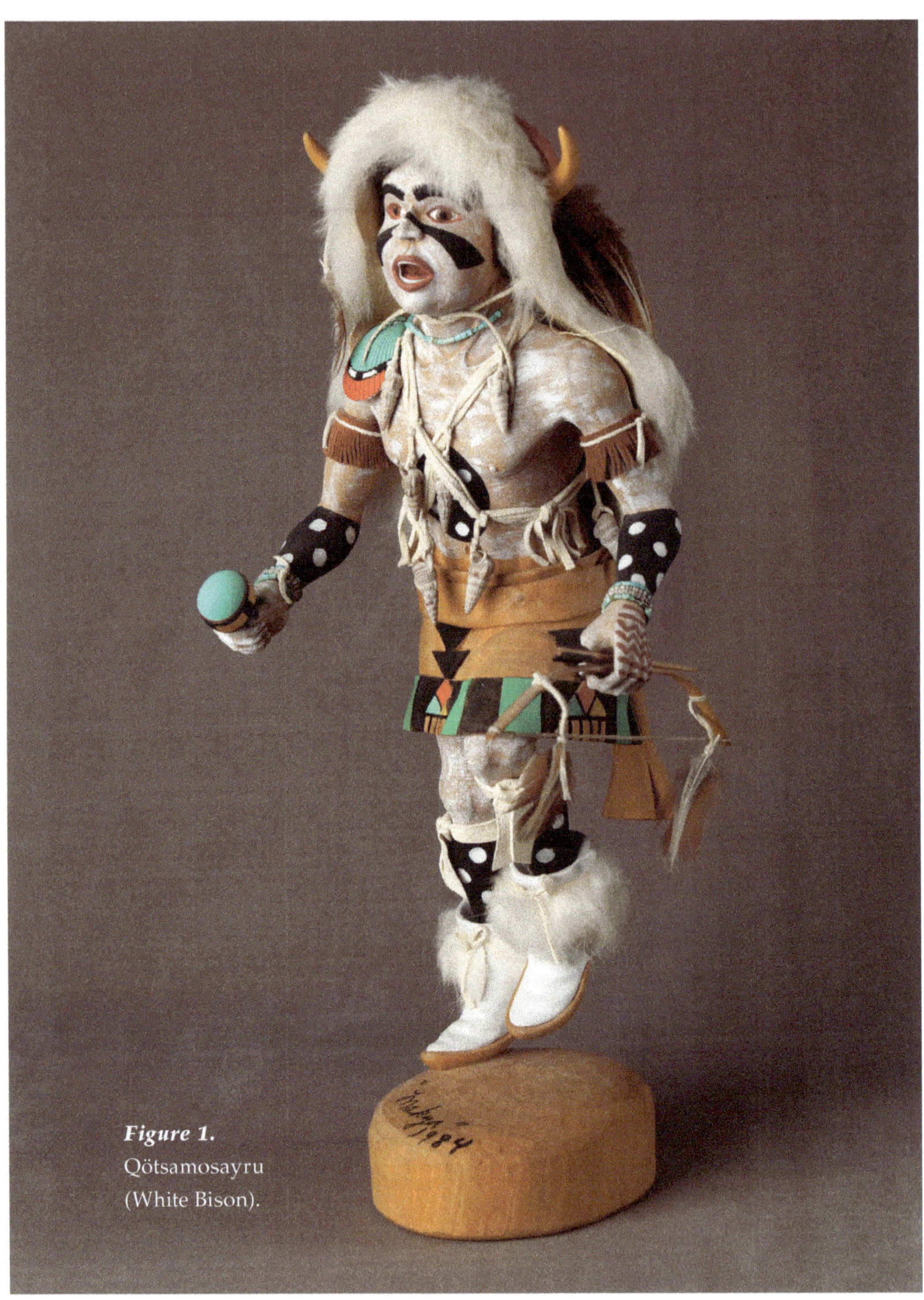

Figure 1.
Qötsamosayru
(White Bison).

ALVIN JAMES MAKYA

Persistent Perfectionist

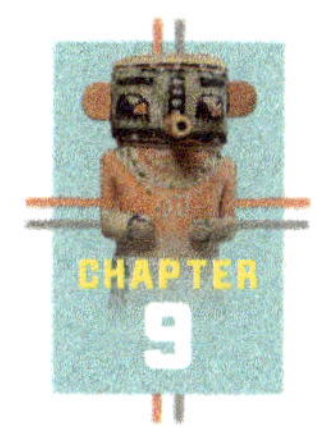

ALVIN JAMES MAKYA WAS BORN in 1936 and passed in 2003. He was Piikyas (Young Corn) Clan and grew up in Orayvi (Oraibi). For information regarding Alvin, I spoke with his eighty-eight-year-old sister, Treva Burton, and Treva's daughter, Beatrice Norton. I also relied on biographical material from books on katsina carvers by Teiwes (1991), Bassman (1991), and Schaaf (2008).

Alvin's education was local until, according to Beatrice, he "was shipped to the Stewart Indian School in Carson City, Nevada." Alvin received training in carpentry there. After high school graduation, he joined the Marines. In the Marines, he was such a fine shot that he became a sharpshooter. I would suggest that his training in carpentry and woodworking, in combination with the precision required to be an expert marksman, resurfaced later in his extremely precise katsina carvings. After finishing his military service, Alvin worked as a union carpenter. Jobs took him all over the Southwest, although most were local to Arizona.

As a young adult, Alvin said he only carved one or two katsinam a year. Teiwes (1991) noted that in 1960 Alvin attended the annual Hopi Artists Exhibition at the Museum of Northern Arizona. There he was impressed and inspired by some of the action figures he saw. He started to carve seriously and within a year won first prize at the 1961 Hopi Exhibition. Very early on, it was clear Alvin had a special gift.

Beatrice Norton noted that Alvin was a perfectionist. While others often raved about his work, she said Alvin was hard on himself, never satisfied, always pushing himself to get better.

Alvin James Makya was an innovator on many fronts in the Ultra-Realistic Style. He rendered the human body with great sensitivity and accuracy. One of his innovations was that he left some portions of the wood on his carvings unpainted so that the grain showed through beautifully. Examples include the unpainted kilt and horns on the Qötsamosayru (White Bison) in Figure 1. These features are only lightly stained with no coloration. Earlier examples of these figures would have been painted white. Alvin explained that he used acrylic paints sparingly and wood preservers (Teiwes 1991). He also used no power tools, working with X-Acto blades and modified paring knives.

Alvin also rendered complex motion and bodily movements as few, if any, had done before. As noted by Teiwes,

> Alvin's strength lies in his ability to carve the human body and the human face realistically. His Hano clowns are known for their athletic prowess, often balancing on one foot or holding a large watermelon high above their heads. (Teiwes 1991, 83)

An excellent example of his ability to render the elaborate movement and grace of a katsina is shown in Figure 2. This is the Kwaakatsina (Eagle) katsina. The elegance of the posture of this katsina was a startling development at the time. And the carving represented very precisely how the Katsina really looks when he dances.

In addition, note the exceptional detail of Makya's renderings of the bodies of katsinam. In Figures 1 and 2, pay careful attention to the carving of the hands, arms, knees, nipples, and toes. These are indeed ultra-realistic. Before Alvin James Makya (and very few others), no one had achieved this skill of carving in wood.

Alvin also experimented in nontraditional ways, making unpainted nude female figures and abstract katsina sculptures. He was one of the first to create bronze sculptures of katsinam. In addition, at times he worked in basswood because the material allowed greater precision in carving details. Alvin and a few peers introduced all of these developments.

By the early 1970s, Alvin's work was becoming famous. He was featured in a book on katsina carvers by Clara Lee Tanner and Ray Manley (1980) and in *Arizona Highways* repeatedly. As noted by Schaaf, "By 1977, Alvin's carvings were valued higher than any other carver at the annual Hopi show" (Schaaf 2008, 199). He won many awards at major competitions during the 1960s, 70s, and 80s.

Figure 3 shows Beatrice Norton, Alvin's niece, with some of the last carvings he made. He was quite ill by the time he created these. A similar carving from this era is shown in Figure 4, a Palhikwmana (Water Drinking Maiden) sculpture. Note that in his old age he continued to experiment in a Sculptural Style.

Late in life, he lived with his sister, Treva, in Orayvi. He suffered from diabetes and required regular dialysis. Despite his infirmity he continued to carve until shortly before his death. He is remembered fondly by family and friends, and within the Indian art world he is universally recognized as a very prominent and influential artist.

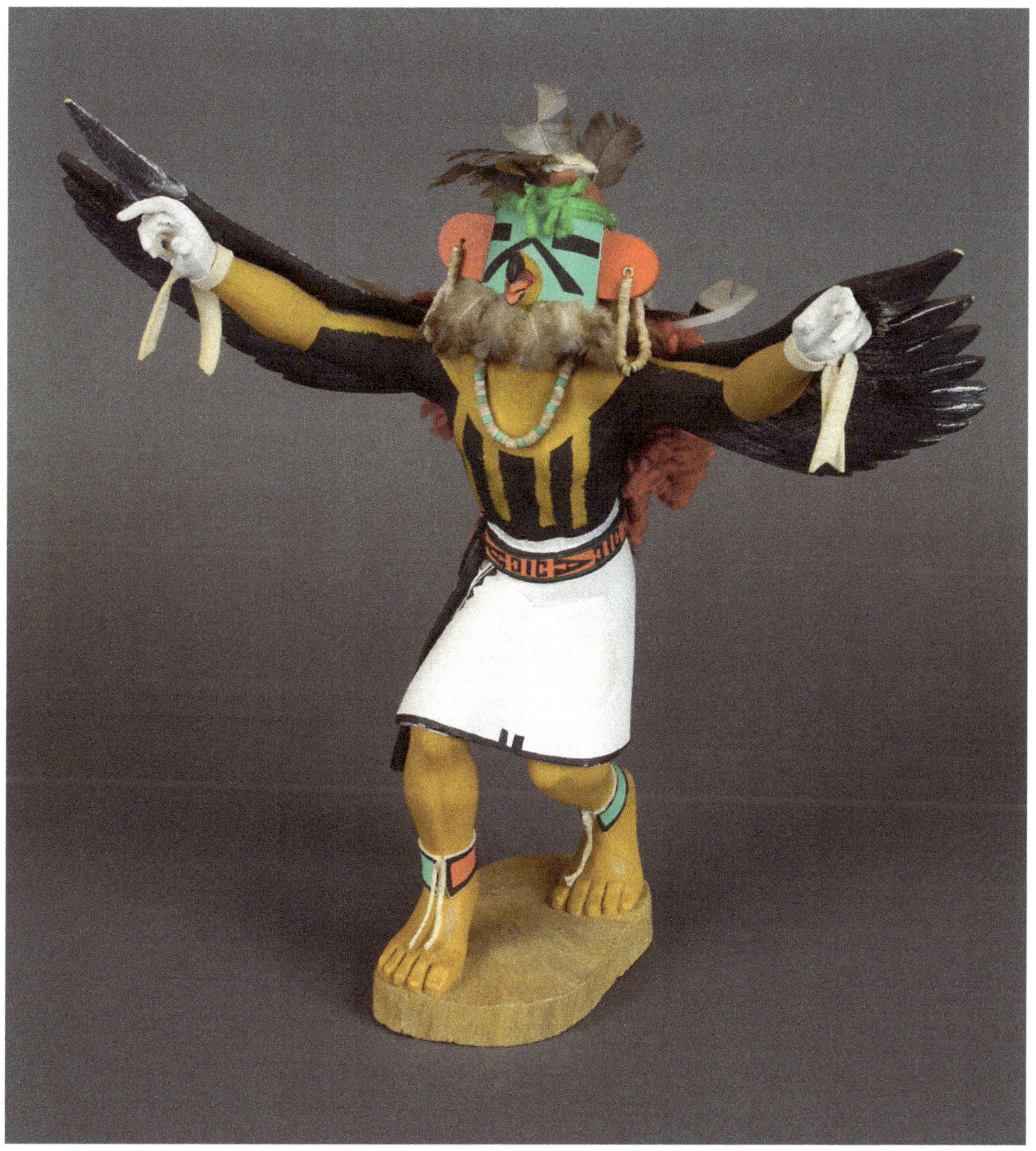

Figure 2. Kwaakatsina (Eagle).

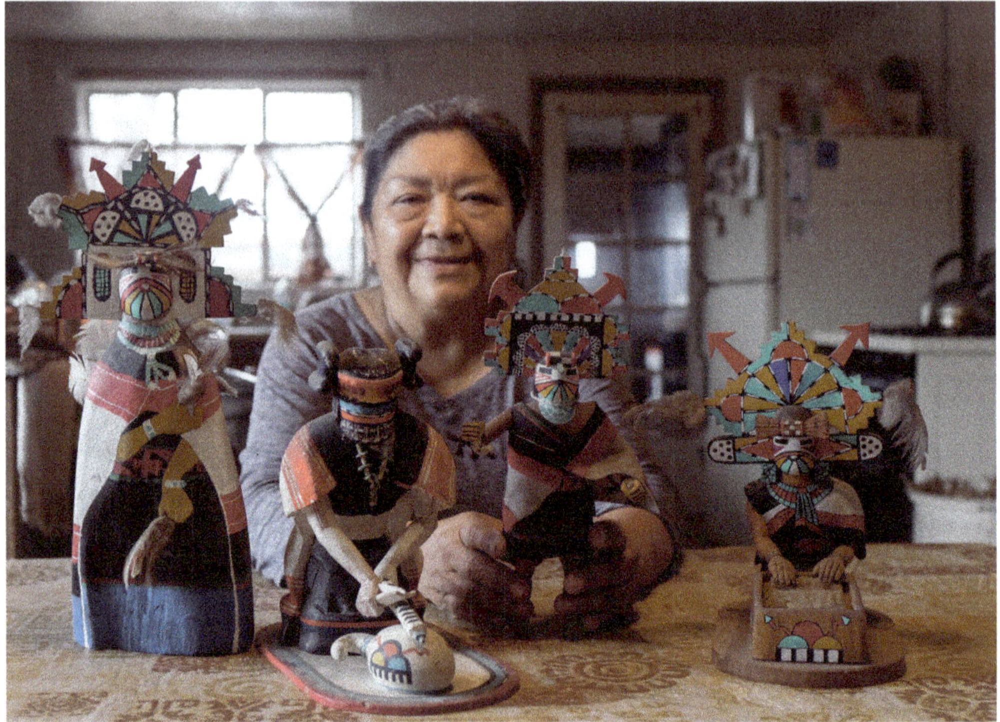

Figure 3. Beatrice Norton, Alvin Makya's niece, shares some of his final carvings.

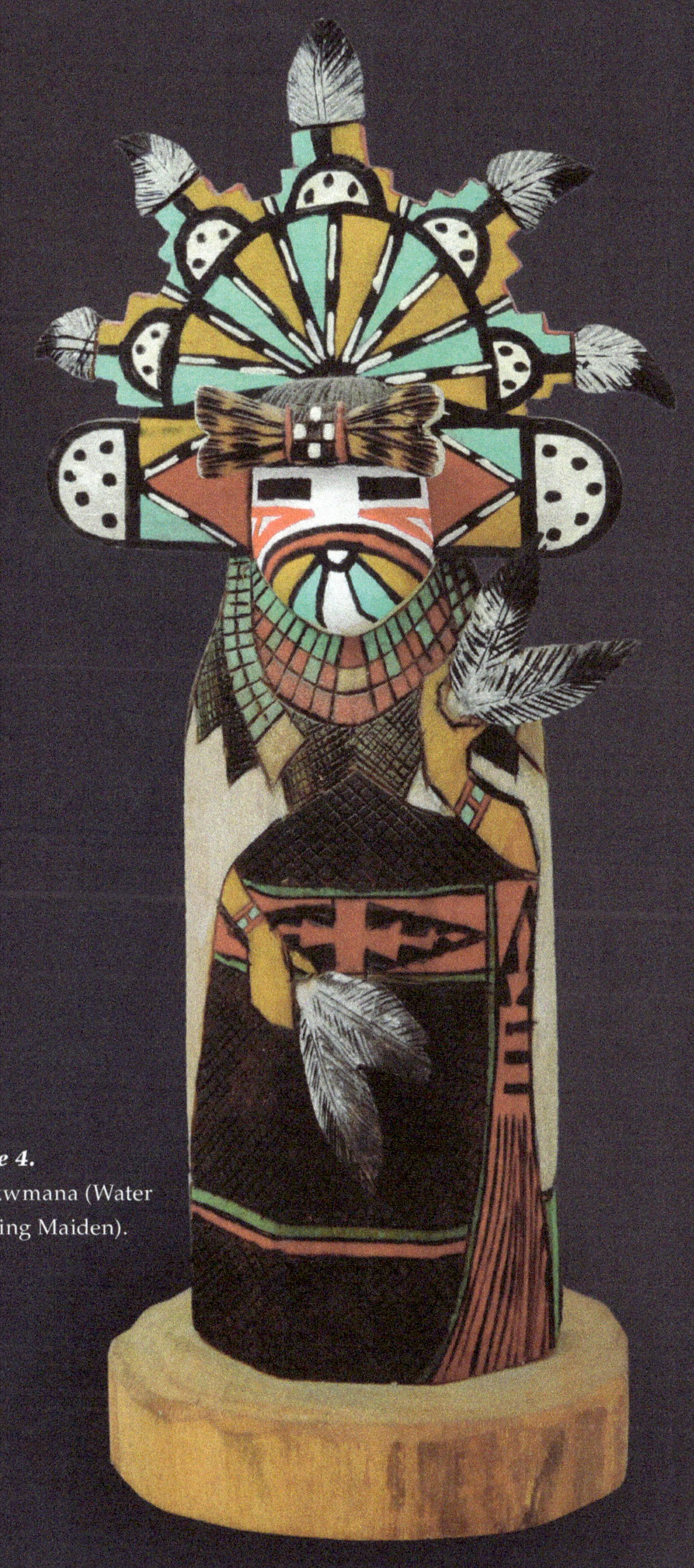

Figure 4.
Palhikwmana (Water Drinking Maiden).

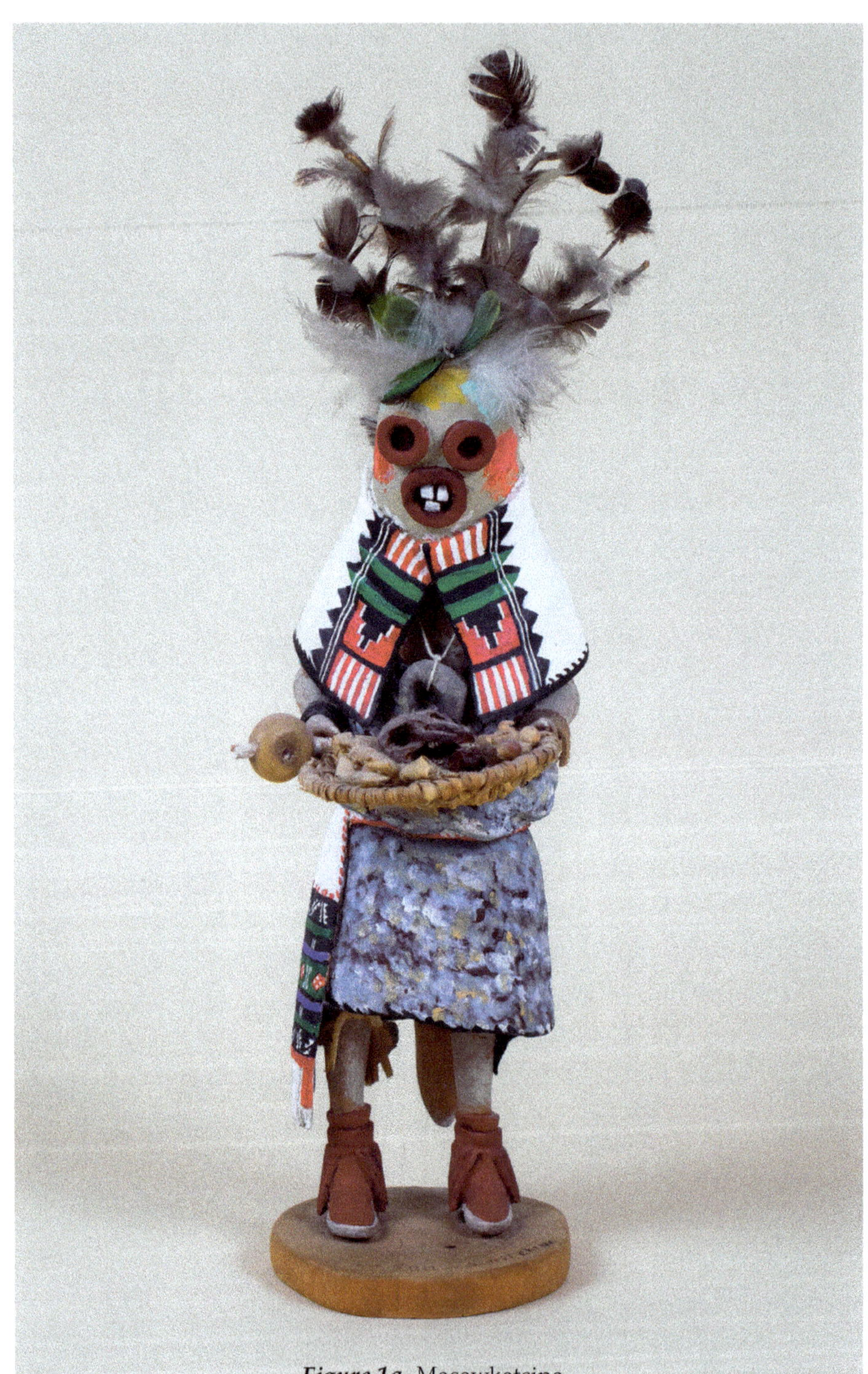

Figure 1a. Masawkatsina.

WILLIAM INGVAYA QUOTSKUYVA

"How They Really Look"

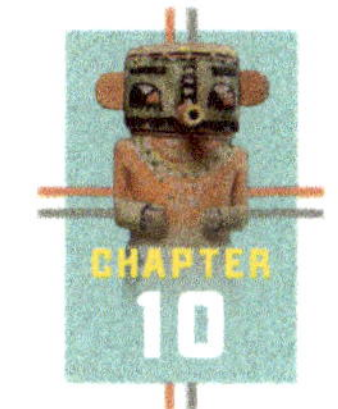

William Quotskuyva—more commonly referred to by his Hopi name of Ingvaya—was not an especially well-known carver outside of Hopiland and Flagstaff. His important influence on the history of katsina carving is in part due to the renown of his Indian trader daughter, Janice, and her spouse, Joseph Day. They have operated a trading post named Tsakurshovi on Second Mesa since the 1980s. They are so widely known on the reservation, around the United States and internationally, that Ingvaya's work became recognized due to their endorsement of his skill. He was not self-promoting.

Ingvaya was born in 1907 in Orayvi (Oraibi) right after the 1906 split and passed in 1999. He was Reed Clan and grew up in Kiqotsmovi (Kykotsmovi). As Joseph and Janice explained to me, the Reed Clan was responsible for growing the reed that allowed Hopi to pass from the Third World to our present world, the Fourth. After this exodus/emergence, the work of the Reed Clan was done, but the clan was still much respected, which is why Ingvaya was frequently asked to smoke in the kiva by members of other clans throughout the years.

Around age thirteen, Ingvaya went to the Sherman Institute in Riverside, California, where Tawaquaptewa, Charles Fredericks, and others were "educated." After several years of schooling, he moved to Hollywood where he acted during the 20s and 30s as an "Indian extra" in several Tom Mix silent movies. He became friends with Iron Eyes Cody, who despite being Sicilian-American, played Native American roles in more than two hundred films over the decades. Ingvaya's acting career was more short-lived. He eventually migrated back to his home of K-town, as it is often called. There he took a job with Babbitt Brother's Trading Company for whom he drove a six-mule team making regular runs between Winslow and Kiqotsmovi. This proved fortuitous as he met his wife, Rose, who was working in a field he passed en route. Their union eventually led to the birth of seven children, including (in order) Joe, Leon, Frances, Willietta, Janice, Joanna, and Glen. Unfortunately, Rose, who was Bear Strap Clan, passed at the young age of 41.

Ingvaya also worked for the farm at the Phoenix Indian School around 1940.

He and the growing family moved to Flagstaff about 1942, where Janice was born in 1943. Later he moved the family back to K-town where he lived the life of a traditional Hopi farmer. Ingvaya was known for his prodigious ability to work. He was close friends with Dick Pentewa, who would help him in his fields. (Note: Dick was the major source of information for the chapter in this book on his father, Otto Pentewa.) Many would avoid going to Ingvaya's fields to help him, as it required great stamina; he could work all day with little evidence of fatigue. He once said to Joseph Day while they were toiling over corn plants, "Where are those hippies who want to live like Indians when we really need them?"

Ingvaya's work as a carver was distinctive, innovative, and brilliant. He was part of a small wave of carvers in the 1970s that rendered Katsinam realistically, but his creations had a special depth and profundity that others had trouble achieving. Consider the Masawkatsina, the katsina aspect of the Maasaw deity, in Figure 1a. Note the detailed face, *paahos* (prayer sticks) on the back of the head, realistic body posture, and rendering of the garment. Note also the special attention paid to the miniature sifter basket with tiny *noqwivi* (a tamale-like food), kernels of corn, and a sheep's skull (Figure 1b). During this period of the 1970s, this level of accurate detail was innovative and surprising. As Robert Breunig, PhD, director of the Museum of Northern Arizona (MNA) at the time, said, "he portrayed the Katsinam the most accurately. He was the best carver." It is no wonder that when William entered a Masawkatsina carving in the MNA's annual Hopi show he won first prize. Two other examples of his fine work are shown in Figure 2. On the left is a Hiilili. Observe the excellent motion portrayed, including the bent legs and arms. This level of accurate dance movement was revolutionary at the time. The same can be said for the Taatangaya (Hornet) katsina on the right. Note the accoutrements in both hands, the felt sash, tiny necklace, and leather armbands.

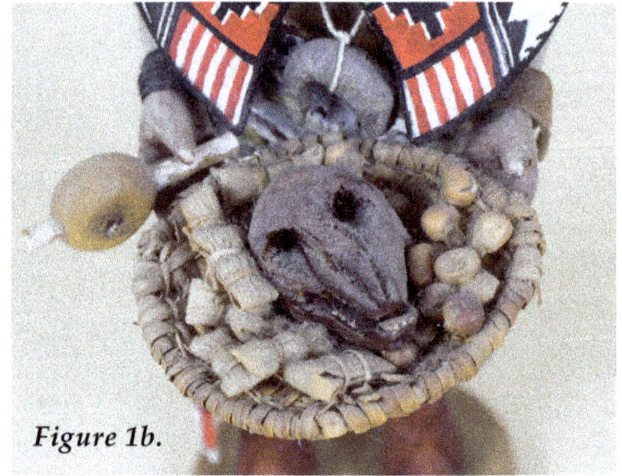

Figure 1b.

Three more fine carvings by Ingvaya are shown in Figure 3. From left to right: an Angaktsina (Longhair), Masawkatsina, and Kooyemsi. Each shows the exceptional, but-not-overdone realism of the Katsinam and "how they really look when dancing." Ingvaya's rendering of bodies is what dancers look like *as individuals* rather than idealized prototypes. Note also his provision of accurately

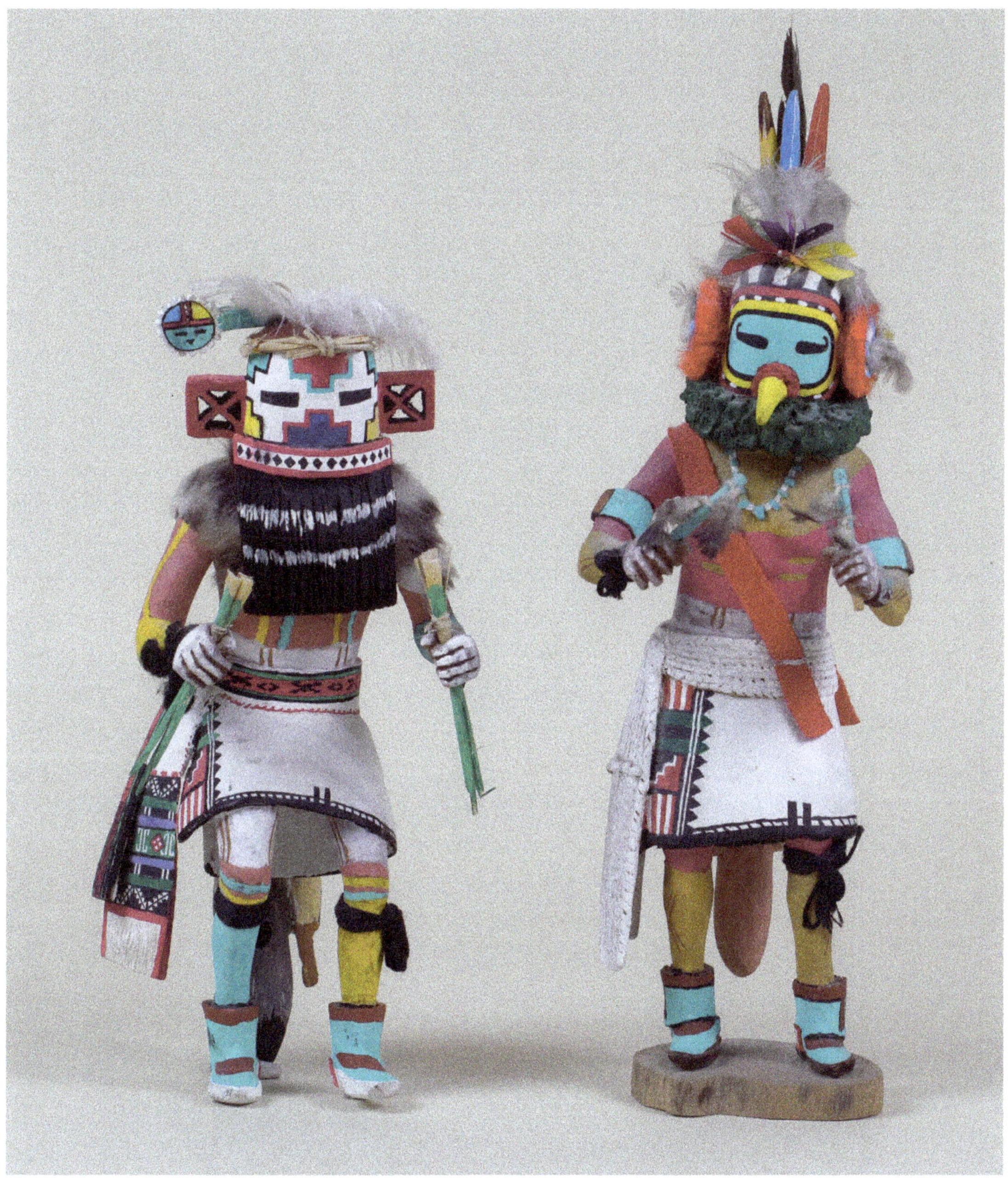

Figure 2. Hiilili and Taatangaya (Hornet).

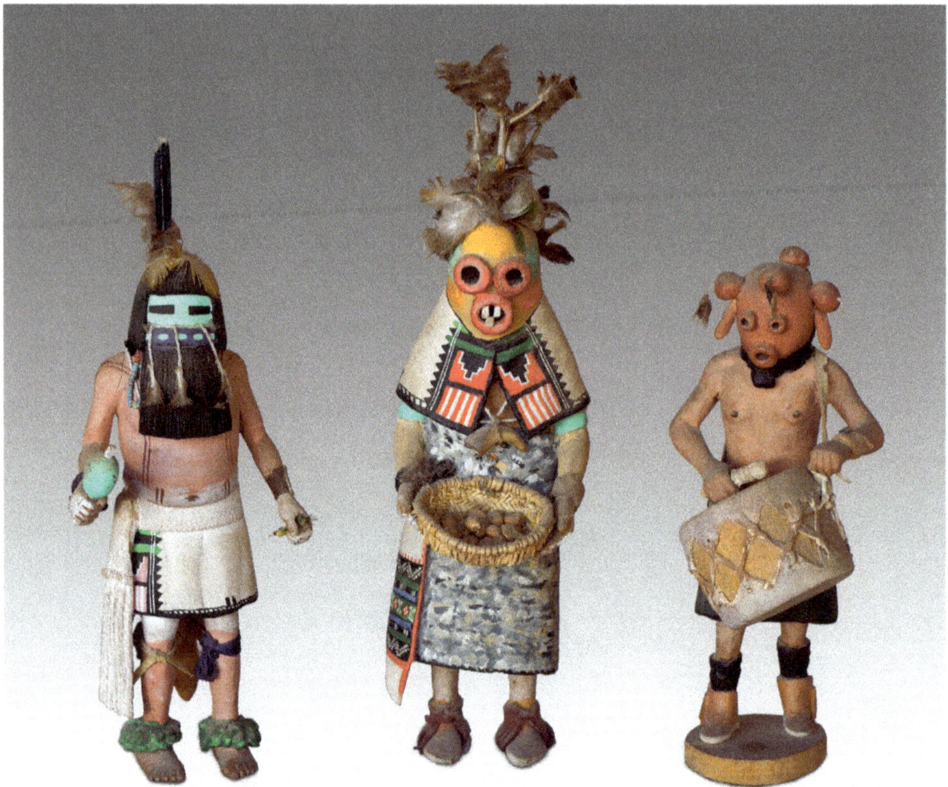

Figure 3. Angaktsina (Longhair), Masawkatsina, and Kooyemsi.

rendered accoutrements, including the Masawkatsina's sifter basket and the Kooyemsi's drum, strap, and pounder.

A very unusual carving by Ingvaya is shown in Figure 4, a Sootangkwaakatsina (Laguna Eagle Dancer). This is the first example I've seen by him of a non-Hopi figure. MNA records indicate that this was acquired by the museum in 1976. It is a dramatic carving and looks rather menacing. Note that the dancer's wings are assembled from real bird feathers.

Hopi carvers generally stay within the pantheon of Hopi katsina figures, in part because the katsinams' features and details are well known to them. In addition, katsinam that are familiar in the marketplace tend to sell better. However, sometimes Hopi individuals visit other Pueblos and may witness another tribe's Katsina ceremony. Inspired by what they've seen, Hopi individuals

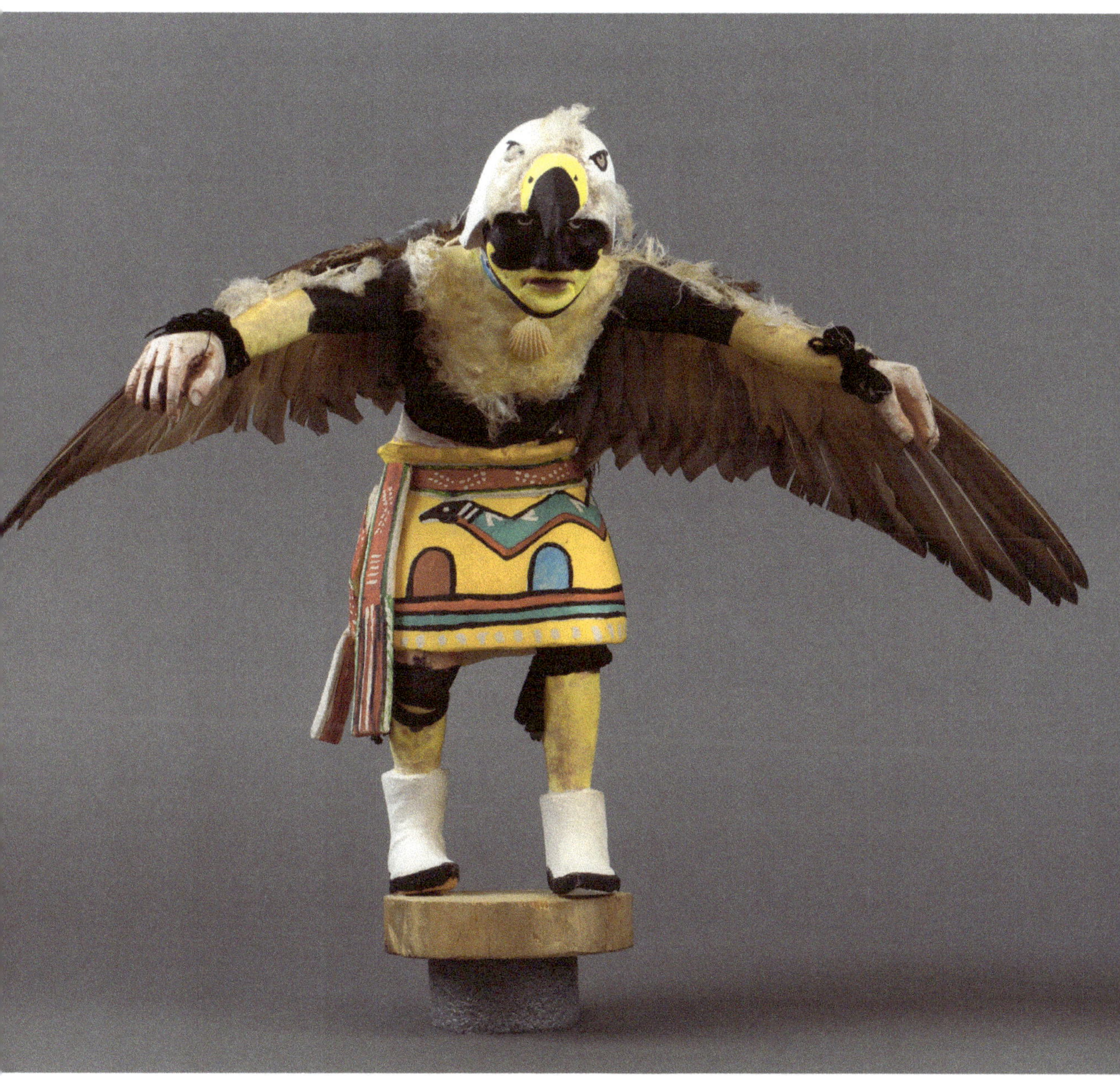

Figure 4. Sootangkwaakatsina (Laguna Eagle Dancer).

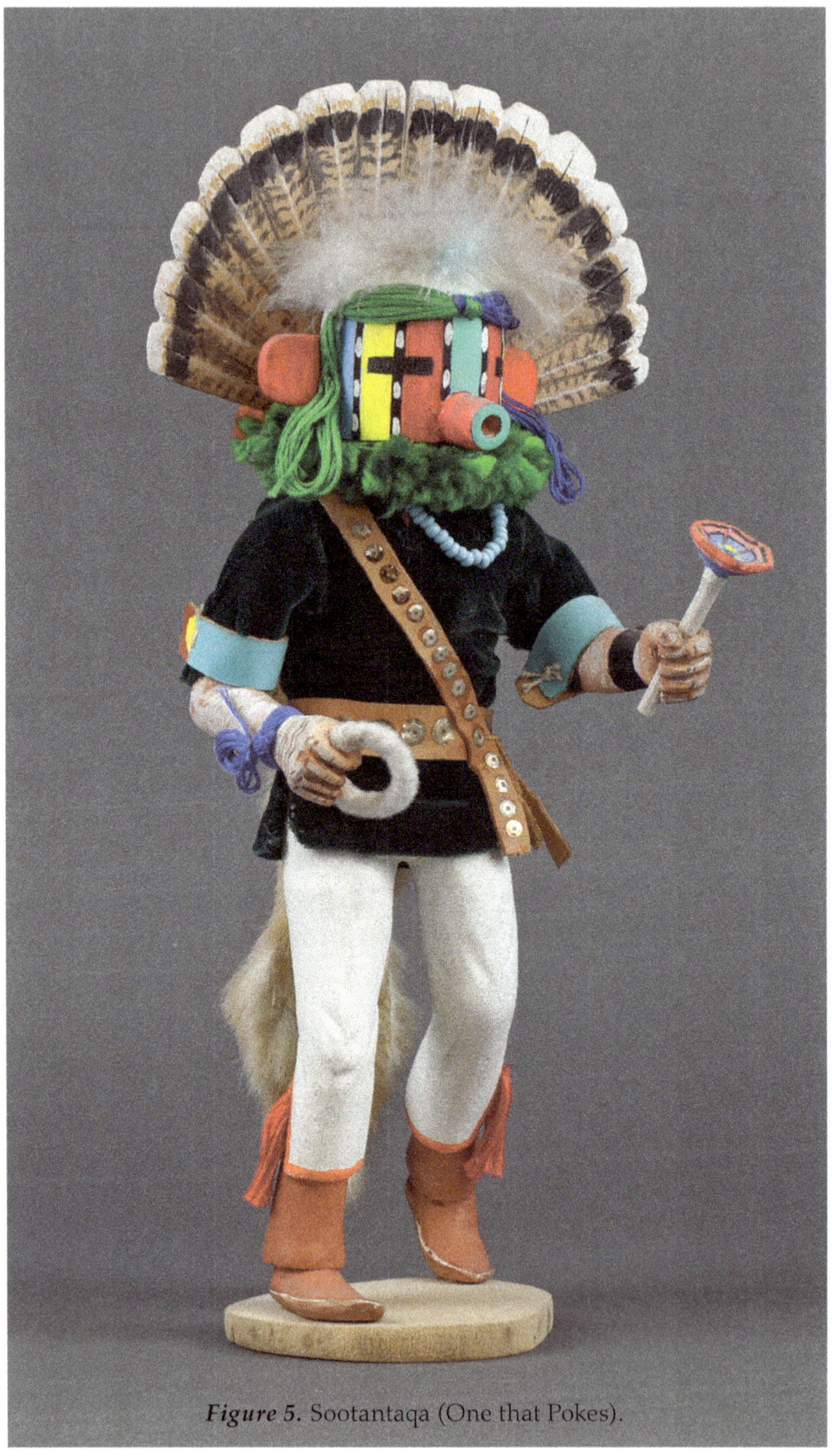

Figure 5. Sootantaqa (One that Pokes).

may later choose to create their own interpretation. I suspect that is what happened with Ingvaya's Laguna Eagle Dancer.

Figure 5 is a katsina referred to as a Sootantaqa, or the "one who pokes at a ring with a stick." Ingvaya's exceptional detail is apparent on the katsina's leather bandolier, garment, dance wand, and wood-carved feathered headdress.

Eventually, Ingvaya created entire katsina dance scenes for the Heard Museum in Phoenix and the California Academy of Sciences in San Francisco. His dioramas of two ceremonies are among the pinnacles of katsina carving from any era. Joseph Day told me he had a role in obtaining the commissions for the two museums because of his contacts in the Indian art world and with the museums specifically. Joseph added, "I offered to promote his work and help make him famous like Henry Shelton and Alvin James Makya, but he just wanted to be a Hopi farmer."

Ingvaya worked in his fields and as a katsina carver into his old age. Known to some as Bill, he was a lady's man, courting women into his eighties. Somewhere along the line, he acquired the nickname "Wild Bill," about which relatives are hesitant to elaborate.

His children were alarmed that he was still operating a vehicle into his late eighties when it was clear his driving skills had diminished. They were relieved when his old battered pickup stopped working, except for reverse. Undeterred, Bill still journeyed to and from the local K-town store and his fields using only reverse gear. He was not known to have done any damage.

William Quotskuyva had a long, colorful, and productive life. At various times, he was an actor, a shoemaker, a carpenter, and a farmer. He is remembered with great fondness by his children and grandchildren. And for those in the know, he is also remembered as one of the great katsina carvers of all time.

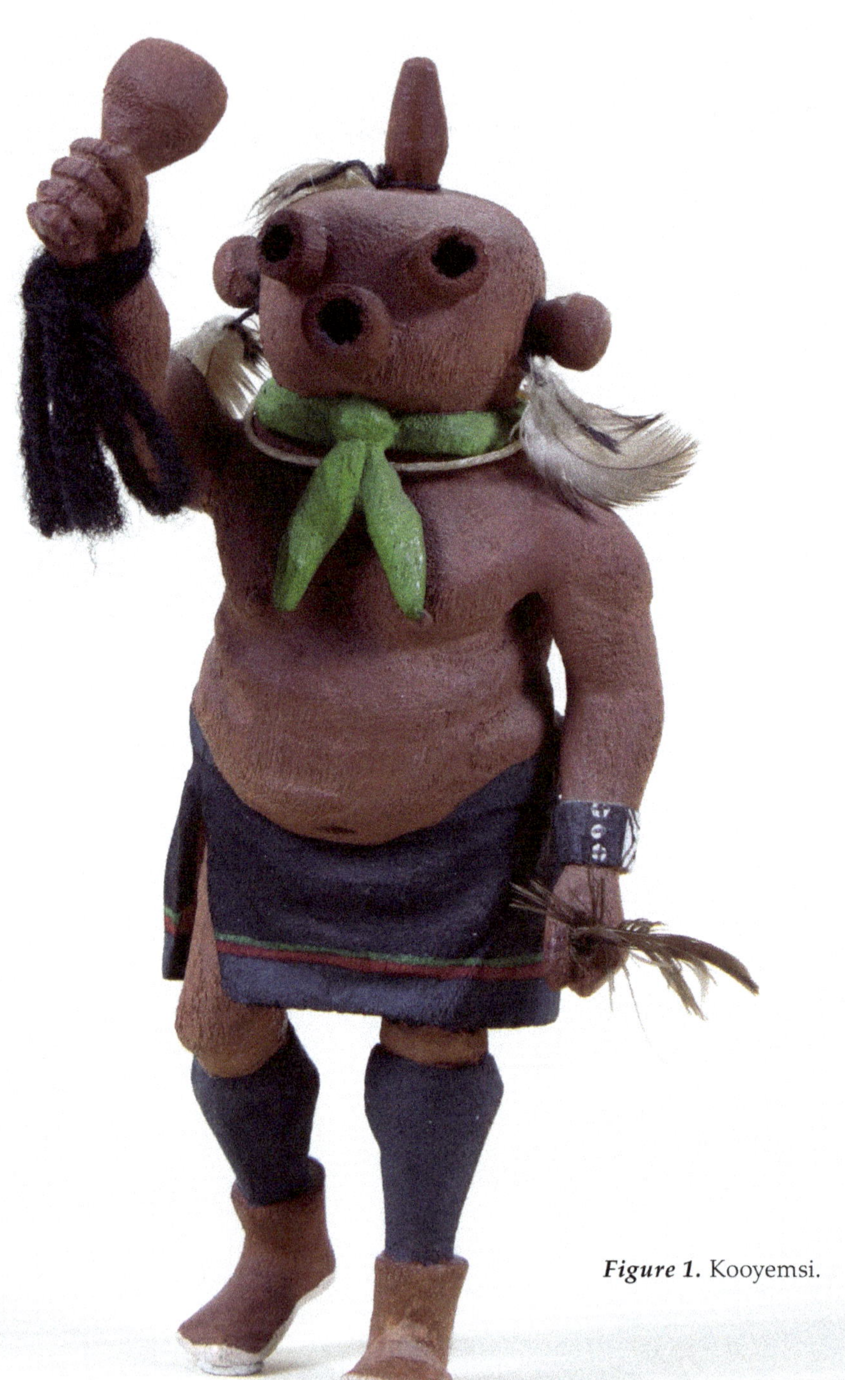

Figure 1. Kooyemsi.

HENRY SHELTON

Black Belt Carver

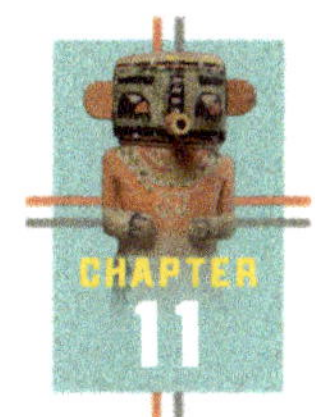

HENRY SHELTON WAS ONE of the seminal figures in the history of Hopi katsina carving. Along with a few others, he moved katsinam from the Late Action Style of the 1950s into the Ultra-Realistic Style of the 60s, 70s, and beyond. My sources for this chapter were Mark Bahti, a long-time Indian trader in Tucson and Santa Fe, who knew Henry well, plus the books by Teiwes (*Kachina Dolls*, 1991) and Schaaf (*Hopi Katsina*, 2008). I was unable to locate family members to assist me.

Henry was born in the 1930s in Kiqotsmovi (Kykotsmovi). His Hopi name was "Ho-Ya'Oma" which means "arrow carrying." He often used an arrow as part of his signature on katsina carvings. In his youth, Henry was a star athlete. He won an Arizona state wrestling championship and a flyweight boxing title in New Mexico. Henry's wrestling and boxing abilities would resurface later in life.

Henry received his high-school education at the Santa Fe Indian School from 1944 to 1949. In 1957 Henry moved to Flagstaff where he worked at Food Town. In 1961 he was offered a job at the Museum of Northern Arizona (MNA) where he joined two other notable Hopi employees, Jimmie Kewanwytewa (see Chapter 5) and Edmund Nequatewa. Henry did quite well at the MNA, being promoted to the position of "preparator," which entailed preparing museum spaces for exhibits and other assembling duties. He also began to give lectures and carving demonstrations.

Henry shared with Teiwes that the Director of the MNA, Edward Danson, encouraged his katsina carving. Henry added that he became "real good at carving by 1966" (Teiwes 1991, 136). Barton Wright, who encouraged Henry in the early 1960s to "carve some Kachinas like they really look," once told me a related story. According to Wright, for Christmas one year Henry gave him a pot-bellied Kooyemsi. This carving is nearly identical to the one shown in Figure 1. The only difference between the katsina Henry gave to Barton and the Kooyemsi in Figure 1 is that its kerchief was red. Barton's gift Kooyemsi can be seen on page 79 of his book *Hopi Kachinas: The Complete Guide to Collecting Kachina Dolls* (1977).

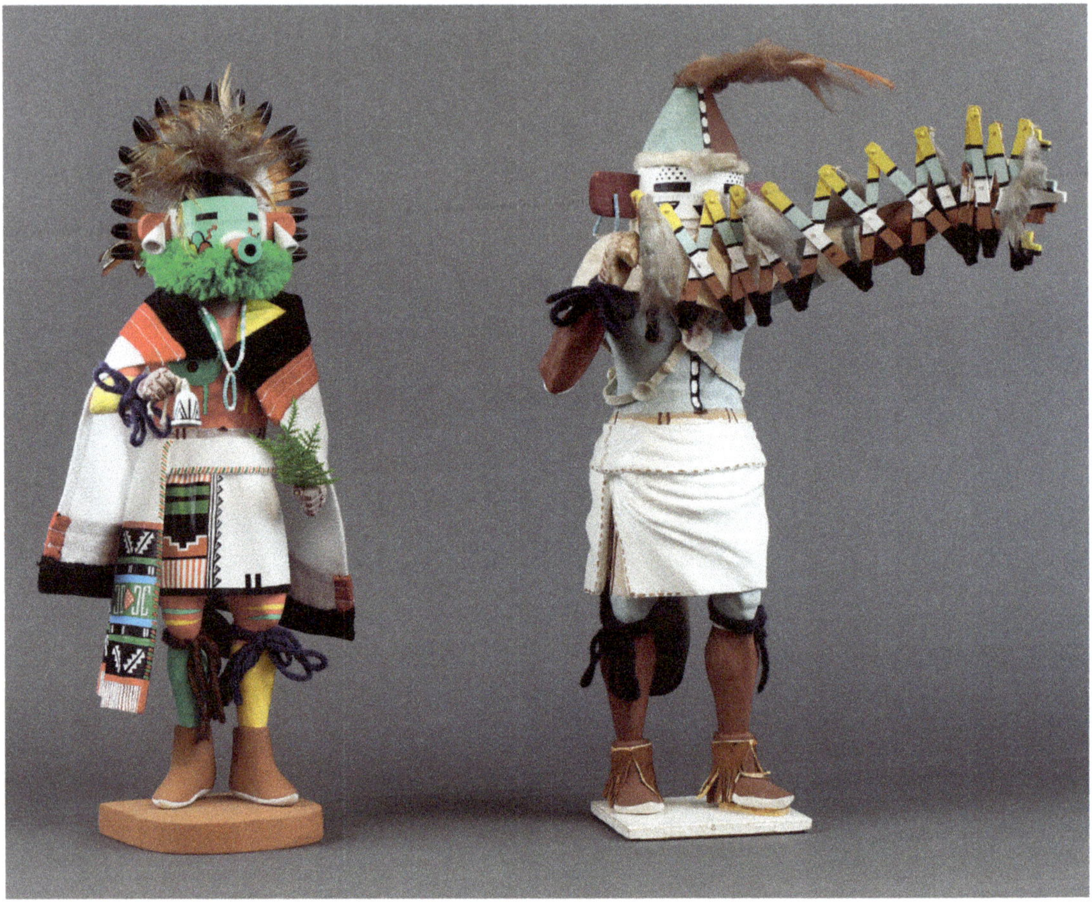

Figure 2. Talavaykatsina (Morning) and Sootukwnangw (Heart of the Cosmos).

Fine detail and ultra-realistic carving became Henry's hallmark. Examples of his work from his time at the MNA are shown in Figures 2, 3a, and 3b. Fortunately, detailed records from the MNA allow us to date these carvings precisely. The Sootukwnangw (Heart of the Cosmos) on the right in Figure 2 received an honorable mention at the 1964 MNA Hopi Show. Note the elaborate lightning bolt extender in his hands. The Talavaykatsina (Morning) katsina on the left in Figure 2 is equally

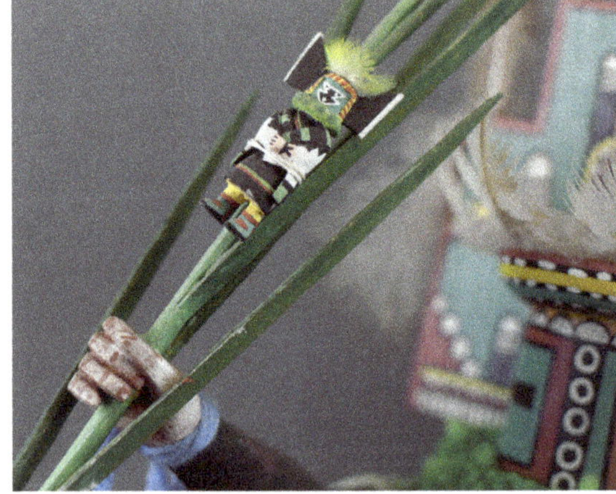

Figure 3a. Putsqatihu (Cradle) and cattails detail.

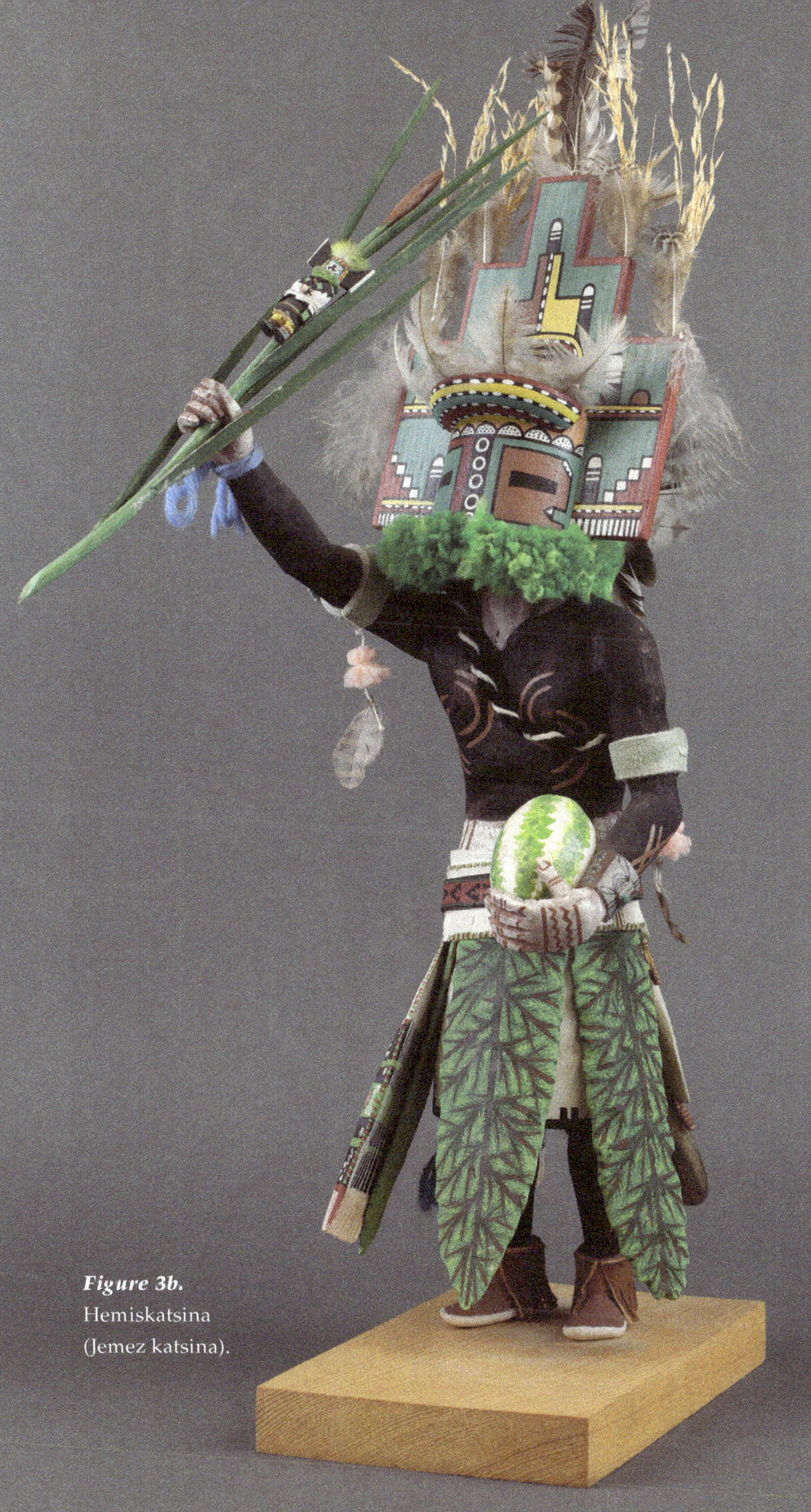

Figure 3b.
Hemiskatsina
(Jemez katsina).

well done. He is holding a bell in his right hand and is wearing a real cloth manta or cape and jacla necklace.

The meticulously detailed and dynamic Hemiskatsina (Jemez katsina) in Figures 3a and 3b was acquired by the MNA in 1965. Note the dramatic movement of the Hemiskatsina, the putsqatihu (cradle) katsina is the katsina's right hand, the cattails, and the well-rendered melon. The cradle katsina represents what would have been given to a lucky young girl attending the Katsina dance. By this time, Henry was really taking katsina carving to a new place. By the way, the price for this katsina in 1965 was $65.00! In today's market, high-quality katsinam by Henry sell in the $1,000 to $2,000 range.

During this period, Henry sold an unpainted Hemiskatsina to a trader named Clay Lockett from Tucson, who had the figure cast in bronze. Henry is believed to be among the first to explore this new media artistically. Henry was also one of the first to create in the Sculptural Style. By now it was clear that this new era of ultra-realistic and sculptural katsina carving was considered by the marketplace to be "fine art," and not simply "arts and crafts."

Examples of Henry's work from more than a decade later are shown in Figure 4. Both the Nata'aska (Black Ogre) and So'yokmana (Ogre Maiden) were acquired in 1978 by the MNA. These katsinam demonstrate Henry's continued use of bright acrylic paints, dynamic body postures, and the addition of time-consuming accoutrements. It's worth noting that Henry never made the switch to stains or diluted paints like other carvers such as Ron Honyouti or Cecil Calnimptewa (see Chapters 12 and 13).

Figure 5 shows Henry at the peak of his artistic powers. This is truly a masterful example of the Ultra-Realistic Style from the 1970s. This carving of a Tsu'sona (Snake Dancer) won First Prize at the Gallup Inter-Tribal Indian Ceremonial in 1974. Note the carefully rendered musculature, folds in the garment, undulations in the snake, fringed clothing, and miniature jewelry. However, the facial expression is the key. The Hopi Snake Dancer is a forbidding, awe-inspiring figure. He performs with a rattlesnake in his mouth, which he has subdued to fulfill his purposes. Henry has captured the spirit of this performance deftly. This type of rendering is why Henry became renowned as an innovative carver.

In 1978 Henry left the MNA, due to his many outside activities. He took up martial arts during this time and eventually earned black belts in both judo and karate (Schaaf 2009). Henry also traveled widely throughout the United States and abroad. In the summer of 1985, he was invited by the British-American Arts Association to demonstrate at an arts festival in the United Kingdom. This event was hosted by the Museum of Mankind, where Henry met Prince Phillip.

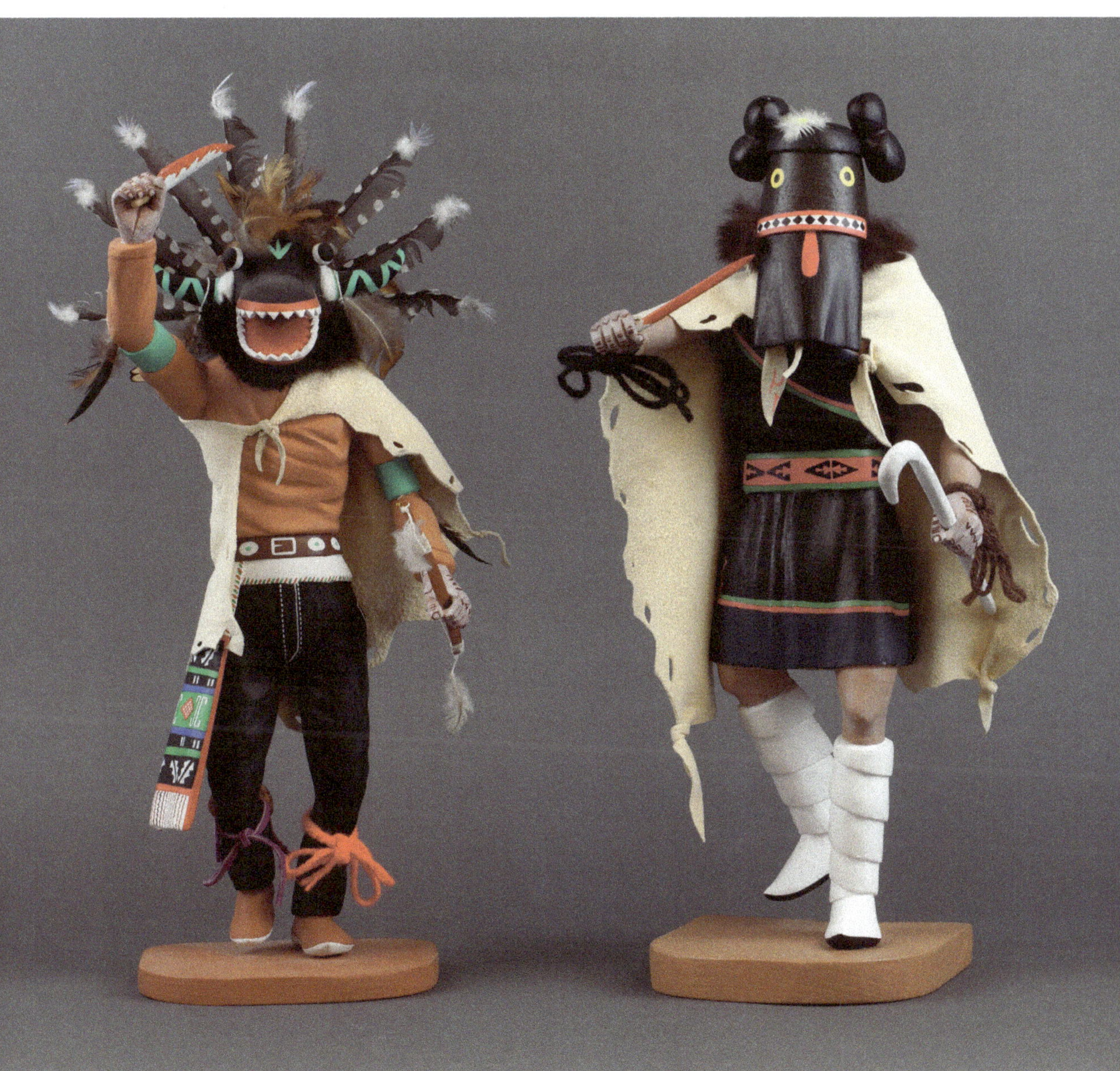

Figure 4. Nata'aska (Black Ogre) and So'yokmana (Ogre Maiden).

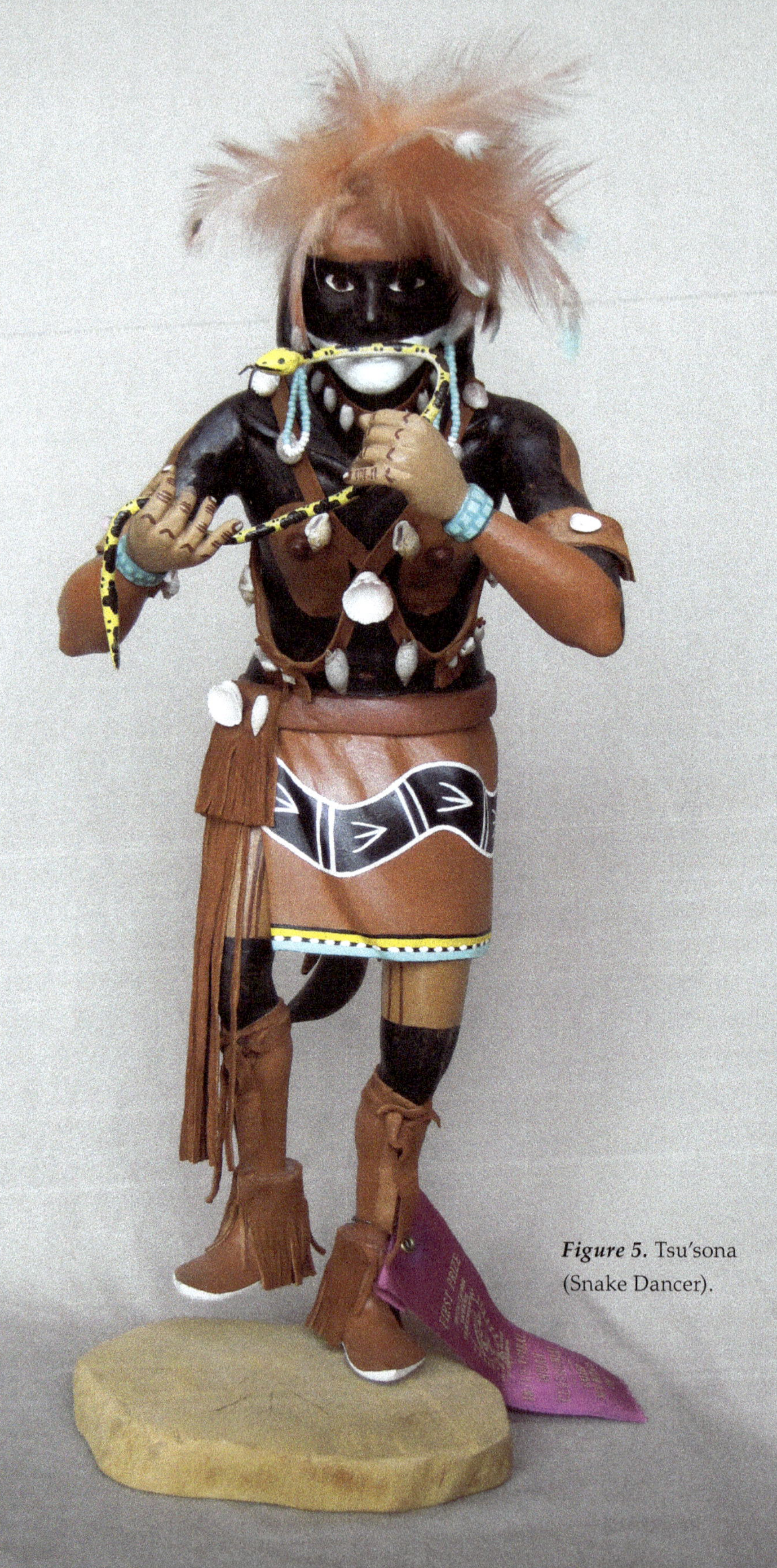

Figure 5. Tsu'sona (Snake Dancer).

Over the decades, Henry won many prizes at the MNA, Heard, Gallup Inter-Tribal, and Santa Fe's Indian Market. His work is in the permanent collection of the National Museum of the American Indian, the Heard, and the MNA. In 1992 he received the great honor of being designated an Arizona Indian Living Treasure.

Mark Bahti recalled Henry fondly from interacting with him at many shows over the years. He noted that Henry had a great sense of humor. Mark recalled that Henry always wore a bright polyester jacket, with patches, indicating his black belt status. Henry was clearly justifiably proud of his martial arts accomplishments. Mark also referred to Henry's older brother, Peter Shelton (Hoyesva), who was a very fine painter and katsina carver in his own right. Mark said that Henry also made jewelry, which is not well known.

Henry continued to produce high-quality katsina carvings well into his old age. Figure 6 shows a small carving by Henry from the 1990s. Although it is only 6 inches tall, the Koyaala includes a great deal of detail, including jacla earrings, a goodie box stuffed with tiny sweets, and lots of dripping candy to convey the clown's gluttonous behavior. It is signed "Henry Shelton, Oraibi," along with his arrow-carrying insignia. Henry was certainly a man and an artist whose aim was true for a very long time. He ranks among the most influential of all katsina artists.

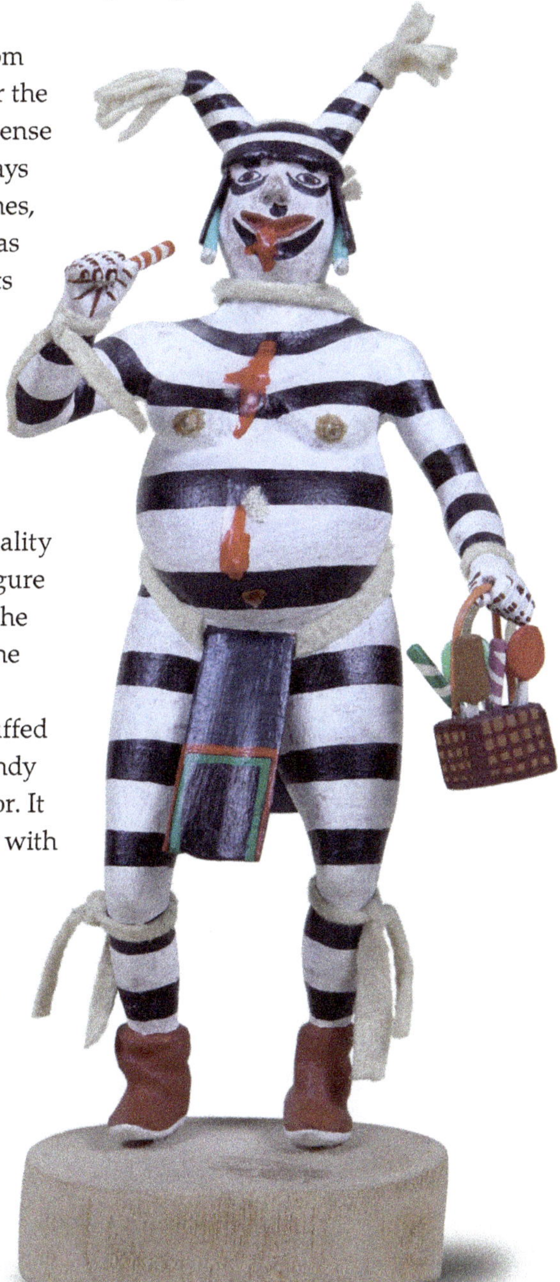

Figure 6. Koyaala.

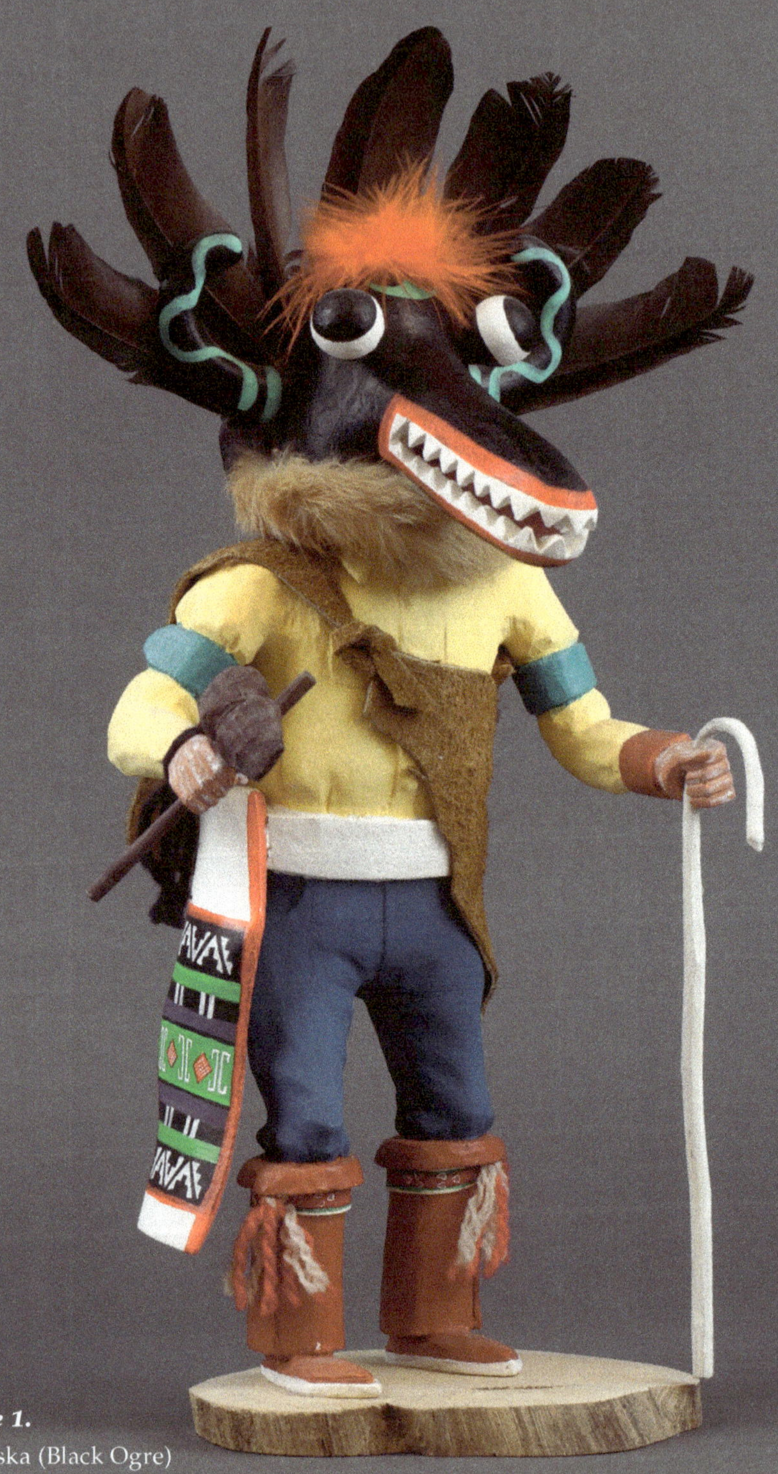

Figure 1.
Nata'aska (Black Ogre)
by Clyde Honyouti.

HONYOUTI FAMILY

Part I: The First Two Generations of Excellence

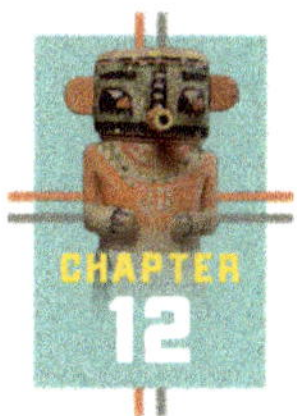

DURING THE PAST 100 YEARS, there have been several accomplished families of Hopi katsina carvers, but few, if any, have matched the skill across generations of the Honyouti family. This chapter will discuss the contributions of two generations of carvers: grandfather (Clyde Honyouti) and second generation (Brian, Lauren, and Ronald). A later chapter (26) will discuss the third generation (Mavasta and Kevin). For this chapter, I relied on interviews with Ronald Honyouti (born in 1955).

Ron is Greasewood/Roadrunner Clan and grew up in Paaqavi (Bacavi). His father, Clyde, was from Hotvela (Hotevilla). From elementary school through junior high, Ron attended the Mennonite Mission School on the Hopi reservation because his mother worked there. He was sent to the Phoenix Indian School for high school, which he said was a difficult adjustment. Ron noted that he had little or no art training in high school. Everything he learned about art came from his family.

Like most Hopi carvers, Ron began making katsinam around age thirteen or fourteen. His major influence was his father, Clyde. Ron noted that Clyde taught by example rather than instruction. Clyde was a traditional Hopi farmer and sheepherder. He reminisced that his father would come home from the fields with a shoulder bag on his back. Within would invariably be a katsina that Clyde was working on while tending the sheep. When Clyde wasn't looking, Ron would sneak a look at his father's current project and learn from viewing the changes in the piece over time. An example of Clyde's work is shown in Figure 1, a Nata'aska (Black Ogre) from the Museum of Northern Arizona's (MNA) collection. This example certainly shows Clyde's skill in making katsinam in the Late Action Style (see Chapter 1).

After high school in Phoenix, Ron received training as a motorcycle mechanic. However, Ron found himself missing Hopi life so he returned to the reservation around 1978. There he married Carla Honani from Hotvela. They eventually had three children, Mavasta, Felicia, and Kevin.

Not long after returning to Hopiland, Ron found himself becoming serious about katsina carving. His major influence was his older brother, Brian. Even

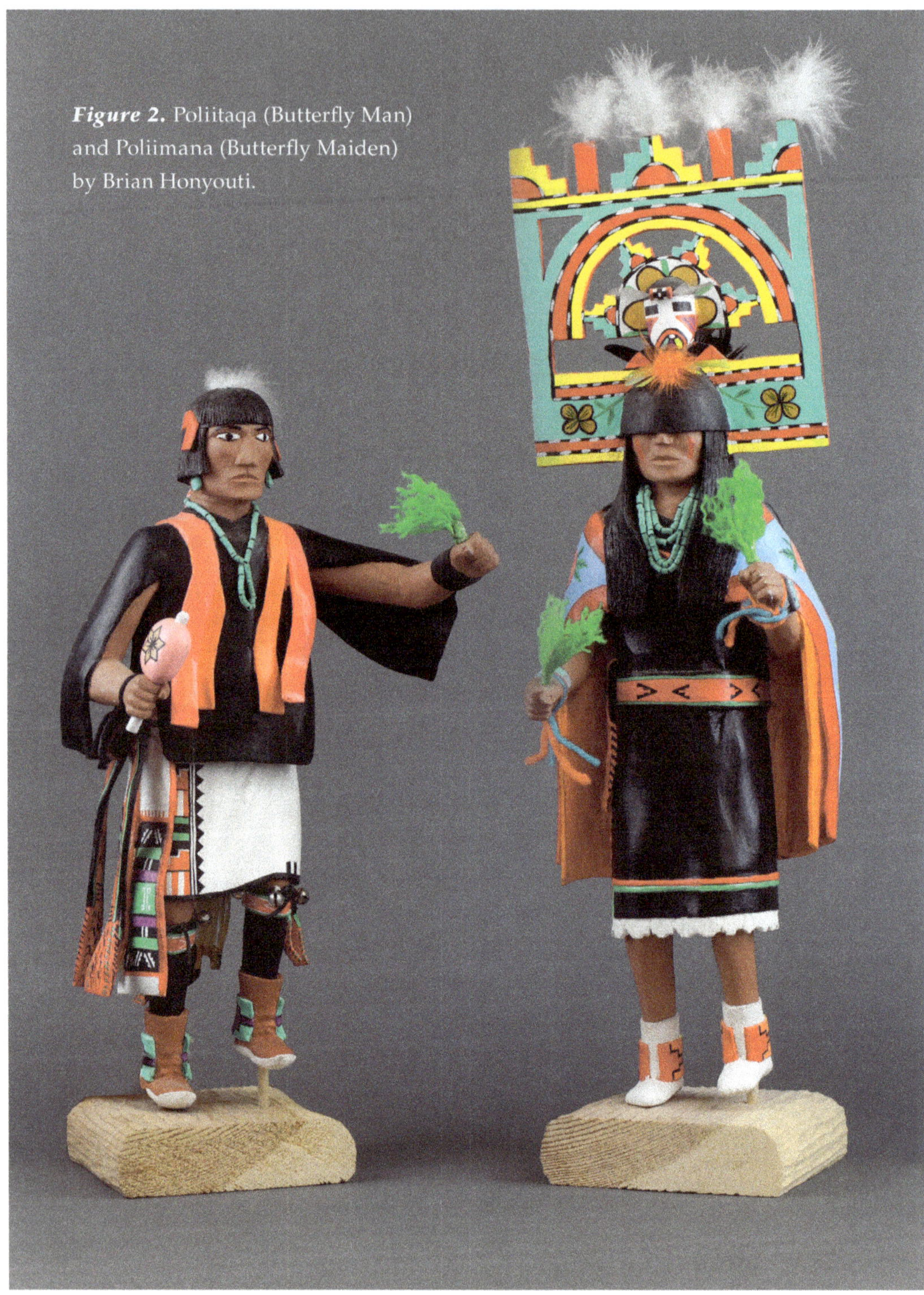

Figure 2. Poliitaqa (Butterfly Man) and Poliimana (Butterfly Maiden) by Brian Honyouti.

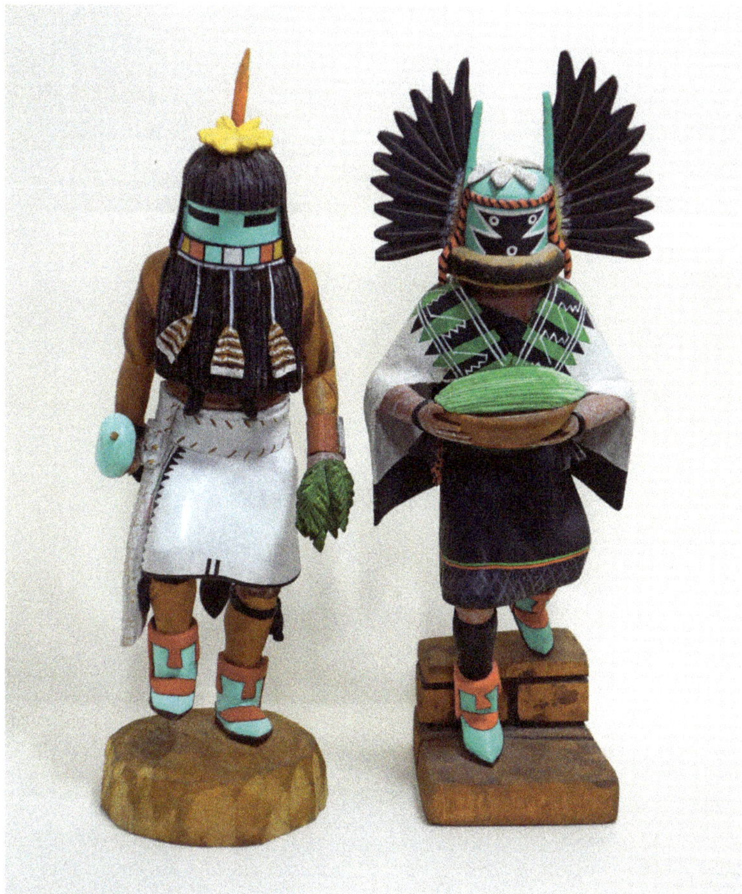

Figure 3. Angaktsina (Longhair) and Angwusnasomtaqa (Crow Mother) by Ron Honyouti.

early on, their work was so well received that Ron said he felt encouraged that he "could make it as an artist." Ron said that he and Brian admired two other carvers during this period—Von Monongya and Alvin James Makya. Ron said their work "developed together." Ron and Brian were at the forefront of the Ultra-Realistic Style, which eventually would evolve into the Sculptural Style.

Two very fine examples of Brian's work are shown in Figure 2. These are a matched pair of social dancers, Poliitaqa (Butterfly Man) and Poliimana (Butterfly Maiden). Not only are they beautifully rendered, they are also quite substantial, at 17 inches and 24 inches high. These two carvings were acquired by the MNA in 1971, so clearly Brian was carving at an advanced level by the early 1970s. Note that the examples in Figure 2 both feature bright and bold acrylic paints. This preference for bright and rich colors was about to change for the Honyouti brothers.

As Ron told me, by the mid- to late-1980s, he and Brian shifted to stains and diluted acrylics to achieve softer tones on their katsinam. Two examples of transitional carvings by Ron are shown in Figure 3. On the left is an Angaktsina (Longhair) and on the right is Angwusnasomtaqa (Crow Mother). Note the bare arms and legs of the Longhair are not painted but rather stained, as is the bowl carried by Crow Mother. The Longhair carving is dated 1981, which demonstrates their gradual shift in paint media.

This "revolutionary" move toward the use of stains and muted paints is further represented in Figures 4 and 5, both of which were created by Ron. The dark katsina with crossed feathers on his face is Owak'katsina, the Coal katsina. This carving is largely stained with only minimal use of diluted acrylics. The shift toward staining is even more dramatic in Figure 5, the Kooninkatsinmana (Havasupai Maiden). With this social dancer, the coloration is almost exclusively light staining with only small color accents. Her garment of pale deerskin is lightly coated with stain as opposed to paints, as is the base. And note the sinuous forms of her dress. This is no longer just an Ultra-Realistic carving; it has become a katsina sculpture. During this period another brother, Lauren, also emerged as a very talented carver. An example of his work is shown in Figure 6. This is Patro, the Sandpiper katsina. The Honyouti family talent is very much in evidence in Lauren's carving, with the deft use of stains and muted paints, the skillful rendering of bodily motion, and the well-crafted base.

Ronald consistently made other innovations as he moved into a predominantly Sculptural Style. Consider the elaborate and exceptional Figure 7a, which features three different types of Hopi maidens, or Manas, including a central Palhikwmana (Water Drinking Maiden). As shown in Figures 7a and 7b, this complex piece features flowers, corn, a rattle, a cradle katsina, dragonflies, cloud

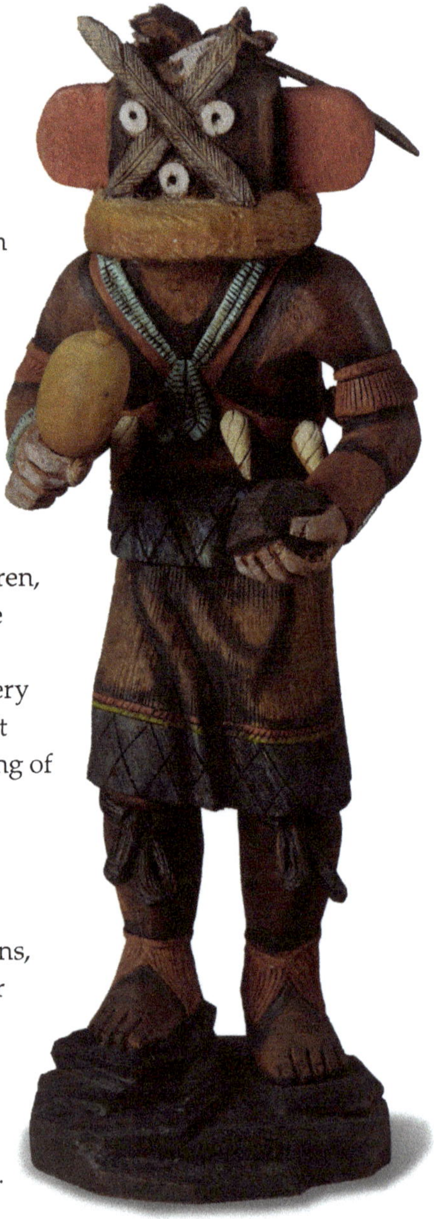

Figure 4. Owak'katsina (Coal) by Ron Honyouti.

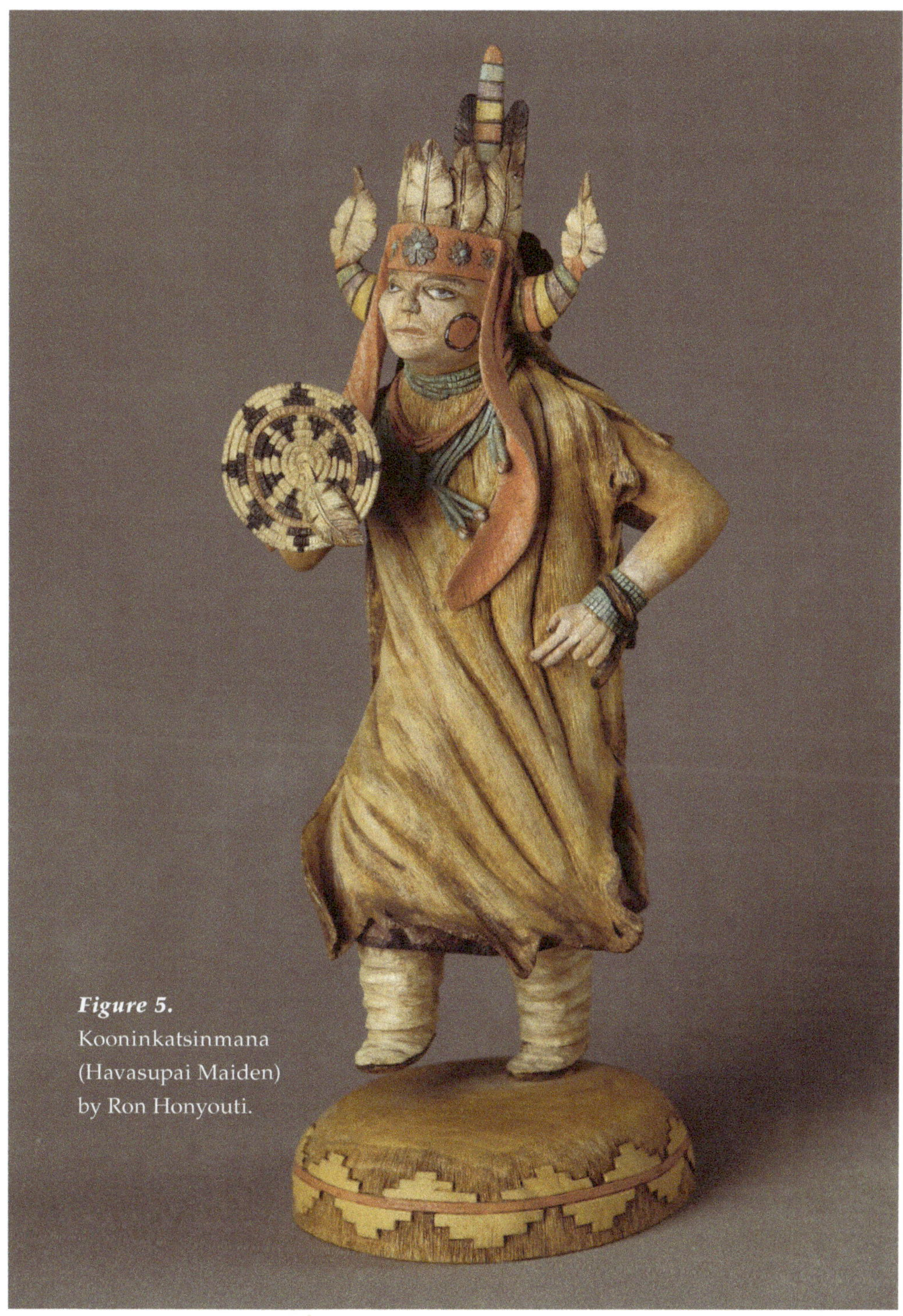

Figure 5.
Kooninkatsinmana
(Havasupai Maiden)
by Ron Honyouti.

designs, and feathers. This work is more than representational; it is thematic and symbolic.

Moreover, it should be noted that this carving requires multiple vantage points. The three figures on the sculpture can only be fully viewed if the carving is fully rotated. The work is best viewed on a rotating stand so that the overall "concept" of diverse Hopi maiden roles is disclosed. This multi-perspectival feature has not been true for any of the other katsinam discussed in this book so far. The evolving work by the Honyouti family is another example of how katsina carvings have moved from an arts-and-crafts tradition into the realm of fine art.

Ron's talent, hard work, and meticulous attention to detail have resulted in countless awards at the Southwestern Association for Indian Arts (SWAIA), the Heard, the MNA, the Gallup Inter-Tribal Ceremonial, and beyond. Yet Ron is rather modest about his myriad achievements. He told me, "I don't consider myself an artist. I just like to play with sharp knives!" Modesty aside, his exceptional creativity has served as a handoff to Ron's two sons, Mavasta and Kevin. Their work is featured in Chapter 26, part two on the Honyouti family.

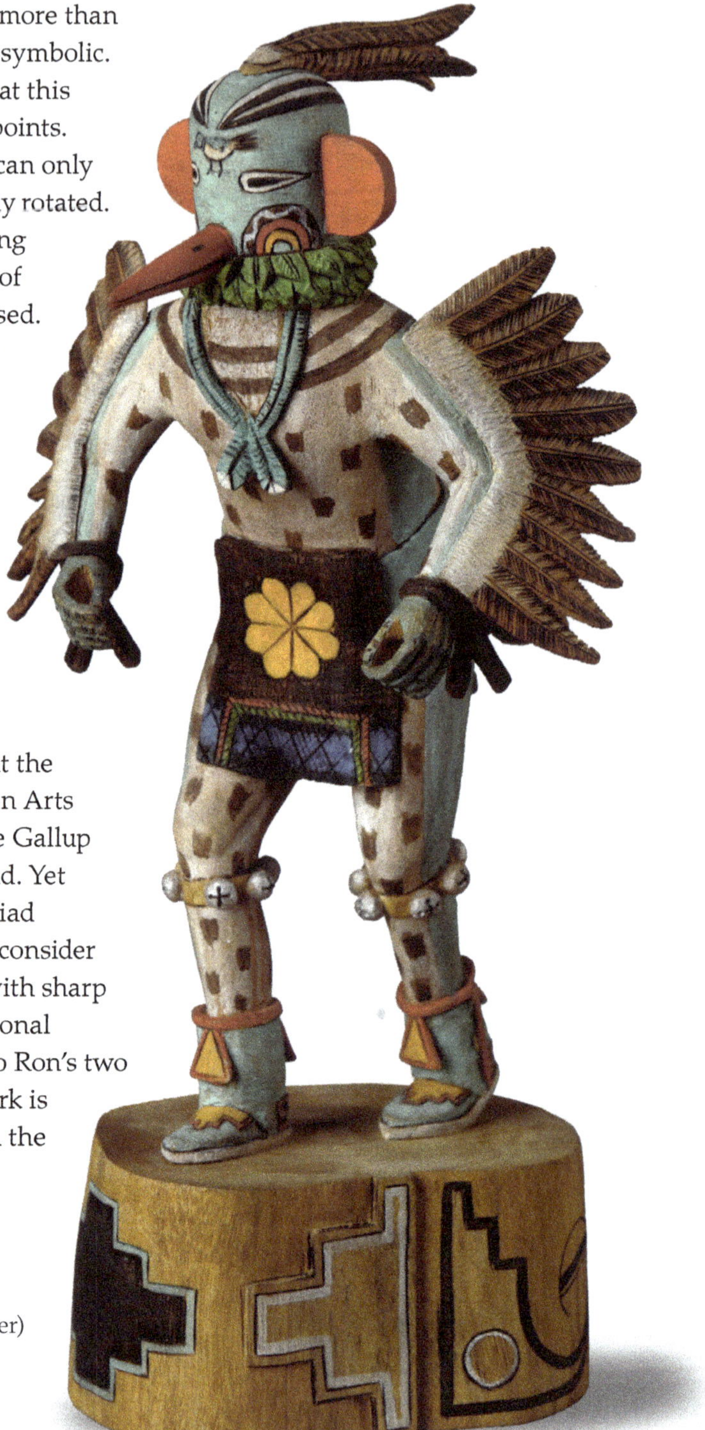

Figure 6. Patro (Sandpiper) by Lauren Honyouti.

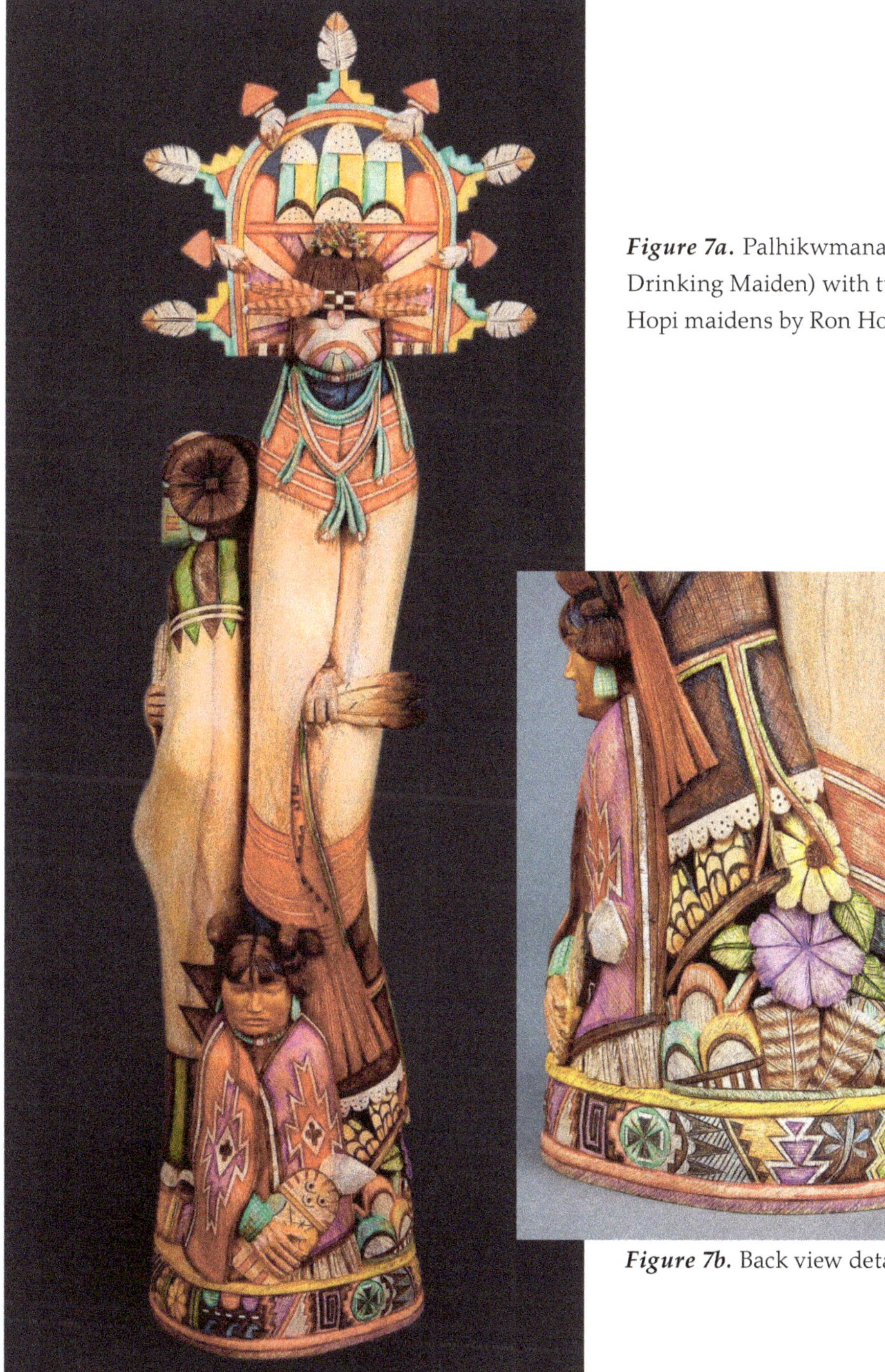

Figure 7a. Palhikwmana (Water Drinking Maiden) with two other Hopi maidens by Ron Honyouti.

Figure 7b. Back view detail.

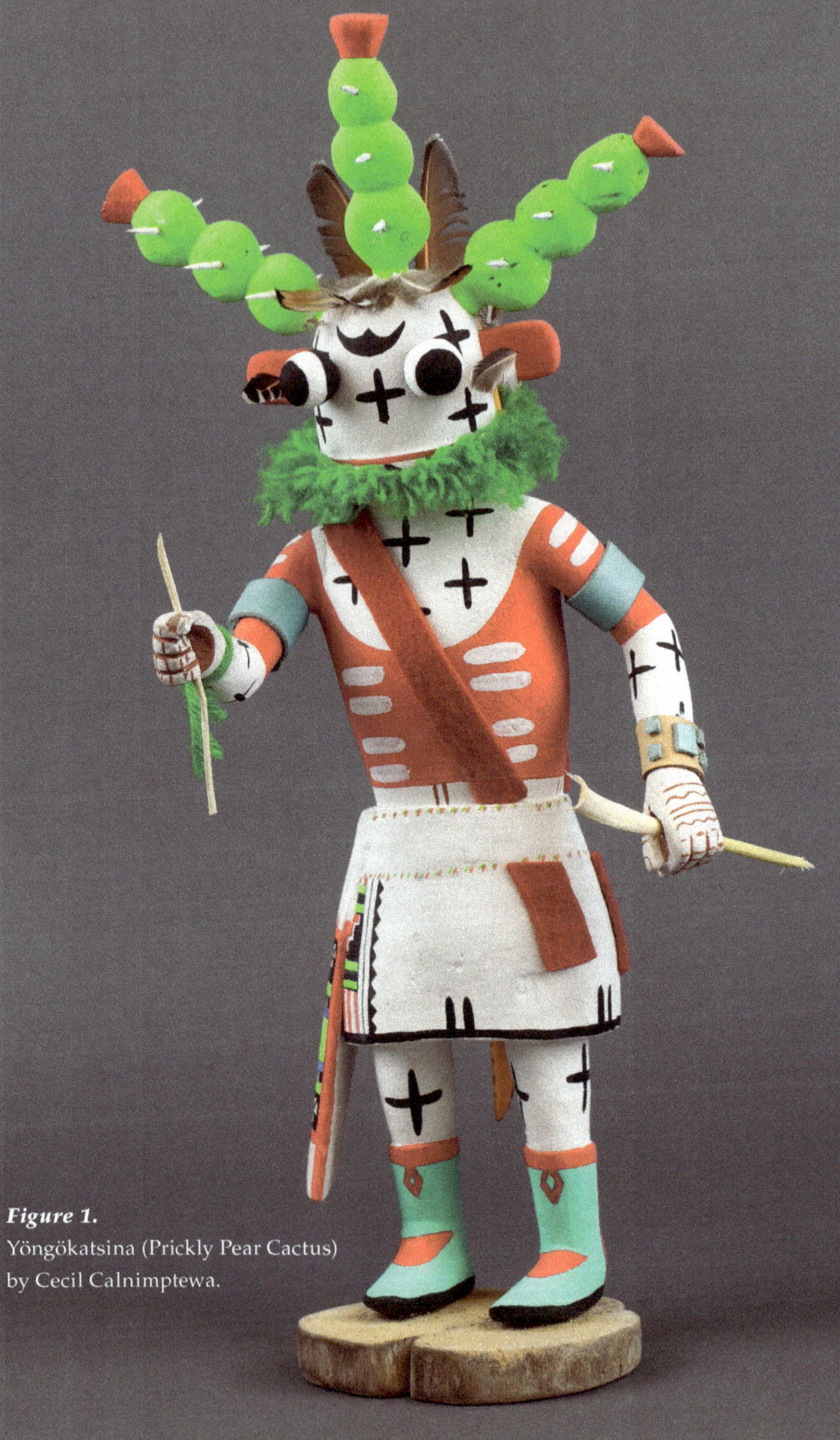

Figure 1.
Yöngökatsina (Prickly Pear Cactus)
by Cecil Calnimptewa.

A GREAT WAVE OF ULTRA-REALISTIC AND SCULPTURAL CARVERS

The 1960s to Present

As indicated in previous chapters on Henry Shelton; William Quotskuyva; Alvin James Makya; and Clyde, Brian, Lauren, and Ronald Honyouti; a major development in katsina carving occurred in the 1960s. Other talented individuals who were at the vanguard of these innovations were Von Monongya, Wilfred Tewawina, and Cecil Calnimptewa, to name a few. From the 1960s onward, a great wave of carvers emerged who moved from the Late Action Style of artists like Jimmie Kewanwytewa and Otto Pentewa, into an Ultra-Realistic Style. Eventually, this style further evolved into what I call the Sculptural Style. These developments had major implications as to the aesthetics and meaning of katsina carvings and their impact on the Native American art marketplace.

During the 1970s and beyond, some of the carvers listed above, and others, became art luminaries. They were featured in one-man shows, and magazine articles and books were written about them. Some sold carvings at prices previously unheard of, such as $10,000 or even $25,000 for a single work. Many of these artists were able to make extremely elaborate carvings out of one piece of cottonwood root. Such carvings often took weeks or even months to complete.

Micro-detailing became the norm. Individual vanes of feathers and strands of hair were incised with wood-burning tools, X-Acto knives, and power rotary tools. Such devices were necessary to successfully execute fine detailing.

Color applications also changed. Diluted acrylics, oil paints, and commercial wood stains became very popular. These materials markedly changed the coloration of the katsinam, often adding a subtlety and muted hues not seen on the Katsina dancers themselves, who manifest bright, primary colors.

During this wave of innovation, some of these Hopi artists were arguably among the best wood-carvers in the world and still are. Not surprisingly, as this type of work entered the world of "fine art dealers," some of these wood carvings were turned into bronze sculptures (e.g., Alvin James Makya, Neil David Sr., and Lowell Talashoma Sr.).

In the 1970s, the move toward ultra-realism also resulted in a revision, retrieval, or protest. For more on that, see the chapters in this book on Manfred

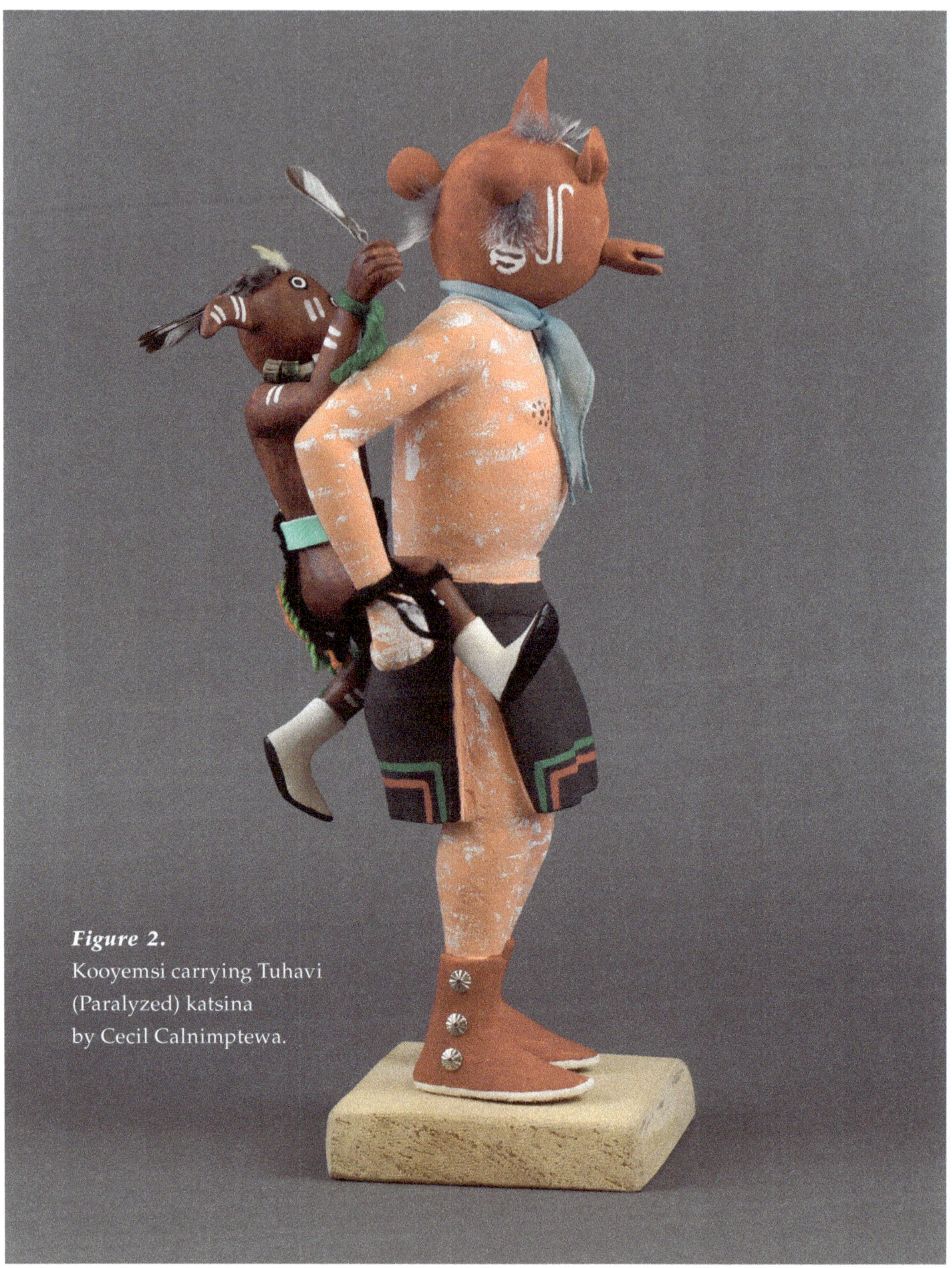

Figure 2.
Kooyemsi carrying Tuhavi (Paralyzed) katsina by Cecil Calnimptewa.

Susunkewa and Walter Howato. Manfred insisted that "something was being lost" with these intricate carvings, so he championed returning to the Traditional Style. Eventually, his move attracted other adherents, including Manuel Denet Chavarria, Philbert Honanie, Clark Tenakhongva, Ferris "Spike" Satala, and many others (see Jonathan Day's book, *Traditional Hopi Kachinas*, 2000).

The emergence of the Ultra-Realistic and Sculptural carvings and the "protest" of the Traditional Style continue to this day. Both traditions have survived well. Only rarely does an artist work in both realms (e.g., Neil David Sr., Ed Seechoma, and Kevin Honyouti).

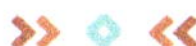

This book will not attempt to review all the Ultra-Realistic and Sculptural carvers who emerged during the 1960s, continuing to the present. There are too many to adequately cover, and many of these very talented individuals have been discussed at length in previous books by Teiwes (1991), Bassman (1991; 1994), Fred Jones Museum of Art (2013), and Pecina and Pecina (2013). What this chapter will do is chronicle the evolution of one of the most recognized creators, Cecil Calnimptewa. Examples from the collection of the Museum of Northern Arizona (MNA) will serve to document his artistic development over time.

The biographical information on Cecil in this chapter comes primarily from Bassman's book, *The Kachina Dolls of Cecil Calnimptewa: Their Power—Their Splendor* (1994), a full-length volume containing a wealth of photos of his work. It is the most extensive source on Cecil's art. Also, contributing to this chapter are sources by Teiwes (1991) and Schaaf (2008).

Cecil Calnimptewa Jr. was born in 1950 in Munqapi (Moenkopi). He is Bamboo Clan. Cecil says that he learned to carve katsinam from his father, Cecil Sr. He shared that he carved his first doll when he was about 18 years old, a Suyang'evu (Left-Handed One), and that his father took it to New Mexico where he sold it for $50. Not a bad start, but what a trajectory would play out!

Early on Cecil used only a pocketknife to carve katsinam, and used poster and acrylic paints. Over time he came to use a band saw to shape basic figures, a Dremel rotary tool to refine the wood, and an X-Acto knife to execute the details. He noted that the meticulous work on details is very time-consuming. Cecil has credited Alvin James Makya, Brian Honyouti, and Ron Honyouti for inspiring him to make ever more elaborate action figures. And he cited the Honyouti brothers and Lowell Talashoma Sr. as influencing him to use wood stains for coloration.

Another major influence on his artwork was his wife, Muriel. He married Muriel in the mid-1970s. Muriel was a niece of Feather Woman (Helen Naha), the renowned potter. Muriel was a potter herself until Cecil and she had their first child, at which point Muriel switched to katsina carving. She was particularly known and highly regarded for her miniatures. According to Teiwes, "Cecil taught Muriel basic carving skills and Muriel, in turn, taught Cecil how to refine his detail carving" (1991, 96). Cecil and Muriel carved together every day until her untimely death from pneumonia in 1988. Cecil noted that it was an extremely difficult time after Muriel's death to raise four children, tend to his farm and livestock, and continue his carving career. He eventually remarried in 1991 to Wanda Talayumptewa who brought two additional children to the family. Another major event was when Cecil opened his own gallery, Calnimptewa's, near Orayvi (Oraibi) in 1990. It is closed now but had a good run during the 1990s and into the early 2000s.

In turning to Cecil's carvings, it is instructive to examine five carvings from the collection of the MNA. The earliest is depicted in Figure 1. This is a Yöngökatsina (Prickly Pear Cactus) katsina. It is essentially done in the Late Action Style first made popular in the 1940s and 50s. It is dated on the base as 1969. Note the use of what appears to be poster paint, the yarn ruff, and the rather stiff motion of the katsina. He has added some detail including a bracelet with turquoise chips, toothpicks representing cactus spines, and a red felt bandolier.

In Figure 2, one can see refinement in Cecil's technique. This is a Kooyemsi with a Tuhavi (Paralyzed) katsina on his back. These katsinam are painted with acrylics, and the motion depicted is more adept. Note that there are yarn, feather, and cloth accoutrements. The date for this carving is 1973. The four-year period between Figures 1 and 2 has resulted in a much more sophisticated carving.

The next example (Figure 3) from the MNA collection is from 2005. This is a very different katsina from the 1973 figure. The human physiology is expertly rendered. By now Cecil has studied the human body and can render it in full motion with great accuracy. There are no fabric or feather add-ons to this carving; it is all wood. The coloration is primarily different shades of wood stain. A small amount of color is added to the Mastopkatsina's necklace, bowguard, and moccasins. The Mastop is a fertility katsina.

A fourth example, from 2010, depicts Palöngawhoya, who is a deity, not a katsina (Figure 4). Once again, Cecil has captured the dynamic motion of the running figure. In this case, the use of diluted oil paints and stain are masterfully combined. The details on the katsina's garment, stockings, and moccasins are exceptional. This is truly ultra-realism.

The final example to be discussed is in the Sculptural Style (Figure 5). The figure is interpretive as well as representational. This Wuyaktaywa (Broadface) is portrayed in a bodily position that a real dancer is unlikely to assume. I've seen

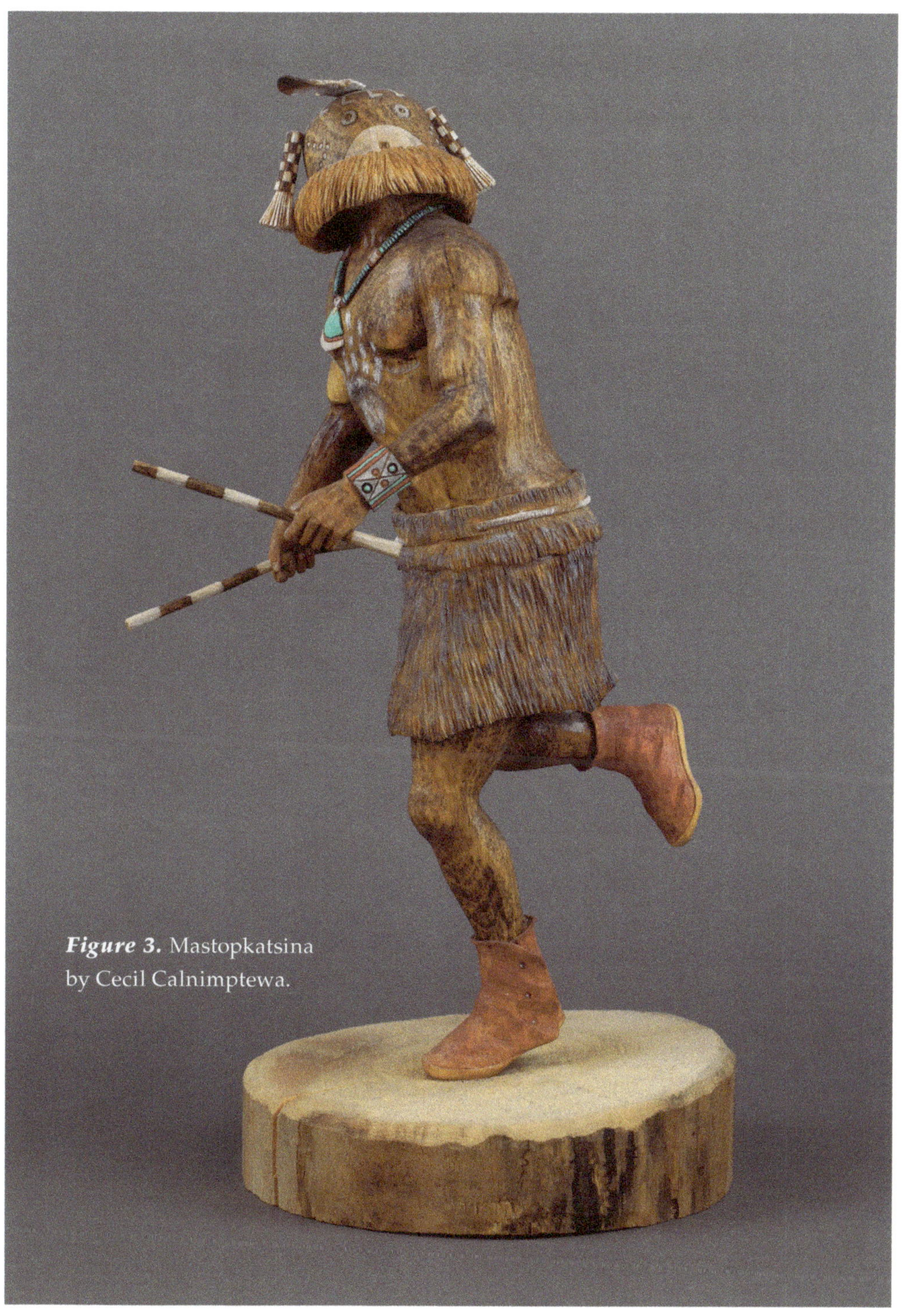

Figure 3. Mastopkatsina by Cecil Calnimptewa.

Broadface katsinam many times at dances and they do not move their heads around as posed. They plod forward at a slow pace, often protecting Crow Mother, and exhibit a great but stolid dignity. I believe that Cecil's intent with this carving was to symbolically represent the katsina's relationship with the heavens. The Broadface is looking up at the ancestor clouds, anticipating rain and related long-life for the Hopi people. Note the exceptionally high level of detail on this piece, including individual strands of hair on the katsina's beard, the cascading lines of red horsehair on the garment and dance wand, the crown of eagle feathers on the head, and the fringe on the moccasins. It is also quite substantial at $15\frac{5}{8}$ inches tall. This is a very beautiful sculpture and katsina doll as fine art.

The explosion of Ultra-Realistic and Sculptural carvings continues to this day, although the extremely robust market for such work has calmed a bit. Artists who produce exceptional work in this style still find a strong customer base for their wares. Examples of carvers currently producing such katsinam are provided later in this book in the chapters on Neil David Sr., Robert Albert, and Mavasta and Kevin Honyouti. Their chapters are meant to be representative. There are many other skilled artisans working in the Ultra-Realistic and Sculptural Styles as well, including Dennis Tewa, Loren Phillips, John Fredericks, Arthur Holmes Sr. and Jr., Michael Dean Jenkins, and several others.

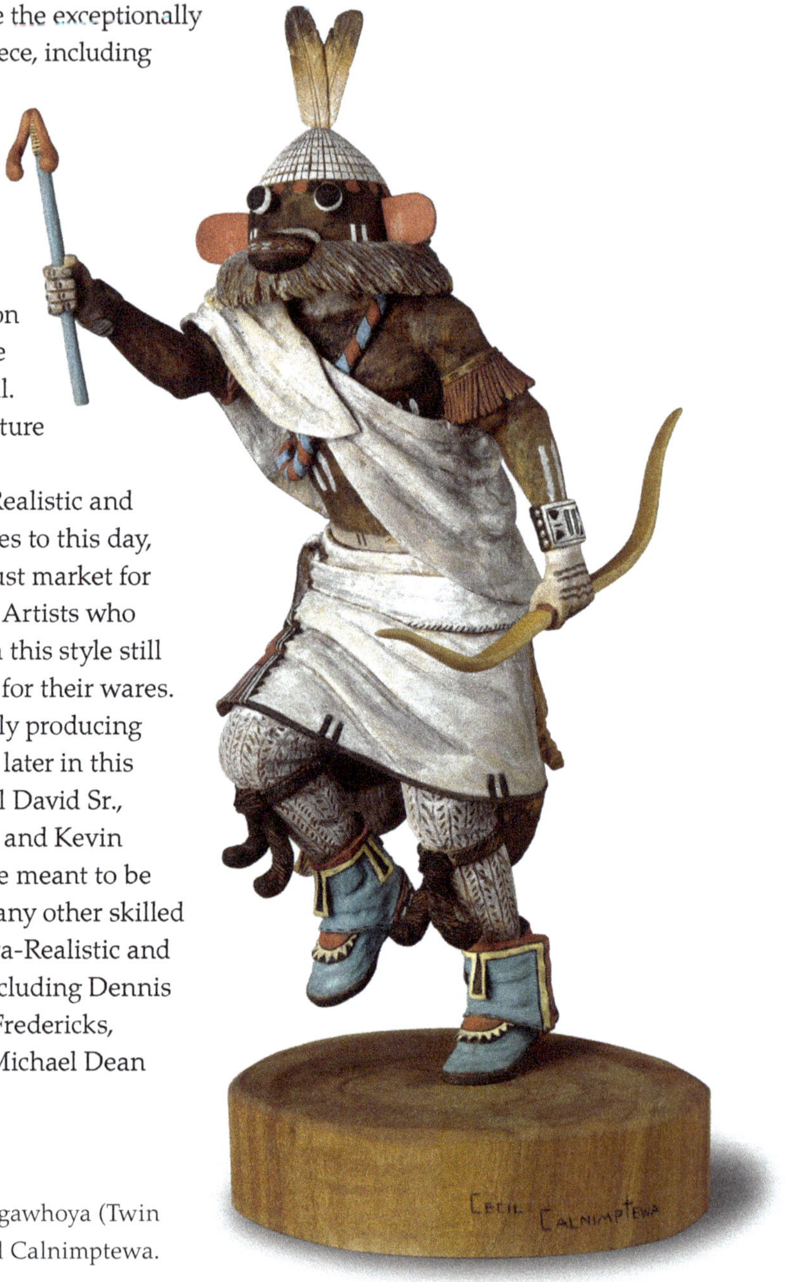

Figure 4. Palöngawhoya (Twin Warrior God) by Cecil Calnimptewa.

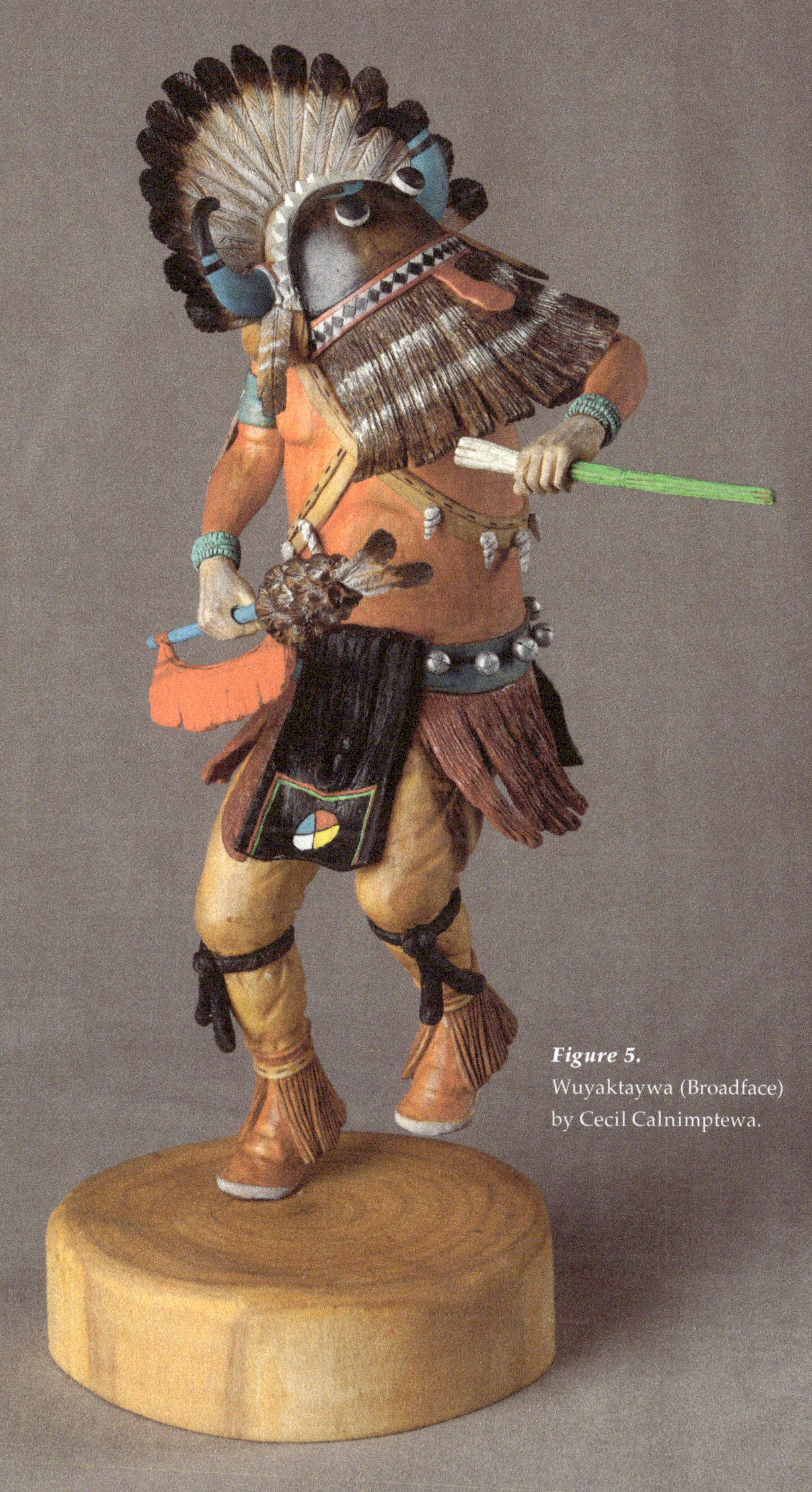

Figure 5.
Wuyaktaywa (Broadface)
by Cecil Calnimptewa.

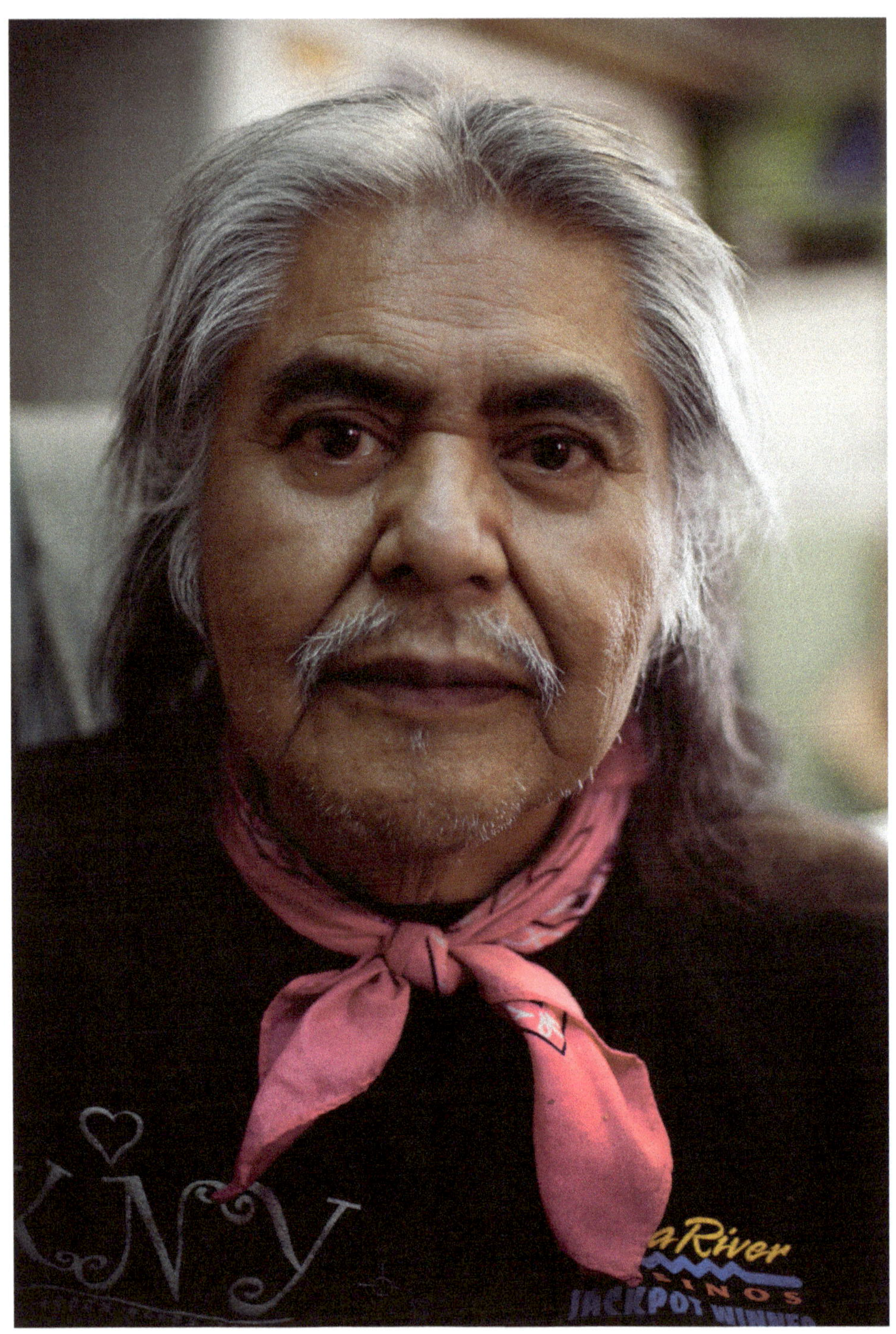

Figure 1. Neil David Sr.

NEIL DAVID SR.

Master of Diverse Media

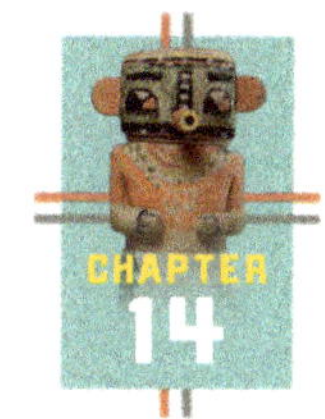

Neil David Sr. is a legend in the Native American art business (Figure 1). He has had a long, uninterrupted, successful career as an artist working in diverse media, including paintings; lithographs; murals; sculptures in clay, bronze, and porcelain; and katsina carvings (in both the Sculptural and Traditional Style). Neil was kind enough to provide me with an extended interview at his home in Polacca on the Hopi reservation. He shared that he was born in 1944 and his maternal clan is Katsina and Parrot. He grew up in First Mesa's Hano or Tewa village. He went to school through the seventh grade at the old Polacca Day School. From eighth through tenth grade he attended high school in Orayvi and as he told me, "when that was abolished, I was shipped out to the Phoenix Indian School in 1963."

Remarkably, Neil said he did not study art in high school, but did have a lot of art classes in elementary school and experienced a rather notable teacher in eighth grade, Fred Kabotie! Fred Kabotie was one of the most celebrated Hopi painters to ever live. He was also a jeweler, author, illustrator, educator, and informal ambassador for Hopiland.

Taught by Fred Kabotie or not, Neil said that like most eighth graders, he "spent a lot of time looking out the window," yet even so he learned a lot from Fred, including how to work with casein. He said that Fred, "saw my potential and encouraged me." At the Orayvi school, he had another remarkable teacher, Charles Loloma! According to Martha Hopkins Struever, Charles is "arguably the most influential Native American, if not North American, jeweler of the twentieth century" (2005). Charles for a time had a workshop at the school where he taught jewelry making. Neil said Charles also recognized his potential. With such mentors, Neil muses that his art "could have taken off at that time, but it didn't." Rather, it took years to germinate. Still, having such encouraging and accomplished role models during his formative years must have hinted at the possibilities.

After he finished high school in Phoenix, he signed up to attend school at the Institute of American Indian Arts (IAIA) in Santa Fe, but he never attended.

Instead, he went to Albuquerque where he lived with an aunt and spent time babysitting. Eventually, he came back home to Hano until he found himself drafted during the Vietnam era into the U.S. Army. In 1965 he went to boot camp in Fort Polk, Louisiana, and from there to Fort Gordon in Georgia. He received advanced training in radio technology. He referred to himself as a "tube changer" in the Signal Corps and remarked on "the huge machines" that were necessary to transmit radio signals back then. Later he was deployed to Germany, where he spent the remainder of his three years in the Army. He said he found Germany "very beautiful. It was so green there, so different from Hopi."

While in Germany, he fortuitously rediscovered his art "toolkit" from eighth grade. He began making portraits, usually in oil paints, of fellow soldiers, who would send them to their girlfriends, wives, and children. This was the beginning of Neil's art career.

When he was discharged, Neil returned to the reservation. He noted that in the late 1960s, "the Europeans were visiting and buying Hopi crafts." Establishing a pattern that survives to this day, Neil recognized a market opportunity and took advantage of it. He began carving katsinam and making paintings, which he successfully sold to tourists. Still, he wasn't sure of his future direction. He considered going back to school via the G.I. Bill.

A key moment occurred when Michael Kabotie, son of his old teacher, Fred, approached Neil about joining the Hopi Arts and Crafts Guild. The guild was an important cooperative that was teaching and sponsoring the creation of Hopi arts and crafts. Neil said Fred and his wife, Alice, were managing the co-op and that Paul Saufkie, another seminal figure in Hopi jewelry, worked there as well. Neil began selling katsinam and paintings to the guild, which at that time was a very successful business.

Michael and Neil began painting together and collaborating on various projects. In 1972 they formed the Artist Hopid group along with friends Terence Talaswaima and Delbridge Honanie. Later Terence exited and Milland Lomakema joined them. The Artist Hopid group comprised young men who were striving to give new interpretations to traditional Hopi art forms (Pecina and Pecina 2011).

Neil recalled that at that time they were all working in a tiny workshop at the Hopi Motel complex, which was so small they couldn't make any larger carvings, paintings, or sculptures. Neil said the Artist Hopid really hit its stride in 1974. The members began doing shows as a group in Tucson, New Mexico, and California. They were also featured in prominent galleries such as Rosequist's and Glenn Green's. Eventually, the group broke up around 1978 as the individual artists went their separate ways.

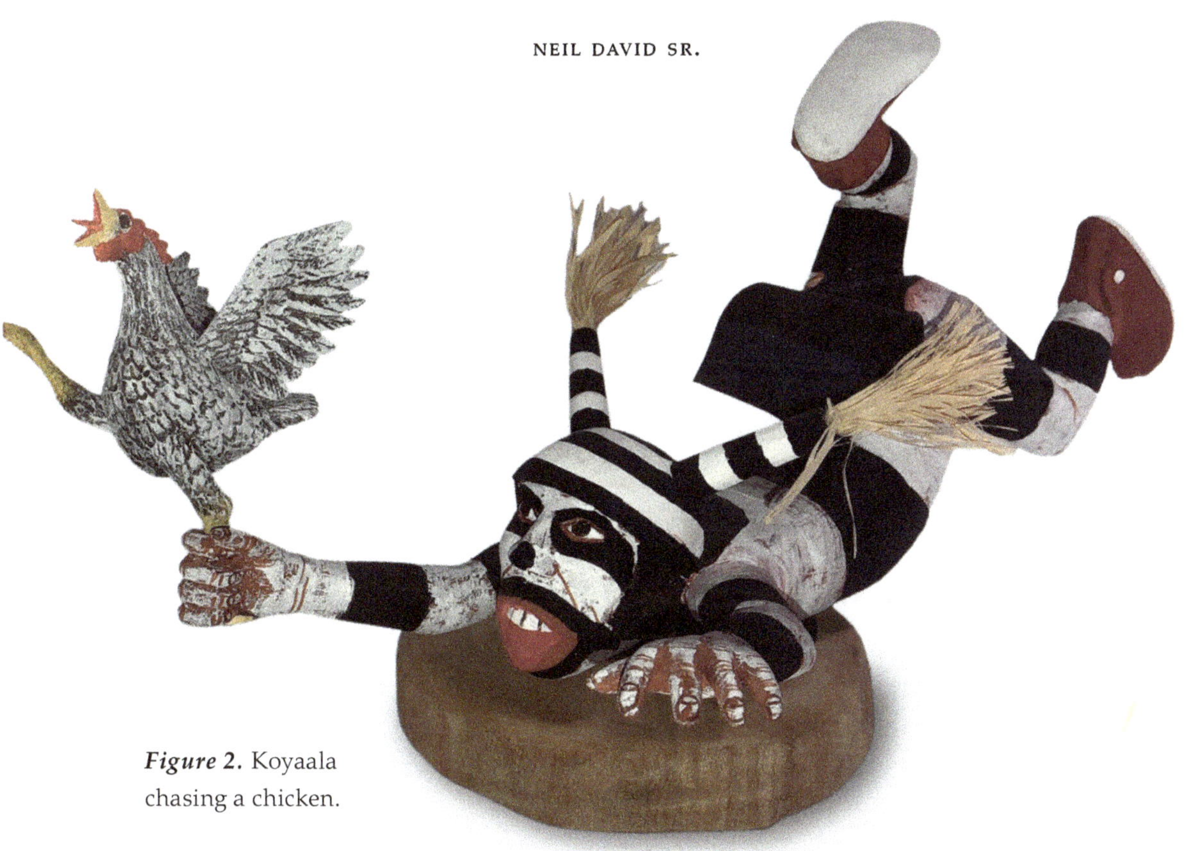

Figure 2. Koyaala chasing a chicken.

One direction for Neil was to obtain a booth at Santa Fe's Indian Market. He recalled that he did this market for about fifteen years. Back then he indicated the scale was much smaller; all the booths were on the plaza only. At the time, a booth at SWAIA cost $125, whereas at the time of this writing it was around $600. Speaking of the plaza in Santa Fe, for years Packard's On the Plaza was a prominent gallery presence. Neil sold very detailed katsina sculptures to them for years until Packard's closed in 2013.

As Neil's career began to evolve during the 80s and 90s, his work took on a diversity that few in the Indian art world can equal. His creation of katsina carvings and paintings has already been noted, but Neil also began to produce bronze sculptures depicting katsinam and other Hopi subjects. For a time, he collaborated on bronzes with another noted katsina artist, Lowell Talashoma Sr. They also produced a series of katsina figures in porcelain that were made in a large factory in Mexico. Additionally, Neil produced limited edition prints of his paintings and lithographs. While the focus in this book is on his katsina carvings, it is important to emphasize Neil's impressive artistic creativity and versatility.

One type of carving for which Neil has been known for many years has been his Koyaala or Hano clowns. A favorite has been his rendition of a

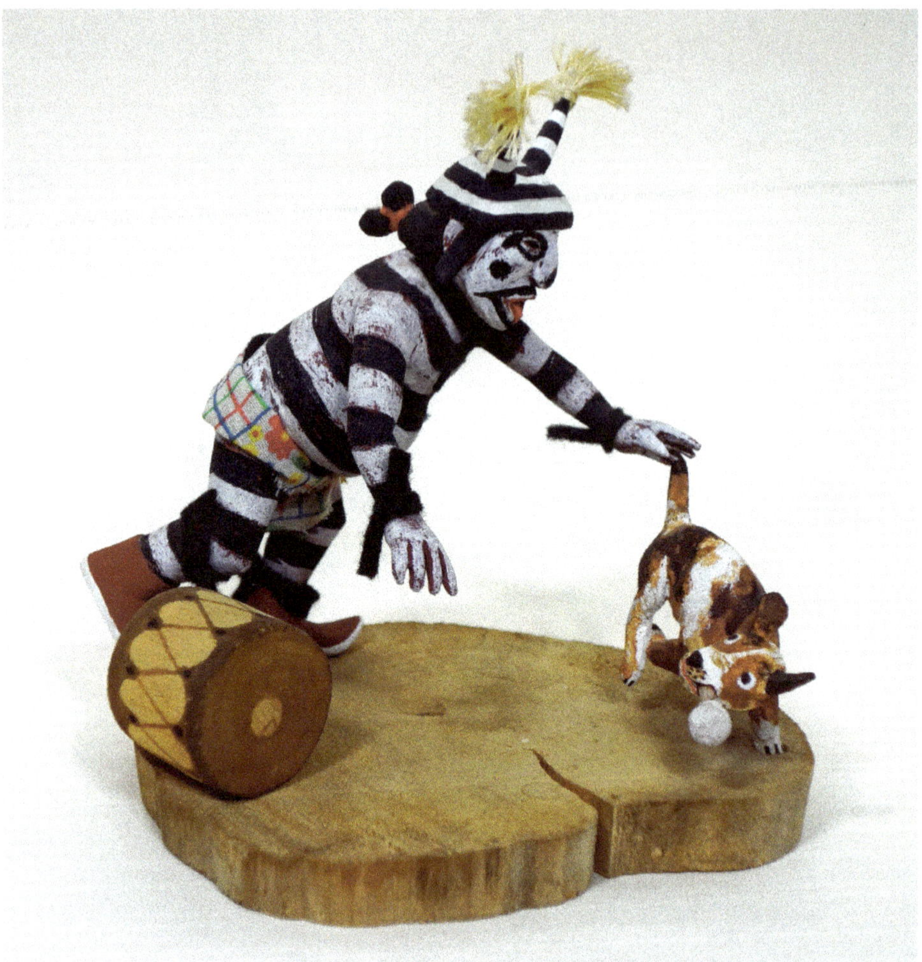

Figure 3. Koyaala chasing a dog.

Koyaala chasing a chicken, as shown in Figure 2. Neil recalled that when he first submitted one of these to a competition in Holbrook he won many ribbons. Since then the Koyaala-with-chicken motif has been a favorite among customers. Neil explains that "I take the clowns I see at dances and exaggerate them a bit more." Or maybe a lot! These carvings are hilarious and charismatic. They have been Neil's signature carvings for decades now. Other examples of Neil's comical Koyaalas are shown in Figures 3 and 4. Figure 3 shows a Clown chasing a dog that has stolen his drum pounder. Figure 4 shows six different Koyaalas engaged in different types of merriment.

Neil said that at times he grows weary of carving Koyaala and chicken figures over and over, but he carries on. After all, Neil has a large family to support. He

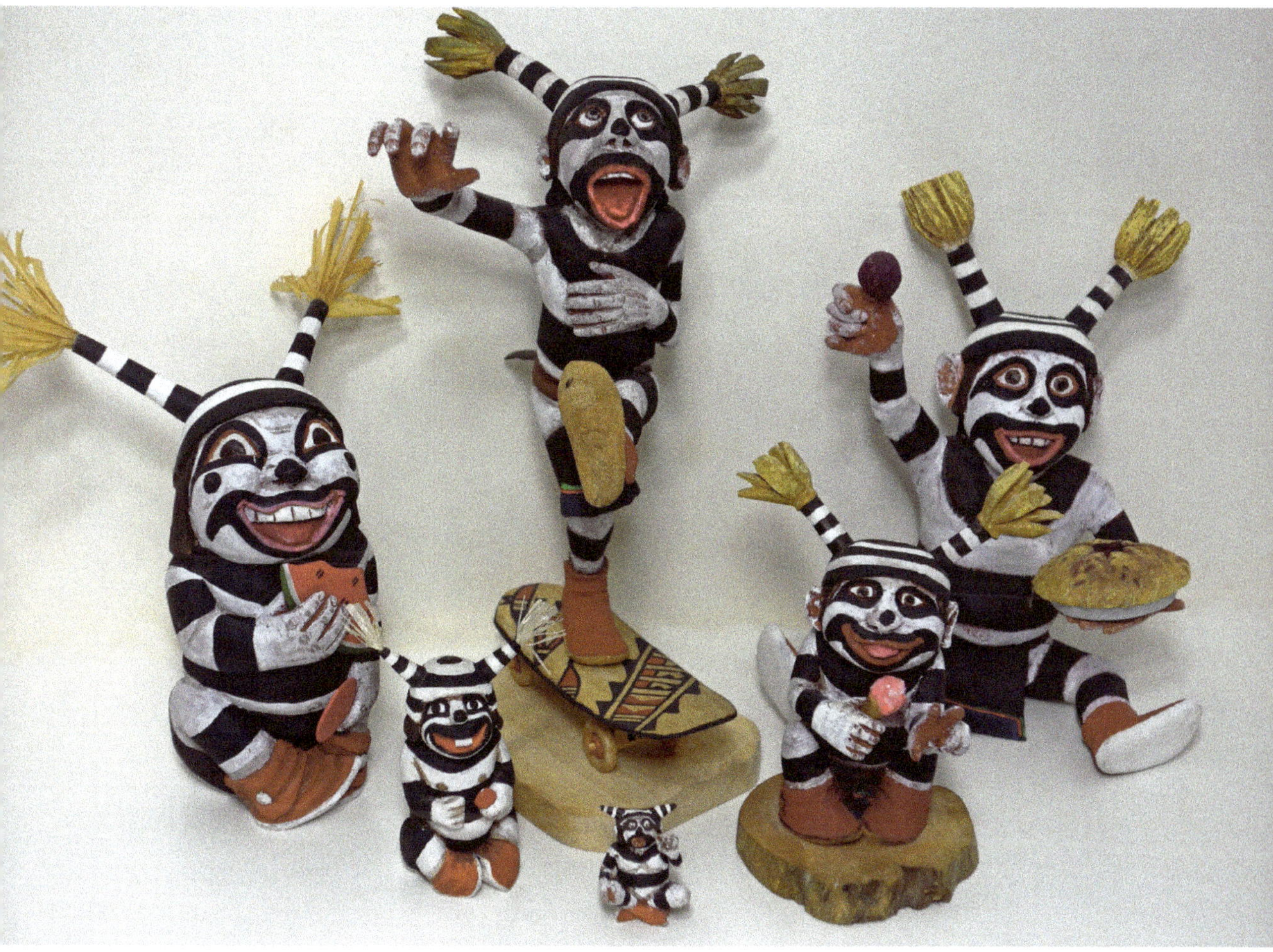

Figure 4. Six Koyaalas.

notes when he gets a call for such special orders, he asks, "What is the figure doing?" "What size do you want?" and "How much detail?" The answers to these questions determine the price, then Neil gets to work.

For years Neil has also made katsinam in the Ultra-Realistic Style. An excellent example is shown in Figure 5. This is the Suyang'evu (Left-handed One). Neil is known on First and Second Mesa as Suyang'ephoya, another term for Left-handed One. Note the exceptional rendering of the kneeling body posture and the detailing of the leather cape, jacla necklace, moccasins, ketoh (bowguard), etcetera.

Always attentive to the vagaries of the Indian art market, about ten years ago (around 2008) Neil began making carvings in the much more simplified

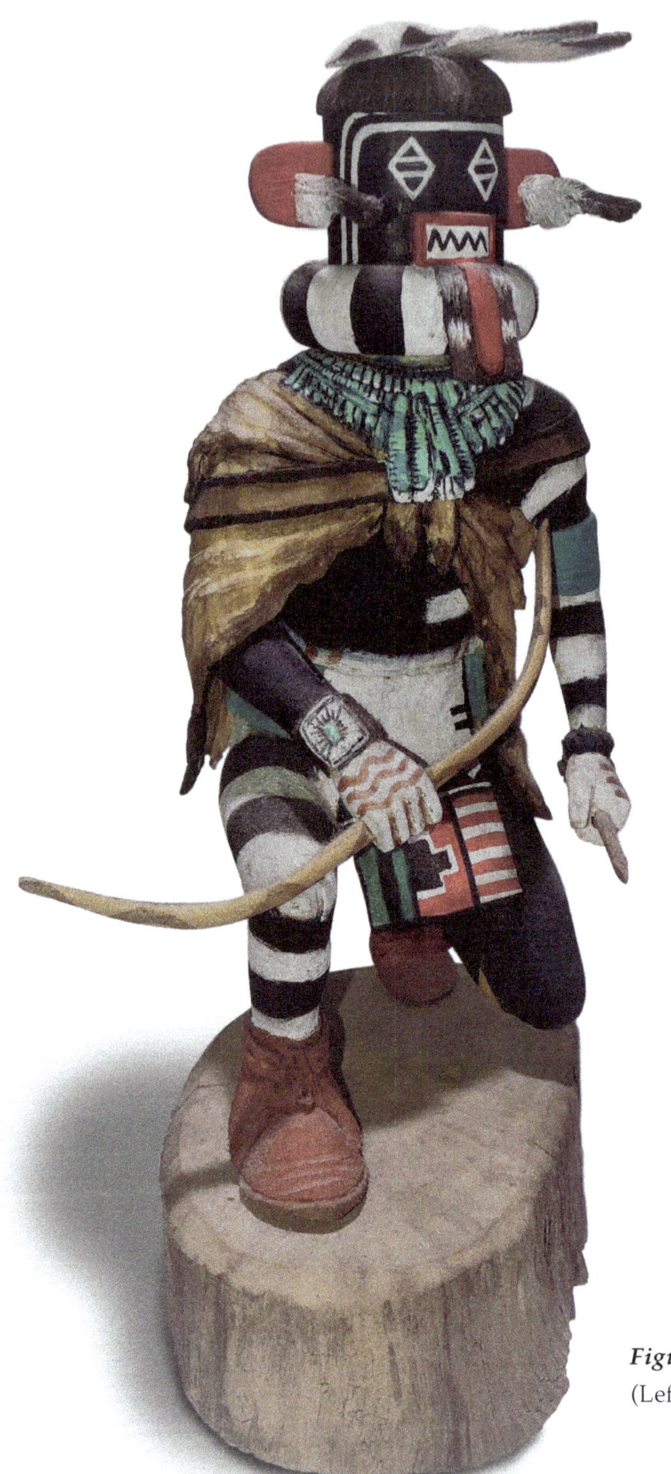

Figure 5. Suyang'evu (Left-handed One).

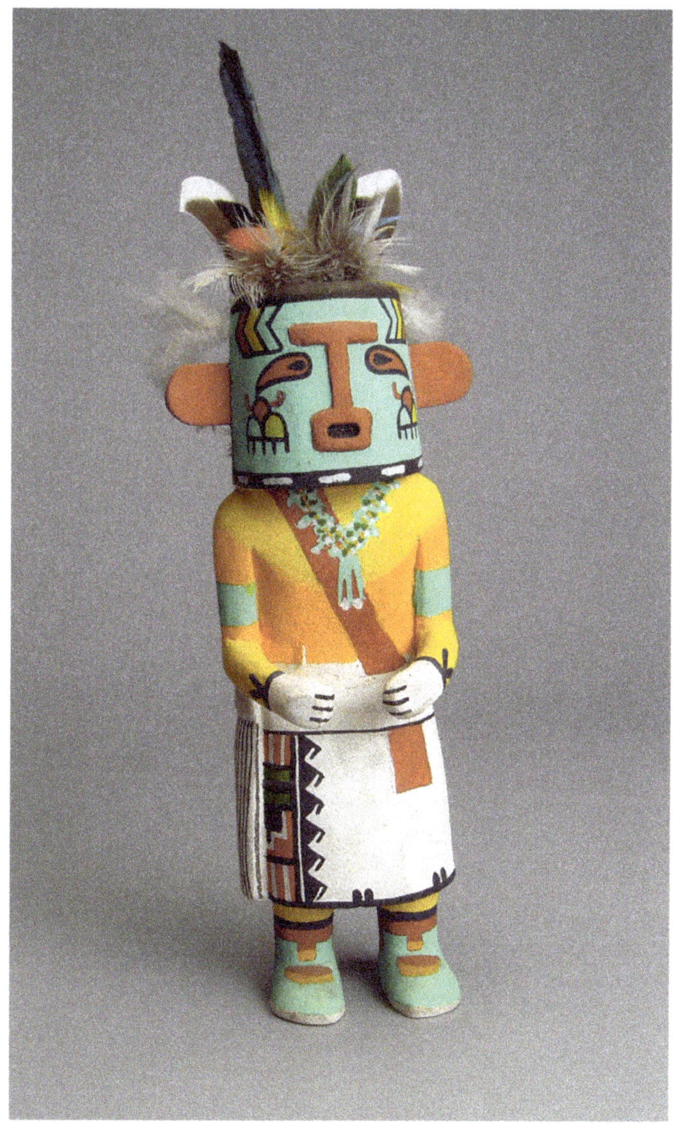

Figure 6. Kuwan Hehey'a.

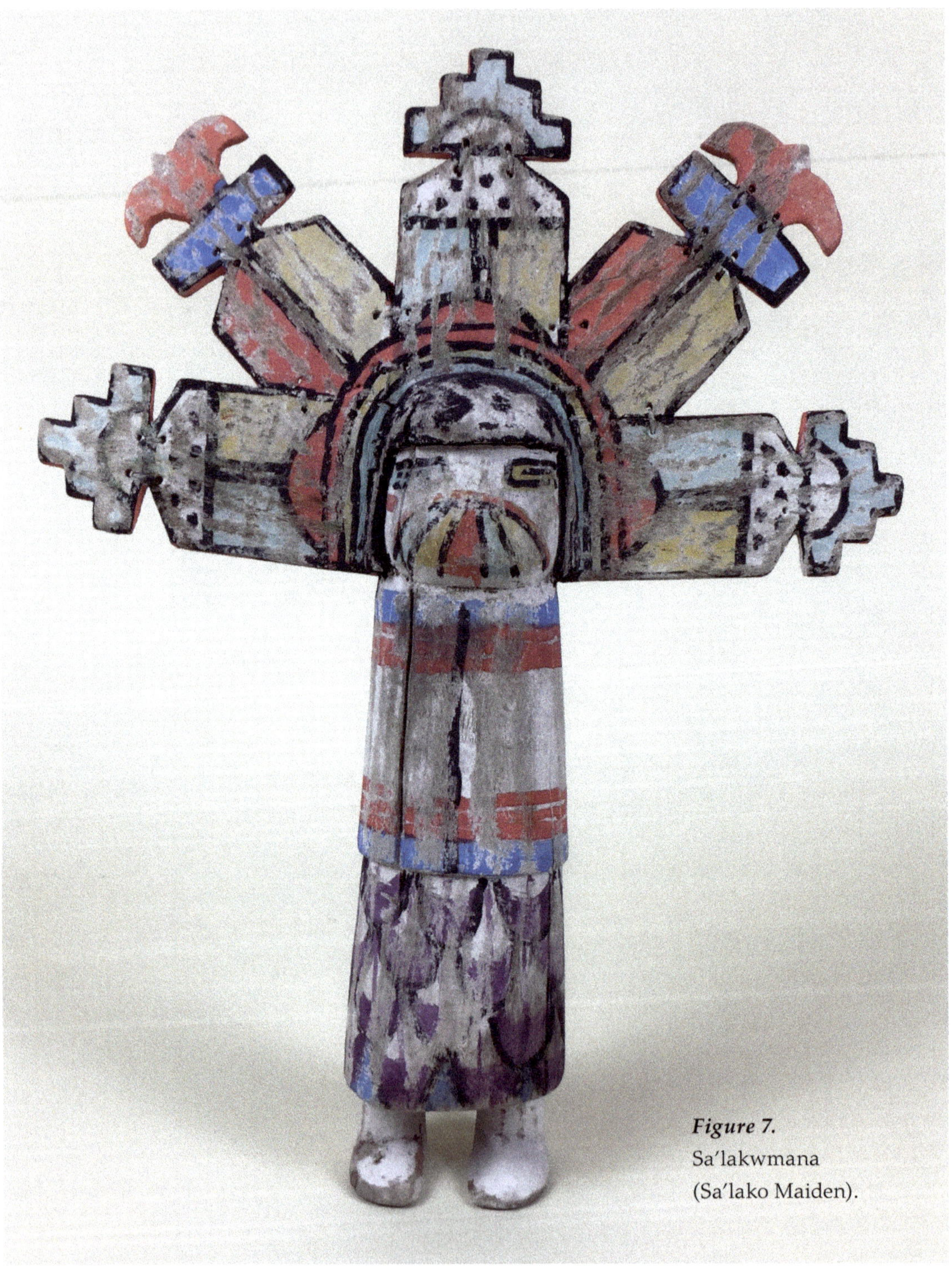

Figure 7.
Sa'lakwmana
(Sa'lako Maiden).

Traditional Style. A good example is shown in Figure 6, a clean rendition of a Kuwan Hehey'a (or Colorful Hehey'a). And at times, Neil has fun making "ancient" katsinam (see Figure 7, a Sa'lakwmana), which he playfully claims to have found in a ruin or cave somewhere. However, his artist's signature on the bottom betrays this charade. Everyone who encounters Neil comments on his hilarious sense of humor.

This humor also manifests in his paintings, which often portray his favorite subject of Koyaalas or Clowns. See Figure 8 for a wonderfully entertaining example. I sure would like to know what they are pointing and laughing at.

More recently, Neil has come to rely less on galleries and art shows and more on special orders; he is so established at this point that business comes to him. Neil prefers to work this way, explaining that galleries often try to impose restrictions as to productivity, deadlines, and exclusivity. He prefers to work on his own terms and finds it gratifying that after all these years he has the freedom to do so.

Neil is very proud of and close to his family. Unfortunately, he recently lost one of these members. He shared that he grieves his oldest son, Loren, every day. Tragically, the family lost Loren to alcohol earlier in 2017. One way that Neil deals with his grief is by his frequent making of humorous figures.

His other children are two sons, Neil Jr. and John Sr., both of whom are katsina carvers, and Rhonda, the youngest, who is less involved in the art world. Neil's grandfather, Victor Charlie, was also a notable carver. An example of his work is shown in Figure 9, a Kuwan Hehey'a katsina. However, it is certainly hard to find any artistic link between Victor's work and Neil's.

When asked about his artistic influences, Neil denies having major mentors. He said, "it has mostly come from within." He notes that he has a large collection of *Southwest Art Magazine*, which he may refer to, and likes to read the biographies of artists and learn from how they discuss their work.

Speaking of print media, Neil has been very involved in illustrating a number of books. Most notable is the 1993 volume, *Kachinas: Spirit Beings of the Hopi*. Neil provided all seventy-nine of the katsina paintings for that book—a major amount of work. The book features many rare katsinam seldom seen in other publications and unfamiliar to many Hopi. Neil's work has also been featured in two more recent books by Ron and Bob Pecina, *Neil David's Hopi World*, published in 2011, and *Hopi Kachinas: History, Legends, and Art*, published in 2013.

Neil David Sr.'s creativity and versatility spanning four decades are indeed impressive. We are fortunate he remains a vital contributor to the world of Hopi katsina carving and the broader art world.

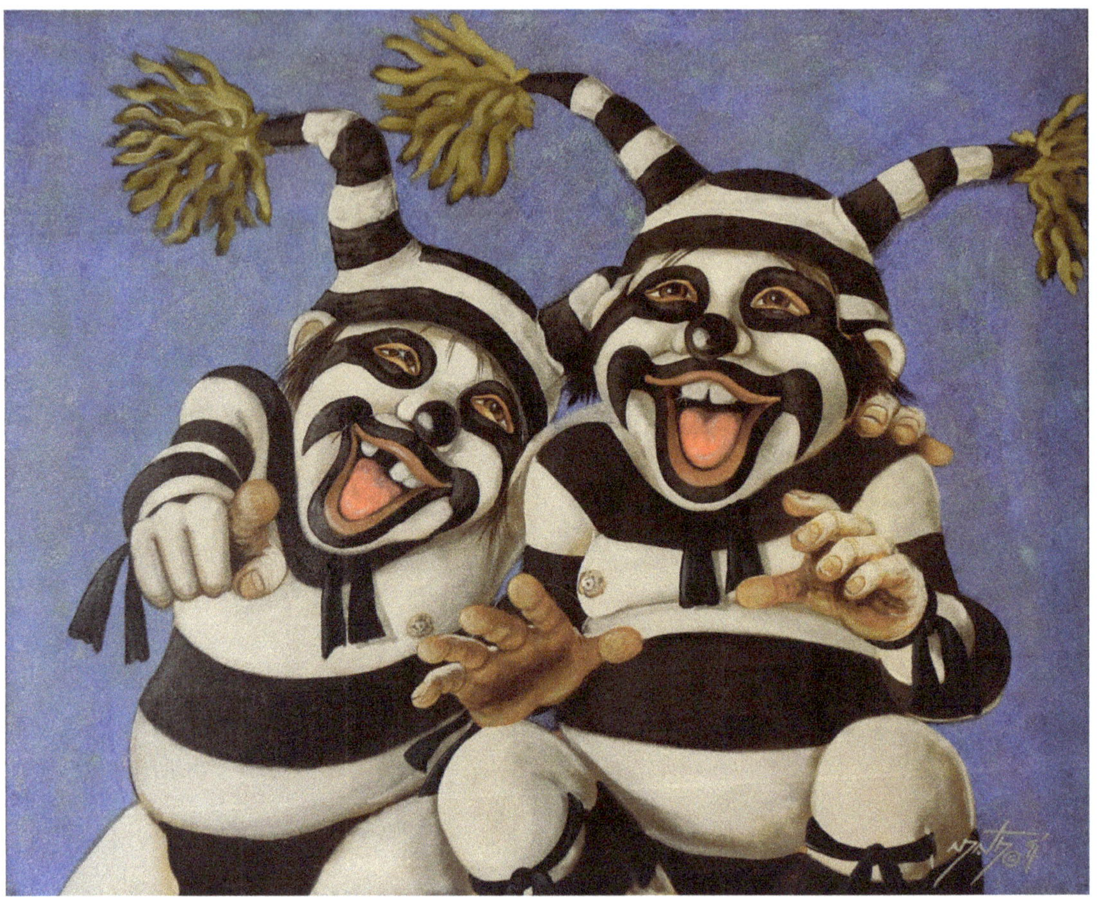

Figure 8. Painting of Koyaalas.

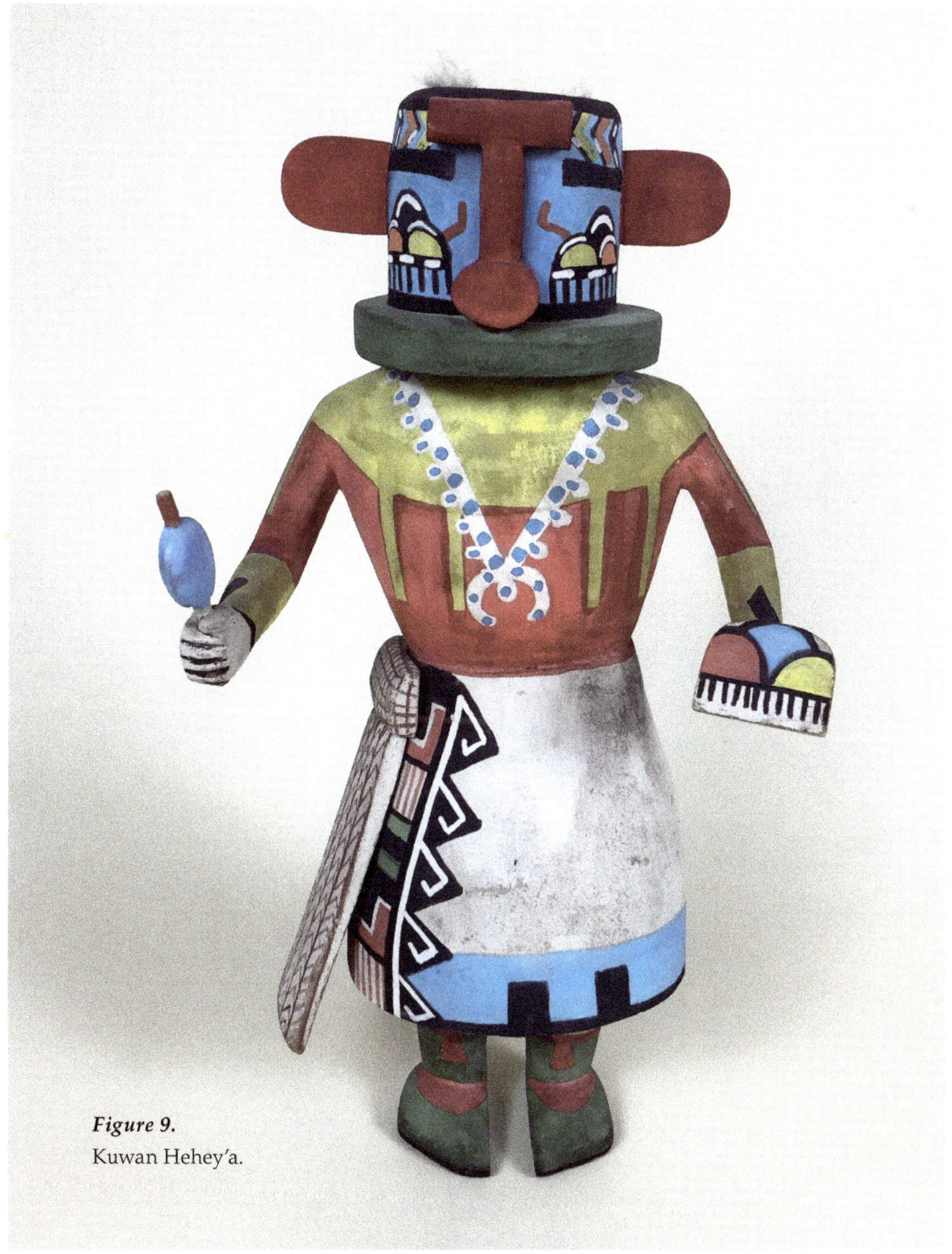

Figure 9.
Kuwan Hehey'a.

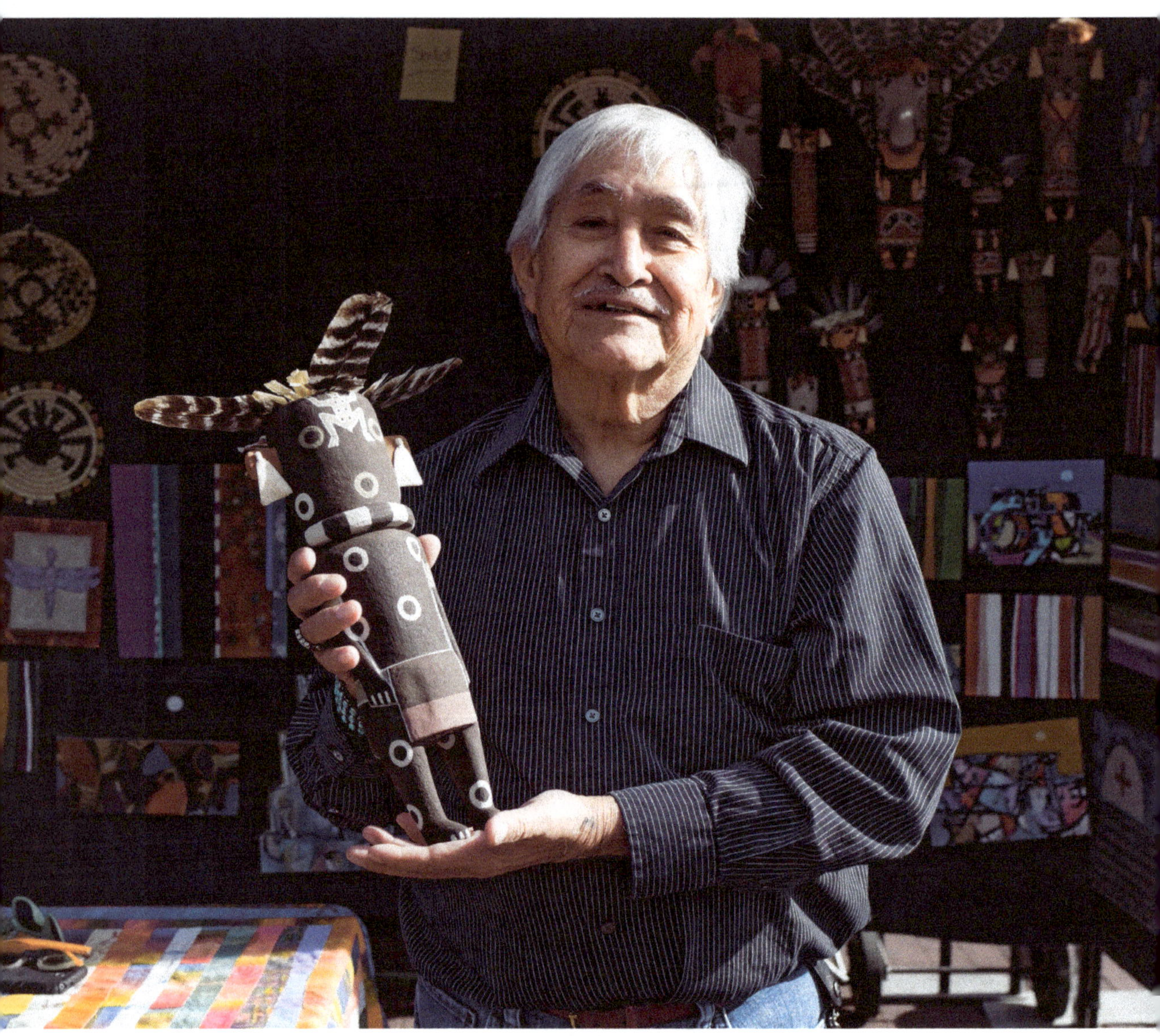

Figure 1. Manfred Susunkewa.

MANFRED SUSUNKEWA

The Originator

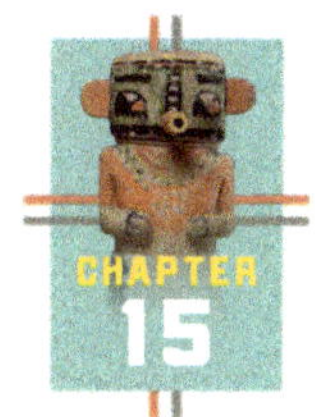

MANFRED SUSUNKEWA (see Figure 1) was born in 1940. His maternal clan is Spider/Bear Strap Clan and his paternal clan is Sand. He grew up in Songoopavi (Shongopavi), Second Mesa.

During his youth and young adulthood, Manfred received a fair amount of education in schools and art settings, but he asked me to concentrate on the development of his katsina carvings and not other aspects of his biography. I have honored that wish.

Manfred is the originator of the "old style" or "Traditional katsina movement." He started making dolls in his minimalist, provocative way "as a protest." He said he "wasn't the first to make katsinam in this way, but the style had disappeared." Manfred explained that what he began in the 1970s "was a revision," and that real katsina carvings were "being forgotten." Referring to the elaborate Ultra-Realistic Style dolls that were all the rage with collectors by the 1970s, Manfred said the dolls "were becoming too pretty." He said his "revision or return was designed to recapture the spirit of the carvings in relation to the Spirit Beings." He elaborated, "I took some things from the past and made them contemporary."

He reminisced that as a child he would sleep on the floor and see the katsina carvings hanging on the walls and they "were scary, not cute." Years ago, he told me how he had seen jet black Owak'Katsinam (or Coal) in the kiva as a child where he "felt a sense of awe and fear." He also recollected that his mother used to point to the wood stove in their home and say, "Do what the Ogre says when he comes to the village or he will throw you in that fire." These were the experiences and emotions Manfred recaptured in making his utterly distinctive katsinam.

Manfred also spoke about his grandfather, Pasyva, a name that means "a flower blooming in Spring."

> My grandfather told many stories. He was a very unusual and profound man. He would talk mysteriously and I would listen. He taught me about the philosophy of the prophecies. I didn't always understand but the stories were in there, in the back of my mind.

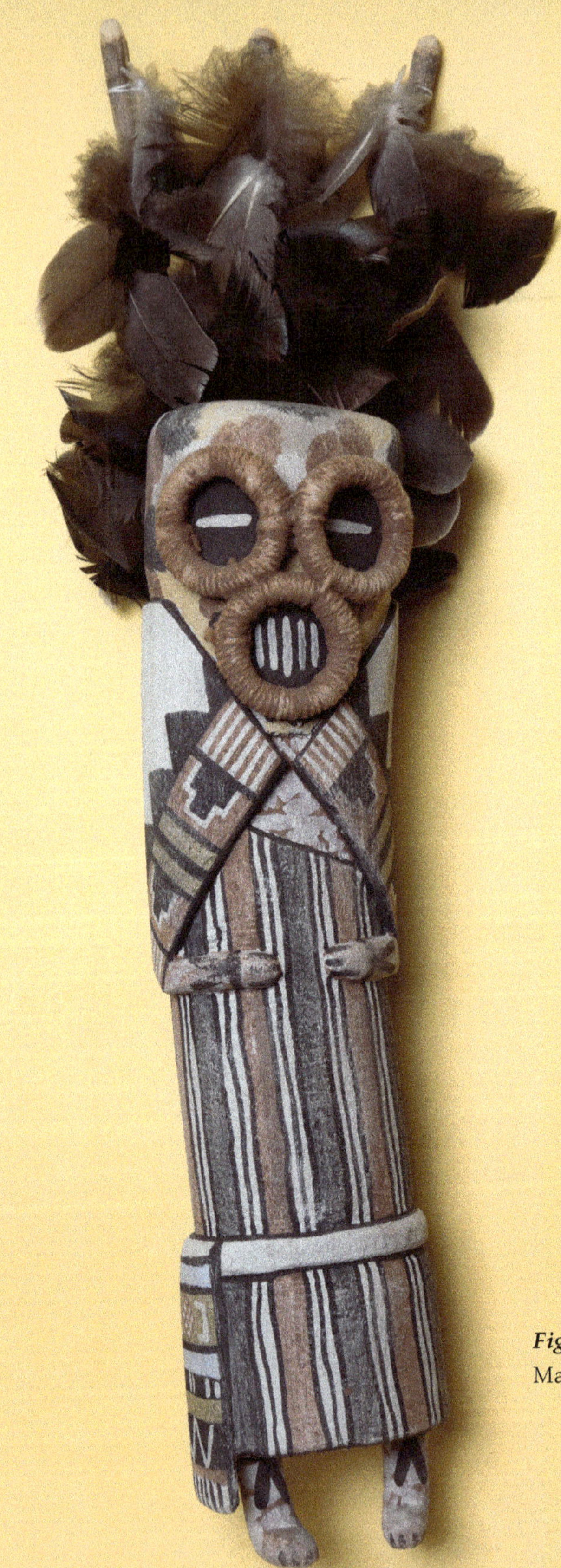

Figure 2.
Masawkatsina.

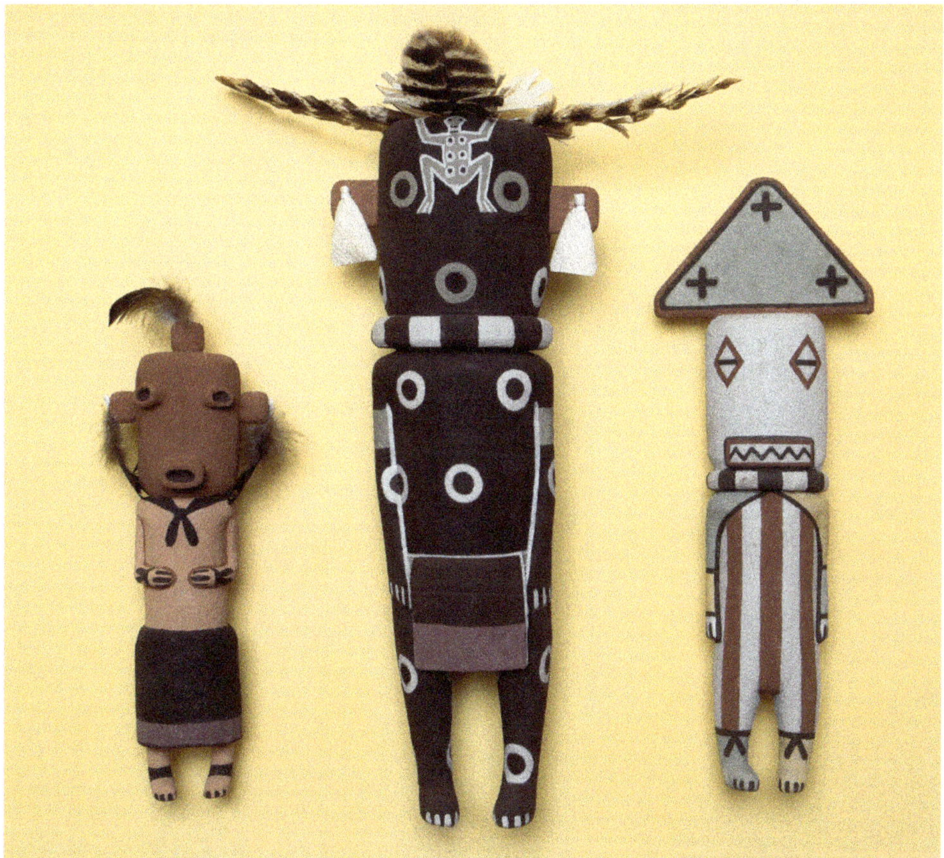

Figure 3. Kooyemsi, Poos'humkatsina (Corn Seed), and Owangaroro (Stone Eater).

Manfred added, "From these experiences I learned the truth and this is how I became what I am today."

This conversation led to a discussion of what has influenced his art. Despite his exposure to prominent artists such as Charles Loloma or Lloyd Kiva New in his formative years, Manfred is adamant that in creating katsinam, his artistic talent and innovation came solely from within. He said that his "artistic influences" were those childhood experiences of awe and fear, his grandfather's stories of prophecy, and the Katsina spirits themselves.

Not surprisingly, in turning to the katsina carvings, they all have a sense of eerie power and spirituality. Let's start with a heavy hitter: a large Masawkatsina I acquired from Manfred in the early 1990s (Figure 2). This is the katsina version of the Maasaw deity. This carving is 21 inches tall. There is nothing "cute" or "pretty" about it. Rather, it is a frightening depiction of the katsina version of the

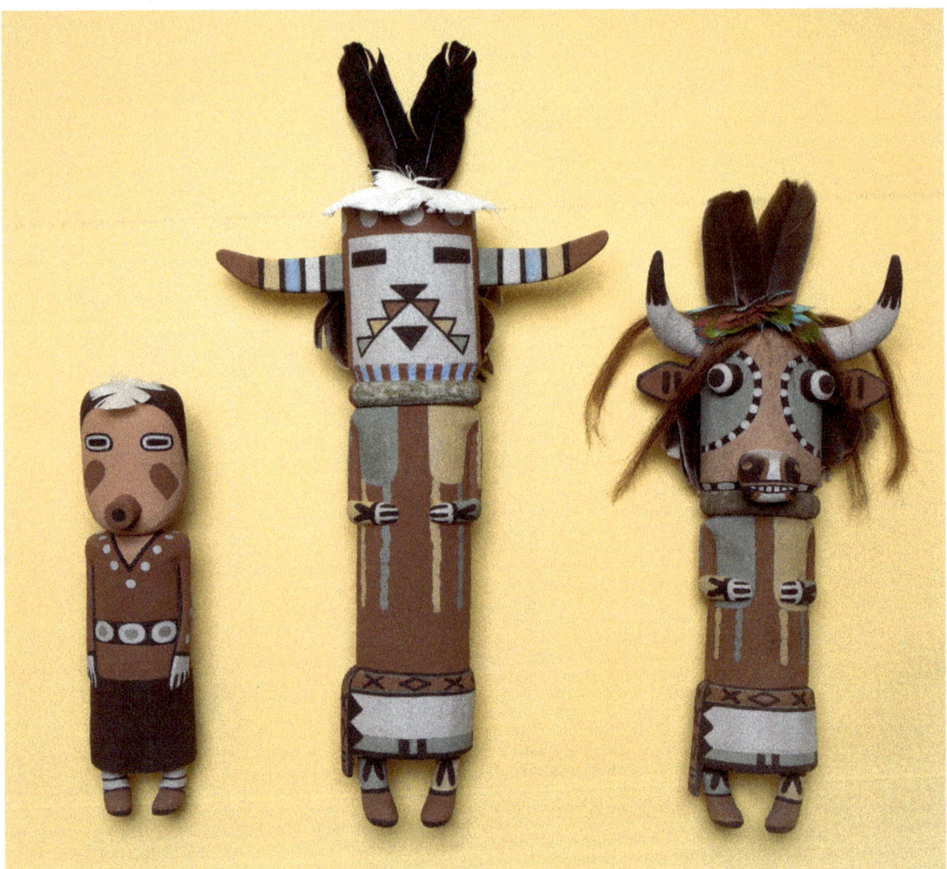

Figure 4. Tasapmana (Navajo Maiden), Kooninkatsina (Male Havasupai), and Wakaskatsina (Cow).

Death Spirit or God of the Underworld and looks appropriately skeletal. Clearly, this carving has recaptured the awe and fear that the young Manfred never forgot. Similarly impactful are the katsinam in Figure 3. These are left to right: a Kooyemsi (frequently referred to as a Mudhead), Poos'humkatsina (Corn Seed; corn is the foundation of life for the Hopi), and Owangaroro (Stone Eater) katsina (a figure so fierce he grinds up stones and rocks with his teeth). All three have a serious, ominous presence.

This is not to say that Manfred does not make beautiful katsinam. Consider the large and stately Hemiskatsina and Siohemiskatsina in Figure 5. They are 20 inches and 17 inches tall respectively. Each is a handsome rendition of a beloved Niman or Home Dance Katsina. Another beautiful figure is a Kooninkatsintaqa (male Havasupai katsina) in the center of Figure 4. Manfred's work can also

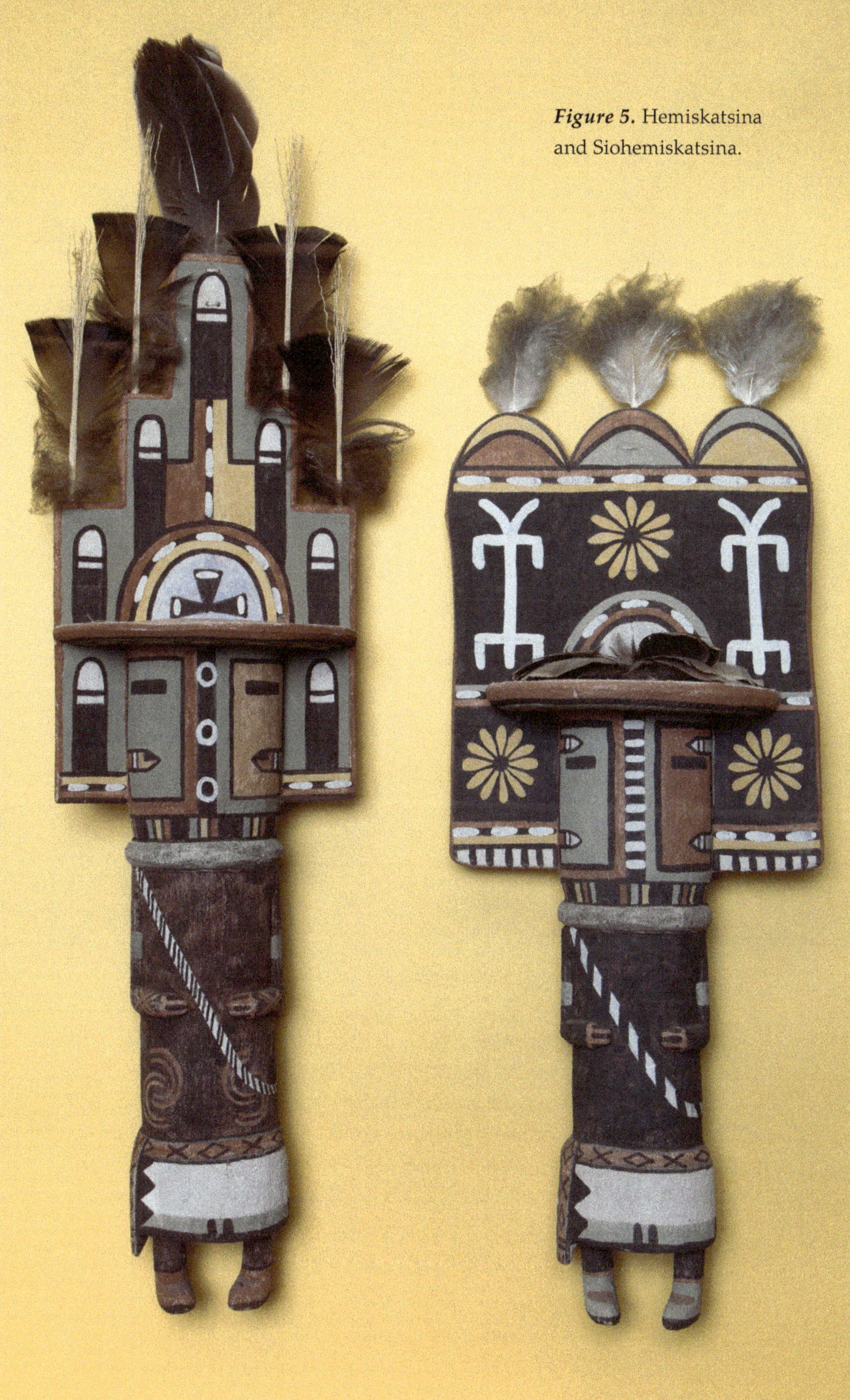

Figure 5. Hemiskatsina and Siohemiskatsina.

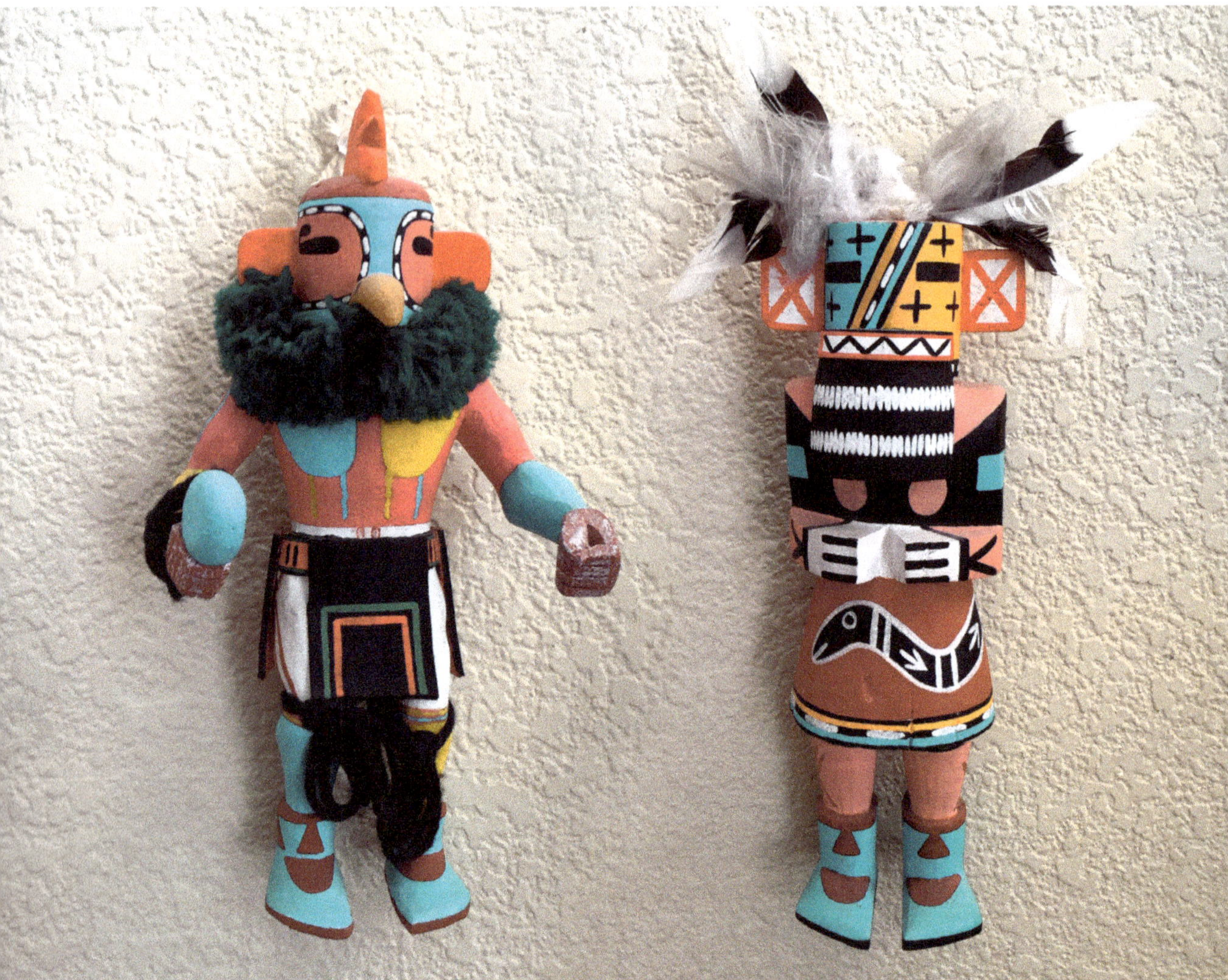

Figure 6. Kowaakokatsina (Chicken) and Hiilili.

have a comic element, as shown on the left and right in Figure 4, where we see a Tasapmana (Navajo Maiden) and a Wakaskatsina (Cow).

Lest you think this style of carving came from nowhere, please review Figure 6. These are early carvings by Manfred from the 1960s; they pre-date his "revision," and certainly show how radical his reworking of katsinam has been. The Kowaakokatsina (Chicken) on the left is done in an Early Action Style and painted with commercial acrylics. The Hiilili (Guard) on the right is done in a very basic Route 66, trading post style and also painted with acrylics. There is nothing unusual or innovative about these early carvings. Manfred was to move far beyond these early efforts.

It is important to describe the specifics of Manfred's revisionist artistic approach. First of all, Manfred uses the simplest of tools in making his dolls. No power devices are employed. He also uses mineral and vegetal paints exclusively. Notice the beautiful hues on his carvings. These colors are full and rich because they all come from the earth. He collects these minerals and plants on Hopiland and elsewhere.

The body postures of his katsinam are reminiscent of the carvings from 1880–1920. Note the simple linear shapes that emphasize the head. The bas-relief arms and hands are almost always in the "stomachache position" found on early dolls. The ding-toed feet do not permit the carvings to stand. They are meant to hang on the rafters, just like in the old days. All the simple, basic components of his carvings are consistent with his return to the "old ways."

Manfred's artistic and spiritual decision to carve in the old style has made him successful in the art world. Over the past forty years, he has received much recognition for his work, and his katsina carvings have become highly collectible art objects. His work is in the permanent collection of the Heard Museum, Museum of Northern Arizona (MNA), Haffenreffer Museum, Arizona State Museum, Denver Art Museum, and others. He has won many prizes at diverse Indian markets, especially in Santa Fe. Perhaps his greatest honor is that he was designated an "Arizona Indian Living Treasure" in 2002. Only three or four artists are given this honor each year.

Manfred also shared that he crossed paths over the years with numerous famous carvers who are no longer with us. He recalled being at a dance in Orayvi in the 1950s and seeing Tawaquaptewa outside his home selling his dolls to tourists. Manfred said he also knew Otto Pentewa. And he noted that Jimmie Kewanwytewa was married to his aunt, Agnes. He said he used to see Jimmie on school field trips to the MNA, where Jimmie worked as custodian, guide, and lecturer. All three of these carvers are featured in this book.

All of Manfred's success has involved family support. He has been married to his wife, Norma, since 1965. She is a skilled maker of *poota*, or coiled basketry. They have three children named Sheryl, Vesta, and Elberta, as well as two grandchildren. Sheryl is an artist in her own right, being an accomplished and award-winning painter.

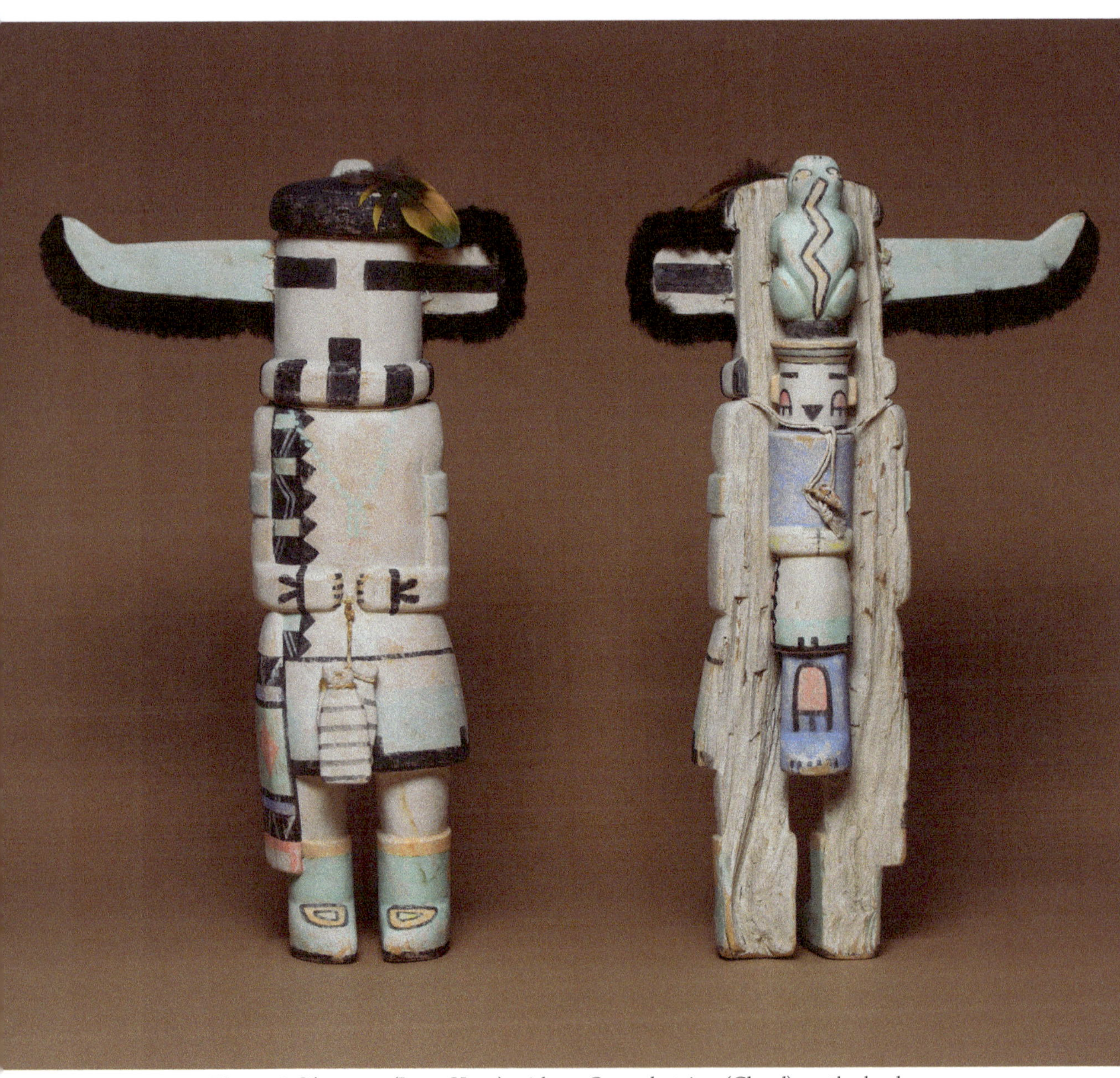

Figure 1. Sáyartasa (Long Horn) with an Omawkatsina (Cloud) on the back.

WALTER HOWATO

Wild Creativity

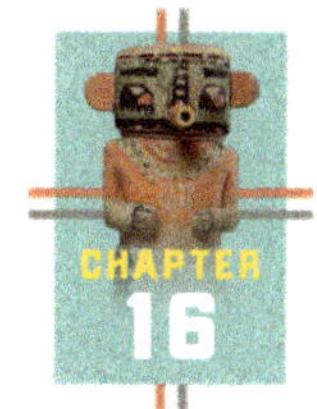

WALTER HOWATO WAS BORN IN 1921 and passed in 2003. As a primary source for this chapter, my old friend, Jonathan Day, author of *Traditional Hopi Kachinas,* was kind enough to share his recorded interview with Walter. This interview dates to about 1999. The recording is a long, rambling, hilarious reminiscence by Walter, including his biography, travels, jobs, and jokes about village occurrences or playful tricks played on *Pahaanas* (white people). From this source and two of his old friends, Janice and Joseph Day, I have been able to prepare this chapter. The most important content is, of course, the examples of his exceptional work.

Walter's maternal clan was Reed. He grew up in Sitsomovi (Sichomovi) or Middle Village on First Mesa. During the Great Depression, Walter attended the Santa Fe Indian School. Upon graduating, he was hired by Walt Disney Studios in California to work as a painter. Disney apparently had an ongoing relationship with the school, which led to Walter's job offer. At Disney Studios, Walter said, "We did a lot of things. Sometimes I played an Indian at Disneyland, and sometimes I painted and did some interior decorating with my friend, R. C. Gorman. R. C. and I painted everything up there." (Day 2000, 42). Gorman, of course, became a very famous painter and a fixture in the Santa Fe art scene.

After his experience in California, Walter returned to Hopiland. However, he found it hard to make a living on the reservation so he left to become a heavy equipment operator. He worked at this job all over the Southwest, including Denver and extensively on the Glen Canyon Dam (Arizona) project. He told Jonathan Day that the dam involved very dangerous work. He was on the dynamite crew, which involved detonating, and then moving rocks after the explosions. He said the turnover in this job was tremendous, yet he remained working there for an extended period of time. He also lived in Florida for a while where he worked for the Osprey Amusement Park and for Ringling Brothers.

In the 1960s while living in the Phoenix area, Walter began spending more time carving katsinam. He developed a relationship with the Heard Museum gift shop, which became his most consistent outlet for decades.

Walter's carvings are utterly distinctive. As shown in the photos in this chapter, their most salient characteristic is that they look to be ancient, at least 100 years old! Walter shared with Jonathan Day in detail how he arrived at his distressed look (although like any accomplished artist or chef, I suspect he left a few steps out). The process is not what one would expect: it did not involve extensive sandpapering. Rather, his first step was to create his own paints by mixing *tuuma* (Hopi clay undercoat) with poster paints. Then, he would apply the first coat to the cottonwood root. Once the paint dried, he would take a "clean, wet brush to remove a bit [of paint] here and there." (Day 2000, 41). He would repeat this process three or four times to produce the worn, antique look. As far as I know, no one else had used this method to create a patina on katsina carvings; it was his innovation. Another feature of his work is that he often used "junk wood . . . cracked and old." The huge cracks in some of his carvings reinforce their look of antiquity. Some appear to have emerged from a long-abandoned cave.

Walter indicated that his preference for this "old style" was not just some artistic affectation. Rather, as he was creating his katsinam, he would close his eyes and remember how they used to look back in his mother's home in Sitsomovi. In a sense, Walter described an artistic "retrieval" like what Manfred Susunkewa expressed in Chapter 15.

In turning to the katsinam themselves, let's start with Figure 1, a complex figure indeed. This is an exceptional example that points to the uniqueness of Walter's work. The photo shows the carving both front and back. The piece is very large at 12 inches wide by 21½ inches tall. (Oversized katsinam were rather common for Walter.) The front is a Sáyartasa (Long Horn) katsina, a Zuni-derived figure. The back is vintage Walter, a creation no one else would have envisioned. The central figure is an Omawkatsina (Cloud) katsina. However, the carving is very unusual in that it has a single unsplit foot. Where else do you see that? And in place of the usual cloud motif on the top of the Omaw's head is a life-sized frog or Paakwa! Note also that the back of the Long Horn to which the Omaw and Paakwa are attached is raw driftwood. Walter made no attempt to sand or paint the back. It was left elemental and basic which increases the effectiveness of the whole composition as to its ancient appearance.

Walter often produced eerie looking figures, as shown in Figure 2. On the right is a strange black-faced figure with horsehair tufts coming out of his head. This appears to be the seldom-seen Kawiikoli, as found on page 132 in Fewkes's book, *Hopi Katcinas Drawn by Native Artists* (1903/1982). He is said to be a "fire carrier," which is why he is carrying torches. A similar surprise is the carving with a blue cone-like head in the middle of Figure 2. This is probably

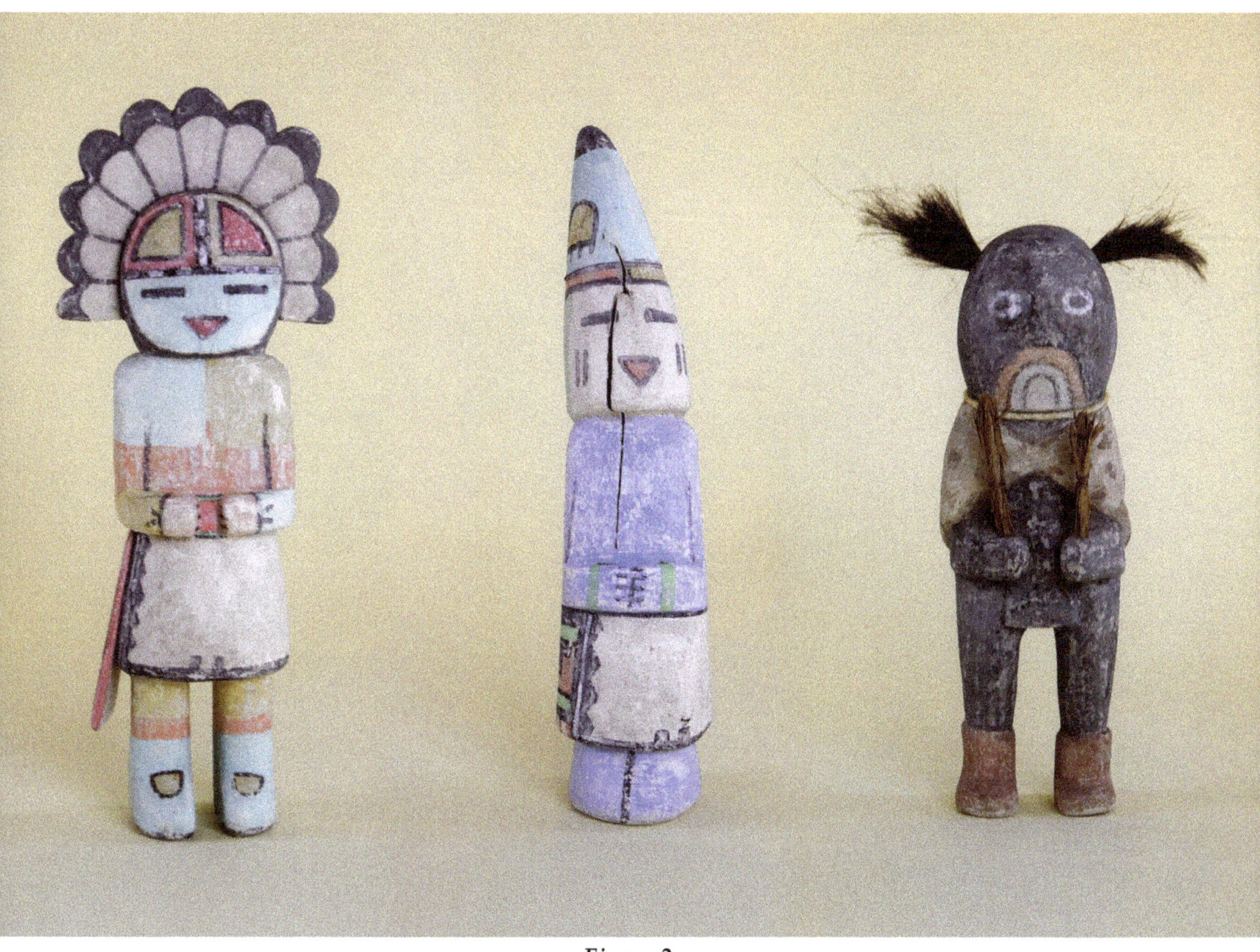

Figure 2.
Tawakatsina (Sun) and possibly a Sootukwnangw (Heart of the Cosmos) and Kawiikoli.

Sootukwnangw (Heart of the Cosmos), but it is so minimalist that identification is speculative. Note that it too has a single foot or base, and only Walter would place a large crack so prominently in the face and body of a katsina. On the left of Figure 2 is a more mainstream rendition. This is Tawakatsina (the Sun) katsina. It is a very direct, beautiful version of the beloved Sun figure.

Another innovative carving is shown in Figure 3. It is a Sa'lakwmana (Sa'lako Maiden) that Walter deliberately left unfinished. No one used cracked, worn, undecorated wood before Walter chose that artistic direction. It was as if the katsinam were only half-emerged from the cottonwood root.

Walter was known, and sometimes criticized, for making figures some Hopi

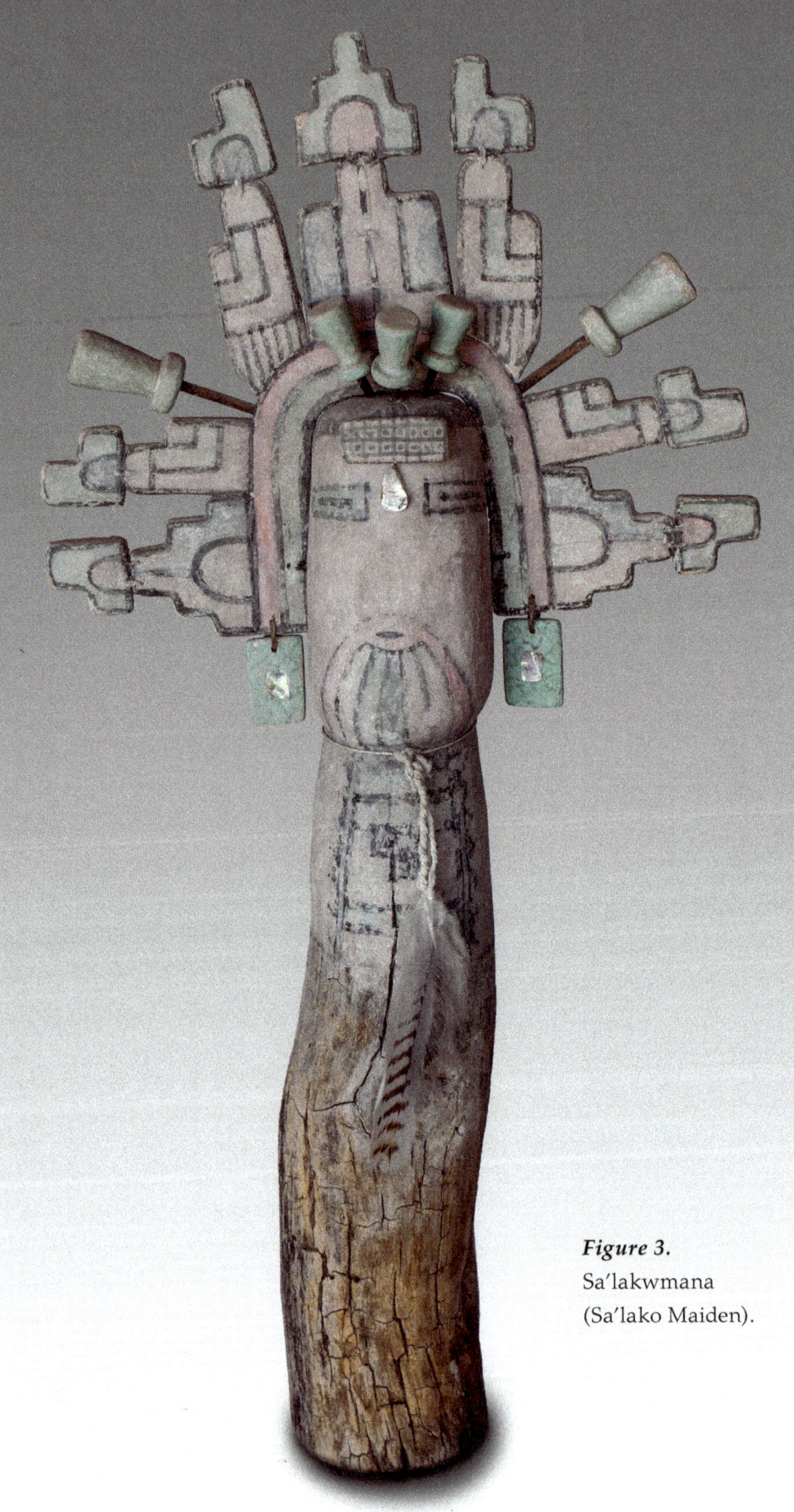

Figure 3.
Sa'lakwmana
(Sa'lako Maiden).

considered to be "sensitive." For example, he occasionally made multi-item sets he called "altar figures," which were controversial. Walter explained that such figures came from his imagination; they did not depict anything secret, sacred, or inappropriate. I believe that Walter may have been a bit less attentive to certain tribal prohibitions because he lived off-reservation for so long. Clearly, he intended no harm.

Of course, Walter often made more conventional carvings, and they can be very beautiful. In Figure 4 there is a simple yet elegant Katsinmana katsina bearing a quail feather "beard." Figure 5 presents another example of Walter's unusual creativity. This Poliimana (Butterfly Maiden) is quite large at 15 inches wide by 21½ inches tall. Look carefully and note the frogs leaping off her tablita. It's as if Walter snuck the frogs in there; they're not that obvious. Creativity just leaped from his work.

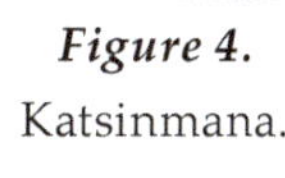

Figure 4. Katsinmana.

Figure 6 depicts three more excellent carvings by Walter, each quite distinctive and unusual. They are left to right: the seldom seen Saaviki (Snake Clan Wuya or Ancestor) with a snake in his mouth and lizard on his forehead, a small Sootukwnangw (Heart of the Cosmos) holding a lightning stick, and a large and imposing Hakto, which means "carrying wood on his head." The Hakto has many accoutrements, including antler dance wands, a jacla necklace, a bowguard with turquoise, and a huge feather pendant. Note that Saaviki is called Tsaana'yo at First Mesa.

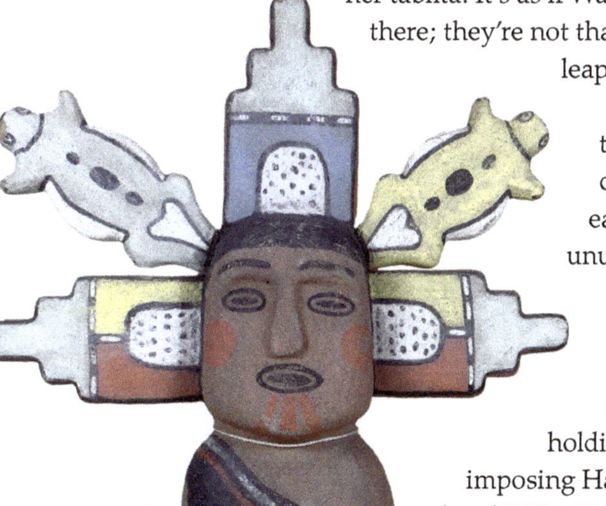

Figure 5. Poliimana (Butterfly Maiden).

In closing, it is fitting to include a motif or scene by Walter. Figure 7 depicts a Tsu'sona (Snake Dancer) and his accompanying handler. This is an eerie carving affixed to a base with cloud and other symbols. It is an example of his most powerful work. The power is derived from the subject matter—the imposing Snake dance with the rattler in the Tsu'sona's mouth—and

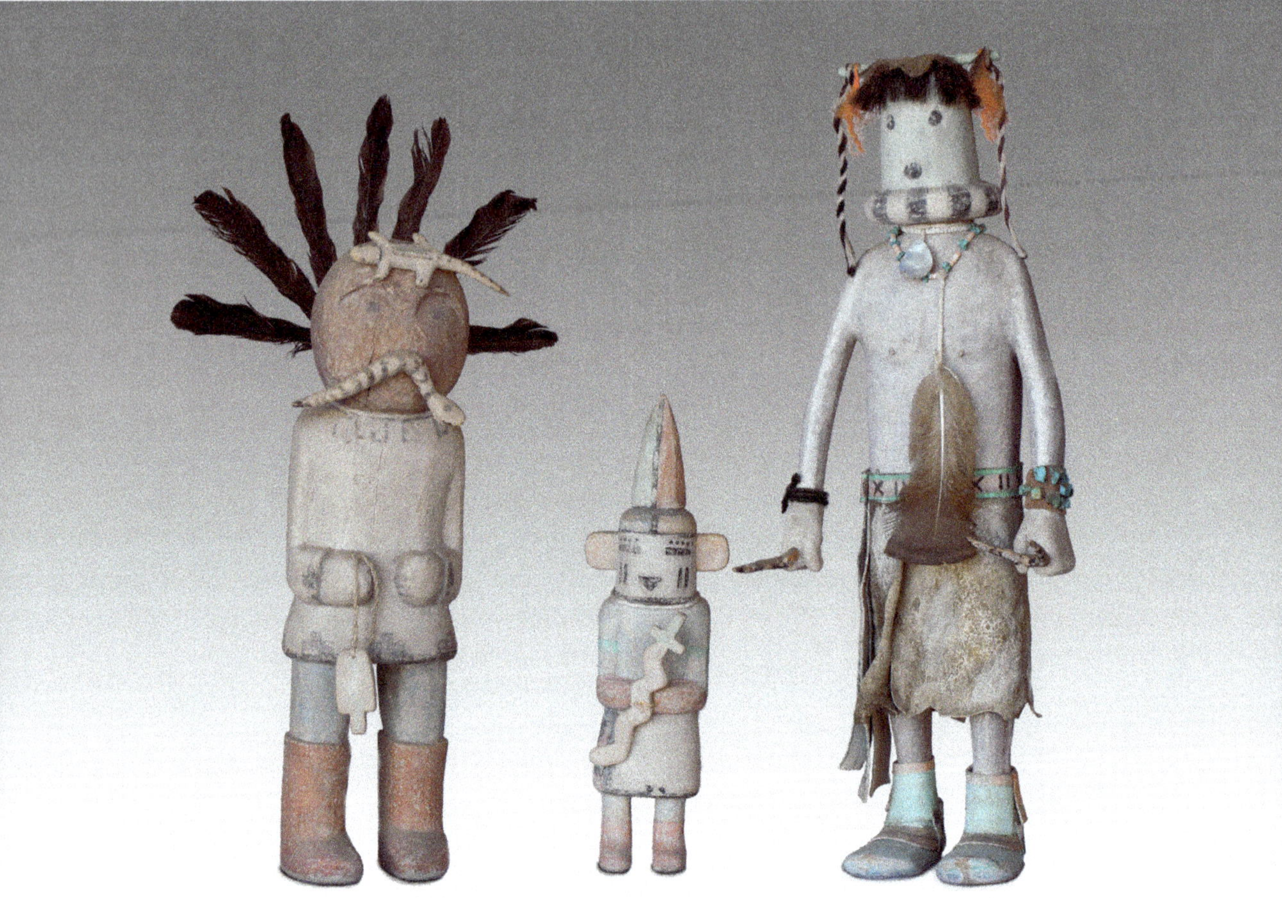

Figure 6. Saaviki (Snake Clan Wuya or Ancestor), Sootukwnangw (Heart of the Cosmos), and Hakto.

also from his antiquing of the paint, which gives the figures an ancient feel.

Walter is generally credited to be the co-creator of the Traditional Style katsina movement, along with Manfred Susunkewa. Walter's work certainly brought back the eeriness and spiritual dimension to the carvings that he made. He was truly one of the special artists in the history of Hopi katsina carving.

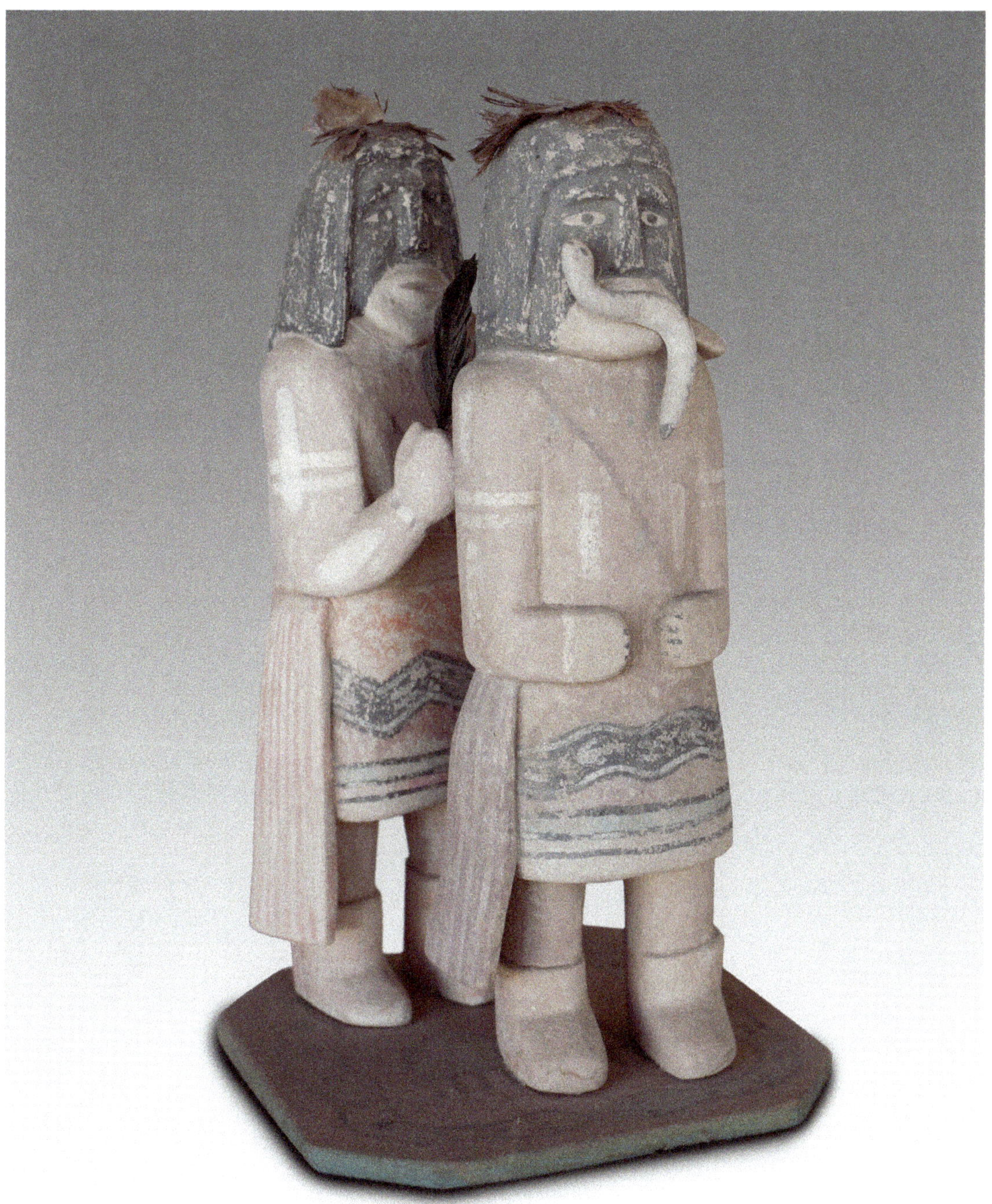

Figure 7. Tsu'sona (Snake Dancers).

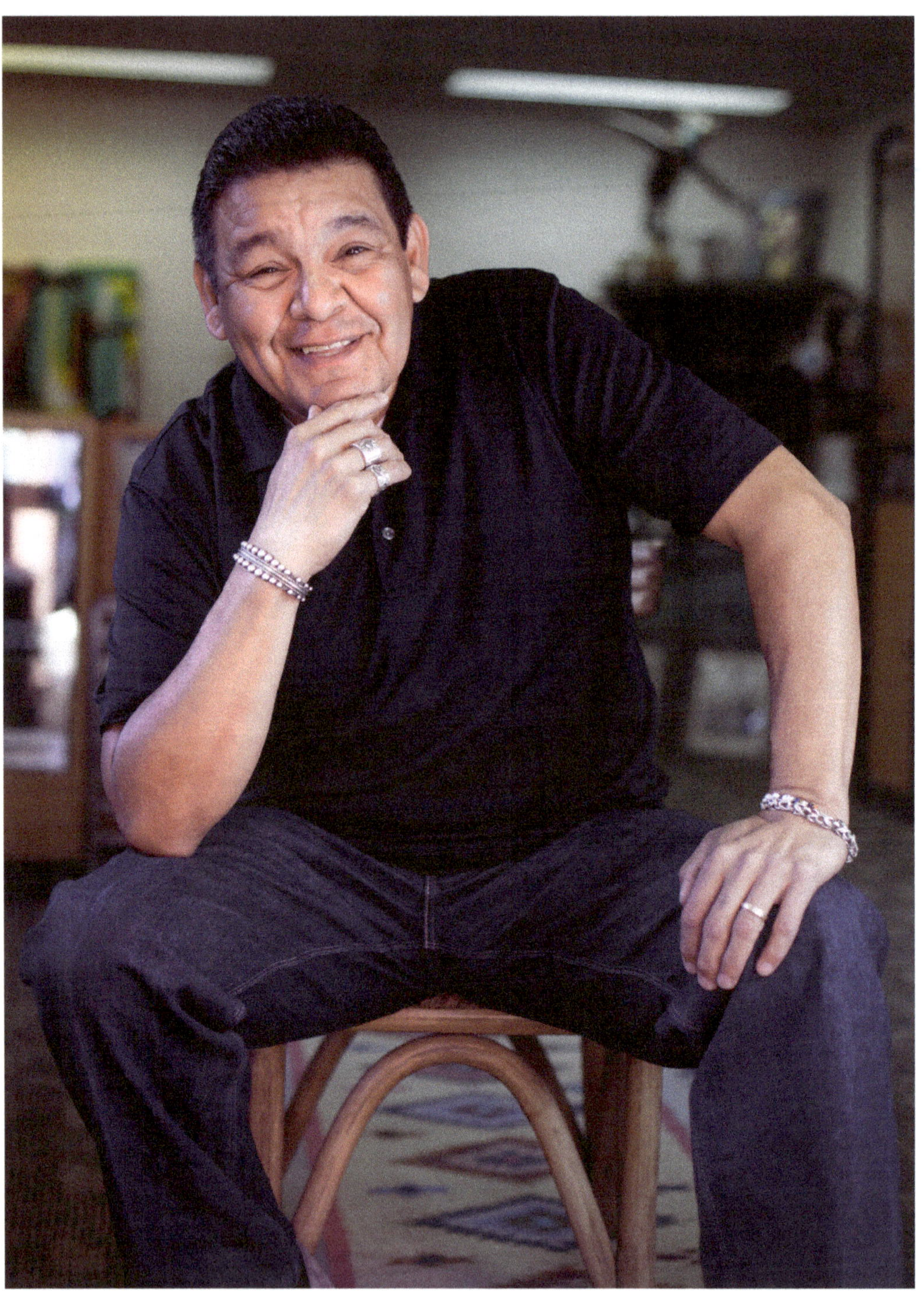

Figure 1. Manuel Denet Chavarria.

MANUEL DENET CHAVARRIA

Diverse Transformations

MANUEL DENET CHAVARRIA IS A HOPI MAN who was born in 1964 (Figure 1). He lives east of Polacca near First Mesa, Arizona. His maternal clan is Butterfly and he often signs his work with a butterfly symbol. Manuel has been making katsinam since he was eleven years old. What is especially remarkable about his work is that his style has evolved dramatically over the years. Some trends have been radical departures from the previous. And as he told me recently, his artistic style continues to be a work in progress. But let's start at the beginning . . .

Manuel attributes artistic influence to many people whom he speaks of with great respect. He shared that his earliest katsina influences were his grandfather, Fred Denet, and his grandmother, Otille Jackson. He noted that Otille was one of the first women to make katsinam, and he emphasized that she taught him something especially important: the business side of the art world. She cautioned him, "never leave home without your tools, because one can make art and generate income no matter where you are." Manuel says he's never forgotten this advice, so his carving tools and paints are his constant companions.

He added that another grandmother, Susan Denet, was also an influence. She was a renowned potter who inspired him to strive to be an artist. And he points to Walter Howato, the legendary master katsina carver as another key influence. He recalled going to the Heard Museum in the 1980s and trying to sell his early work with little success. He would walk around the Heard gift shop and see Walter's work and be in awe. At the time, he was attempting to carve in the Realistic Style that was popular in the 1970s.

That all changed in the late 1980s with some encouragement from trader Joseph (Joe) Day who had recently opened Tsakurshovi on Second Mesa with his Hopi wife, Janice. (Manuel notes that this was so early in the existence of Tsakurshovi that their signature "Don't Worry, Be Hopi" t-shirt only came in red!). At the time, Joe had a few dolls by Manfred Susunkewa for sale. Pointing to them, Joe urged Manuel "to try something different" and make something in the "Traditional Style." As Joe likes to emphasize, the early and Late Traditional

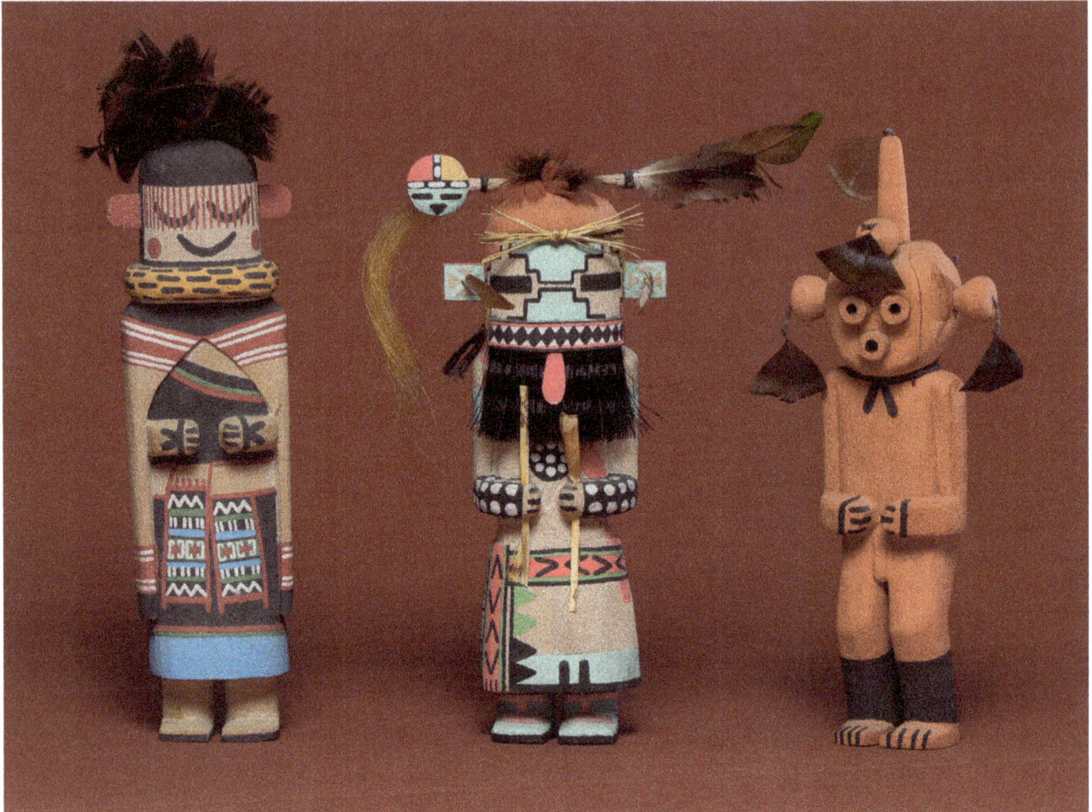

Figure 2. Hahay'iwuuti, Hiilili, and a Kooyemsi.

Style katsinam never died out on the reservation. They still were given as gifts at *Powamuya* and *Niman* ceremonies, but were largely ignored and forgotten in the art world.

So, with Joe's encouragement, one day Manuel "stayed up all night and made a Koyaala" (or Koshare). Joe bought it immediately and the rest is history. Manuel has been carving in some version of the Traditional Style ever since.

Please note examples of early carvings by Manuel from the early 1990s in Figure 2. These are, left to right, Hahay'iwuuti, Hiilili, and a Kooyemsi. Work from this era had bright colors. The execution was notably fresh, clean, and crisp, without being fussy. The body types were linear and simple and resembled the Early Traditional katsinam from 1890–1920. Work from this era was well received. Manuel's carvings were included in *Arizona Highways*, and later in Jerry and Lois Jacka's book, *Art of the Hopi*. He also won prizes at shows at the Museum of Northern Arizona and the Heard Museum. Manuel was realizing his dream of being a full time, self-supporting artist.

During this period, Manuel received his first invitation to have a booth at Santa Fe's Indian Market—which he refers to as the "Super Bowl" for young artists. He recalls the first time he attended and watched Arizona Living Treasure, Manfred Susunkewa, from afar. Manuel said he was too intimidated to approach him but observed how Manfred arranged his booth, interacted with customers, and discussed his katsina carvings. He watched Manfred all day, adding that "this is how we Hopi learn. We don't read texts or manuals. We observe." He added that as he became more confident, he eventually shared this story with Manfred and they had a good laugh.

While Manuel was having some success at this time, he was not healthy or well. As Manuel shared with me, he had developed a problem with alcohol. He dates this challenge to his time in the United States Army at Fort Knox from 1986–1989. He added that after discharge he brought his alcohol abuse back with him to the reservation. There were some positives to his return to Hopiland as he renewed his relationship with an old girlfriend, Marlinda Kooyaquaptewa. She eventually became his wife and mother of their three children. But Manuel notes that he struggled with alcoholism on and off for twenty years. By 2009 Manuel had been diagnosed with diabetes and weighed as much as 250 pounds, and was in an extremely unhealthy place. This is when one of his transformations occurred.

Manuel realized he was "becoming a diabetic who would waste away and die." With a great deal of family support, Manuel regained sobriety. When he reached his first year of sobriety, he began working for the Detox Stabilization Center in Holbrook, Arizona. Manuel became a peer-support worker helping others in their recovery. Early on he found this work meaningful and that it supported his own recovery as well. He noted that this was his "first real job." Even so, he said, "My identity as an artist was calling me back to my heart." Manuel also noted that working at home as a carver allowed him to be closer to family (which by now included thirteen grandchildren).

Manuel became heavily involved in cycling, a major contributor to improving his health. He rides three to five days per week and has competed in long-distance races. In recent years, Manuel has ridden twice in the Tour de Sih Hasin (Navajo for "hope"), a seven-day tour cycling three hundred miles in the summer. He has since joined the Board of Directors for this event. In addition, Manuel and others started a biking program for Hopi youth in four of the nine villages. Because of his emphasis on fitness, he lost forty pounds and does not require insulin.

Having returned to the life of a full-time artist, Manuel carves three to five days a week. Since resuming, his style of carving has undergone a profound change. Note the katsinam shown in Figure 3. These are a So'yokwuuti (Ogre

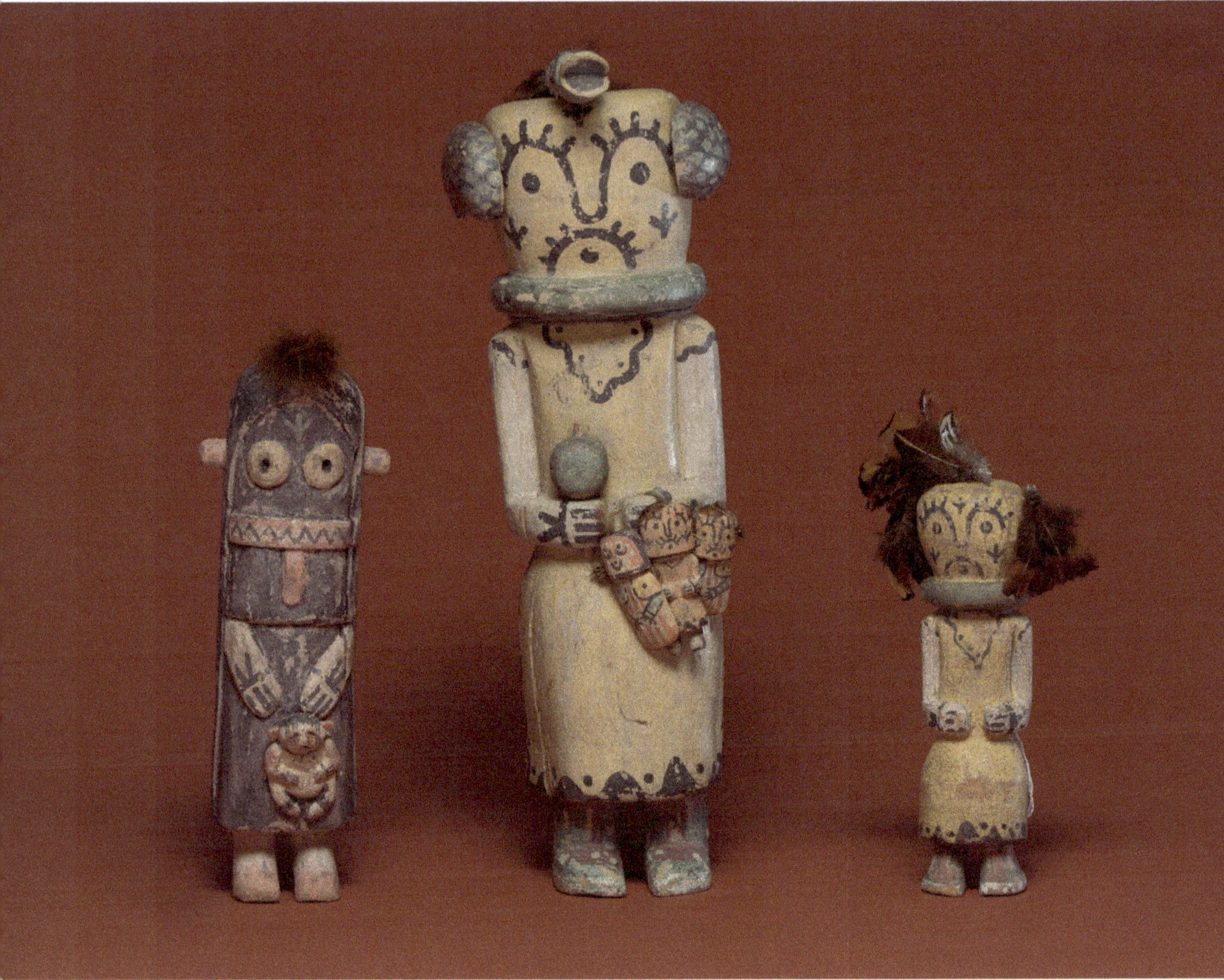

Figure 3. So'yokwuuti (Ogre Woman), large Qöqlö, and small Qöqlö.

Woman) on the left, followed by a very large Qöqlö, and a smaller Qöqlö. The style of these carvings is radically different from his work from the early 1990s (Figure 2). The paints are muted and subtle, and he now uses what he calls "a distressed style." Asked how he arrived at this style, Manuel said it came from visiting museums and seeing antique dolls. He said he loved how they look and decided to "replicate it." He also noted the influence of his old idol, Walter Howato, yet Manuel has made the style his own. Two other recent examples in this style are the Ogres shown in Figure 4. On the left is the rarely seen Atosle

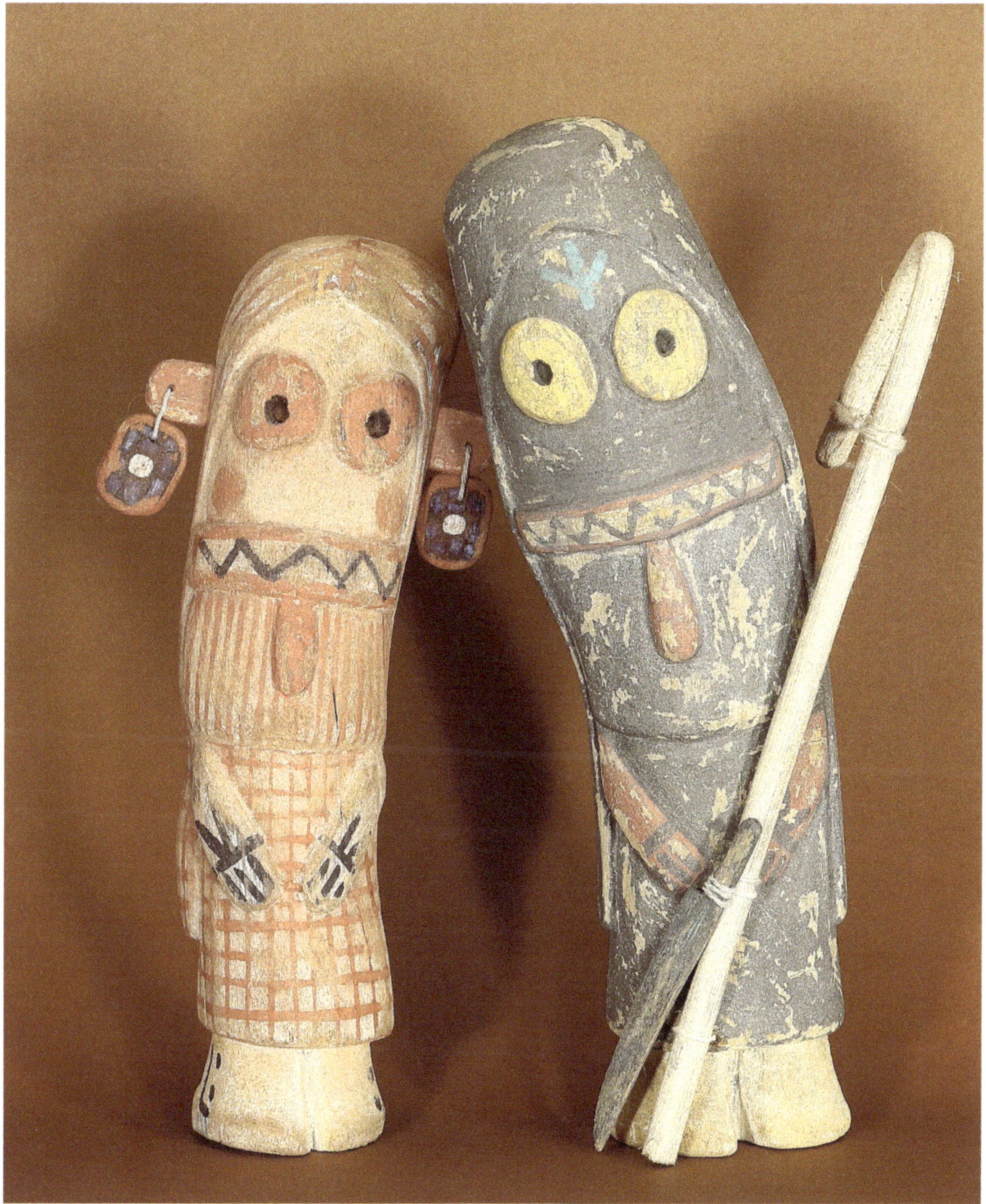

Figure 4. Atosle and So'yokwuuti (both Ogres).

(another form of Ogre Woman) and on the right, a So'yokwuuti.

One aspect that differentiates his work from Walter's is his tendency to add miniature dolls and other items to his carvings. For example, the So'yokwuuti in Figure 3 is holding a small Hehey'a, and the large Qöqlö is equipped with Hahay'iwuuti and Qöqlö cradle katsinam, and a full-figured mini Qöqlö.

Manuel's newer style of carving calls for very large pieces. A fine example is shown in Figure 5. This is a Yöngökatsina (Prickly Pear Cactus). It is a whopping 11 inches wide by 18 inches tall. The cacti on its head bear more than 500 inserted toothpick spikes! Another example in this oversized trend is shown in Figures 6a and 6b. This is another large Qöqlö—but a very different version—which is carrying a mini Qöqlö (shown in Figure 6a below), a Matyawkatsina, (One with Handprint on His Face), and a drum with pounder.

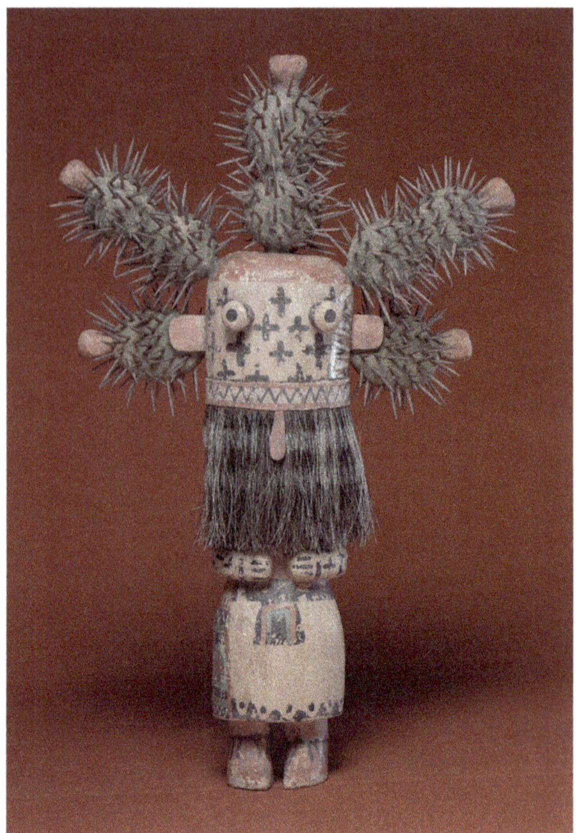

Figure 5. Yöngökatsina (Prickly Pear Cactus).

Even more dramatic is the Palhikwmana (Water Drinking Maiden) shown in Figure 7. This is an amazing example of Manuel's work. The Palhikwmana is more than 20 inches tall and nearly as wide. It is not able to stand on its own; it is a wall-hanger. The tablita is one of the most extensive I've seen and is assembled in the old, nineteenth-century method, hand-tied with cotton cord. Great time has been taken to add the hand-made *tu'oynàanaqa* earrings and necklace. Note that she has genitalia, a characteristic of nineteenth-century carvings.

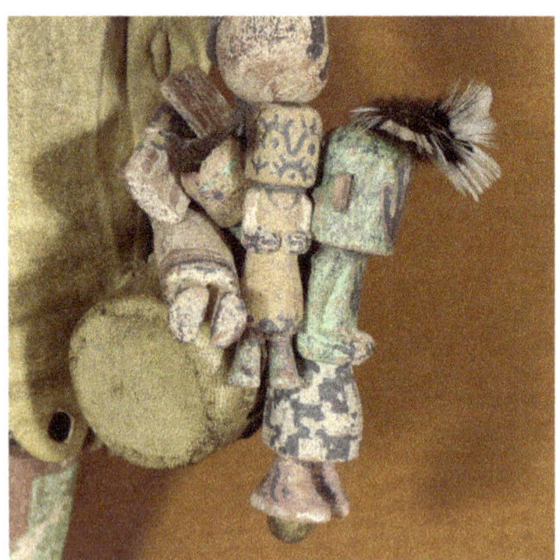

Figure 6a. *Detail of 6b on page 153.*

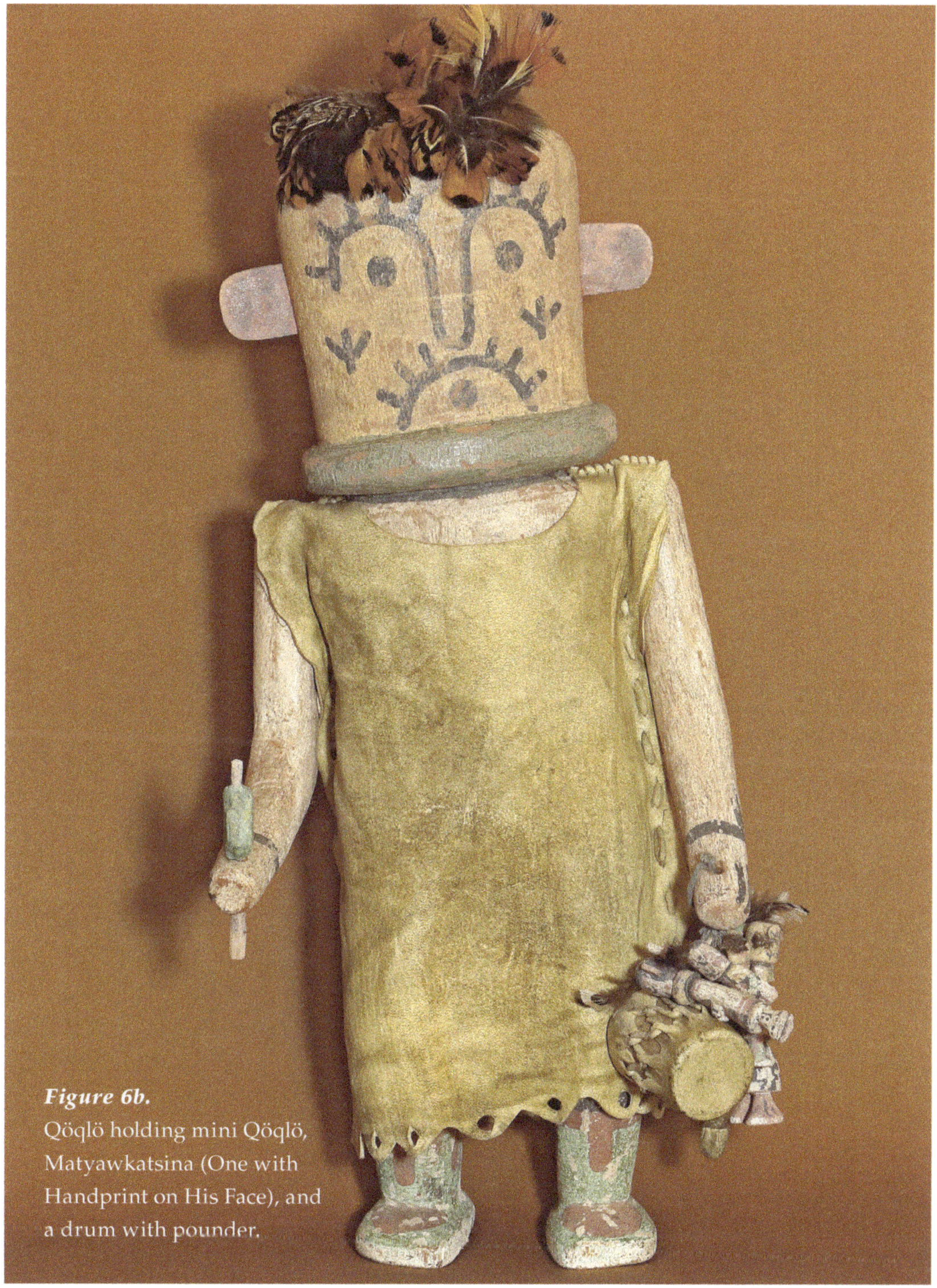

Figure 6b.
Qöqlö holding mini Qöqlö, Matyawkatsina (One with Handprint on His Face), and a drum with pounder.

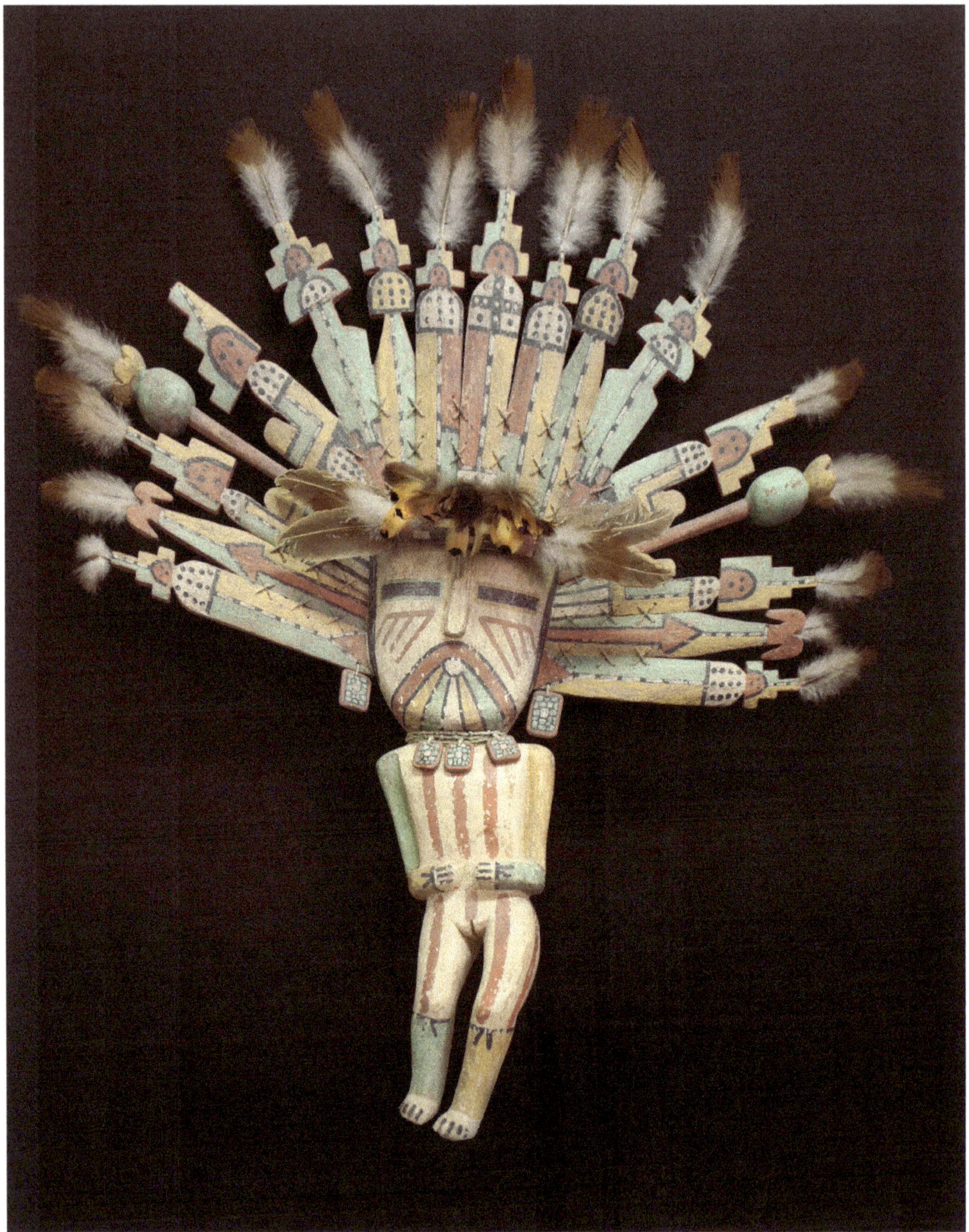

Figure 7. Palhikwmana (Water Drinking Maiden).

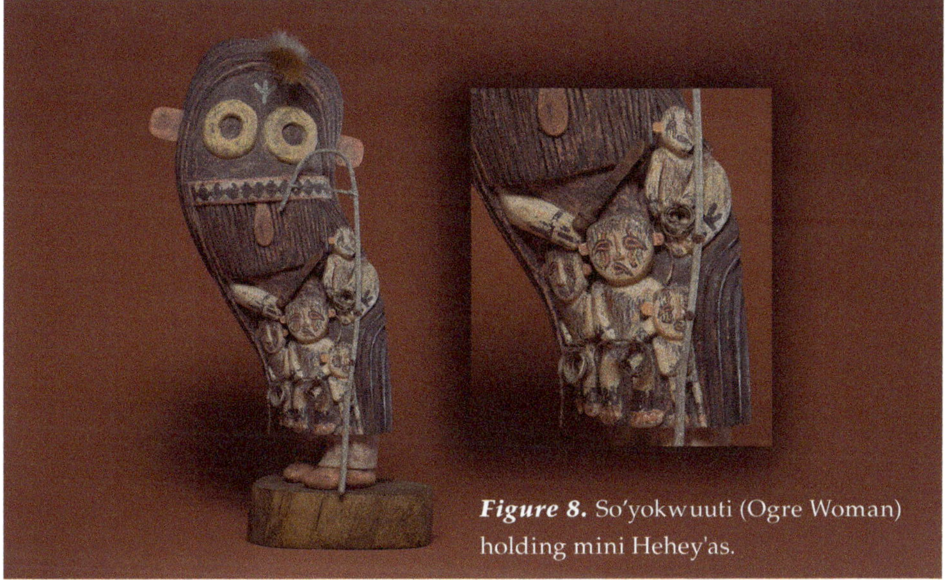

Figure 8. So'yokwuuti (Ogre Woman) holding mini Hehey'as.

While Manuel has worked in this distressed style for several years, he originally made two prototypes in this manner as early as 1990. And he said, "Even now I'm not set in one place; I'm still evolving."

A case in point is the recent carving shown in Figure 8. He described this remarkable piece as a "mixture of the contemporary and old style." Note the exceptional detail on this work of art. The So'yokwuuti (Ogre Woman) is holding a crook to capture naughty children and a knife with a copper blade with which to chop off their heads. Hopi mythology as to the role of Ogres is not for the faint of heart. Carved in bas-relief on her torso are her assistants, four mini Hehey'a katsinam, with three of these holding twine lassos. The movement of this large figure is undulating and the shaping of the hair and garment are synchronous. This sculpture is 7 inches wide by 18 inches tall and secured to a base, unlike almost all his other work. Clearly, Manuel's artistic development is ongoing.

Manuel notes he has learned to work in a healthier manner. He used to carve in a frenzy to get ready for shows or competitions; he wouldn't take breaks to rest and would eat candy bars, chips, and soda to keep going. He said, "I was like a car running too hot." One night several years ago while working in this manner, he said he "almost flipped out." "I went to a dark, scary place and when I came back, I decided to change things." So now Manuel paces himself, takes a break, eats healthily, rides his bike, reads a book, and spends time with the grandkids. These are all part of the transformations of Manuel Denet Chavarria. We can all look forward to his next artistic directions.

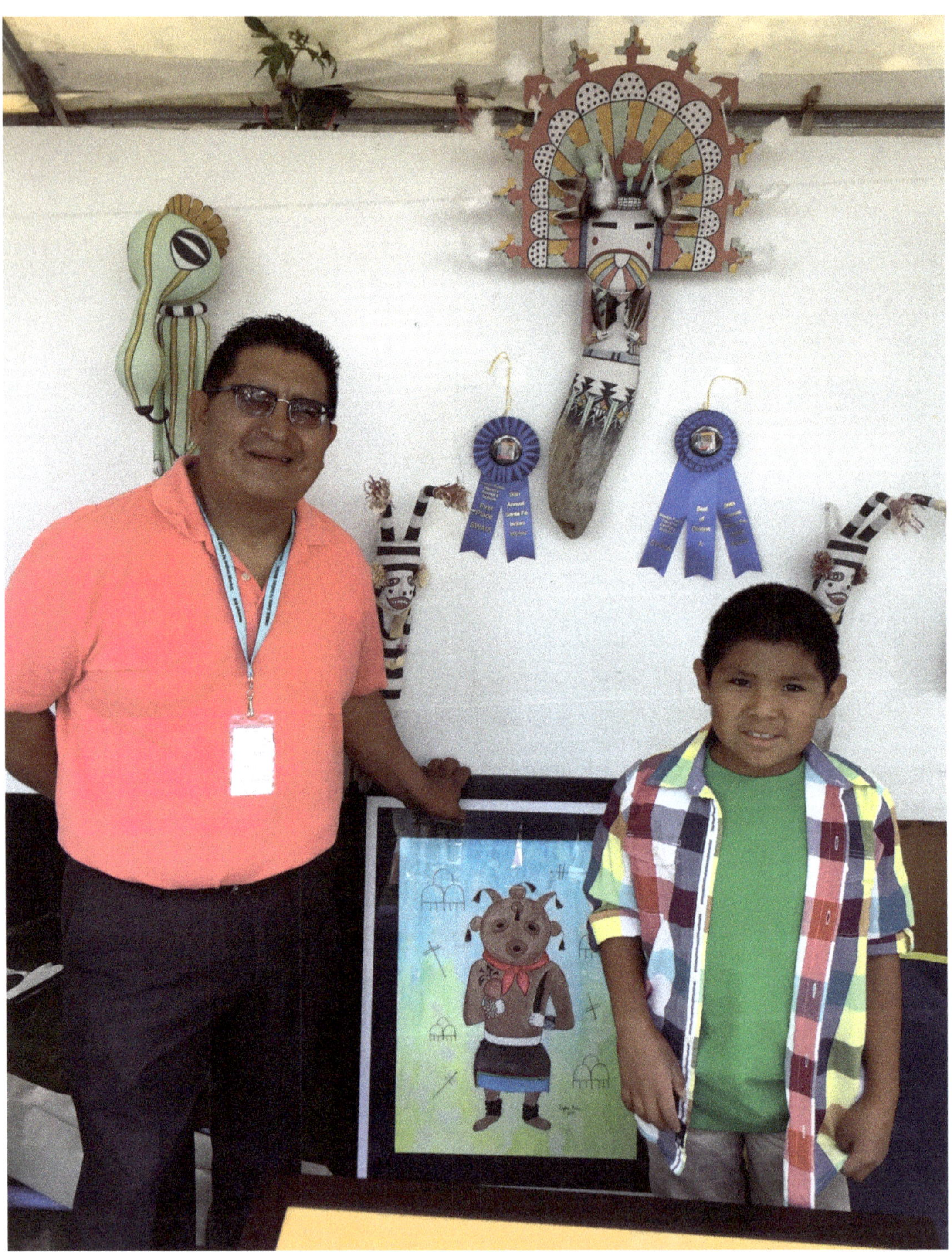

Figure 1. Clark Tenakhongva and his grandson, Suyma Malo.

CLARK TENAKHONGVA

So Many Chapters

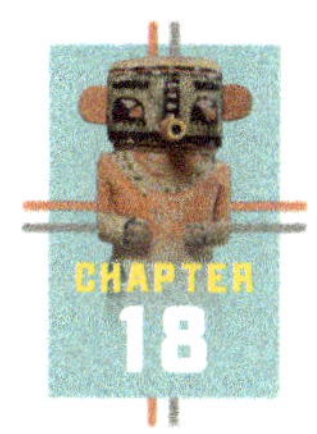

CLARK TENAKHONGVA (shown in Figure 1 with his grandson, Suyma Malo) has had a complex, colorful life. He was born in 1957, and grew up in Hotvela (Hotevilla). His mother Louise's clan is Rabbit/Tobacco. Early on, he attended Hotvela Day School, followed by the day school in Kiqotsmovi (Kykotsmovi). Later he graduated from Winslow High School where he ran cross-country. This talent resulted in an athletic scholarship to Central Arizona College. Clark said he only lasted one year at the college because he "got into the wrong side of life, heavy drinking." However, he said he must have had "some sense of maturity" because after doing this for a few months, he decided to "start over." He recalls being with a group of friends one day and they were challenging each other to enlist in the armed services. One offered Clark $500 if he would do it. So, Clark followed through with the dare and enlisted. He mourns to this day, "I'm still waiting for that $500."

Impulsive or not, this decision led to a major chapter in Clark's life, a ten-year stint in the United States Army. He served in Missouri, California, Germany, Panama, Alaska, and Oklahoma—talk about climate variation.

While in the Army he received intensive training for two occupations. He was a heavy-equipment operator and also worked in "combat arms" with an expertise in explosives and demolition. His highest rank was Sergeant First Class. Clark served in a combat operation when he was deployed to the island of Grenada during the brief U.S. invasion in 1983.

After his years in the service, Clark decided to "opt out" in 1984. While he was tempted to continue toward the goal of twenty years, he decided he "didn't want to raise our family in a military environment." Back in 1979, Clark had married his wife, Ann, and by the time of the opt-out, they already had two boys. So, they decided to return to Hopiland after a very long absence.

Clark noted that "reintegration was tough." To assist, he went through a traditional Hopi reintegration ceremony. He also recalled a large family picnic in his father's cornfield that welcomed him, Ann, and the children back to the reservation. He said this event was "one of the highlights of my life," and during

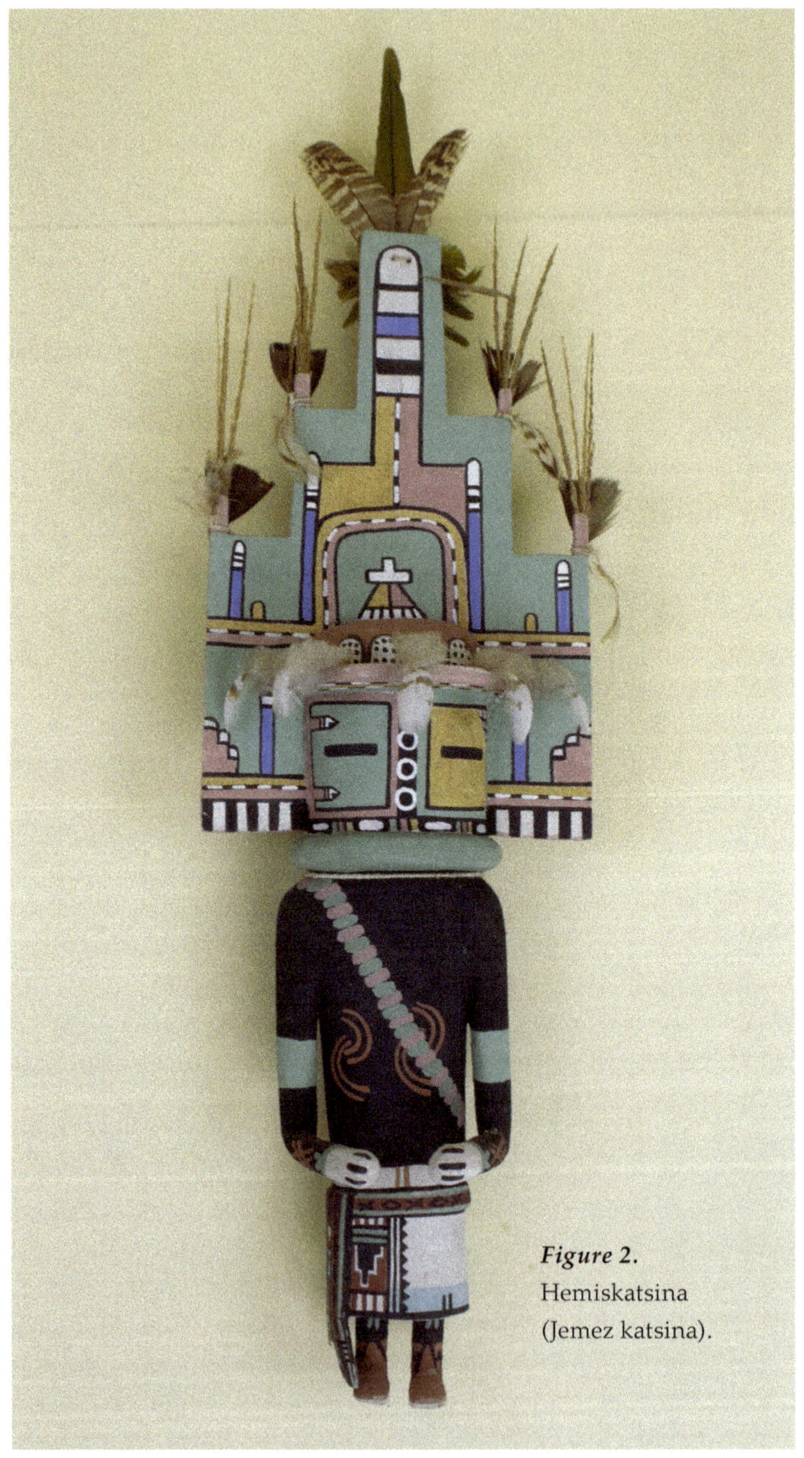

Figure 2. Hemiskatsina (Jemez katsina).

this reunion he realized how glad he was to be back. Clark added, "My father was a great dry farmer. And I realized I was born into corn, our lifeline is like corn, and we die like corn." He said, "we are here to provide nourishment to family and society, just like corn." Clark and his family have resided on Hopiland ever since. Asked if he had doubts about returning to the reservation and making a go of it, Clark replied, "I knew I could make it. Hopi people are survivalistic."

In turning to the topic of carving, Clark said he began making katsinam about 1985. He had always been artistic but also started carving in order to "help make ends meet." He noted that in 1986 he ran into Manfred Susunkewa, whose work made a big impression on him (see Chapter 15). When he first saw Manfred's dolls in a booth at an Indian market, he thought to himself, "What museum vault did he get these from?"

Prior to seeing Manfred's work, Clark tried to make what he calls, "Michelangelo dolls." He joked, "You know, the correct size of the penis and all that!" He said his influences during this period were Von Monongya, Alvin James, and Henry Shelton. However, after his encounter with Manfred, he decided to move away from the Ultra-Realistic Style of carving and attempt the Traditional Style. He recalls saying to himself, "I think I can do this." A common theme in Clark's life is a bedrock of self-confidence.

Once he and Ann added two daughters to the family, Clark began to make dolls in a simpler style. One time, Joseph Day, from Tsakurshovi came by his home and noticed some of these more basic katsinam hanging on the wall. He encouraged Clark to fashion some dolls in this style for the marketplace. Clark quickly took advantage of this offer. Soon after, he was selling not only to Tsakurshovi but also to the gift shops at Museum of Northern Arizona and the Heard, and to Mark Bahti, of Bahti Indian Arts in Tucson.

Clark's success in selling to these diverse major outlets was due to the distinctiveness and charisma of his katsinam. Consider the artistic range shown in several of the carvings in this chapter. For example, Figure 2 is a stately looking Hemiskatsina (Jemez katsina). The katsina effectively portrays the dignity and beauty of this important figure. This katsina and the Kooyemsi in Figure 3 both show characteristics that were typical of his early work: large heads and carefully sanded arms and hands that turn at a right angle.

However, over time Clark added to his carving style by creating very different head and body types. See Figure 4. On the left is a soaring Hehey'a and the right a veering Sikyatsuku, the Yellow Ritual Clown. On these carvings, the heads, bodies, and arms are much different from the examples in Figures 2 and 3. Both the Hehey'a and Sikyatsuku have a comic impact in part due to their very extended shapes and the bending of the cottonwood root, suggesting motion, vitality,

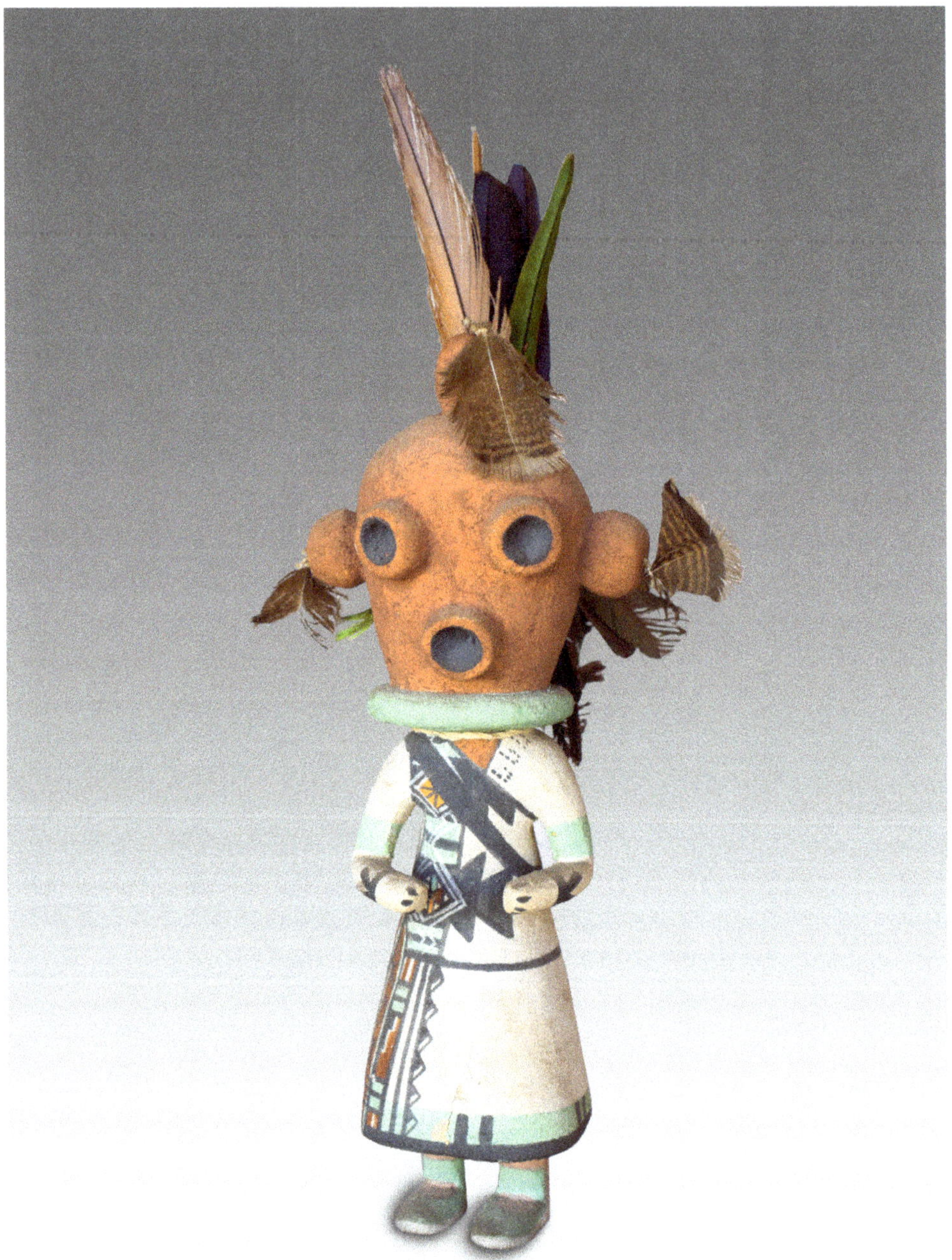

Figure 3. Kooyemsi.

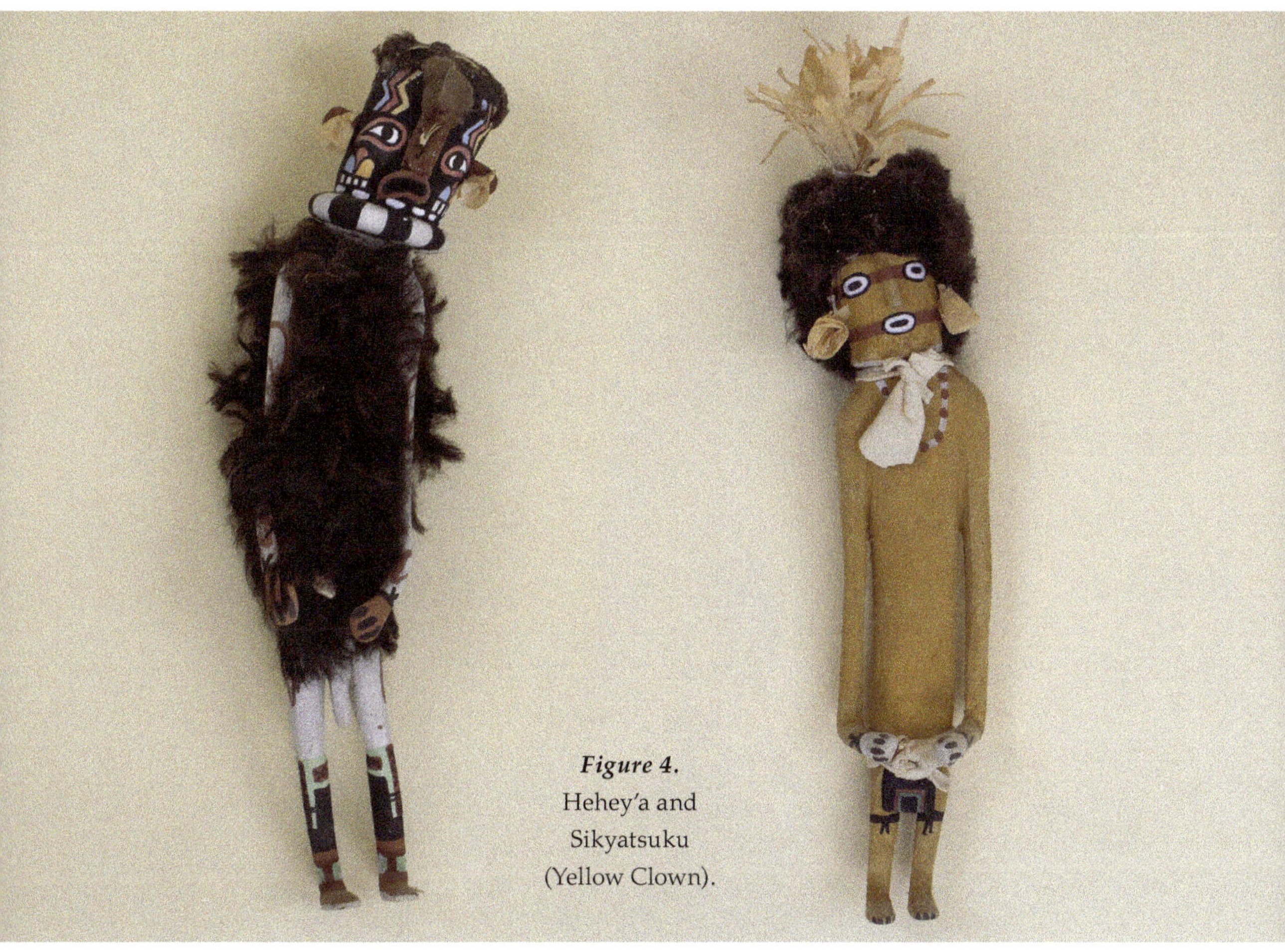

Figure 4. Hehey'a and Sikyatsuku (Yellow Clown).

and humor. The bodies and arms of these carvings in some ways resemble the Volz dolls depicted earlier in this book. Those katsinam from around 1900 may have had an influence on Clark's work; he is very much aware of katsina-carving history.

A spectacular example by Clark is shown in Figure 5. It is a beautifully rendered version of the beloved Palhikwmana (Water Drinking Maiden). This carving is a remarkable 25 inches tall. It is certainly among his best work with the elaborate tablita, featherwork, and lovely colors. Note the signature on this Palhikwmana, as shown in Figure 6. Regardless of style, he generally uses these elements for signing: his initials and Rabbit Clan. Overall, Clark created an utterly distinctive style that has made him popular with collectors for decades.

In discussing his career as an artist, Clark said learning how to deal with the business side required a whole new skill set. He said, "You have to learn how

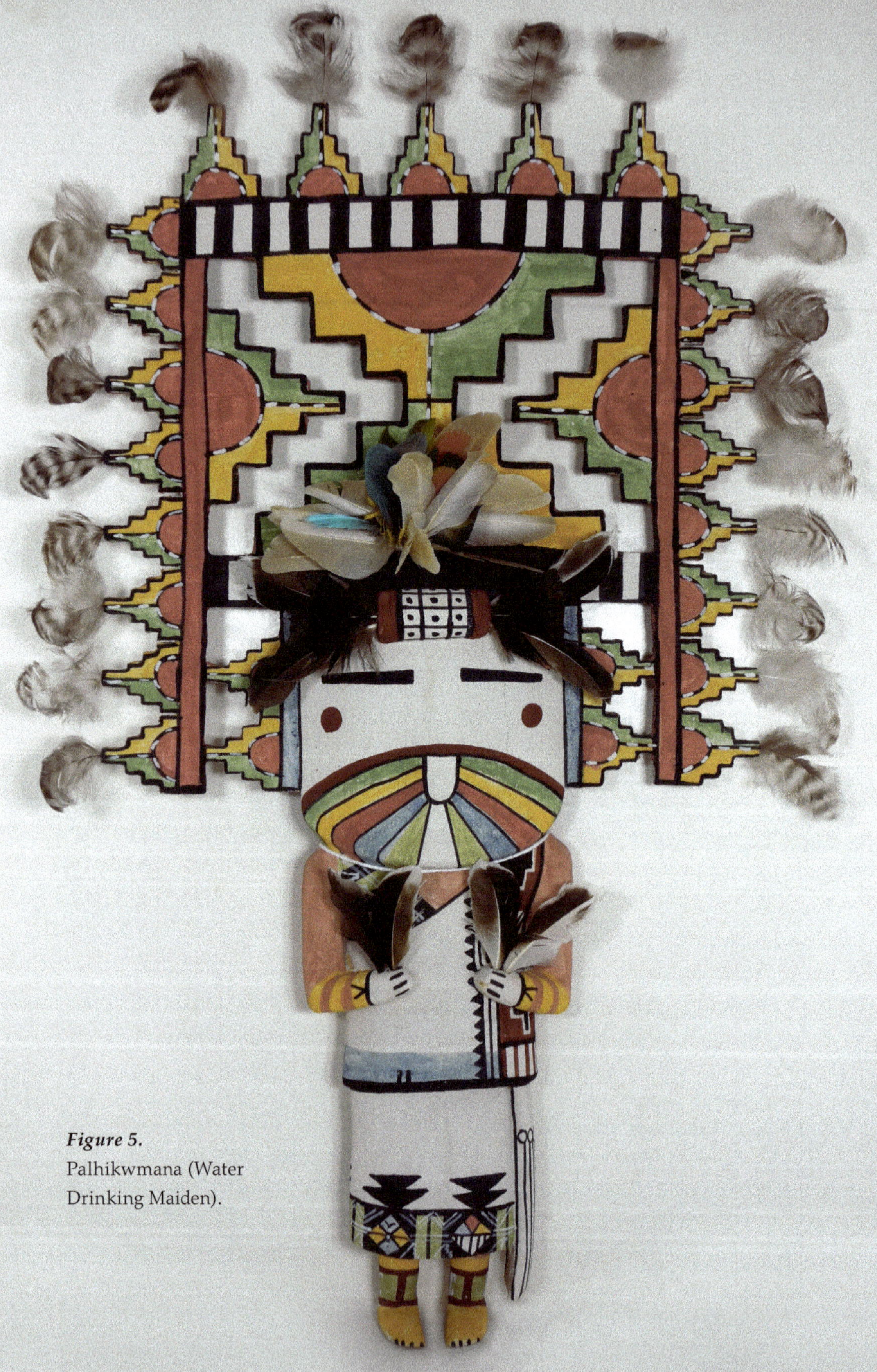

Figure 5.
Palhikwmana (Water Drinking Maiden).

to manage your time devoted to carving, obtain materials consistently, learn how to apply to the shows effectively, afford booth fees, etcetera." It's clear that some carvers move into this world seamlessly, while others struggle with or avoid it altogether. With Clark, it seems likely that his worldwide travels while in the Army made these transitions less difficult. He was used to dealing with Pahaanas (Anglos) and their diverse, puzzling, sometimes aggressive ways.

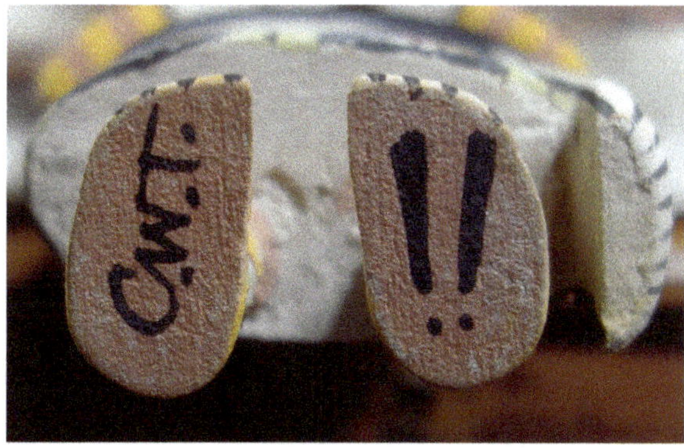

Figure 6. Tenakhongva's signature.

Clark has participated in Santa Fe's Indian Market since 1989. He has won many ribbons at the August SWAIA competitions and has a booth on the plaza annually. In 2017 he shared that booth with his nine-year-old grandson, Suyma Malo, who is quite a painter and has won ribbons in his own right. See Figure 1 showing both Clark and Suyma with their work.

Another chapter in Clark's life emerged in the early- to mid-1990s. Clark began working for the Assistant Prosecutor for the Hopi Police Department and later for the Hopi Legal Services Public Defender's office. Although Clark doesn't have a law degree, he became very knowledgeable about legal matters. From 1997– 2000 he became involved in Hopi politics when he worked as staff assistant to the Chairman of the Tribe. His exposure to military bureaucracy and organization was helpful in this role.

In 2000 Clark began working for the United States Department of Veterans Affairs (VA) where he remained for seventeen years, retiring in the summer of 2017. Clark worked as an outreach counselor for the VA. In this capacity, he covered a territory the size of West Virginia, including the Hopi, Navajo, Apache, Zuni, and Supai reservations. He was often on the road three weeks per month, traveling and sleeping in an RV. Clark provided counseling to veterans with substance abuse problems, helped them obtain VA benefits, and even set up satellite dishes for telemedicine purposes. Much of his territory was far away from VA offices and clinics, and he interacted with a lot of combat vets with post-traumatic stress disorder. He indicated being a vet himself made all the difference. They would trust and confide in him. He added, "My greatest approval was the 'thank yous' at the end of meetings."

During this same period in Clark's life, he began to volunteer as a DJ at the Hopi radio station, KUYI. He played diverse roles in educating the Hopi public, including providing language lessons in Hopi and playing recordings of Hopi elders. Clark's role evolved in some unusual directions. He did the first play-by-play in the Hopi language of a high school basketball game, for which he had to make up words that don't exist in Hopi. For example, in referring to the "rim" of the basketball hoop he used the word in Hopi for the rim of a sifter basket! He did the same thing for Hopi football games where he used the Hopi word for a twenty-five-cent coin to refer to the "quarterback." These broadcasts were very well received by the Hopi public.

Eventually, all this exposure took Clark in another unexpected direction. Canyon Records—known for its Native American music recordings—contacted KUYI looking for someone to record Hopi music. The station manager suggested Clark because at times Clark had sung Hopi music with drum and rattle accompaniment on the air. So began Clark's recording career with Canyon Records that dates from 2002 to the present. To date, he has recorded numerous CDs. His music career has taken him to perform in Canada, Mexico, Belize, France, Spain, and Italy. He has been nominated for, and won, a Native American Music Award (NAMMY) for his recording "Po'li." He was also nominated for a Grammy Award, which resulted in him attending the ceremonies in Hollywood. Clark noted that he wore traditional Hopi clothing to the Grammys, not some out-of-context tuxedo.

An interesting aspect of Clark's katsina making is that he has maintained a successful career as an artist despite his many other roles. He belongs in this book of accomplished carvers because his work is utterly distinctive and effective. Despite his extensive work commitments, he has made time to carve while on the road or on weekends, and has remained committed to the craft. Clark made time to create art for the various shows and competitions—this participation keeps his name in the marketplace.

He credits Mark Bahti for tiding his family over during times of need. He said a couple of his children went to college in Tucson near Mark. "Over and over again, Mark would advance credit to my kids and I would ship dolls to him later on."

The education of Clark's children is noteworthy. To date, very few other Hopi families have children as educationally accomplished as Clark and Ann's. Michael, the oldest, graduated from the Air Force Academy. He served for six years in the Air Force after graduating and retired with the rank of Captain. Michael has since been teaching at Hopi Junior/Senior High School, where he is chair of the math department and a coach for the cross-country team. Their teams have won the State of Arizona Division 4 championships for an astounding twenty-seven consecutive years!

The Tenakhongva's second child is Sam. He graduated as salutatorian of his high school and attended college at the University of Arizona in Tucson where he majored in fine arts. Sam eventually went back to school to acquire credentials to be a teacher. He is currently a fourth-grade teacher at First Mesa Elementary and is very involved with serious responsibilities in his village of Waalpi (Walpi).

The third child, Carlene, outdid her brother Sam by graduating as valedictorian of her high school class. She graduated from Dartmouth College with a degree in American Indian Studies and Government. Clark noted that as far as he knows, she is the first Hopi person to graduate from an Ivy League school. Subsequently, she attended and graduated from law school at the University of Arizona (more loans from Mark Bahti). She is currently Deputy General Counsel for the Hopi Tribe.

The youngest child is Simana. She is still attending school and studies child psychology. Simana has two children and works in a domestic violence program in Keams Canyon.

Clark and Ann certainly deserve much credit for fostering such educational advancement in their children. I asked Clark for the keys to this success. He said one aspect has been the family's faith, belief, and prayers. He added that discipline came from his father, who worked for more than forty years as a custodian for the Bureau of Indian Affairs. And it came from Clark's experiences in the military, along with the structure of his grandfather's traditional Hopi teachings. "In our family, there are no sorries," meaning, "no excuses or sympathies." He added, "we taught our kids to be hard-core. We emphasize having feelings for others but also discipline and structure within ourselves."

The latest chapter in Clark's life is very recent. In 2017 he decided to run for Vice Chairman of the Hopi tribe. He won the primary election in September 2017 and was victorious in the general election in November 2017. He was sworn in as Vice Chairman on December 1, 2017. This is a significant achievement indeed. Clark is already involved in major issues affecting the Hopi, such as opposing the proposed development of Bears Ears National Monument. He has traveled to Washington and testified to members of Congress to advocate for the protection of Bears Ears.

In a life of many chapters, Clark is pursuing yet another major endeavor. Somehow, he'll find time for carving katsinam as he pursues his new activities as Vice Chairman of the Hopi tribe.

Toward the end of one of our conversations, Clark shared a trenchant thought. He said, "Art is a wonderful world, but a hard and cruel life." That certainly applies to many of the life stories presented in this book.

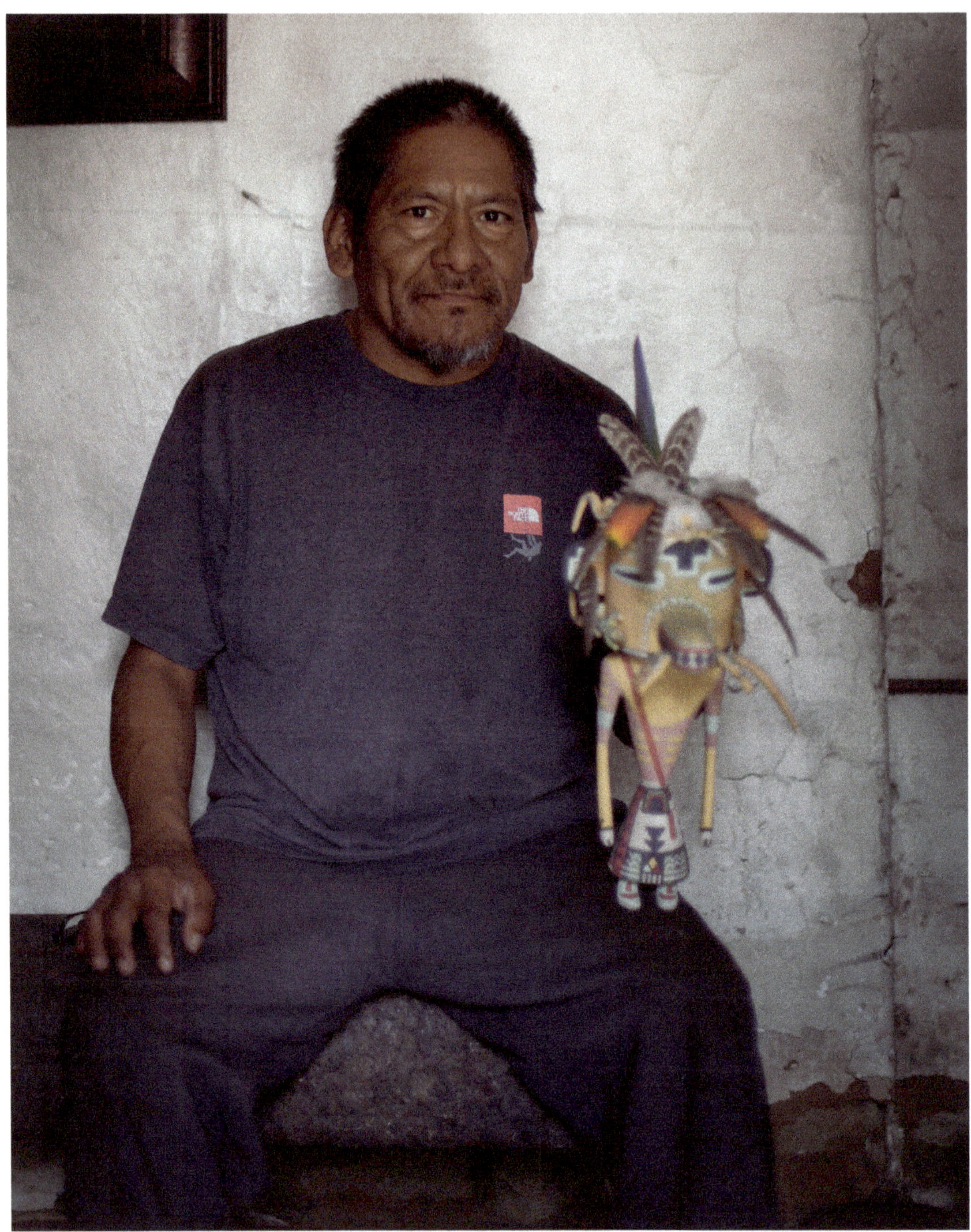

Figure 1. Ferris "Spike" Satala.

FERRIS "SPIKE" SATALA

"It's Mystic"

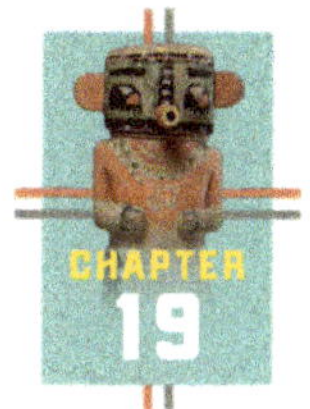

FERRIS "SPIKE" SATALA (Figure 1) was born in 1965. His maternal clan is Bear, and he grew up in Sitsomovi (Sichomovi). He later moved to Songoopavi (Shongopavi) where his mother still resides. At the time of this writing, Spike was living in Waalpi (Walpi). Spike has three children, who attend Winslow schools. Spike suffers from both renal failure and diabetes; these require dialysis treatment three times a week. Yet when I met with Spike several times, he came across as clear and vibrant and quite excited to talk about his art.

Spike shared with me the origins of his nickname. It derives from his Hopi baby name, which is Szi-viyu-dio-ala-at-yamakto, which means "little buckhorn" or the "spike" of early antlers on an antelope. Now there's a nickname with some character.

Spike attended kindergarten on Second Mesa, elementary school at the old Polacca Day School, junior high at Keams Canyon, and high school in Winslow. Although he took art classes throughout his schooling, back in high school he thought he'd end up being a truck driver. Spike exclaimed, "Not sure what happened to that!" He said throughout all levels of his schooling he won awards for drawing and other forms of art.

Like most Hopi males, Spike didn't start carving until age twelve or thirteen, after initiation. He began by sanding dolls for his grandfather, Elmer Satala. He noted that Satala is originally a Tewa name related to a tobacco clan from Santa Clara. He shared that his grandfather "was the last Tewa Chief at Hanoki (Hano) village." Spike indicated he is a third-generation carver. His maternal grandmother taught him which katsinam *not* to carve (such as the Water Serpent or Paalölöqangkatsina). He has honored her warnings to this day.

Spike's career as a katsina maker runs more than thirty years. During that time Spike has worked in two distinct styles. The first was unique to him: carvings with large heads, elongated skinny arms, and tiny feet. See Figures 2 and 3 for excellent examples of this first style. Figure 2 is a Hiilili from the 1990s in a rather typical 7–8 inch size for Spike. Figure 3 features a Manangya (Lizard katsina), an exceptionally large piece for Spike at 6 inches wide by 14 inches tall.

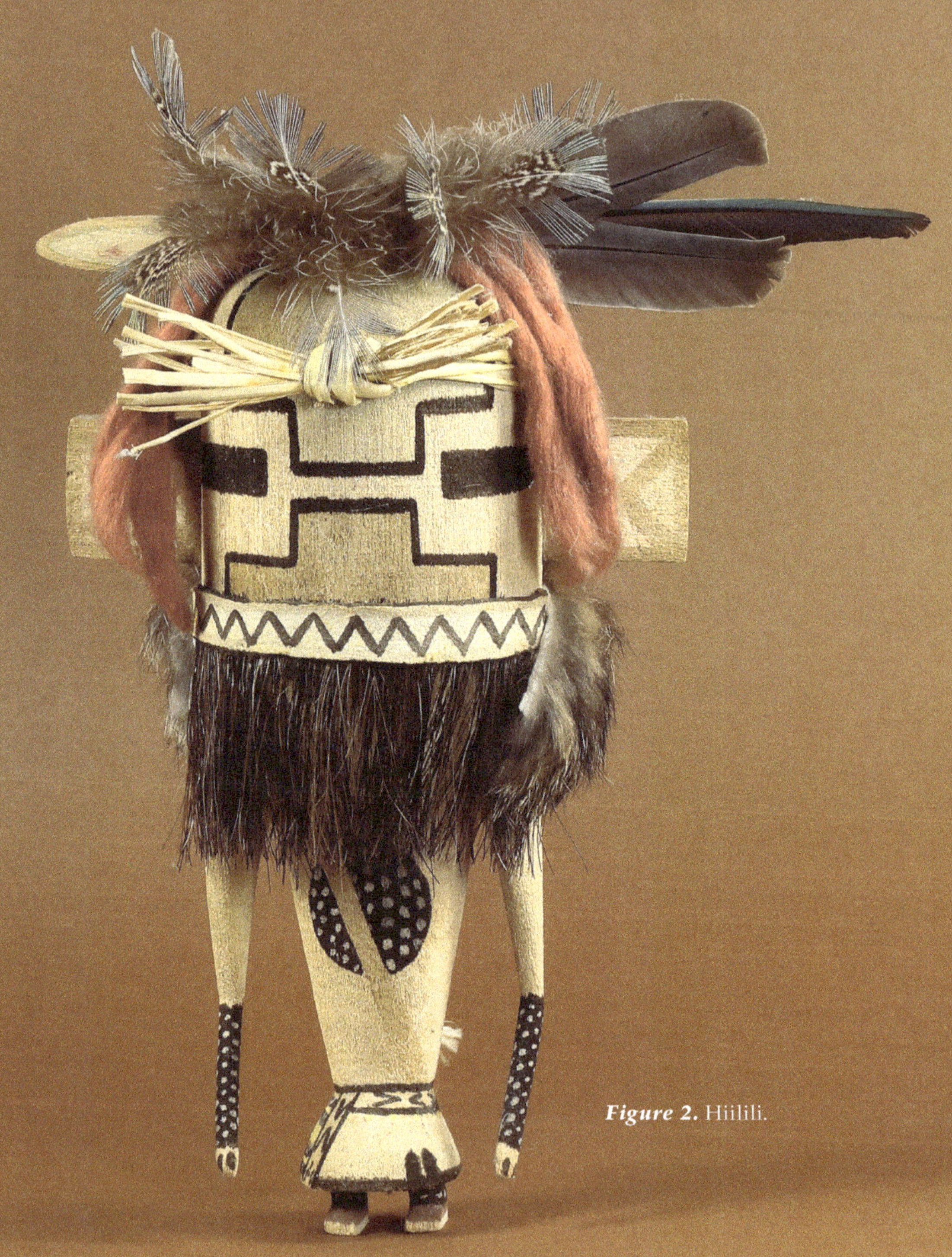

Figure 2. Hiilili.

The Manangya also has remarkable detail with four life-sized lizards attached to its head and one in its mouth. Spike told me he created the unusual stippling on its face with a toothbrush!

When I asked Spike how he arrived at this earlier style, his response was very philosophical. He said the tiny feet are meant to indicate, "Take your time. Go slowly. Be patient. Art can't be rushed." Regarding the thin arms, he said, "Life is fragile. Be careful not to break it." And the very large heads? He explained, "Watch your ego." Although I have known Spike for many years I never took the time to ask about his style of carving; I sure am glad I did. His explanations tell us a lot about his art and him.

Spike elaborated on his feelings about his artwork. He said, "My whole life has been about art. Katsina making is essentially a craft. To be an art, to call it that, it has to be original." And that's exactly what Spike achieved with his early work. One never needed to look for a signature to identify a Spike Satala katsina. The originality leapt out.

Spike noted that when he first introduced these markedly different katsinam to the marketplace, they were not well received right away. One of the initial collectors to appreciate his work was Barbara Rice from Pennsylvania. He also began selling to Winter Sun in Flagstaff and Tsakurshovi on Second Mesa. Eventually, he started winning prizes at competitions, including a blue ribbon at the Museum of Northern Arizona in 2000 and at Indian Market in 2005, and began selling to galleries and museum shops in Phoenix and Santa Fe.

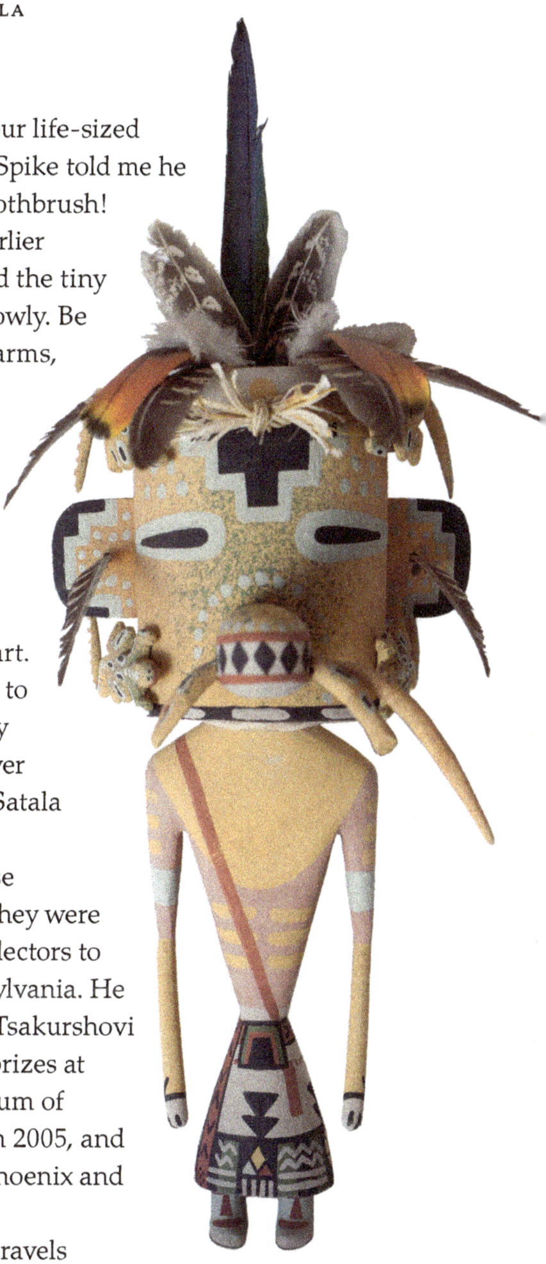

Figure 3.
Manangya (Lizard).

More recently, due to his health problems, he travels less, doesn't compete at shows, and sells primarily to his old reliable outlets: Winter Sun and Tsakurshovi. Coinciding with this change in his life has been a major change in his style of katsina carving. Note two examples shown in Figure 4, a very eerie looking Kooyemsi, and Figure 5, an endearing Pavatya (Tadpole or Pollywog). Spike said he changed his style in part because he felt the market had grown tired of his previous work. He believes most of the serious collectors already had several dolls in this style and were looking for something different.

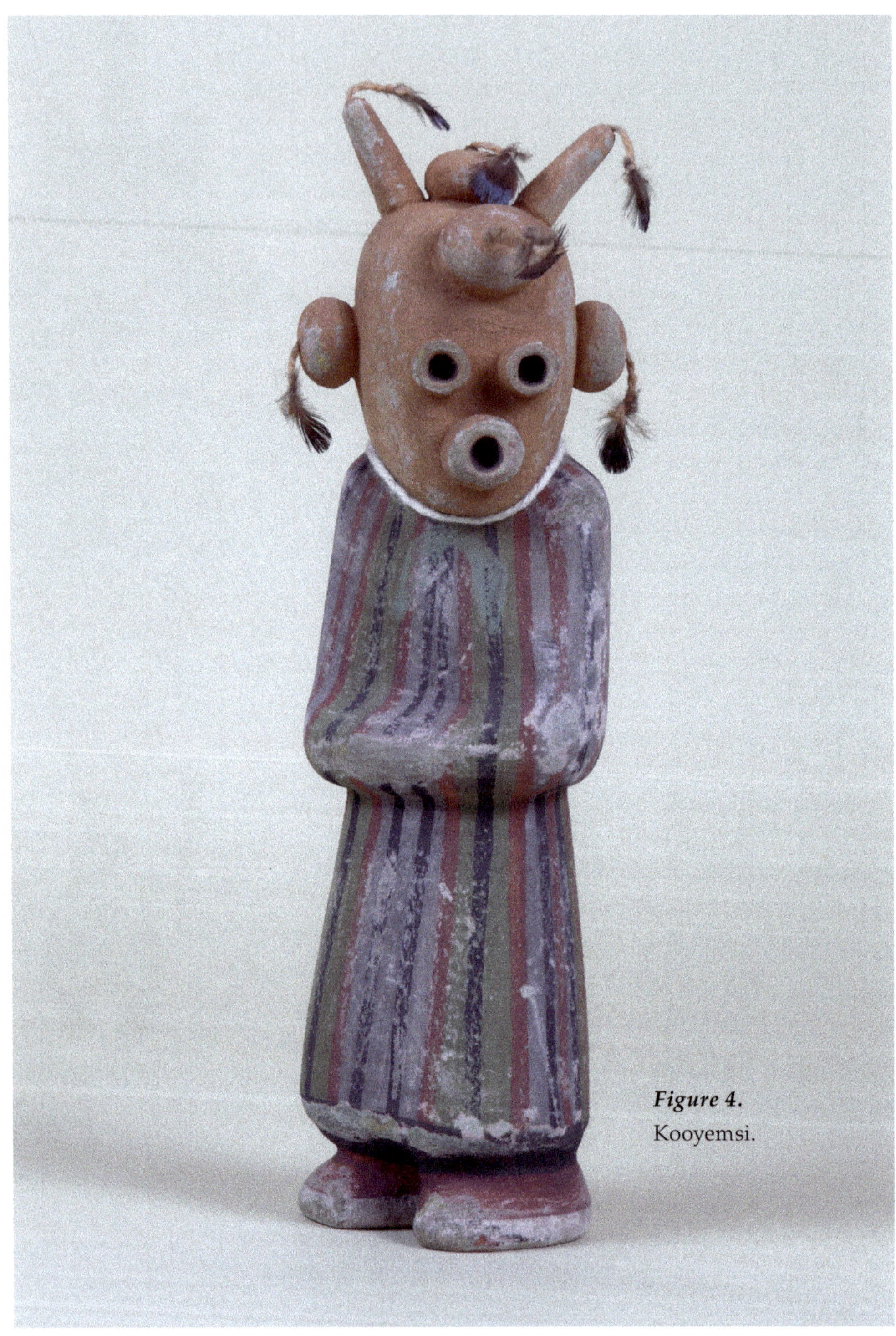

Figure 4.
Kooyemsi.

Spike also noted he would hear collectors in shops asking for katsinam that had "been played with," meaning given to children at dances. He also credited someone I considered to be an extremely unlikely source of influence: Martha Stewart! He said he was watching her show one day and she spoke about how to distress furniture. Spike indicated that he learned several tips from her. Talk about an unusual cross-fertilization . . .

Spike also identified some more conventional influences. Philbert Honanie affected his work early on, and his uncle, Delbridge Honanie, was also instrumental. Strangely, he denies that Walter Howato had an impact on his second style (Walter originated the distressed style back in the 70s). Nonetheless, he says his decision to switch to a more antiqued style essentially came from himself. He also likes the work of several contemporary carvers including Brandon Kayquoptewa and Lester Quanimptewa.

Spike thinks the distressed style is the "future of katsina carving," and I agree that his carvings in this style are especially effective. For example, the Kooyemsi in Figure 4 looks to me like an "old soul"; he is provocatively ancient in his appearance. The distressed style goes way beyond sanded paint to convey the antiquity of the Katsina spirits themselves. The same can be said regarding the Tadpole (Pavatya) katsina. Spike explained this figure is a *Hisot* (Ancient One) seldom seen anymore, and that the posture is "looking up" because that is how tadpoles appear in the water. Consider also the Sakwahote (Blue Hoot'e) by Spike in Figure 6. In this case, the eeriness comes from the feathers surrounding the katsina's head and body. It too looks otherworldly and ancient.

It is quite remarkable that Spike has been so successful in two very different styles. He indicates that there is a common characteristic across both styles: "All my paints are just barely touching each other. I still work that way after all these years."

Like some other carvers in this book, Spike shared that he has had problems with substance abuse in the past and links his current health problems to those behaviors. He is now sober and trying to regain his health, walking long distances very frequently. He commented on the more general problem on Hopiland and said, "Addiction is what's going to beat us if we're not careful." He said, "We better be careful or we'll be talking about the Katsina religion as something we *used to* have." Consistent with this statement, he noted that he is ceremonially involved at Waalpi village. Again, turning philosophical, Spike said, "I've earned my spot in Waalpi and on Hopi; life is all about earning your spot."

Toward the end of our time together, I mentioned to Spike that I'd been coming to Hopiland for thirty years and I wondered what drew me back again and again. Spike smiled at me and said, "It's mystic." And so is Spike in his own way. Thank you!

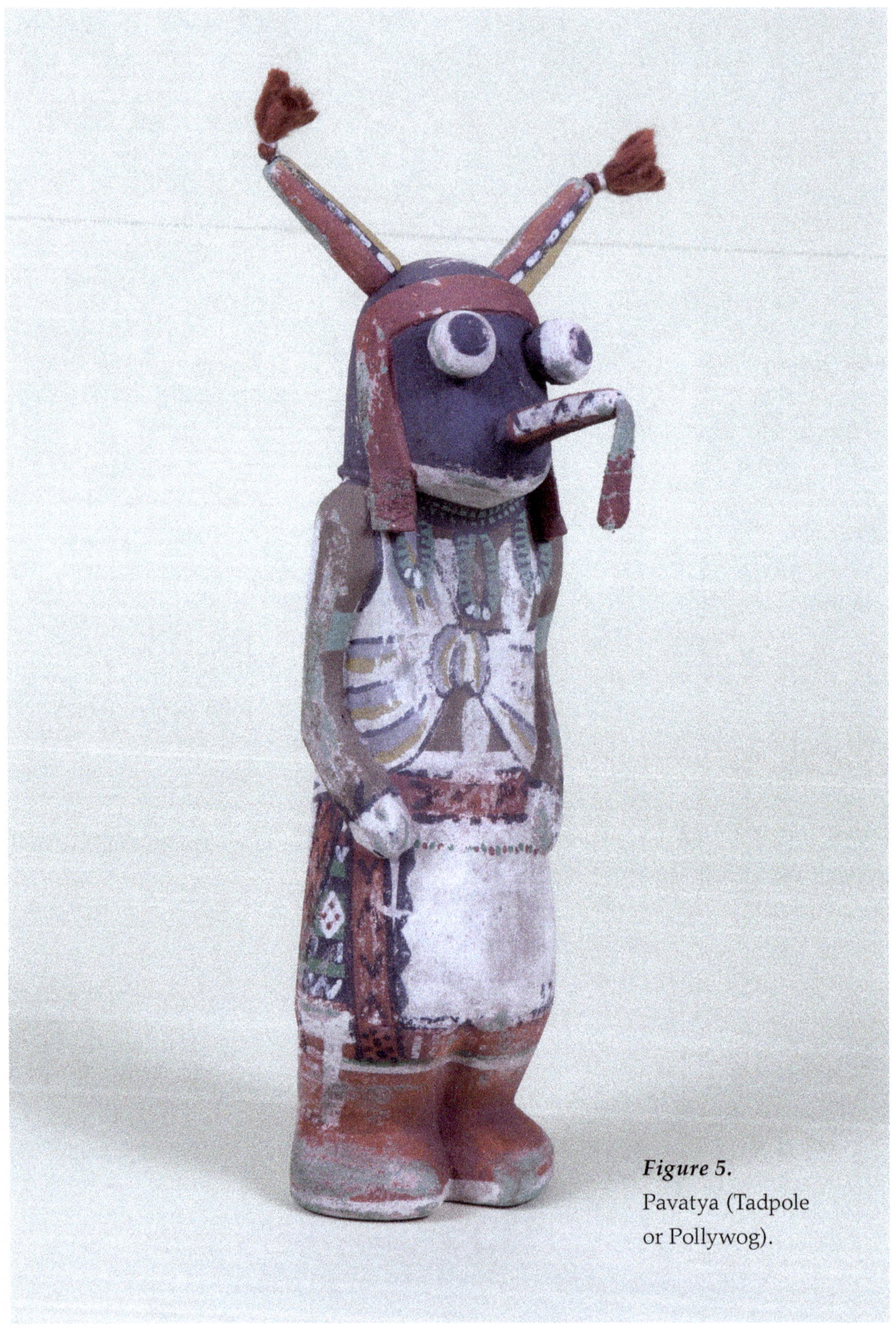

Figure 5.
Pavatya (Tadpole or Pollywog).

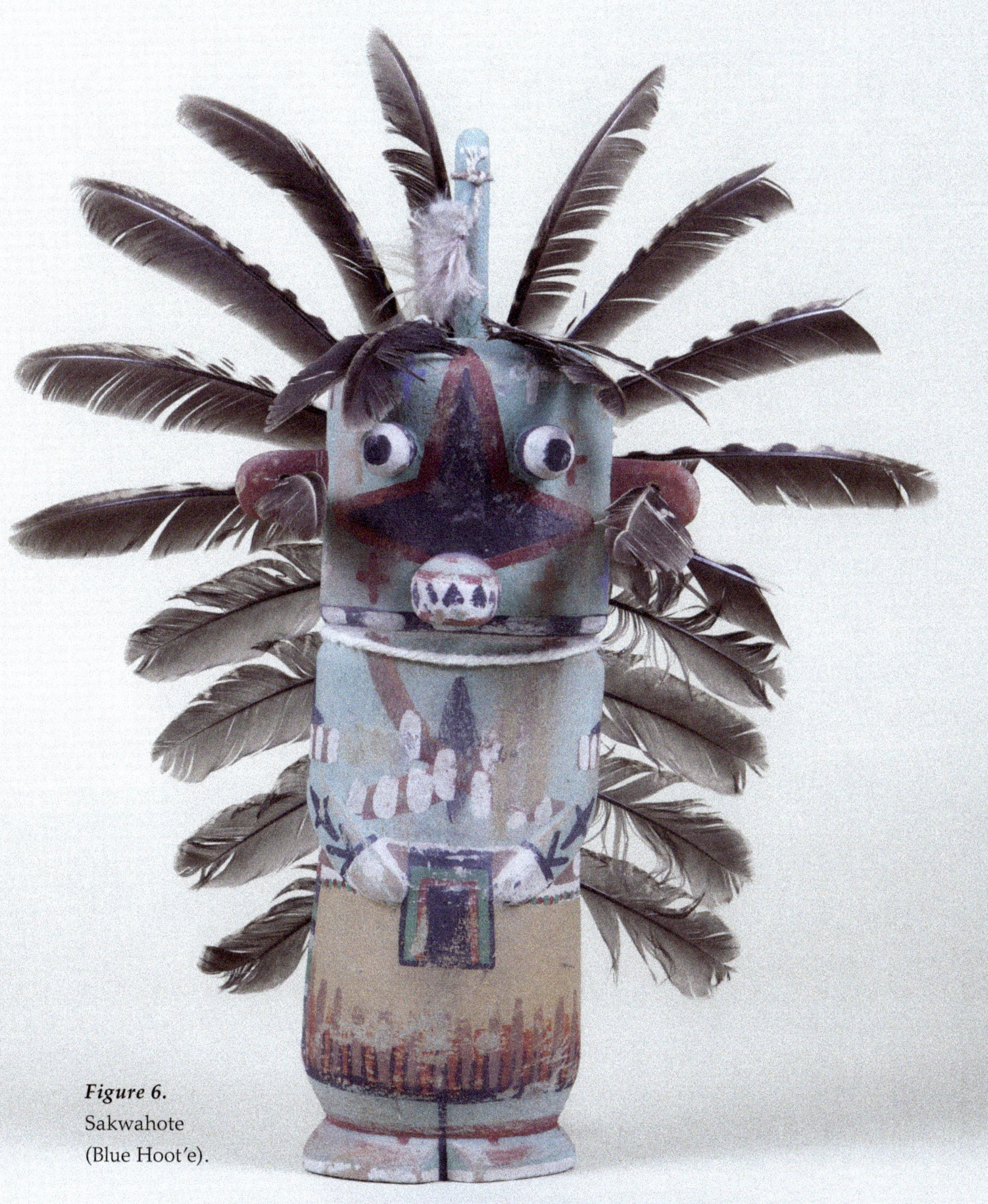

Figure 6.
Sakwahote
(Blue Hoot'e).

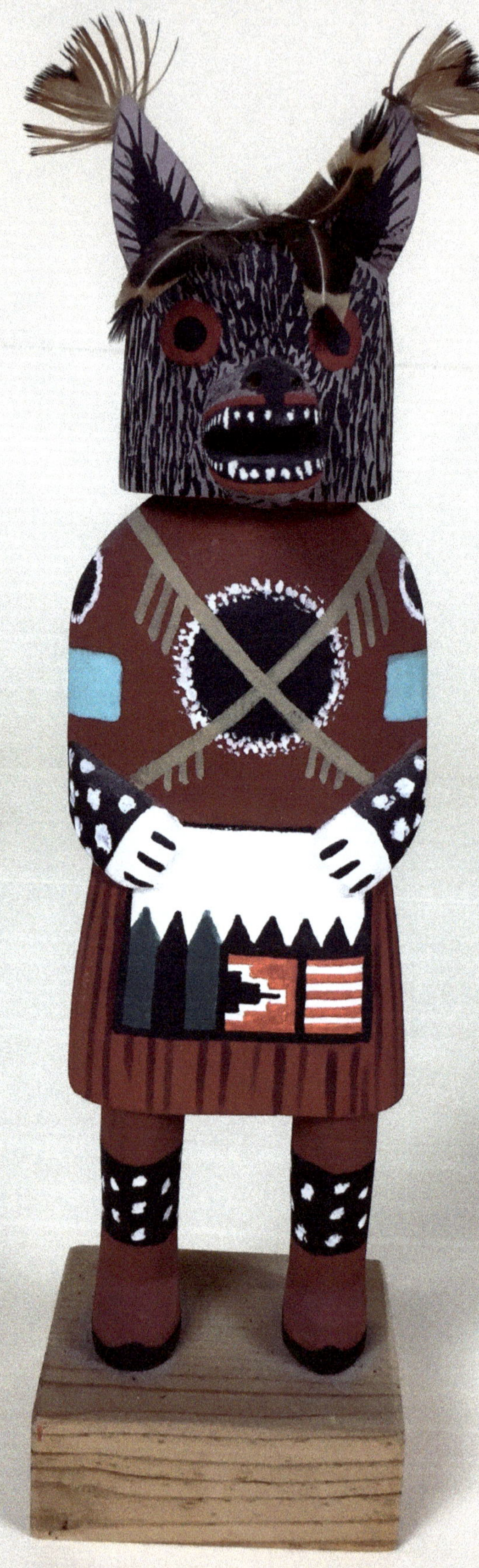

Figure 1.
Kwewu (Wolf).

ERNEST "ERNIE" MOORE

"A Full Hopi…Out of the Wilderness"

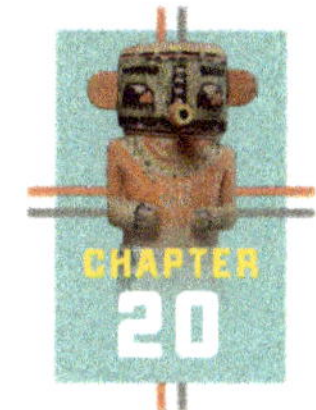

Ernest Moore, better known as "Ernie," was born in 1934. His maternal clan was Reed and his paternal clan was Fire. Most other carvers in this book have described how they began making katsinam at around age twelve or thirteen after being initiated. The route for Ernie Moore was far different and requires an extended explanation.

My sources regarding Ernie were rather limited. I spoke with Darance "Makwesa" Chimerica, who is also featured in this book; Darance and Ernie were friends toward the end of Ernie's life. I also drew heavily on an article on Ernie by Patty Talahongva from a 2004 *Native Peoples* magazine. Adobe Gallery in Santa Fe provides a brief bio on its website, and Greg Schaaf provides some information in his book, *Hopi Katsina* (2008). I was not able to find family members as sources.

The most extensive biography on Ernie is provided by Ms. Talahongva's 2004 piece. She noted that Ernie was born on the Hopi reservation but lived off-reservation for more than fifty years. The specific chronology follows. Ernie was born in Munqapi (Moenkopi), and when he was six his father took a job in Keams Canyon, which moved the family to the other end of the reservation. When Ernie was eleven, the family relocated to New Mexico before settling on the Colorado River Indian Tribes Reservation. In the 1950s, Ernie enlisted in the United States Marines and after his tour of duty, he settled in Phoenix where he remained for decades. In Phoenix, he worked both as an art teacher and a graphic artist. This work fostered his artistic skill and attention to detail, but remarkably Ernie had nothing to do with katsina carving, or any other Hopi arts and crafts, for decades.

Ms. Talahongva noted that in the late 1990s—when Ernie was in his sixties—he became ill with thyroid disease, and experienced problems with alcoholism and family difficulties, which led to a divorce. These challenges caused him to reflect on his life and where it was going. As noted by Ms. Talahongva, "…buried in the man was a wish to one day return to his childhood roots and renew his Hopi way of life." (Talahongva 2004, 59). So, after this period of reflection, Ernie moved back to the reservation to rediscover his roots and culture. Given his artistic training and experience, it was only natural that he eventually tried his hand at katsina carving.

As noted on the Adobe Gallery (Santa Fe) website, Ernie didn't start carving katsinam until he was a senior citizen—in stark contrast to most Hopi peers who generally started around twelve to thirteen. From the beginning, he carved in a rather straight-up Traditional Style. An example of his early work is shown in Figure 1, which shows a Kwewu (Wolf) katsina. Frankly, this is a rather basic katsina. It is 7 inches tall including the base. If Ernie's artistic development had stopped here, he would not have become a highly regarded carver. Note also in Figure 2, at this early point in his development, he was signing his work with his name, "Ernie." This Wolf is cleanly executed and reasonably competent, but his work is nothing special…yet.

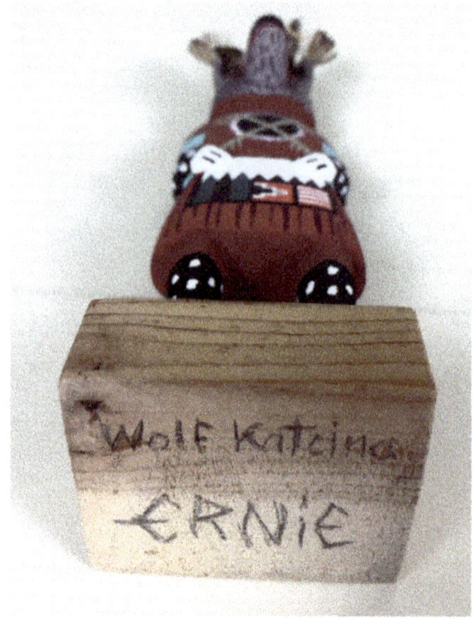

Figure 2. Moore's early signature.

Progress in Ernie's artistic development can be seen in Figure 3. This is a Masawkatsina, the katsina version of the Maasaw deity. This carving is much larger and well developed than the Wolf. It is 15¾ inches tall and is a more ambitious and self-confident work. With this example, one begins to see the precision derived from Ernie's years as a graphic artist. Note the lines of Masawkatsina's garment and the rendering of the kilt over his shoulders, and the care he took in applying the quail feathers to the paahos (prayer sticks) on Masawkatsina's head. This katsina is signed with the Reed and Fire Clan symbols of his parents and the name, "Ernie." A similarly fine carving is depicted in Figure 4. This is the Yöngökatsina (Prickly Pear Cactus). This work is just under 20 inches tall. Note the fine detail on the face, beard, garments, and cacti. The detail and precision of the carving and painting are exceptional and the size is imposing.

Another advanced carving is provided in Figure 5, representing Angwusnasomtaqa (Crow Mother). This is a masterwork. It is 15½ inches tall. Ernie's artistry captures the dignity and presence of this centrally important Katsina. Crow Mother is holding individually carved and painted yucca whips. Note the meticulous attention to detail on the crow wings, ruff, manta, and sash.

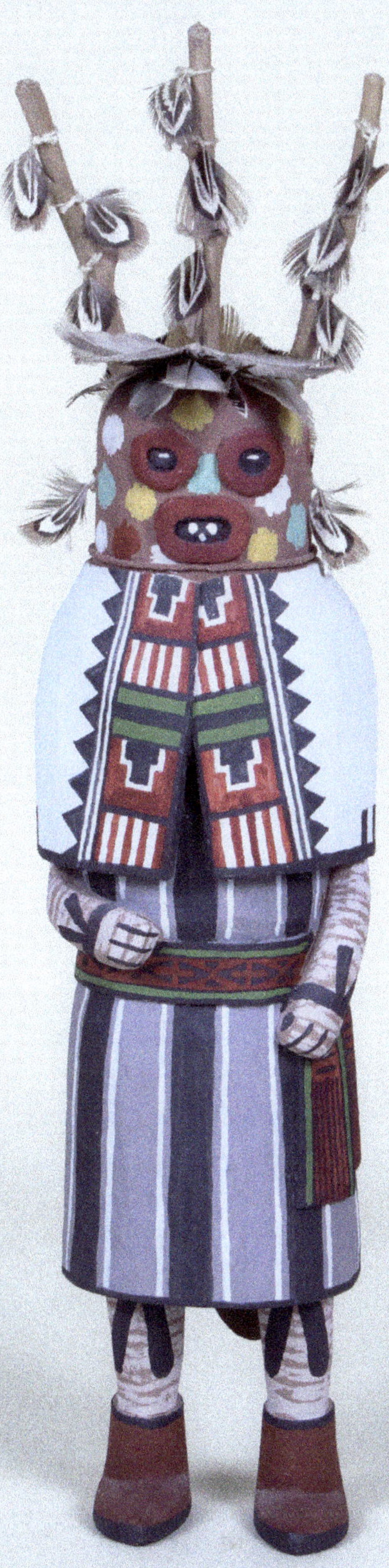

Figure 3.
Masawkatsina.

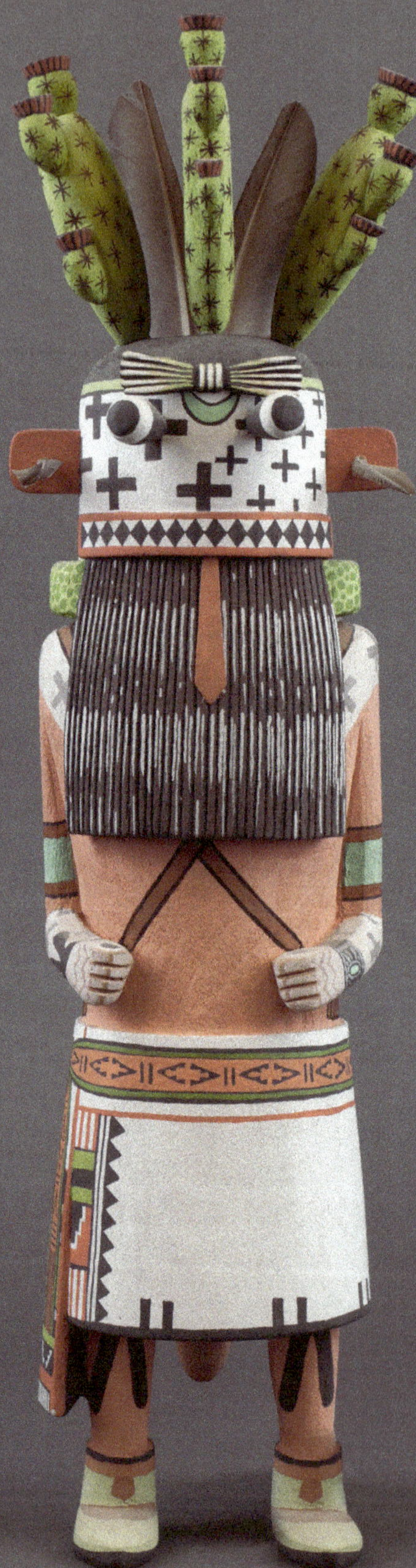

Figure 4.
Yöngökatsina
(Prickly Pear Cactus).

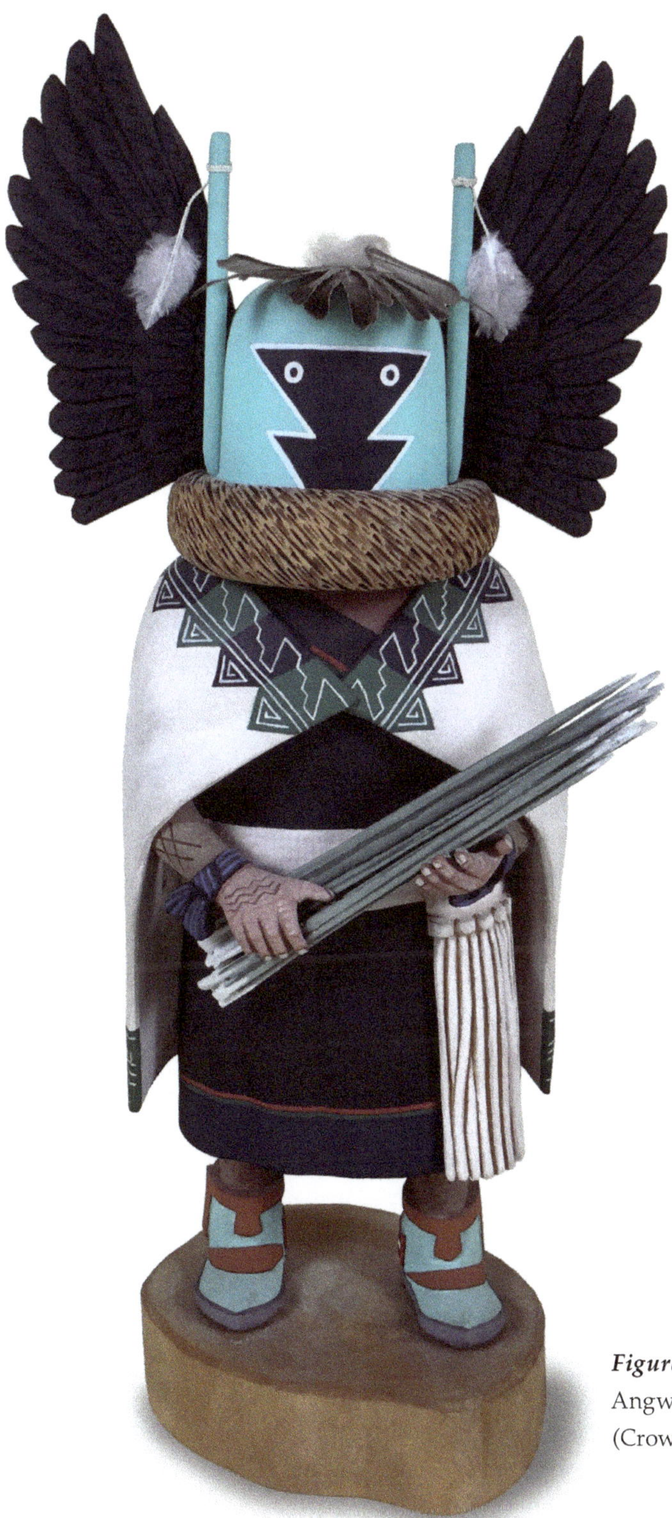

Figure 5.
Angwusnasomtaqa (Crow Mother).

Figure 6. Moore's later signature.

By this time in his career, Ernie was signing his work with his Hopi name, Quanhoyeoma, which means "soldier" or "guard," and symbols for the Reed and Fire Clans, as shown in Figure 6. His transformation from "off-res Indian" with distant memories of Hopiland to reintegrated Hopi Native was now seemingly complete.

Ernie's artistic accomplishment eventually resulted in considerable recognition. In 2003, he created a depiction of a Palhikwmana dance with twenty-four individually carved figures. (For an example of these katsinam, see Figure 7). This carving is signed with only the symbols of his mother and father's clans). Ernie entered this Herculean effort of twenty-four pieces in the Heard Museum annual show where it won Best of Show. He later sold this tableau to the American Museum of Natural History in New York for $20,000.

According to Makwesa Chimerica, this whopping sale changed Ernie's life. It enabled him to buy a single-wide trailer which he placed on Hopi Partitioned Land near Red Lake, Arizona, and he acquired a truck. After this, he lived a rather quiet existence on his land, enjoying its beauty and quiet. As he said to Ms. Talahongva,

> I want this area where I live to be calm and peaceful. The storm will go away and the calm will set in and the rainbow will appear.... I've had a very stormy life, and... I'm a recovering ka-Hopi. My instinct now is to be a full Hopi;... I'm really beginning to feel that I have a purpose and that I'm part of something important. I'm no longer out in the wilderness. (Talahongva 2004, 60)

Toward the end of his life, Ernie concentrated on selling katsinam three times a year: at the annual Heard and Museum of Northern Arizona shows, and Santa Fe's Indian Market. He once told Makwesa that he would sell on average about fifty dolls at the Indian Market each year. I recall going to his booth at the Market and he would be mobbed by eager buyers.

Ernie passed in 2009. He was buried in the backyard of his beloved single-wide trailer. Remarkably, his carving career lasted only about ten years. Yet he became one of the more notable katsina carvers of all time and his talent will not be forgotten. All who knew him were glad he achieved such peace and success in his old age.

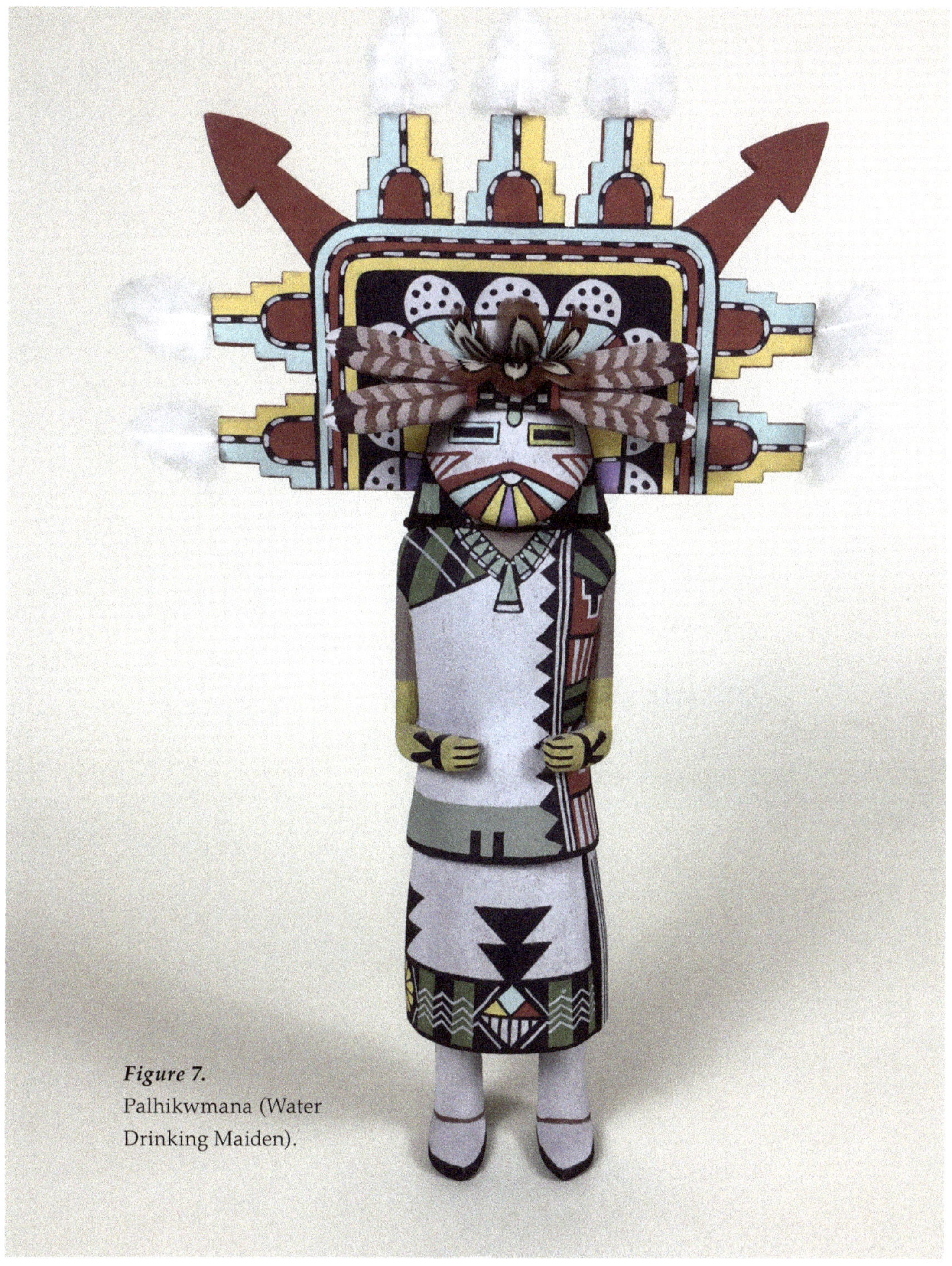

Figure 7.
Palhikwmana (Water Drinking Maiden).

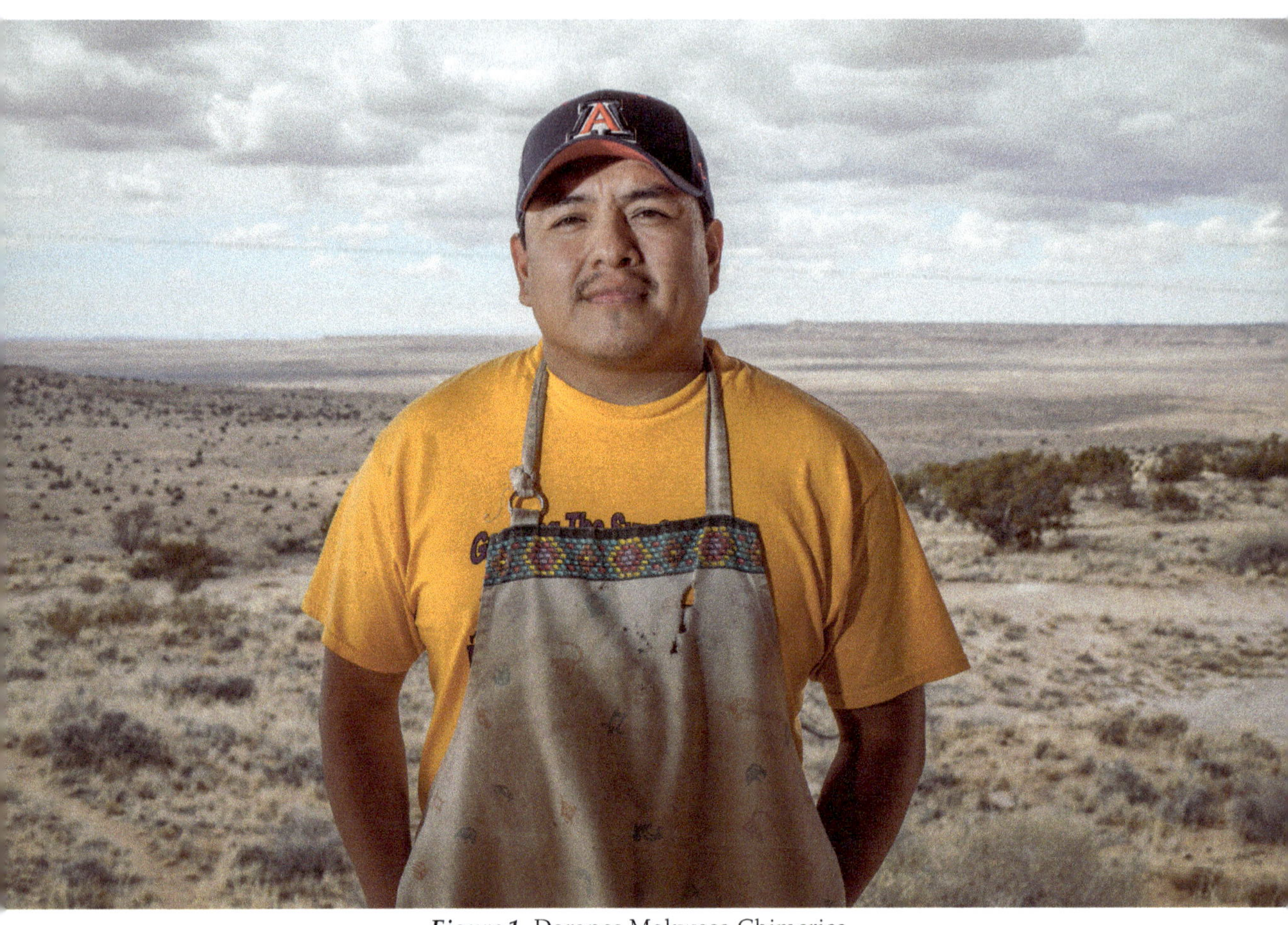

Figure 1. Darance Makwesa Chimerica.

DARANCE MAKWESA CHIMERICA

Unerring Tradition

CHAPTER 21

DARANCE MAKWESA CHIMERICA (Hopi spelling "Tismoqa") is a Hopi man born in 1979 (Figure 1). His maternal clan is Fire and his paternal clan is Sun. He grew up in Munqapi (Moenkopi) and currently lives in Hotvela (Hotevilla) with his Hopi wife, Jessica, and two young children, Potima, and Siin-Mana. The non-anglicized names of their children point to the values of Darance and Jessica. *Potima* means "Maasaw checking the earth," and *Siin-Mana* refers to "a Coyote Clan flower."

As reflected in these names, the first thing to be said about Darance is that in many ways he is a very traditional Hopi. Although he lives in a home with electricity, plumbing, and even solar panels, he is very involved in his village ceremonially and is serious about his traditional Hopi farming. He also raises a herd of cattle with his father, brother, and a nephew.

His emphasis on Hopi tradition pervades how he creates katsinam. He is a Traditional Style carver. He always starts with a douma (white clay) undercoat, and uses natural pigments exclusively, noting that when needed he goes over a color two or three times to achieve the shade he wants. Darance shared that he obtains his blue pigments from Colorado, red from New Mexico, purple and black from Ganado, yellow from near Kiqotsmovi (Kykotsmovi), and green from a nearby Hopi wash. He says that when traveling he is always on the lookout for interesting stones, colors, and minerals. And the same goes for when he is jogging, always scanning for promising materials.

These practices were not always the case for Darance; they have evolved over time. He started carving katsinam in 1997. An early influence was Irving Charlie Talawepi. Darance's aunt was married to Bendrew Atokuku, a well-regarded carver, who also impressed him. And acclaimed artist, Ernie Moore (also featured in this volume), was a close friend. Darance described how he used to visit Ernie at his home near Red Lake and Tonalea, Arizona. He said Ernie offered to teach Darance how to carve in his very distinctive, meticulous style, but Darance—like most accomplished artists—decided to go his own way.

Darance shared that noted collector and dealer, Peggy DeMouthe, bought one of his first carvings in 2000 at Tuhisma (the October Hopi marketplace). This very doll, Angwusnasomtaqa (Crow Mother), is shown in Figure 2. To compare this carving to his current work is very striking, and emphasizes his substantial artistic development. An unusual feature—to say the least—is that he appears to have used pink insulation material to create the border on Crow Mother's face. Darance would never use such unconventional material on a katsina these days.

Another early carving of a Kooninkatsintaqa (male Havasupai) is shown in Figure 3 on the left. A recent katsina, the rarely seen Tewa Pohaha (Four Horn) katsina, is shown on the right for comparison. The Hopi name for this katsina is Nalöq'ala. Note the earlier carving has a much smaller body and tiny feet. The smaller example on the left shows the work of "an artist as a young man," still finding his way, while the larger carving on the right is the work of a confident, established artist who knows his craft. Yet even in the early example, signature aspects of Darance's work can be found, including precise wood carving, careful painting, and a fine eye for coloration. His ability to apply color so well may in part be derived from his experience painting with acrylics in high school art classes.

The consistently high quality of Darance's recent work is shown in Figures 4, 5, and 6. Figure 4 shows a set of Hemiskatsinam rarely seen as a group. On the left is the standard Hopi Hemiskatsina seen at many Home Dances. In the middle is a Siohemiskatsina, the Zuni depiction of the katsina, and on the right is the seldom seen Qötsahemiskatsina (White) version of this figure. Figure 5 shows an ancient figure with an elongated jumping frog on its extended tablita. Darance told me he has only seen this figure in a book and found it so unusual he decided to carve and paint it. Figure 6 shows even more of Darance's artistic range. On the left is his version of a Pakiwkatsina (Fish) katsina, in the middle is Yöngökatsina (Prickly Pear Cactus), and on the right is his interpretation of a Wilson Tawaquaptewa carving (see Chapter 3 in this book). Regarding his work, Darance simply states, "I would say my carvings remind me of how things are supposed to be in physical form."

Because I have known Darance for several years, I felt I could ask him a blunt question: "How have you been able to avoid the chaos, poverty, and substance abuse that can be so common on Hopiland?" Darance's reply was quite revealing. He said, "It's because of my upbringing. My parents were strong role models, both have jobs, and are successful. They didn't drink. And they disciplined us." He added that his involvement in Hopi tradition is also key. Darance realized after graduating from high school in Tuba City that more schooling was not for him. He said he was drawn back to Hopiland, that "when something is going on in the kiva, I want to be there." And for Darance the link to his kiva in Hotvela reaches as far back as his great-grandfather. He also knew he wanted to marry

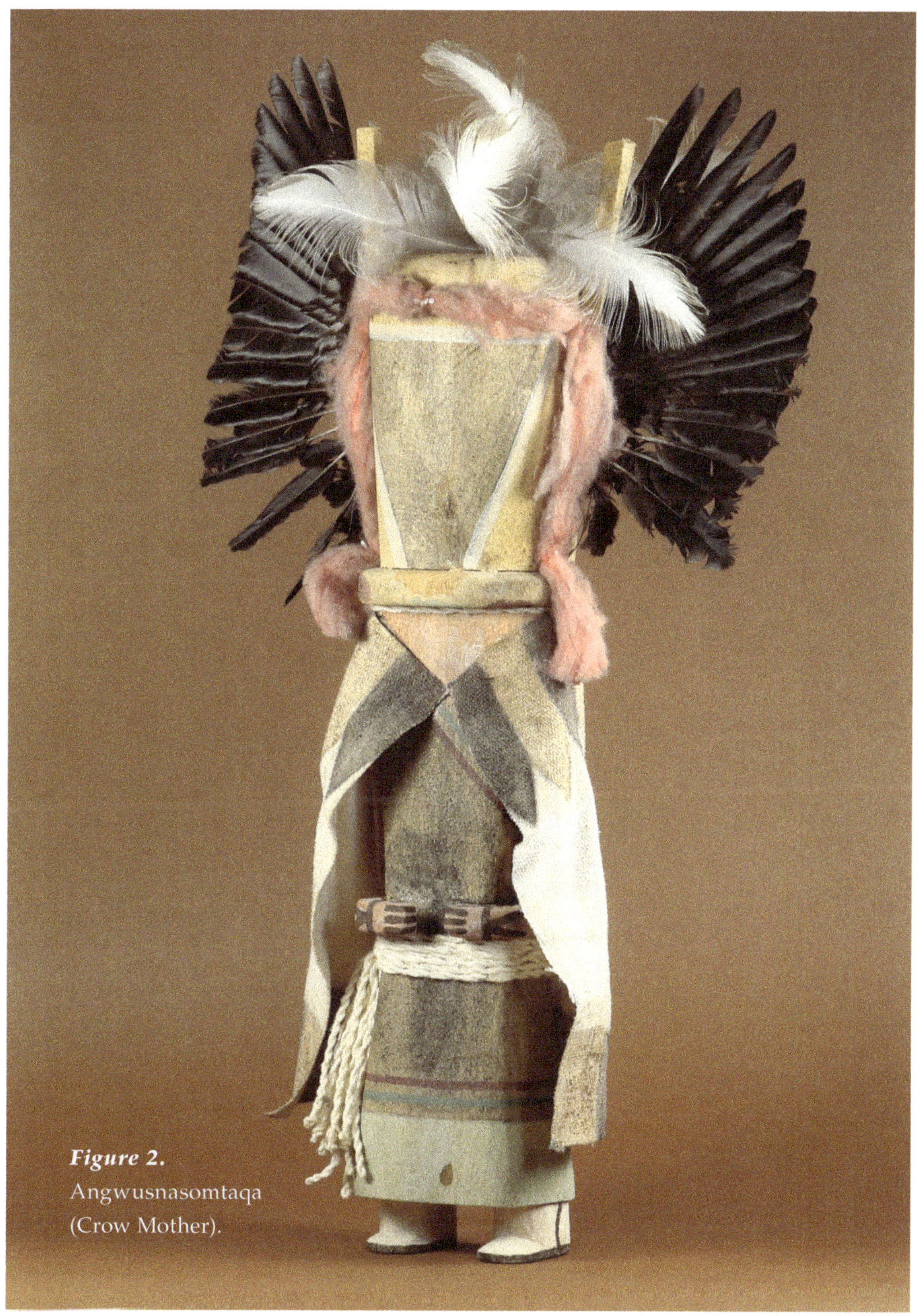

Figure 2.
Angwusnasomtaqa
(Crow Mother).

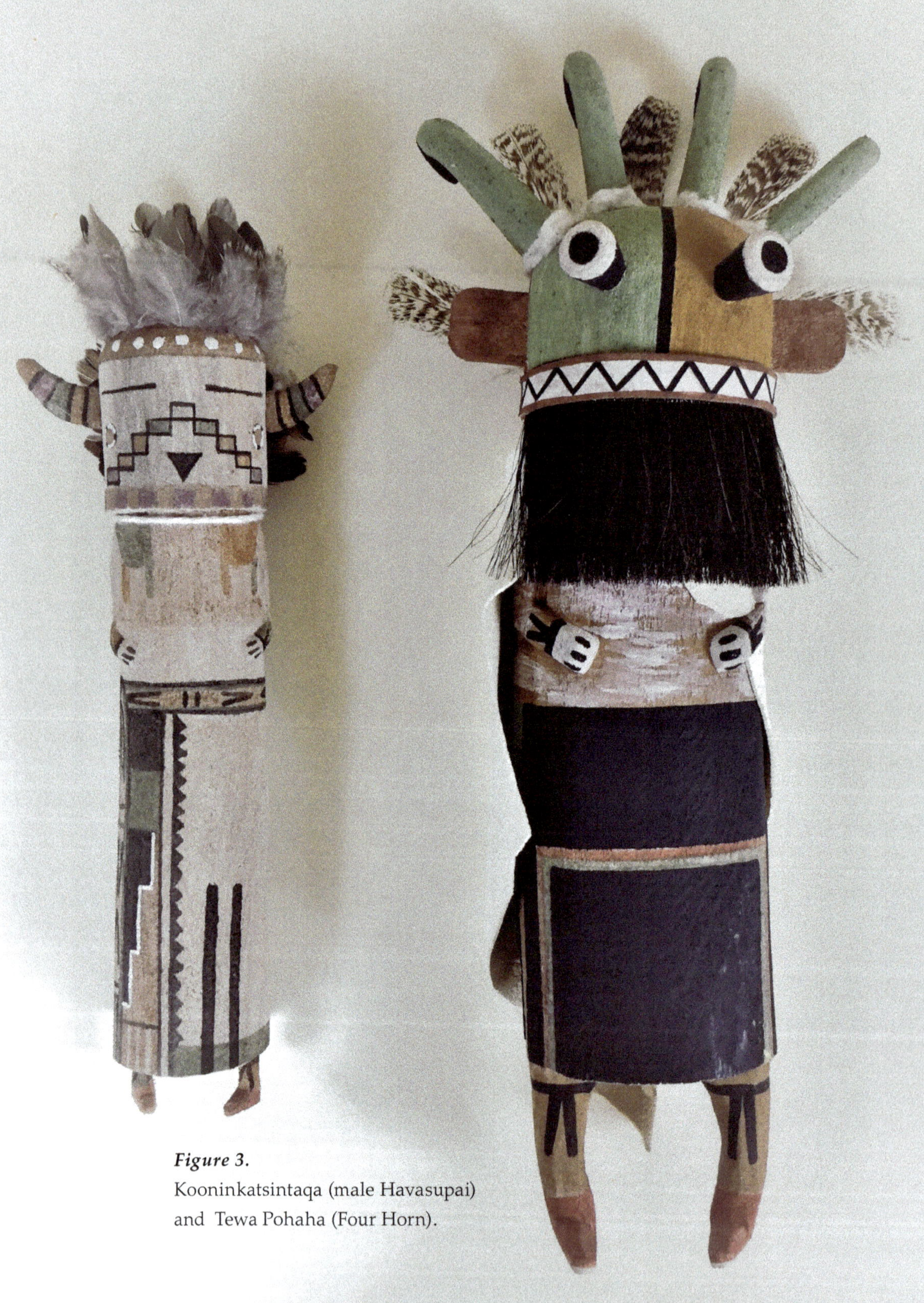

Figure 3.
Kooninkatsintaqa (male Havasupai) and Tewa Pohaha (Four Horn).

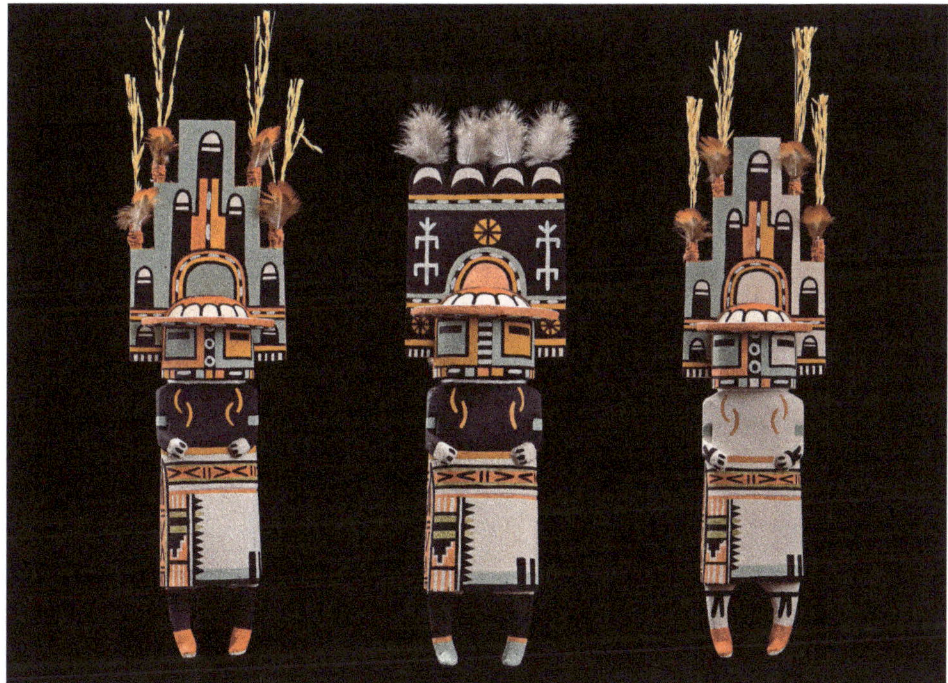

Figure 4. Hemiskatsina, Siohemiskatsina, Qötsahemiskatsina (White).

a Hopi woman and raise children on Hopiland. Fortunately, he met Jessica at an Apache social dance and they were married in 2012.

While Darance values being able to work at home and be with his children every day, he has traveled extensively. Darance has participated in shows at the Cabot Museum in California, the Eiteljorg in Indiana, and the Museum of the Native American in New York City. He has had solo shows with Santa Fe Crafts in California as well as at Buffalo Barry's Indian Art in Massachusetts, which is owned by the author of this book. Darance participates consistently at the winter and summer Santa Fe Indian Markets. He has traveled to Japan twice, once for a show in Tokyo and a second time as part of a delegation reviewing a collection of Hopi material at a museum in Osaka.

Darance is one of the most consistent, artistically pleasing, Traditional Style katsina carvers. As is required to be included in this volume, his work is instantly identifiable with no need to look for a signature (which in Darance's case is "a cloud symbol with rain in the middle"; it also looks like a D tilted on end with a dot in the center). His work is based in tradition, and his values are reflected in every carving. He is adept at dealing with others in part because he is such a centered and focused individual. Darance knows who he is and where he is going. Wouldn't we all like to be able to say the same?

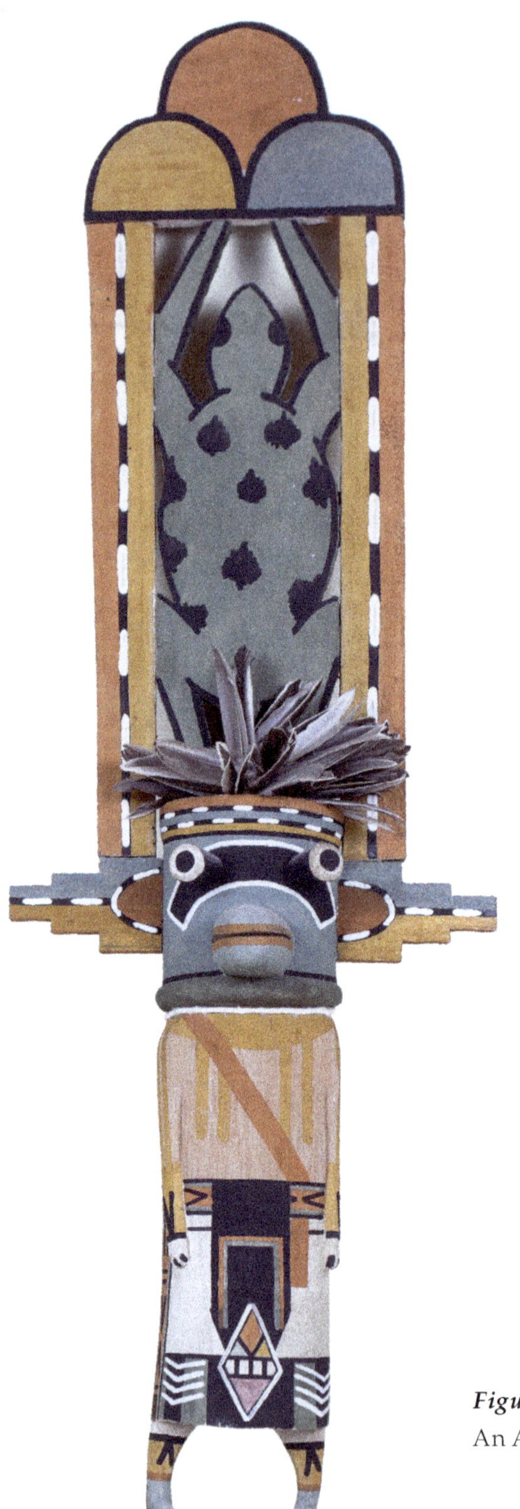

Figure 5.
An Ancient Figure.

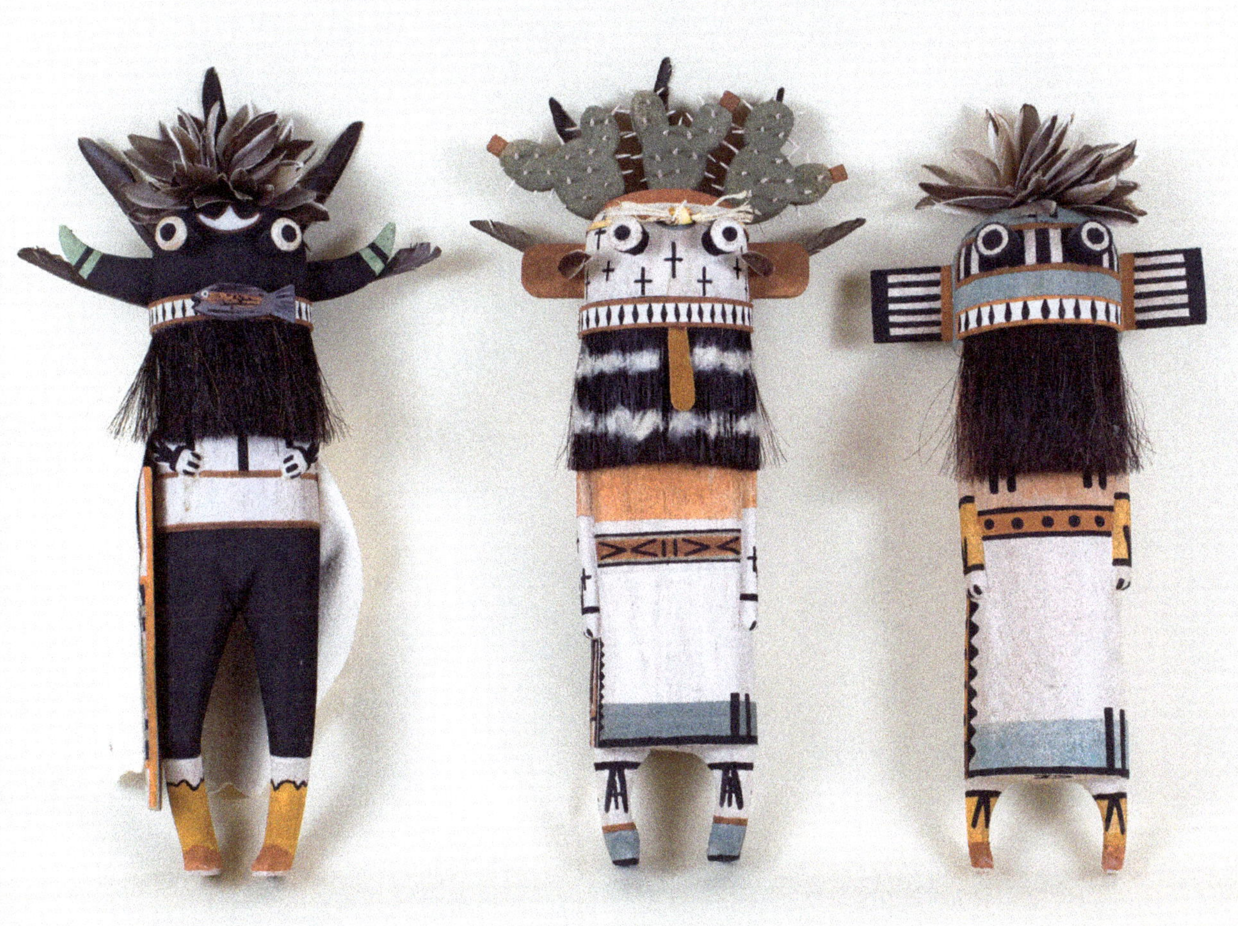

Figure 6. Pakiwkatsina (Fish), Yöngökatsina (Prickly Pear Cactus), and an interpretation of a Wilson Tawaquaptewa carving.

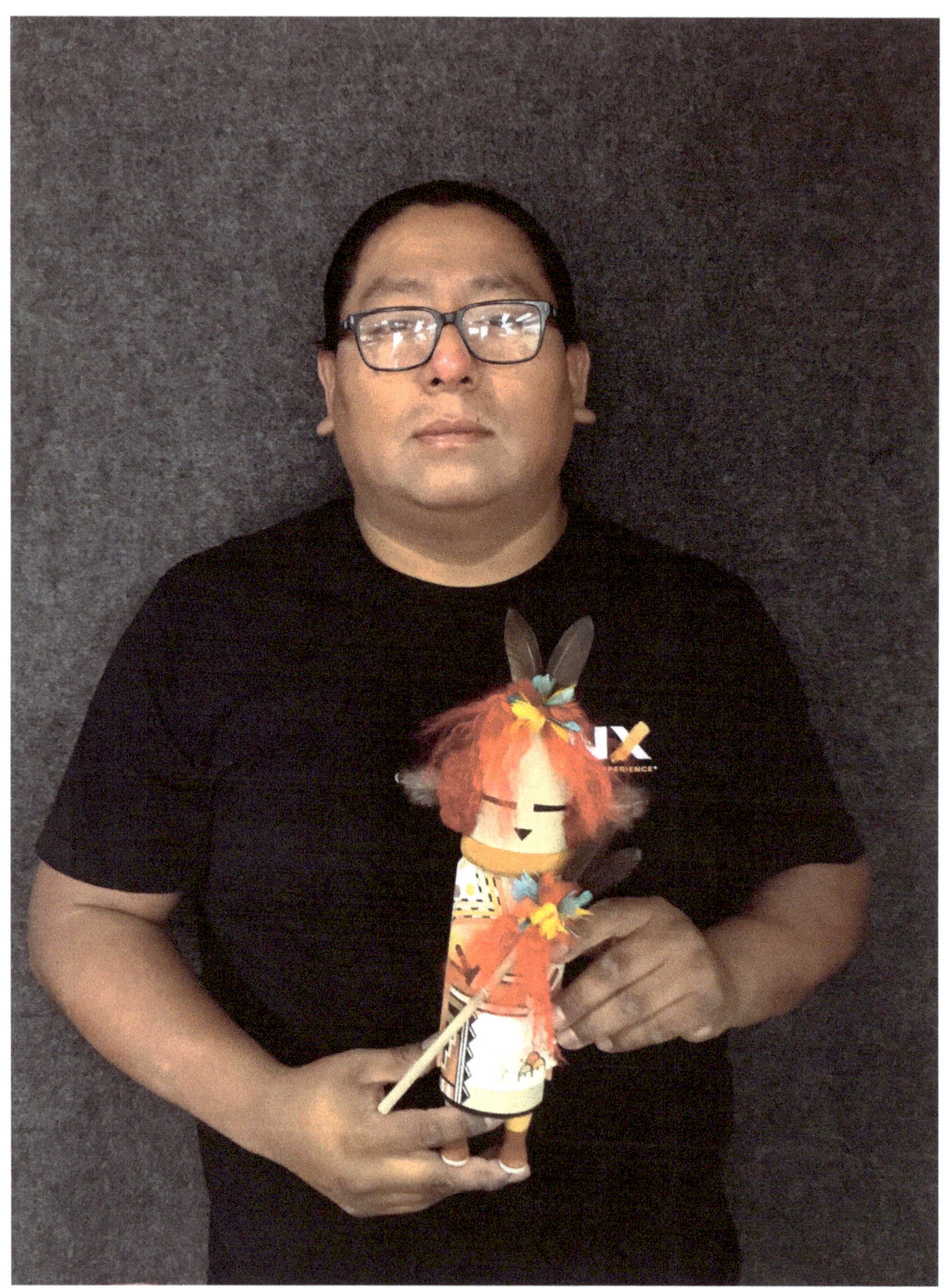

Figure 1. Ryan Gashweseoma.

RYAN GASHWESEOMA

Fine Boxes and Katsinam

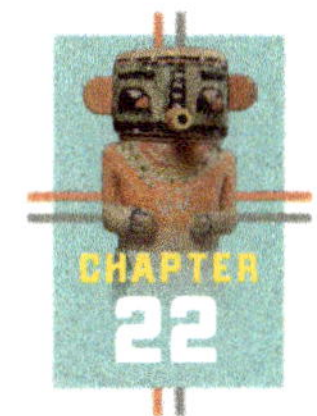

HAVING PURCHASED KATSINAM and wooden boxes from Ryan Gashweseoma (Figure 1) via Facebook and email over the years, I was glad to finally meet him face-to-face at his home in Flagstaff. He shares his home with his wife, Rainbow, and their three young children. Ryan's mother is Katsina Clan and his father is Spider Clan. Ryan grew up in Munqapi where he attended the day school. Later, he graduated from Tuba City High School.

Ryan dates his artistic development to his early schooling. As early as fourth-grade, teachers would tell him he had a special knack for art. In terms of katsina carving, Ryan said that his uncle, Christopher Wytewa, was a big influence, as was his grandfather, Benjamin Wytewa. He noted that his grandfather made katsinam in a style similar to Henry Shelton, who was married to Ryan's grandmother's sister. Henry Shelton is another carver featured in this book.

Ryan is adept at working with wood in myriad ways. He works as a builder in the Flagstaff area constructing houses from scratch. He started his business with a friend several years ago, and often has several houses under construction at the same time.

Ryan originally learned construction skills in Las Vegas where he moved in 2008 after high school. While there for three years, he took classes in woodworking and joined a carpentry union. To this day, these skills serve Ryan well as he supports his family with his home building and his art.

Ryan's skill with wood, combined with his long-recognized talent in art, has evolved in diverse ways. When Rainbow was pregnant with their first child, Ruby, Ryan made a dresser for his wife. This was so well received that Ryan started making fancy and finely constructed wooden boxes, as shown in Figure 2. The boxes were originally gifts for family members, but soon were being purchased by art collectors. Ryan believes he was the first artist to put katsina figures on the front of wooden boxes, as shown in Figure 2. Note the fineness of the presentation of the Hiilili katsina and the water serpents and cloud symbols on each side.

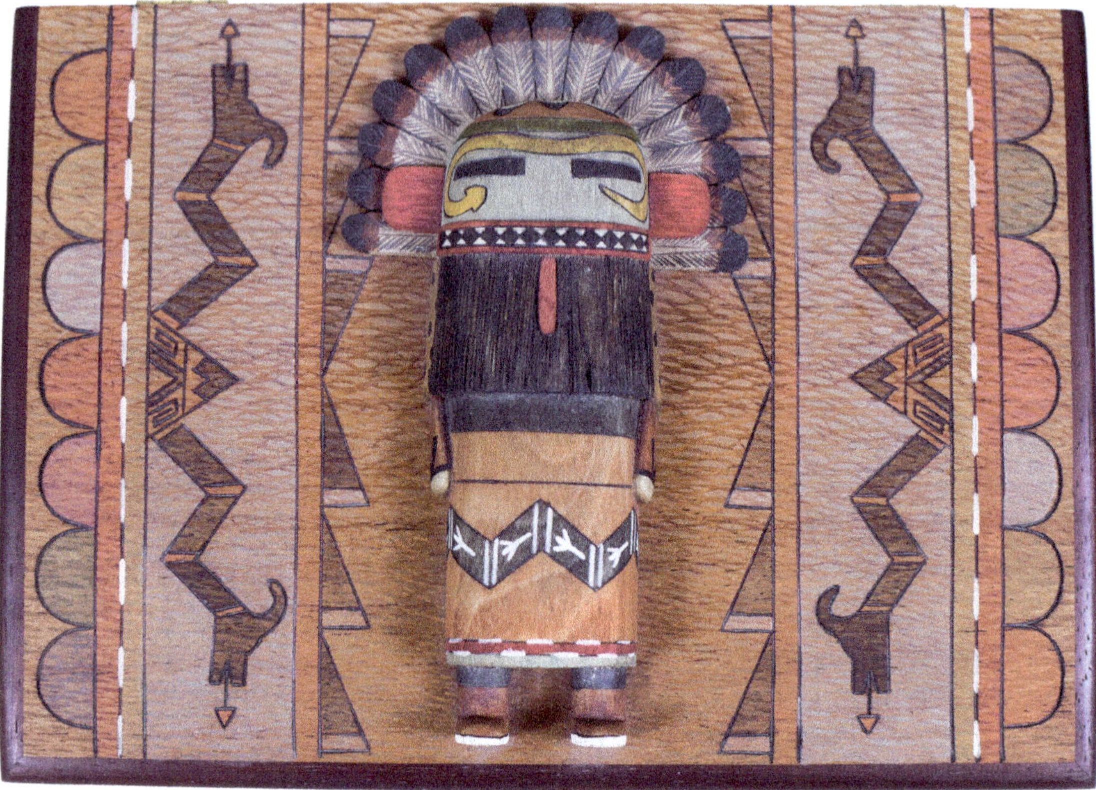

Figure 2. Wood box with Hiilili, water serpents, and cloud symbols.

I asked Ryan if he has always been such a fine and precise painter. He responded that acquiring this skill actually took a great amount of practice over three to four years. He showed me one of his first boxes (Figure 3), which, compared to Figure 2, demonstrates how far along his execution has come. Ryan uses exotic woods, such as paduk, lacewood, and purple heart, to create his boxes. Ryan has won many prizes for his boxes at various museums, including the Heard, Museum of Northern Arizona, the Autry, and the Eiteljorg. He has also had a booth at Santa Fe's annual Indian Market for several years where he sold out on a few occasions.

In terms of his involvement in art, Ryan says he currently spends about 60 percent of his time making katsinam and 40 percent creating boxes. He started making katsina carvings in 2010. One of the reasons I decided (with input from others) to include Ryan in this book of great carvers is his precise execution in terms of woodcarving and painting. Consider the set of the Hisot (Ancient) katsinam in Figure 4. When I bought this set from Ryan several years ago, he

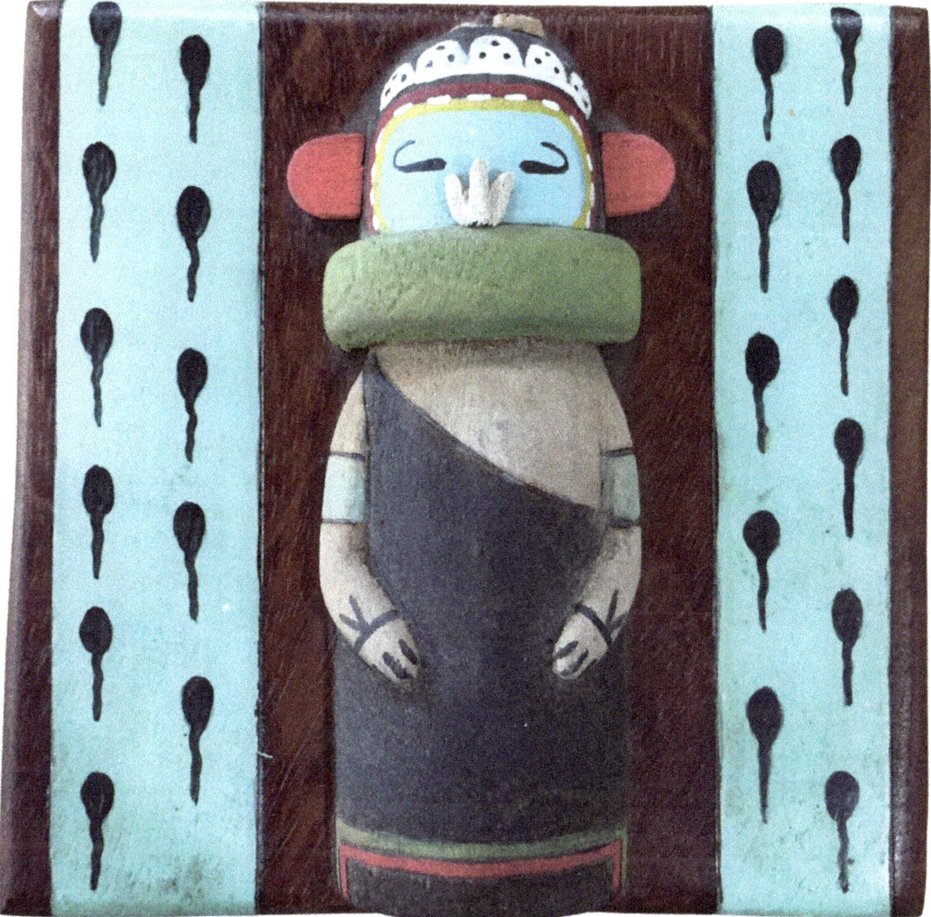

Figure 3. Korowista, one who brings seeds.

told me he created them from a Jo Mora photograph from 1904. He said his uncle identified for him that these were old, ancient, or Hisot katsinam, not seen anymore. That is to say these Katsinam have not appeared in any Hopi ceremonies for decades. Whether they will return or not is known only to the Spirit Beings.

Regarding the set of three, note the precise carving, meticulous painting, and creative body postures. Also remarkable are the elaborate feathers and headdresses. These pieces are unique and exceptional. Ryan told me he "is kind of OCD about featherwork." He added, "I will do and redo until I've mastered it." I would argue that this obsessive-compulsive perfectionism is true not just for the featherwork but for all aspects of his creations. Meticulous and passionate attention to detail is often a desirable trait in an artist.

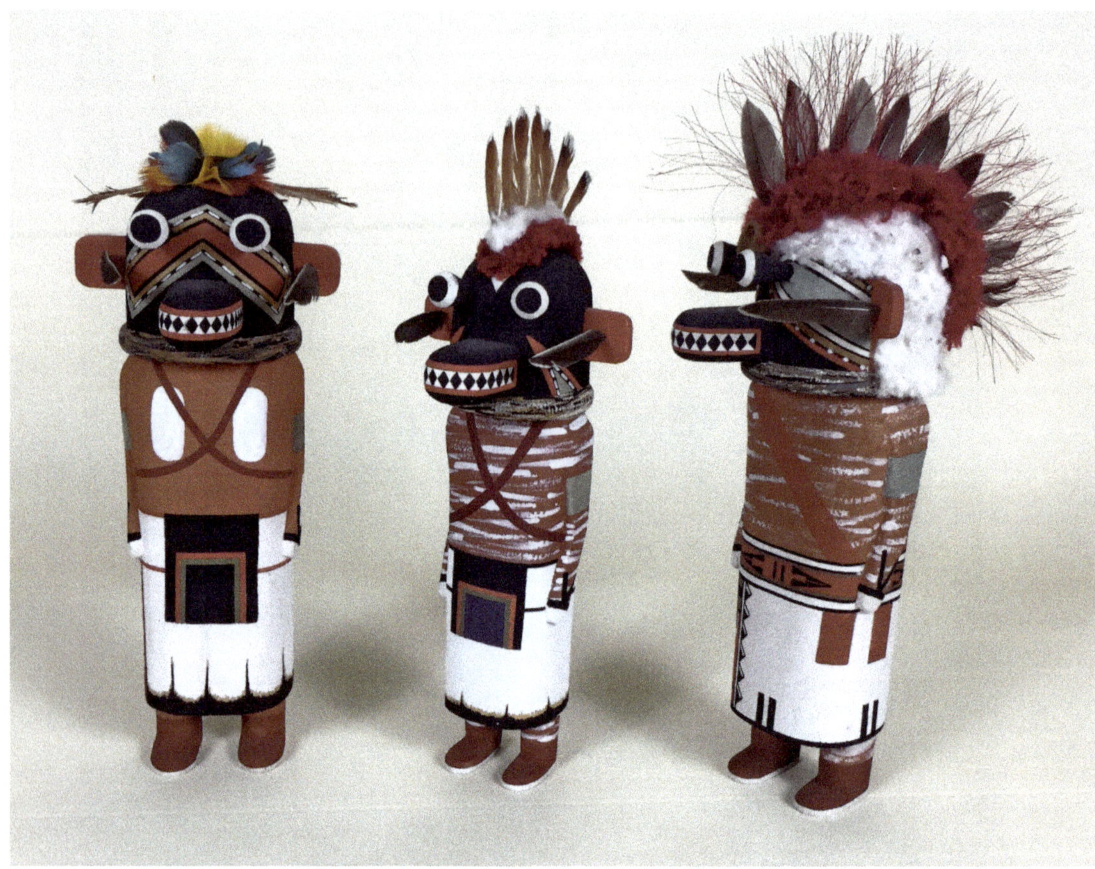

Figure 4. Set of Hisot (Ancient) katsinam.

Figure 5 shows two additional fine examples of Ryan's art. On the left is a Wupamokatsina, a significant personage and guard. On the right is Masawkatsina, the katsina version of the Maasaw deity. Once again, the execution is perfect, including the cornhusk frame on Wupamo's face and the featherwork on the back of his head. The same can be said for the paahos on the back of Masawkatsina's skull. Other fine examples are shown in Figures 6 and 7. Figure 6 is Ryan's interpretation of an Angwusnasomtaqa (Crow Mother) from the 1920s that is in the collection of the Heard Museum. The katsina in the Heard has an extremely unusual cloud design on the top of her head. Neither Ryan nor I had ever seen this feature on a Crow Mother before, so Ryan was inspired to create a new version. Figure 7 depicts another rare katsina, a Tiwenu, a figure said to have migrated from one of the Rio Grande pueblos.

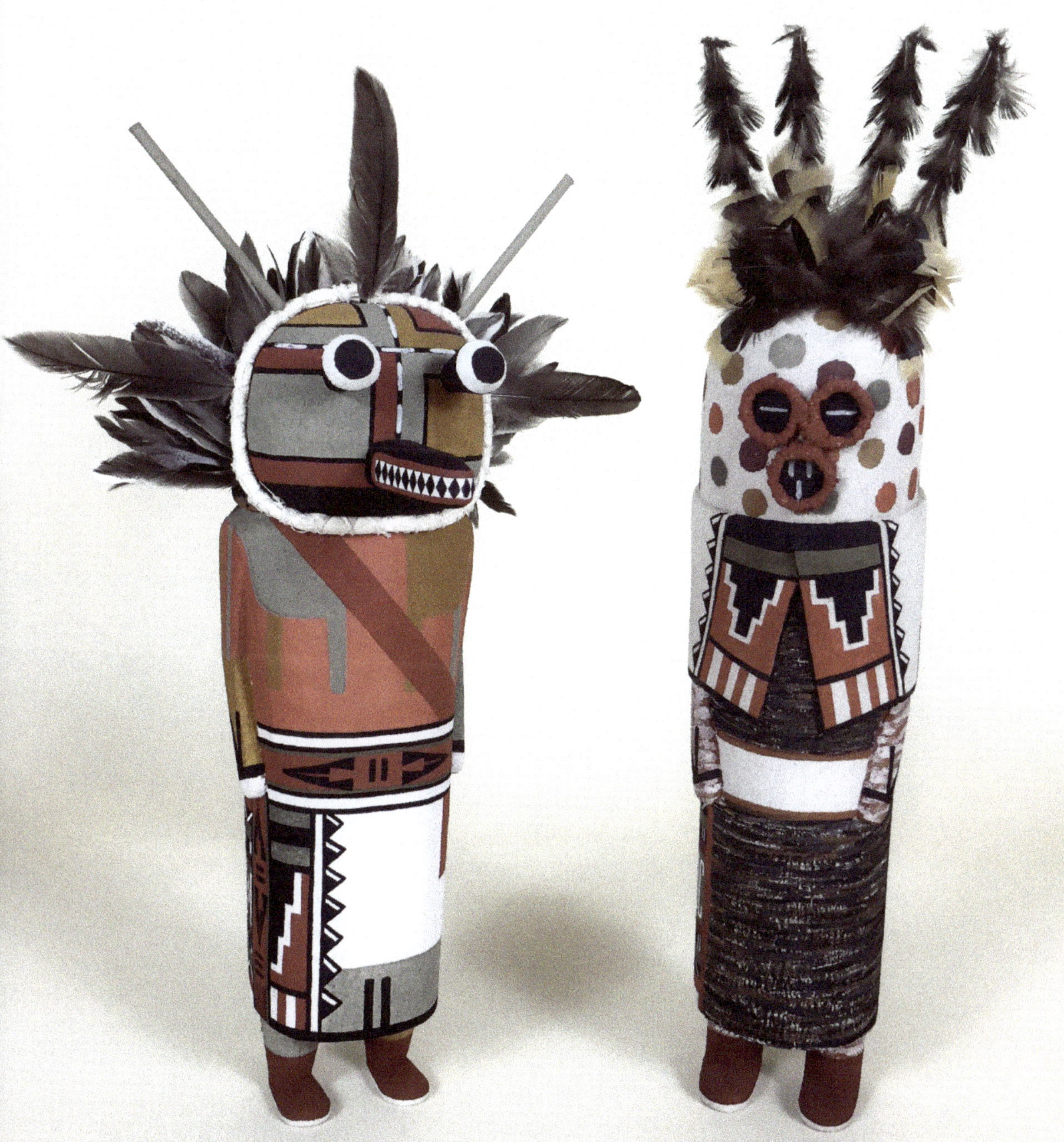

Figure 5. Wupamokatsina and Masawkatsina.

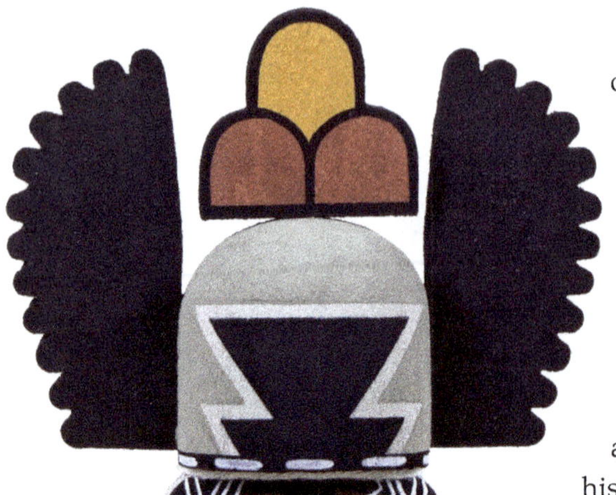

Figure 6.
Angwusnasomtaqa (Crow Mother).

I asked Ryan about artistic influences or other artists he admires. Somewhat surprisingly he cited his uncle, Michael Dean Jenkins, who is one of the most accomplished artists working in the Ultra-Realistic, Sculptural Style. Perhaps the connection between the two is precision rather than an artistic style. Ryan says he also appreciates the work of another uncle, Mark Taho, and admires the katsinam made by his brother, William Gashweseoma. He indicated that Clark Tenakhongva, who is a clan relative, is an inspiration. Lastly, he mentioned Ed Seechoma and Randy Brokeshoulder as carvers he appreciates.

Many katsina makers with whom I have visited have tiny carving huts, or work off to the side in a kitchen, porch, or bedroom. Ryan is very fortunate to have a large workshop that is detached from his home; the dimensions are about 20 by 30 feet. He has power tools for working on his boxes and a separate area for katsina making. This space allows him to work on about twenty to thirty boxes, and five katsinam at a time.

Ryan is a modern individual who frequently sells his work via Facebook and Instagram. Once he posts an item, it often sells within a day or two. He also receives a lot of special orders through social media. On a political note, Ryan has had success selling Kwikwilyaqa (Mocker) katsinam in the image of Donald Trump. The Mocker katsina is a figure who irritatingly imitates others to an absurd degree at Katsina ceremonies. Ryan has created caricatures of other political figures as well.

I know we all look forward to the next creative expressions from the diversely talented Ryan Gashweseoma.

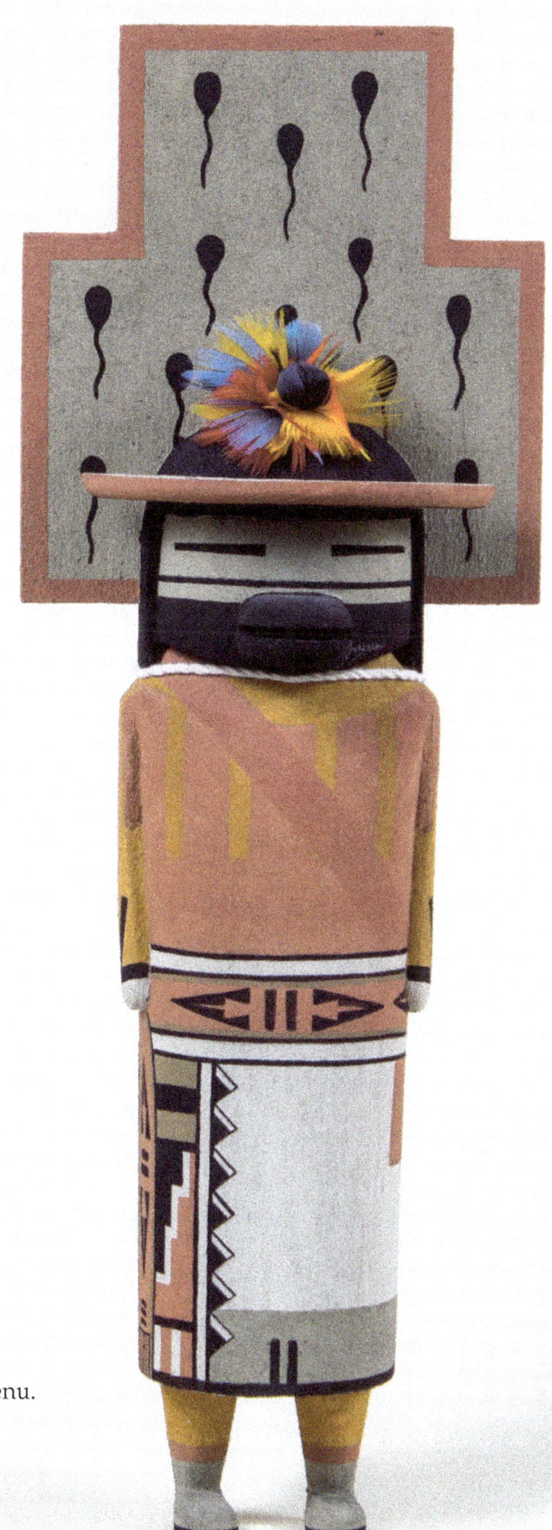

Figure 7. Tiwenu.

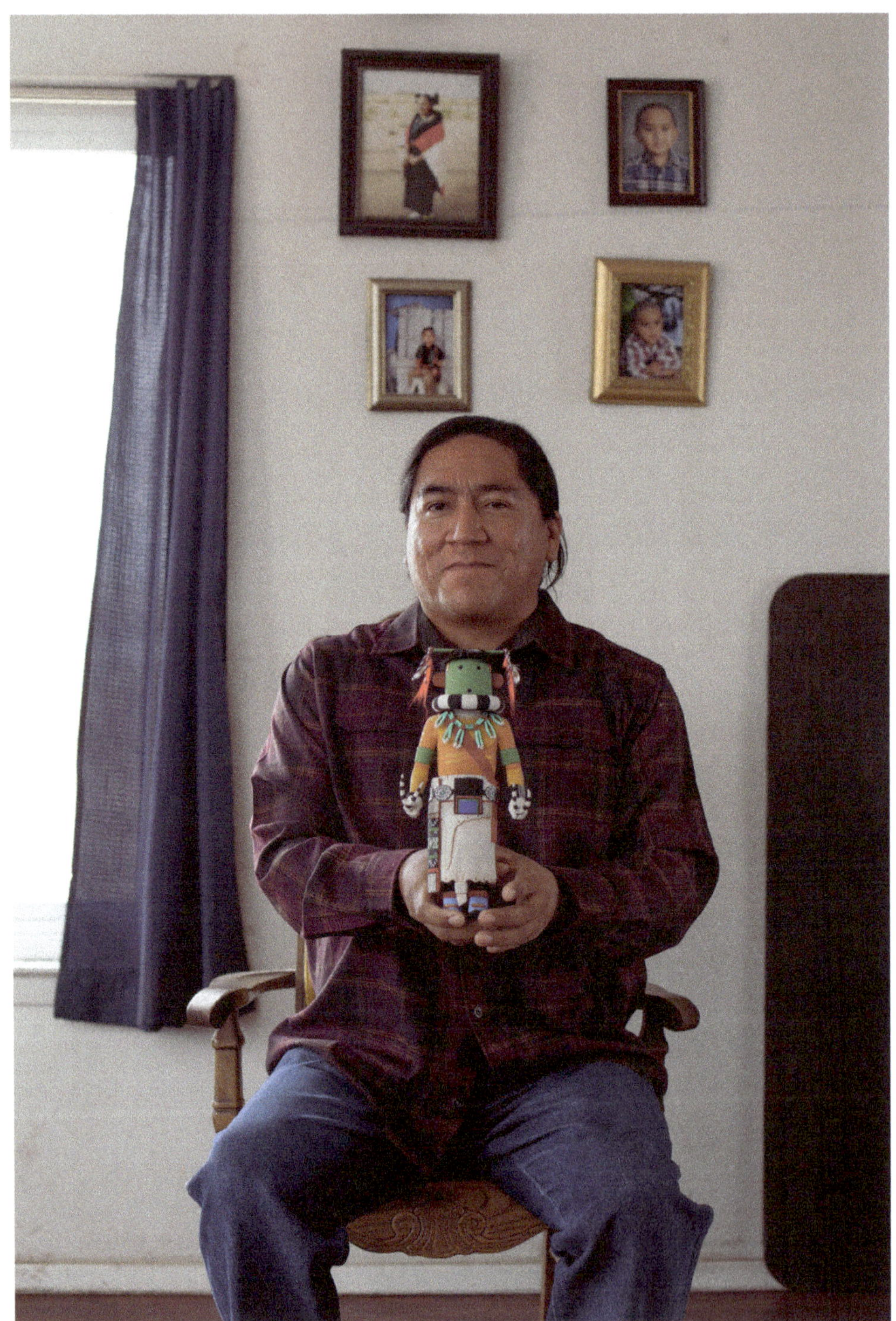

Figure 1. Ray Naha.

RAY NAHA
Humble Precision

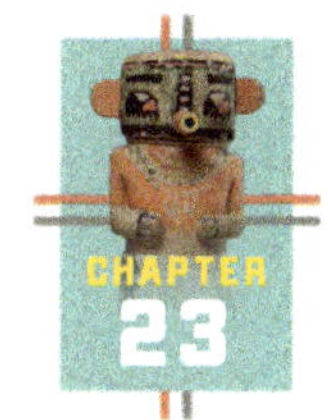

ARTIST RAY NAHA LIVES IN POLACCA, Arizona, near the base of First Mesa (see Figure 1). Ray was born in 1977. His mother, Emmaline is Roadrunner Clan. "Emma" Naha is a well-known potter; Ray's father, Benedict, is better known as Benny. Benny and his extended family are descendants of the renowned potter Nampeyo (1859–1942). Nampeyo was arguably the most important Hopi potter of all time. She used ancient Hopi pottery designs, reinterpreted them, and created an entirely new pottery tradition. Many of her descendants continue to be among the most influential of all Hopi potters (Kramer 1996).

Ray grew up in Sitsomovi (Sichomovi) and attended the Polacca Day School in his early years. Later he went to Hopi High School where he took a lot of art classes. He supplemented this education by attending art programs at Northern Arizona University, where he took classes in jewelry, photography, and painting. When asked how he became such a precise painter on his katsina carvings, he said this began back in high school when he made colored-pencil drawings. Also, his father and uncles sometimes paint in acrylics and he learned from them by observation. He said his biggest influence has been his father, Benny Naha.

Ray's namesake, renowned painter Ray Naha (1930–1976), was his grandfather. This patriarch is generally recognized to be one of the greatest Hopi painters of all time. Ray indicates that another major influence on his carvings is his uncle, Orm Nahee. For an example of Orm's work, see a carving of a Yowe (Priest Killer) katsina (and a soon-to-be-eliminated priest) on page 35 in Eric Bromberg's book, *The Hopi Approach to the Art of Kachina Doll Carving* (1986).

Ray originally started carving when he was in his early teens. He would make small sculptures using wood-burning tools, stain them with linseed oil, and sell them to tourists who were on the Waalpi (Walpi) tours. His carvings have come a long, long way since then!

Ray is one of the finest artists working in the Traditional Style. Let's start by reviewing Figure 2, one of the best carvings I've seen by Ray. The detail on the Palhikwmana (Water Drinking Maiden) is quite remarkable. Note the hand-sewn and hand-painted garment made of duck cloth. Also, note the miniature

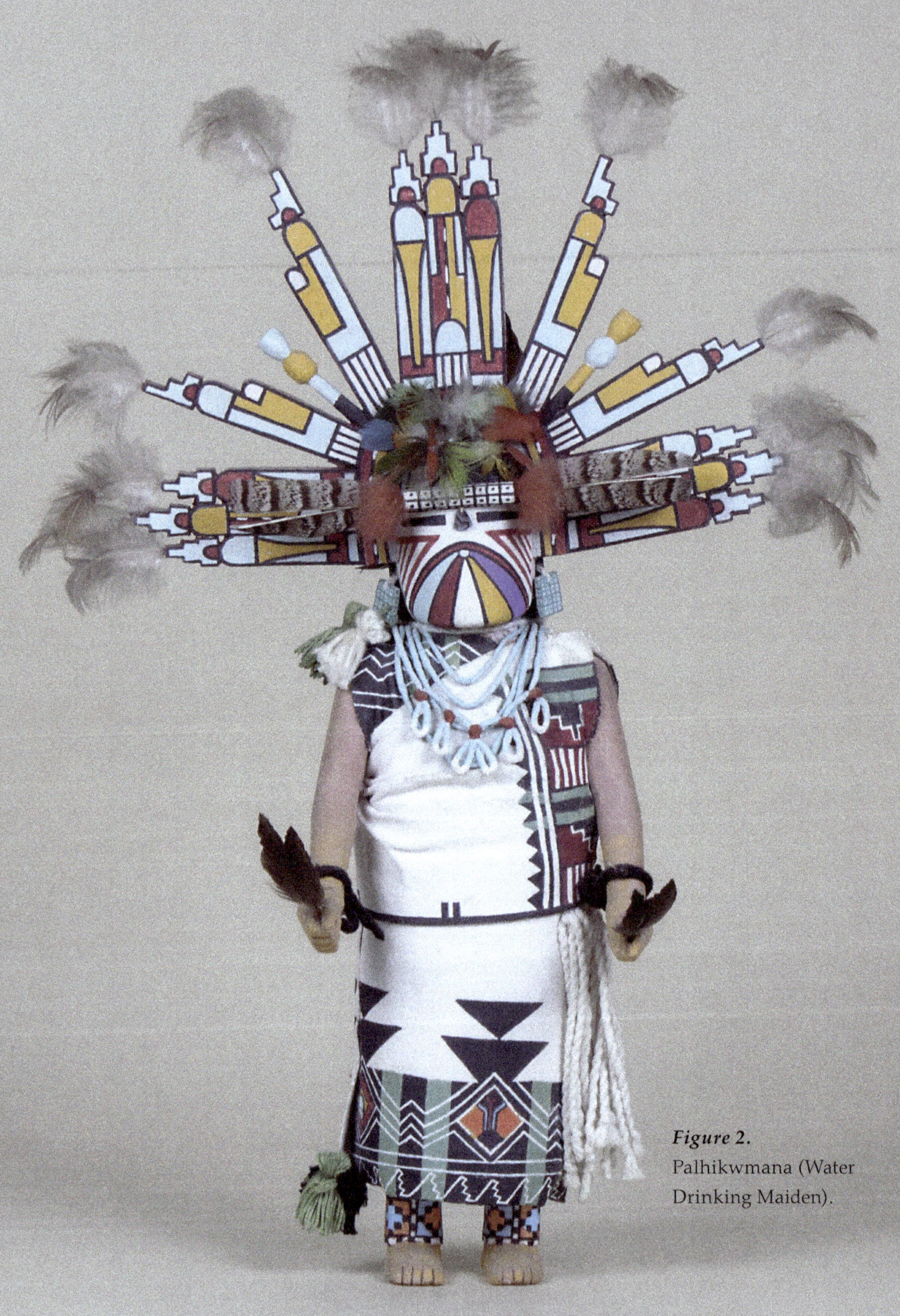

Figure 2.
Palhikwmana (Water Drinking Maiden).

rain sash and tassels attached to her dress. Another exceptional feature is the elaborate *kopatsoki* (tablita), so precisely made and painted, as is the miniature representation of the jacla necklace. This piece is clearly Traditional Style katsina making as an art. The dimensions are 10 by 17½ inches. Ray said these elaborate pieces can take anywhere from one to four weeks to complete.

Ray was influenced by carvers Jimmie Kewanwytewa, William Quotskuyva, Henry Shelton, and Ernie Moore as he moved into carving with so much attention to detail. All four of these makers are featured in this book. Clearly, Ray's work was impacted by some of the finest carvers in history. Yet, he has been able to develop a style all his own. Consistent with one of the criteria to be included in this book, Ray's work is immediately identifiable. No need to look for a signature or tag for identification. A distinctive feature of Ray's work is that he adds the details and accoutrements characteristic of Henry Shelton or William Quotskuyva, but he does *not* incorporate movement into their body postures. His carvings are not in the Late Action or Ultra-Realistic Style. Rather, his katsinam are made from straight wood, and do not depict bodily movement, which is consistent with the majority of works in the Traditional Style.

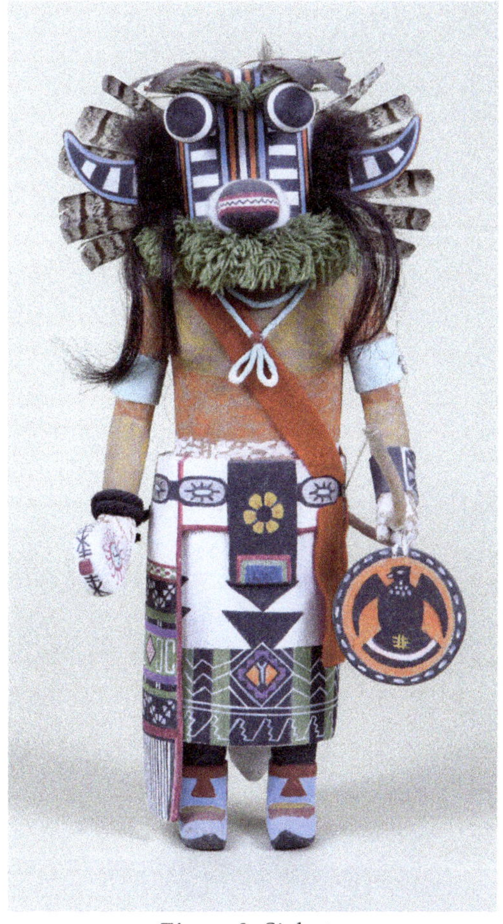

Figure 3. Siohote.

Another fine example is shown in Figure 3. This is the infrequently seen Siohote katsina (Zuni Hoot'e). Once again the carving features extremely fine painting technique and ample accoutrements. The latter includes a hand-carved and painted eagle *yungyapu* or wicker plaque, a strung-bow, and a removable rattle. The figure also bears real leather armbands, a red felt sash, and a jacla necklace. The elaborate painting on the kilt, ketoh, and concho belt is truly exceptional. Ray spares no attention to detail in his work.

Consider the Mosayrukatsina (Bison) katsina in Figure 4. On this katsina the fine details include a removable rattle, a miniature necklace strung with real heishi (shell) and turquoise, and a lightning stick, which moves in the figure's hand. The katsina's head is crowned with black rabbit fur, which approximates the bison fur on the actual Katsinam.

Ray sometimes creates paintings when he needs a break from carving. An example is an acrylic painting of a Palhikwmana shown in Figure 5. Ray's meticulous style is just as effective in this medium as on three-dimensional katsinam. Note the beautiful rendering of the face and the kopatsoki (tablita). By the way, the person in this painting is Ray's niece, Leigh, who is his brother Shannon's daughter. Ray is one of three brothers: Marty is the oldest, then Shannon, with Ray being the youngest. All live in Polacca and are katsina carvers, although Ray is the most prolific.

A marked contrast in style is shown in Figure 6. Ray made this simple carving of a Kwasaytaqa ("one with a dress") for village use rather than the marketplace. The precision of the painting is still there, but the details and accoutrements are not.

Ray noted that about ten to fifteen years ago he began selling to Tsakurshovi, and also sells to collectors in New Mexico. However, during the growing season he is very busy taking care of his fields, in which he grows corn, beans, and melons in the traditional Hopi way.

Overall, Ray comes across as living a very traditional Hopi lifestyle. He presents as a somewhat reserved and humble man. I'm not sure he fully realizes how talented he is. He clearly prefers to focus on his carving, painting, village responsibilities, and fields; that's about it. This approach to life certainly seems to be working for him. Streamlining might benefit all of us.

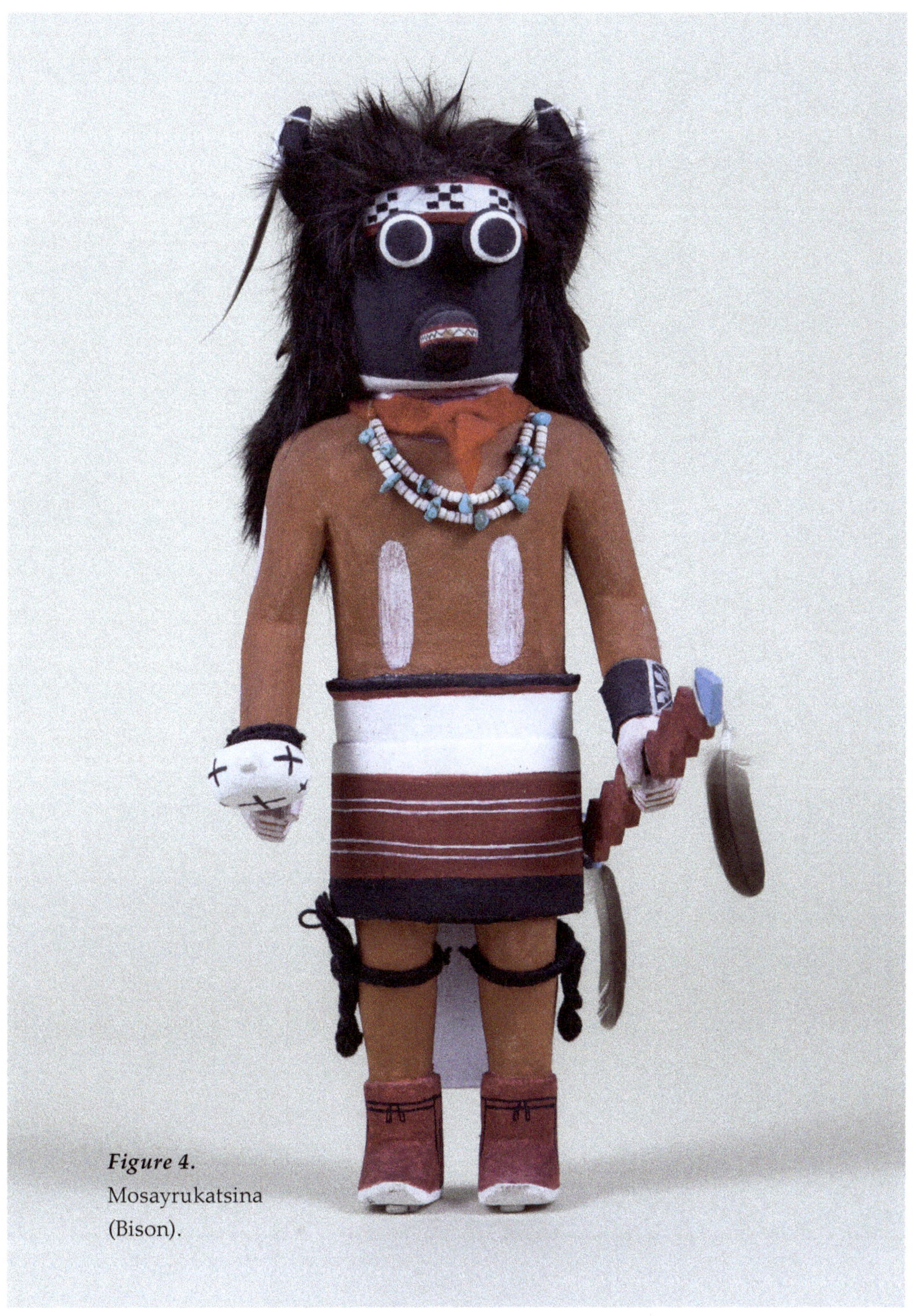

Figure 4. Mosayrukatsina (Bison).

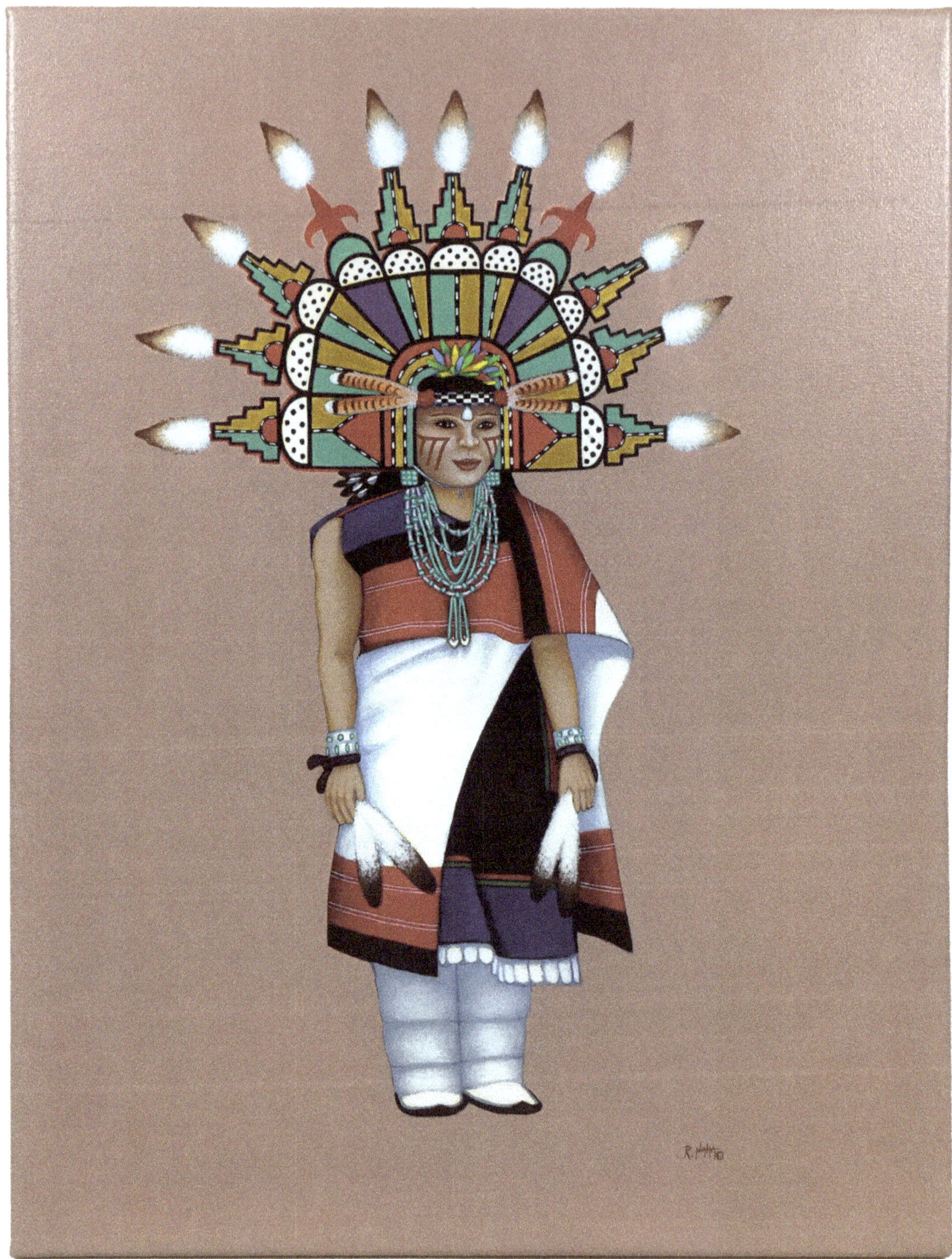

Figure 5. Acrylic painting of a Palhikwmana (Water Drinking Maiden).

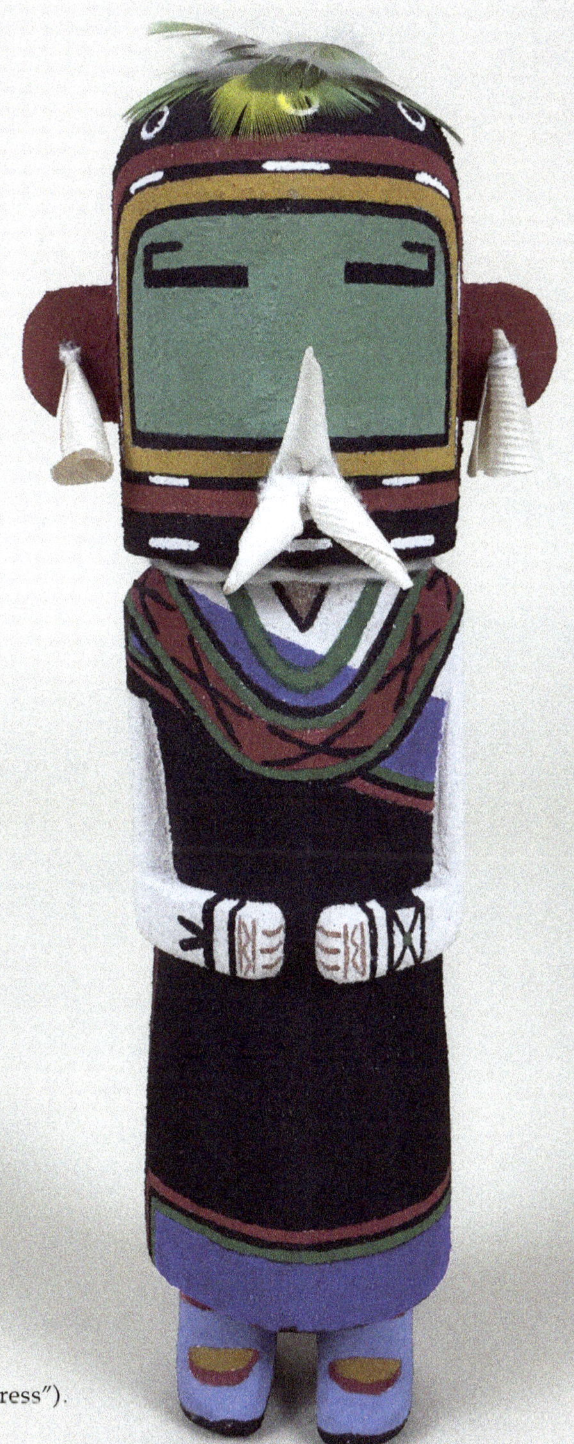

Figure 6.
Kwasaytaqa
("One with a dress").

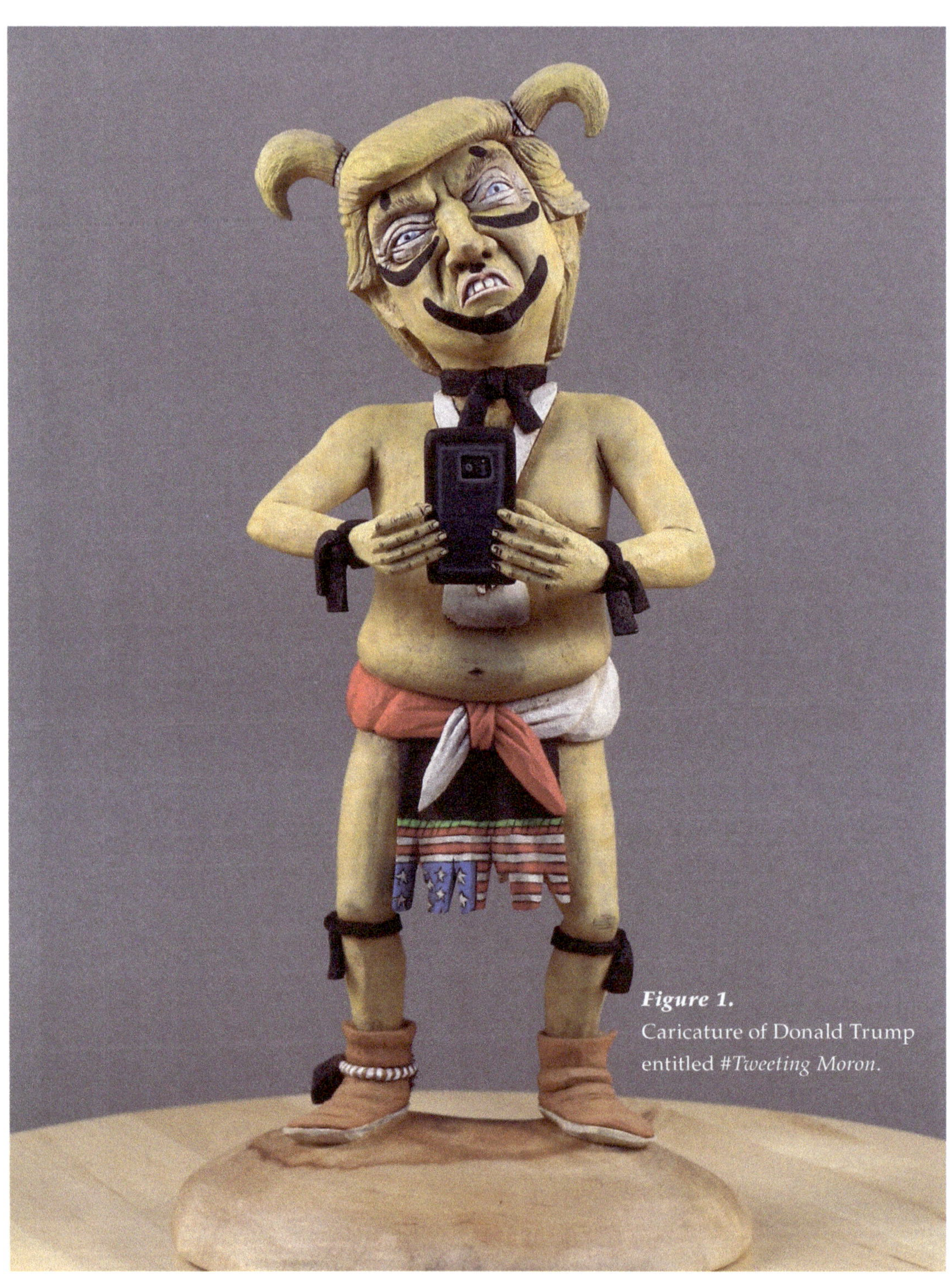

Figure 1.
Caricature of Donald Trump entitled #*Tweeting Moron*.

ROBERT STEPHEN ALBERT

Koyaalas to the Rescue

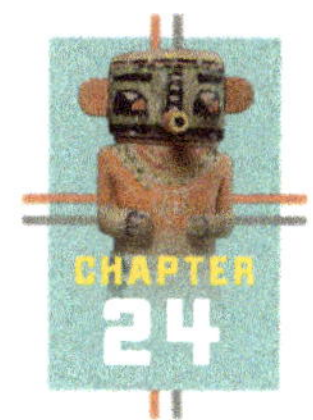

ROBERT STEPHEN ALBERT is named after three grandfathers: Robert Sakiestewa, "Sakhongva"; Stephen Albert Sr., "Hole-cioma, also known as Holatsi"; and Albert Dawavendewa, "Havima."

He is a friendly, approachable man who jokingly refers to himself as, "the greatest katsina carver you've never heard of" (Figure 2). He has a point; I've been dealing in katsinam since the late 1980s and was unaware of his work. Moreover, he was not included in the three main books that featured those who carve in the Ultra-Realistic and Sculptural Styles, Theda Bassman's *Hopi Kachina Dolls and Their Carvers* (1991), and *Treasures of the Hopi* (1997), and Helga Teiwes's *Kachina Dolls* (1991). There is only one example by Robert in the more recent book, *Hopituy* (Ahtone 2013). However, when I saw his work, I was immediately impressed and recognized that he met the criteria for being included in this book: distinctiveness, creativity, and high quality within a particular style of katsinam.

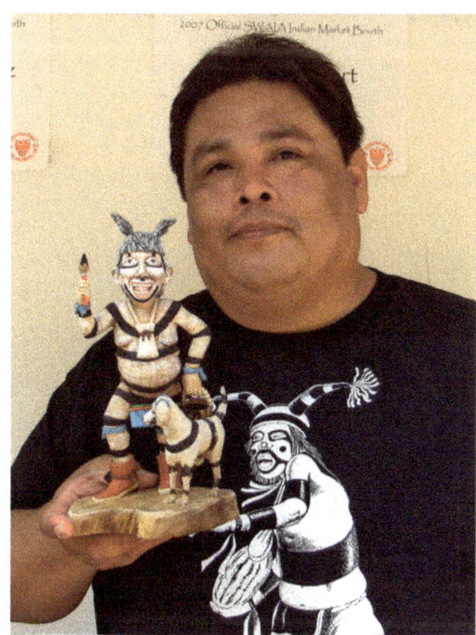

Figure 2. Robert Stephen Albert.

Robert was born in 1964 into his mother's Snake Clan (Velma Sakiestewa, "Talas Wunka") and his father's Sun Clan (Stephen Albert Jr., "Woung Viya"). Robert's Hopi name is "Sakbipmewnewa," which means, "freshly cut or green tobacco laid out straight to dry." His father held jobs away from the Hopi reservation for much of Robert's childhood. As a result, Robert was born in Ganado and spent his first few years in Chinle. For a brief time, the family lived in Munqapi, before his father took a job in Phoenix, where Robert spent the rest of his childhood from the age of three through high school. Robert's dad had good paying jobs working as an engineer and a surveyor for building roads. Robert attended public schools in Phoenix as opposed to the Phoenix Indian School.

Robert was consistently drawn to art from about age four to five. He said he was "always sketching, drawing, and making cartoons." However, he added that he never took art seriously or considered himself an artist until he graduated from high school. He identified a seminal moment in his life: as he was about to graduate, he met with a school counselor for career advice. The counselor recommended working in air conditioning (as Phoenix is very hot) or construction. However, later on, Robert's Native American school counselor, Patricia Helton (Lakota), took a different approach. She asked him, "What do you like to do? What makes you happy?" Robert replied, "Art." So she recommended he apply to the Institute of American Indian Arts (IAIA) in Santa Fe. He followed her wise advice, applied, was accepted, and enrolled in 1983. He graduated in 1986 with a degree in "two-dimensional art."

At the IAIA, Robert experienced a revelation. He had his first exposure to other Natives and their cultures. His eyes were opened to a broad world of Indian art he didn't know existed. His idols became Fred Kabotie, Pablita Velarde, Helen Hardin, and Ray Naha. While at the school, he learned to paint in diverse media and also found himself drawn to return to katsina carvings.

Robert was initiated at age nine and became involved in his kiva in Munqapi (Moenkopi) by age twelve. He frequently spent school and summer vacations on the reservation immersed in Hopi culture. He credits his uncle, Orville Talayumptewa, for giving him his start as a carver. Robert said early on he was not comfortable making katsinam. Instead, he made bows and arrows, rattles, and some flat dolls. However, he would also carefully watch his uncle making full-figured katsinam when Orville was between jobs. One day his uncle threw him a piece of cottonwood root and said, "try it." Robert said his father was also a big influence as he was very artistic.

Shortly after graduating from IAIA, Robert returned to school at the National Education Center where he obtained an associate's degree in commercial art. He thought at the time he needed a backup profession in case his goal of becoming a self-supporting artist didn't work out. He learned useful things at this school, including "how to sell, present myself, and my product." Robert has used these skills ever since in achieving his goal of being a full-time katsina artist.

Robert dates his career as a professional katsina carver to 1990. At that time, he was living in Tucson where he would sell his dolls initially to Silver Bell Trading, and later to Kaibab Shop, Medicine Man Gallery, Bahti Indian Arts, and Grey Dog Trading. Back then he sold rather simple carvings for about $200–$300. He describes this period as one of "just surviving" financially.

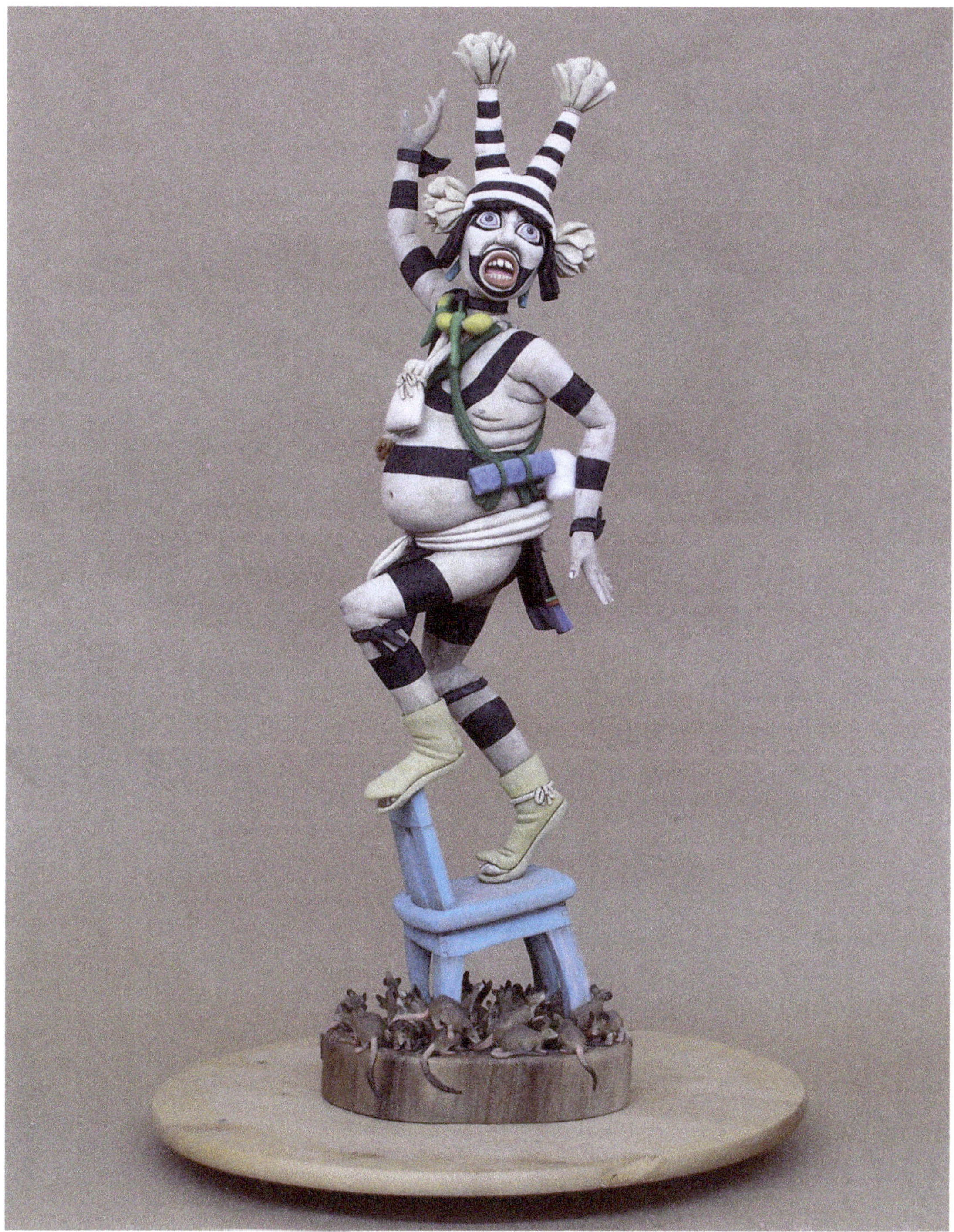

***Figure* 3.** *Hantavirus on the Rampage.*

He said in 1997 he "really turned the corner." He was admitted to Santa Fe's Indian Market and that same year began to win prizes for his work. Over time these prizes have come from not only the Santa Fe Indian Market but also the IAIA, Pueblo Grande Museum, the Museum of Northern Arizona, Gallup Inter-Tribal Indian Ceremonial, and the Heard Museum. He noted he was disappointed he didn't win "Best of Show" in Santa Fe in 2017, but that he aspires to win that award eventually.

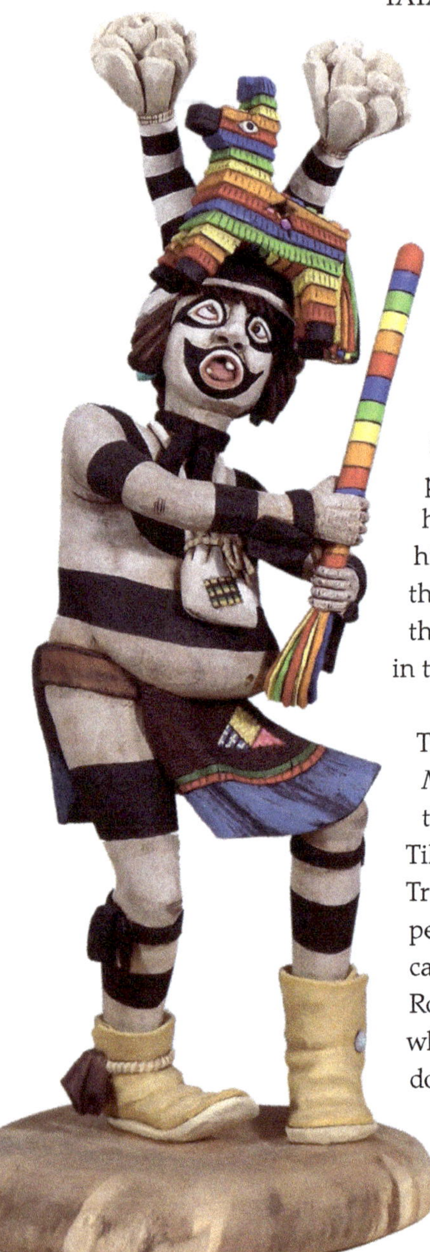

Figure 4. *Candy Crush.*

Asked about his early artistic influences, he cited Alvin James Makya, Neil David, Arthur Holmes, Sr., and Cecil Calnimptewa. Robert elaborated that there are many great carvers (in the Ultra-Realistic and Sculptural Styles) today. He noted that he is in awe of the way some katsina artists can portray musculature and the strands of every hair. Robert believes that his distinctive talent is his ability to capture facial expressions in wood that others cannot. Some prominent examples of this remarkable ability are shown in the figures in this chapter.

Let's start with his caricature of Donald Trump tweeting in the carving entitled *#Tweeting Moron* (Figure 1). Robert said he came to this title after a story on the news about Rex Tillerson, former U.S. Secretary of State, calling Trump a "moron." Regardless of one's political persuasion, this example is an astonishing carving in terms of executing facial expression. Robert noted that he usually makes black and white Koshare or Koyaala clowns, but chose to do a Hopi Sikyatsuku (Yellow Ritual Clown) to match Trump's hair color. This carving is a hilarious achievement; it's not easy to exaggerate Trump's facial expressions!

Other examples in his Koyaala-mode are shown in Figures 3 and 4. Figure 3 shows a carving that is both terrifying-yet-humorous. Robert titled it, *Hantavirus on the Rampage,* referring to a serious rodent-born epidemic that swept the reservation several years ago. Note the panicked facial expression on the clown and the sickening swarm of deer mice below. Such a nightmare image, yet comic! Robert's incredible attention to detail is very evident in this carving, including the worn paint on the blue chair, the clown's feet protruding through the toes of his shoes, the piki bread in a holster, portly body, mice, and most of all the facial expressions and teeth. This is truly masterful work.

Another example of his exceptional skill is shown in Figure 4. Once again, his achievement is not only seen in the carving execution but also his choice of topic. Here we have a Koyaala or Koshare so confused and discombobulated that he is trying to destroy a piñata positioned on his own head. This carving is titled *Candy Crush.* Note the comic details of the Koyaala's crossed eyes and missing teeth. This is great humor captured in cottonwood root. It takes a creative, zany mind to come up with such a theme.

Speaking of creativity, Robert indicated that at times having such a mind can be a curse. A few years ago, he found himself so obsessed with thinking about his katsina carvings that he couldn't "put them down." He was so focused on carving and executing them perfectly that "it was driving me insane." He explained that a turning point emerged when he began carving clowns as shown in Figures 2–4. He said that when he began making Koyaalas, "all the pressures went away," as they provided "an avenue not to be so restricted," and that "I found greater freedom." There is no doubt there is a free-flowing artistic mastery, humor, pathos, and satire in these carvings. Another example is shown in Figure 5, a depiction of five cavorting Kooyemsis (Mudheads) titled *Sliding Kooyemsi.* He has captured such motion and dynamism in this work that one must remind oneself it is made of cottonwood root. Robert's work is certainly among the most impressive and inspired of all those working in the Sculptural Style.

Another exceptional piece is shown in Figure 6, *Honey Bandits.* This amazingly detailed sculpture shows four terrified Koyaalas, who are in the midst of trying to steal honey, only to be interrupted by the "rightful owners," a pair of large bears. Note the astonishing level of detail not only on the clowns but also on the bears, pots, katsinam, and rope at the base of the carving. This is a very complex sculpture with many components that are well balanced and integrated into a cohesive whole. Very few carvers alive could attempt such a work.

Not surprisingly—given such carving skill—Robert has found consistent success in the Indian art market. These days he mostly sells to private customers and fulfills special orders. He noted that his smaller, ten to twelve-inch carvings sell in the $2,500–$4,000 range and that his elaborate, large multi-figure

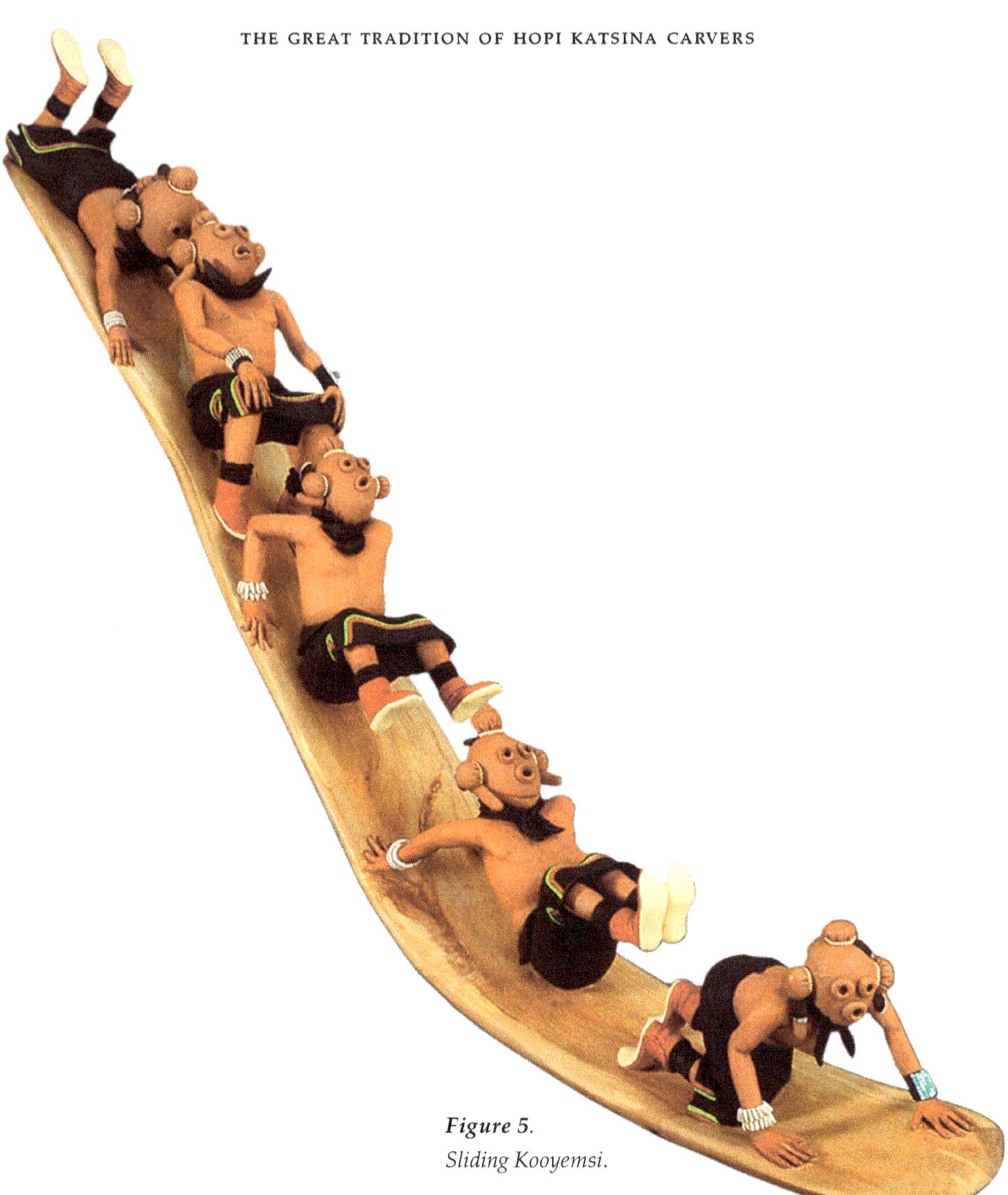

Figure 5.
Sliding Kooyemsi.

carvings, such as shown in Figure 6, range in price from $10,000 to $25,000.

Robert Albert has lived in Gallup since 2004. He has been married since 2001 to a Navajo physician, Adriann Begay, and has fulfilled his dream of becoming a successful, full-time artist. He is one of the leaders and most accomplished artists working in the Sculptural Style. The Indian art world can express appreciation to that Lakota school counselor who provided such sage advice all those years ago. "What makes you happy?" she asked, and Robert has been pursuing art ever since with ever-expanding talent and inspiration.

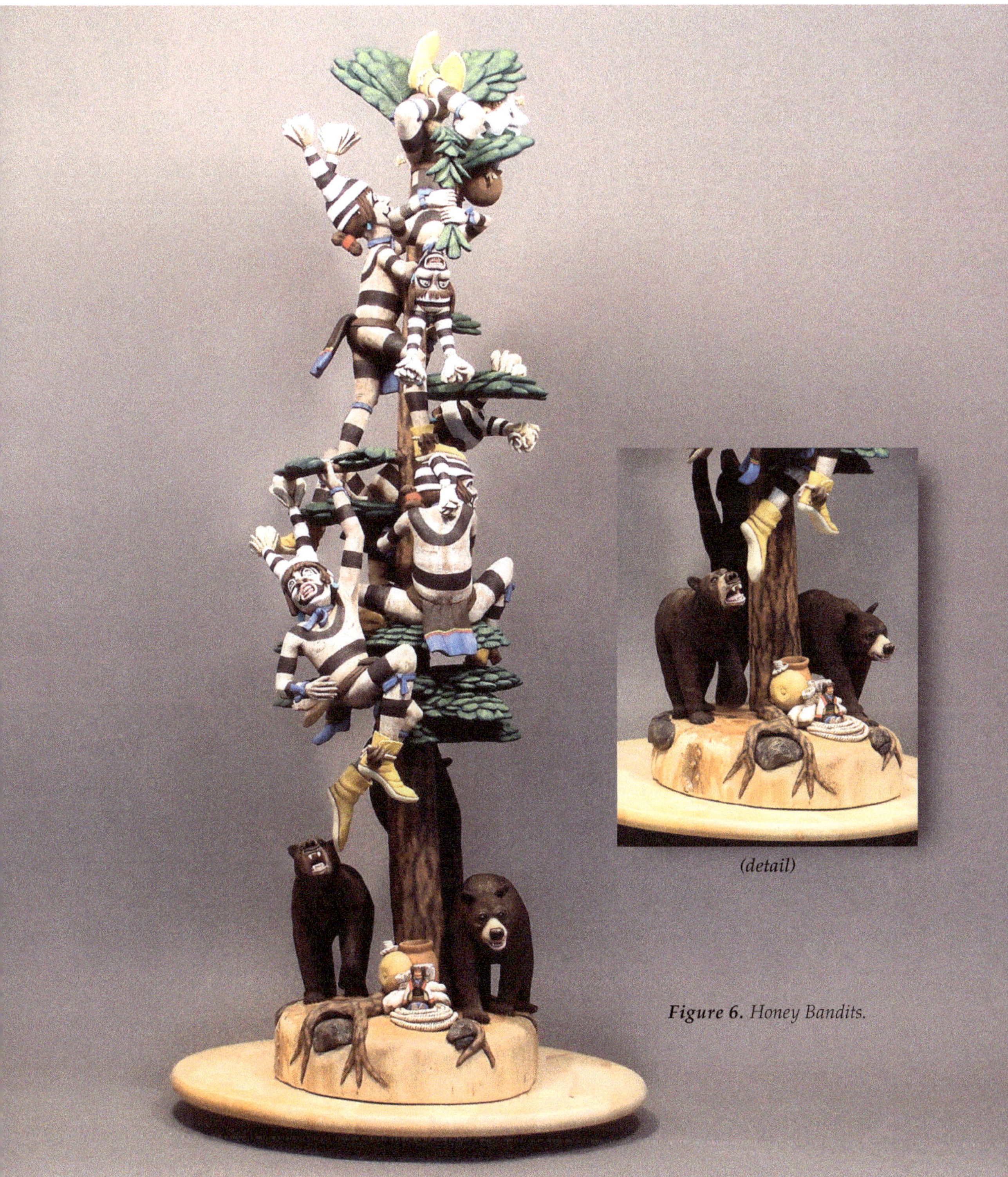

(detail)

Figure 6. *Honey Bandits.*

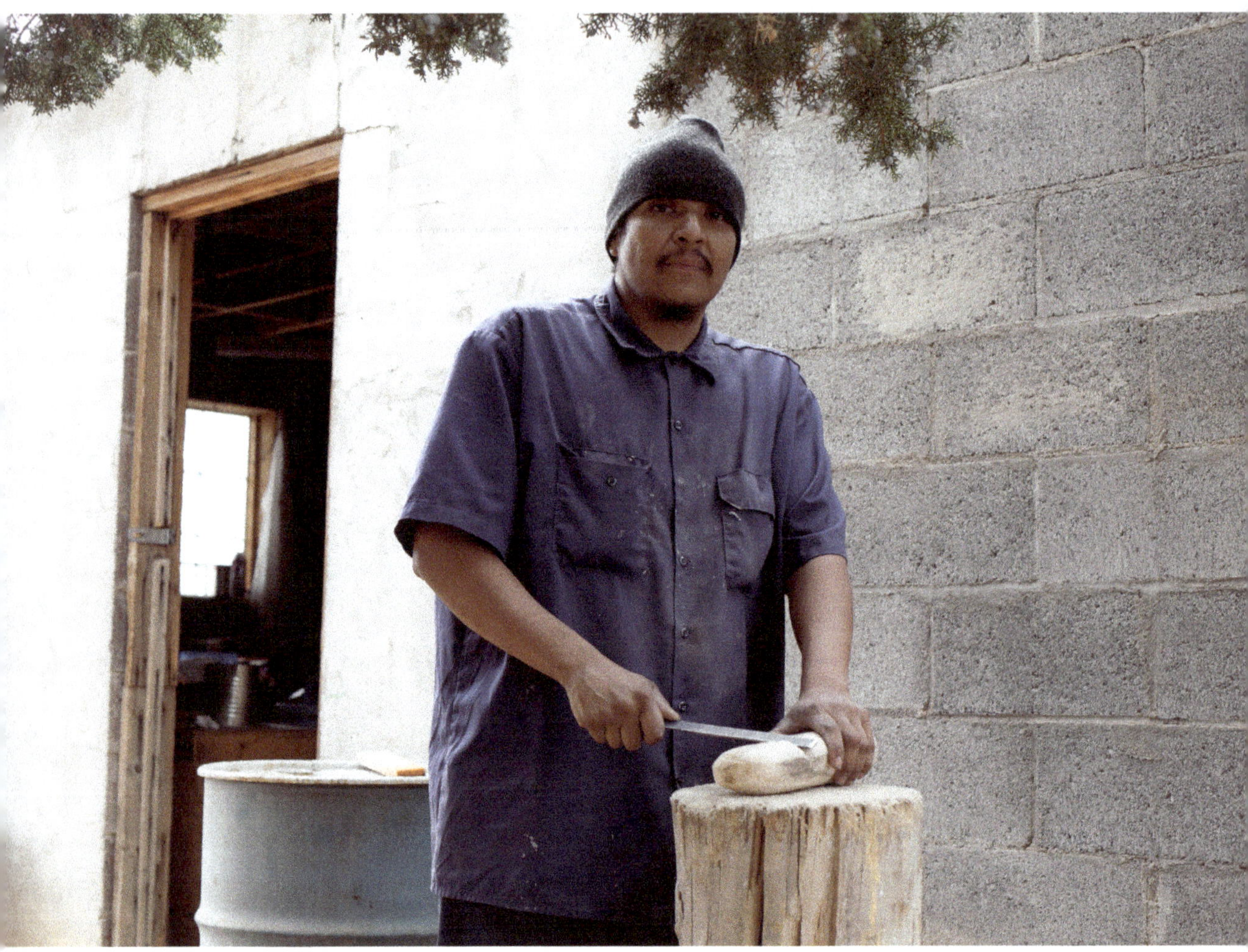

Figure 1. Cimmaron Grover.

CIMMARON GROVER

Between the Katsinam and the katsinam

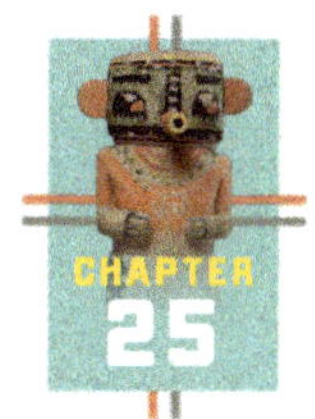

THREE MILES WEST of the town of Hotvela (Hotevilla) lives a carver whose artwork is uniquely interesting. I met with Cimmaron Grover (Figure 1) several times to prepare different versions of this chapter. Ultimately, he requested that I not emphasize his biography, or "ego accomplishments," but rather write about his katsina carvings and their relationship to the Katsina Spirits. By way of biography, I will only say that Cimmaron was born in 1978 and is of the Water Clan.

Cimmaron's view is that the word "Katsina" is "split in half." He told me that "Ka" refers to "body" and "tsina" to spirit. Therefore, a Ka-tsina is an embodied spirit being. (Note: throughout this book, I use the capitalized word, *Katsina*, to refer to the Hopi Spirit Beings, and the lower case *katsina* to refer to the wood carvings.) He emphasized that the Katsina is your friend, and added, "We all have to have a friend, to seek help, to cry, to laugh, and to mourn. The Katsina," he said, "can be your best friend, your spirit friend."

Cimmaron stated, "The spirit of Katsinam come in their own form so we human beings can see them, feel them, and know that our soul is real." He noted, "We must remember that this all relates to our creator. . . .The life we live, breathe, and speak does not belong to us. It is forgotten that our life plan belongs to the great spirit, our father creator. Also, Katsina is the one who reminds us, encourages a long happy way of living life to Hopiland."

Cimmaron cautioned, "The Hopi way of life is in danger of disappearing due to selfishness and Western society influences." He added, "All this about life goes to the Katsina. Katsina is life and when we depart from this world we become a Katsina. [After death], the ancestors put a cloud on our faces (in fact the clouds in the sky are our ancestors) and we become the clouds above. . . .Some people foolishly chase away the clouds, complaining about rain or mud. But, we too will become the clouds and will travel with the clouds. All Katsina songs talk about clouds, rain, crops growing, moisture, and happy hearts."

Cimmaron stated, "These Spirits live among the Hopi. Is it true? Are they real? The non-Hopi will never fully understand. Katsinam are real. The Hopi live amongst them. . . .Before anything else was invented, the Spirit World existed.

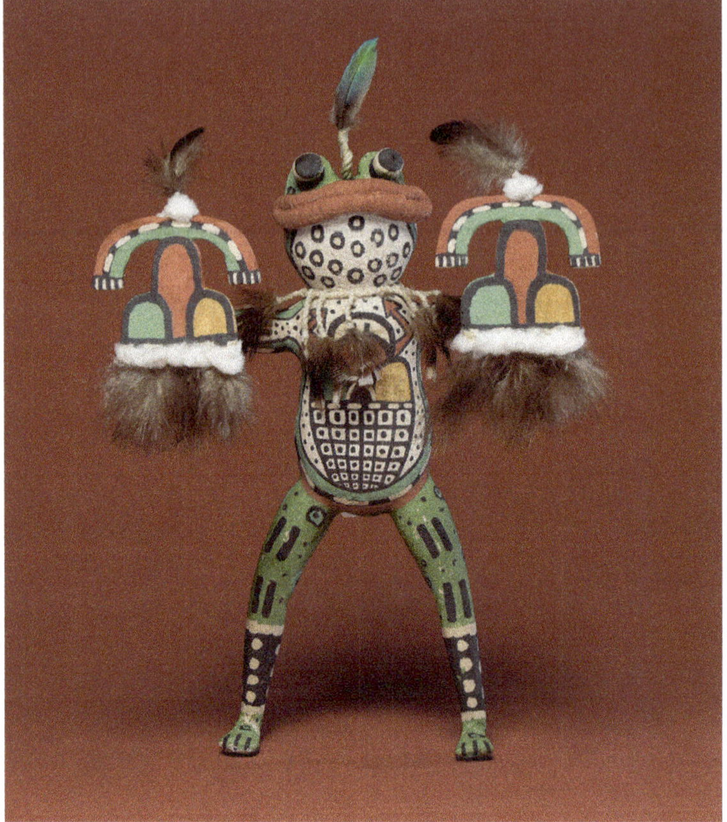

Figure 2. Paakwa Wuya (Frog Ancestor).

Once the Hopi emerged, over time they turned to 'selfishness' and became 'I, me.'" This is one reason Cimmaron focuses on the Katsina spirits rather than his biography.

Cimmaron and I moved to discuss his katsina carvings. He noted that his "carvings are made with arms out to welcome everybody." He said they are made "like when you haven't seen your friend for years and want to meet him with open arms." He added, "everyone looks at body language. People don't want closed or crossed arms. They want to be welcomed."

Cimmaron said, "there is no difference between a Katsina spirit and the wood carvings." He added the carvings "are our teachers, our elders. They are not idols." He explained, "they are visual proof, teaching tools, instructors, that there is a higher power."

Also, "katsina dolls are given to the girls at a young age so that they can learn how to raise, care, and love their own children. That is why some dolls are given with yucca woven cradles."

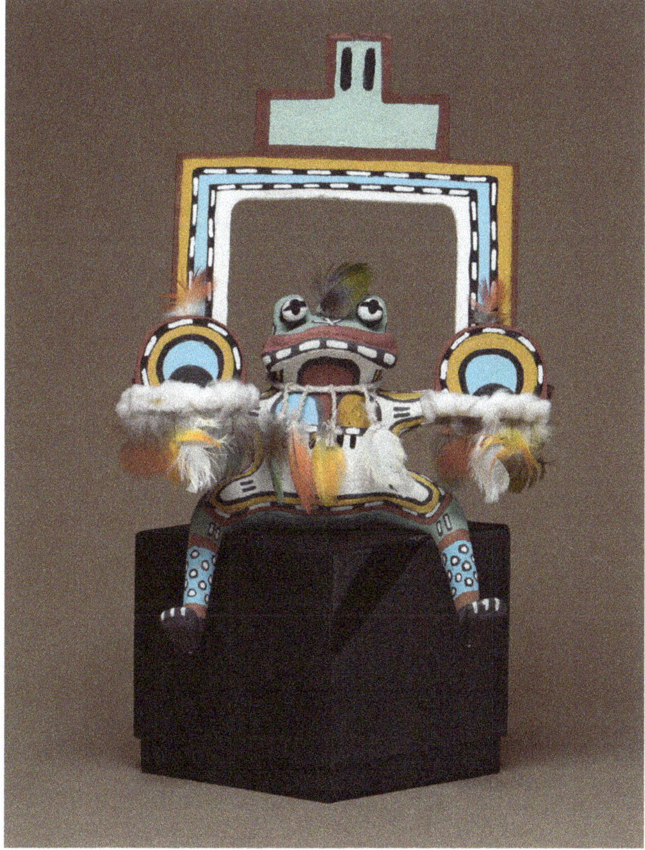

Figure 3. Paakwa Wuya (Frog Ancestor).

Cimmaron expressed that when carving a Katsina in wood, it is an image of oneself. As a person is carving, one becomes that Katsina. He added that when finished, the carver returns to being a regular human being. He then said—quite profoundly in my opinion— "the in-between is sacredness."

In turning to Cimmaron's carvings, let's begin with what he identified as a Paakwa Wuya (Frog Ancestor) in Figure 2. Although I have seen many carvings of Paakwa katsinam (Frogs) over the years, I have never seen one that resembles this exceptional piece. I find it both eerie and charismatic. Cimmaron told me an extended story about this Paakwa. First of all, he said that his native Water clan has a special relationship with frogs, which "represent fertility, rain, and ponds." He added, "we accept frogs, we don't own them." He said that "frogs can hibernate for ten years and that when the water comes, they emerge. They are forever. Without water, there is no life. So, water is life."

He explained how he came to carve a Frog like the one shown in Figure

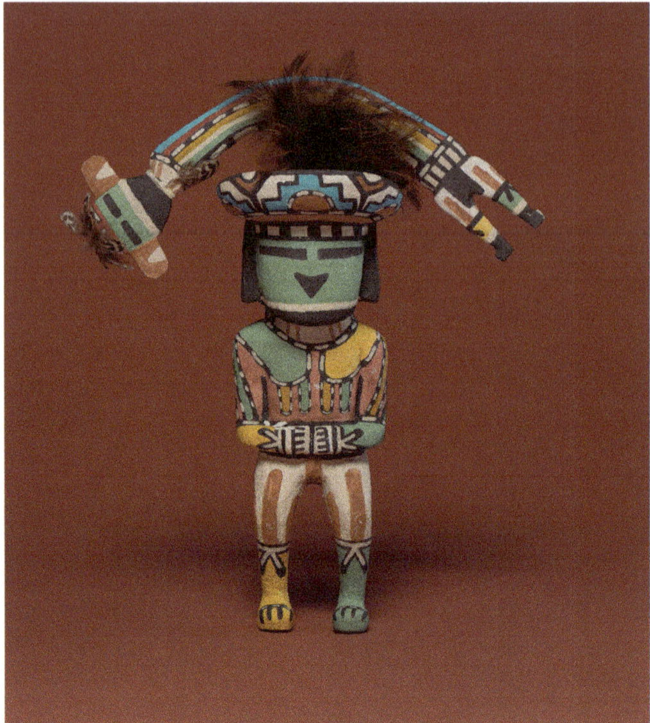

Figure 4. Rainbow Man, a Zuni figure.

2. He said that he "had never really been interested in carving an amphibian before." But one night as he approached a Palhikwmana dance in a kiva, he looked down the opening to see—to his great surprise—a female Paakwa Wuya (Frog Ancestor) figure. He was so taken by this experience he has been carving versions of the Frog ever since. The Frog in Figure 2 is male.

Figure 3 is a different version of a Paakwa Wuya (Frog). This example is holding a kopatsoki (tablita) and is offering it with outstretched arms as a gift or blessing. Note that this carving is made to hang on a wall or to sit on the edge of a table or shelf. I've not encountered other carvings deliberately made to sit on a corner or shelf's edge. Cimmaron does a lot of unusual things!

Another unusual carving by Cimmaron is shown in Figure 4. I have never seen this figure made by any other Hopi artist. Cimmaron saw this Rainbow Man at a dance at Zuni Pueblo and decided to represent it. It is a very dramatic carving indeed and rare because it is a non-Hopi figure interpreted by a Hopi artist. Rainbow Man is one of the most important figures in Zuni cosmology.

In keeping with how unusual many of Cimmaron's carvings are, consider

Figure 5. This is the seldom seen Kookyangwso'wuuti (Spider Old Woman or Grandmother). Cimmaron told me that the large white structure on her head made of raw cotton is her nest for baby spiders. I've only seen one other Spider Woman in the past thirty years and it was a miniature, only 2 inches tall. I was excited to acquire this rare example.

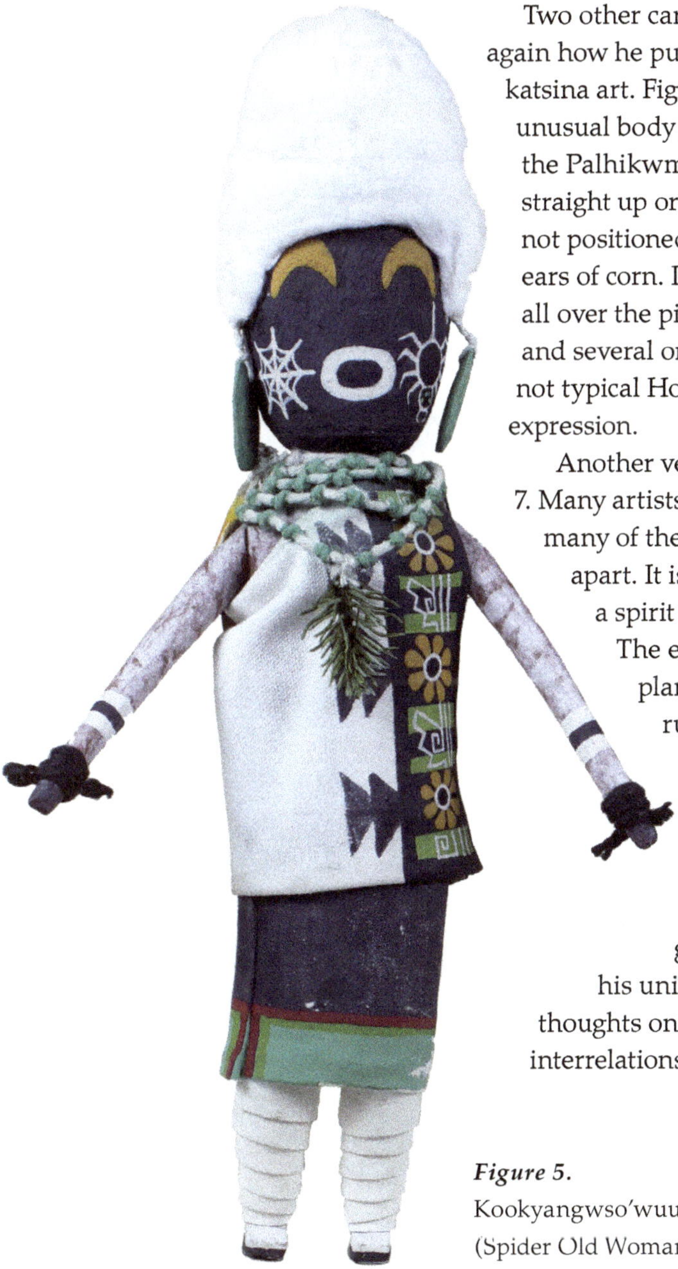

Two other carvings by Cimmaron show yet again how he pushes the limits of Traditional Style katsina art. Figure 6 is a Palhikwmana with a very unusual body posture for this figure. Normally, the Palhikwmana is portrayed as standing straight up or kneeling and grinding corn; she is not positioned with arms outstretched holding ears of corn. In fact, the carving has corn symbols all over the piece—on her arms, legs, and feet, and several on the very elaborate tableta. This is not typical Hopi symbolism. It is a very creative expression.

Another very unusual work is shown in Figure 7. Many artists make Wakaskatsinam (Cows), and many of them are rather "cute." This one stands apart. It is eerie and looks to be halfway into a spirit world that few persons can access. The eyes are haunting and the dried plant material used for the katsina's ruff is very atypical. The antiquing of the paint also gives it an ancient feel. This "otherworldly" aspect is a consistent element in Cimmaron's work.

It has been my privilege to get to know Cimmaron, appreciate his unique work, and to hear his profound thoughts on Katsinam and katsinam and their interrelationship.

Figure 5.
Kookyangwso'wuuti
(Spider Old Woman or Grandmother).

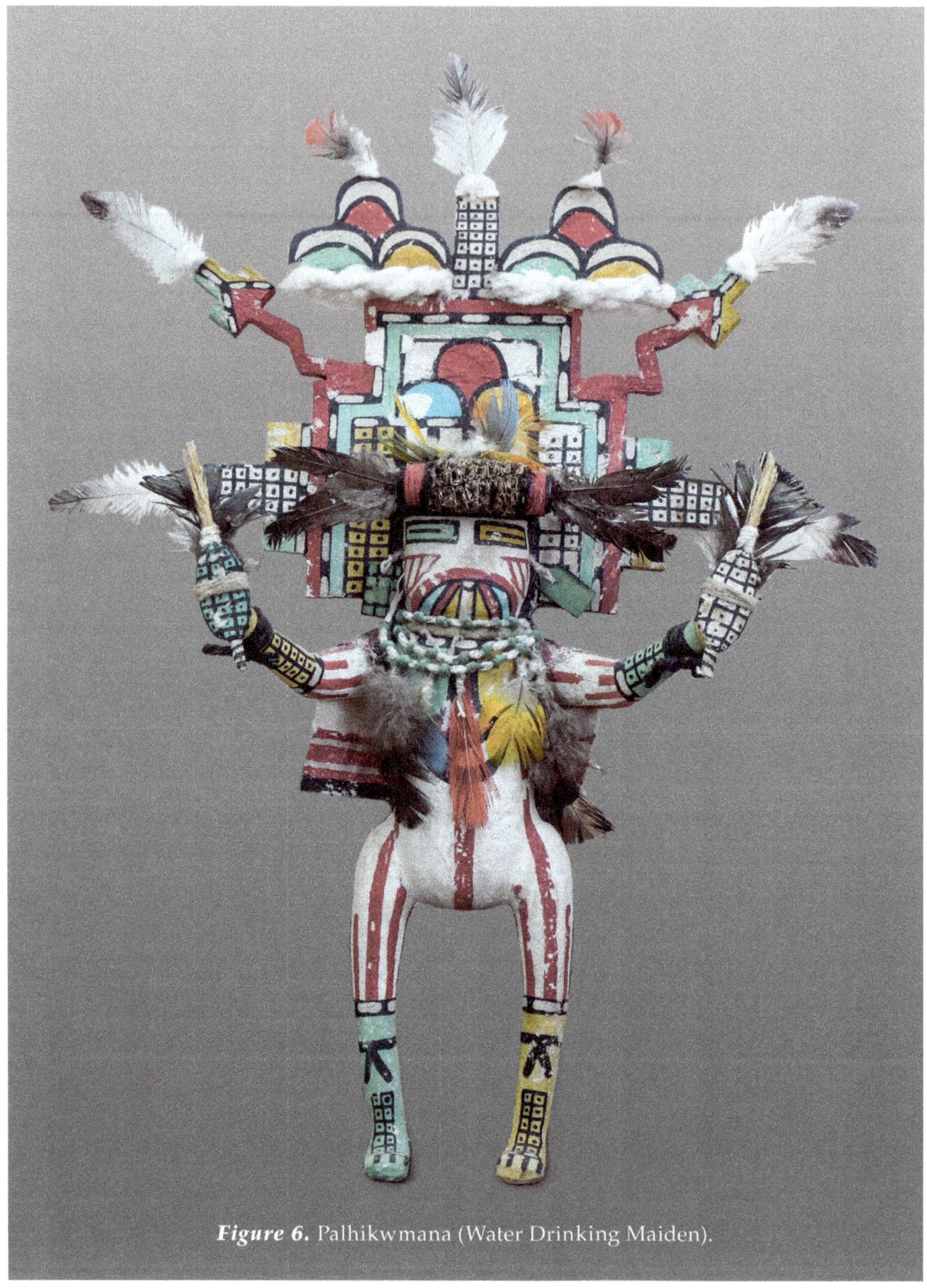

Figure 6. Palhikwmana (Water Drinking Maiden).

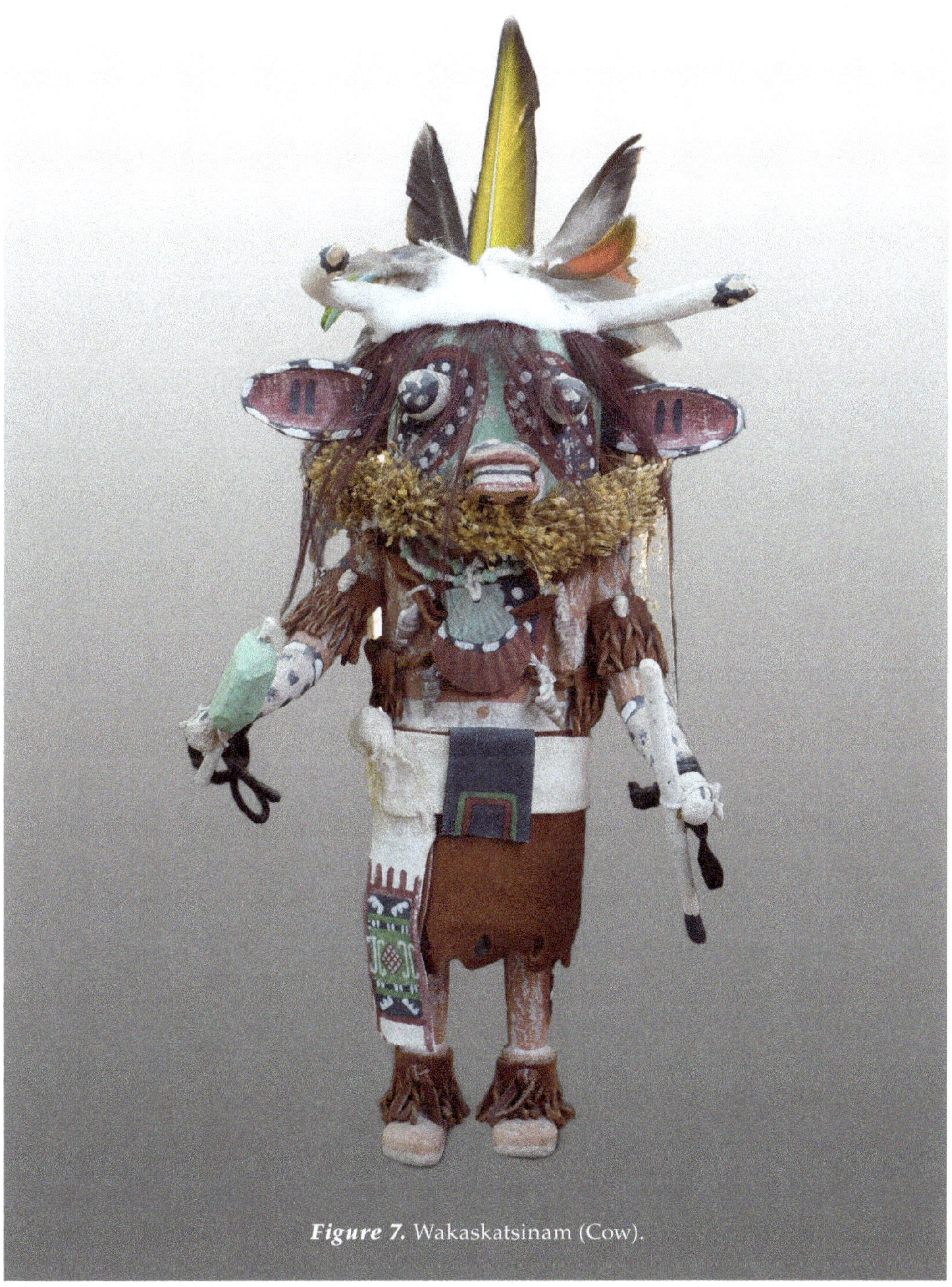

Figure 7. Wakaskatsinam (Cow).

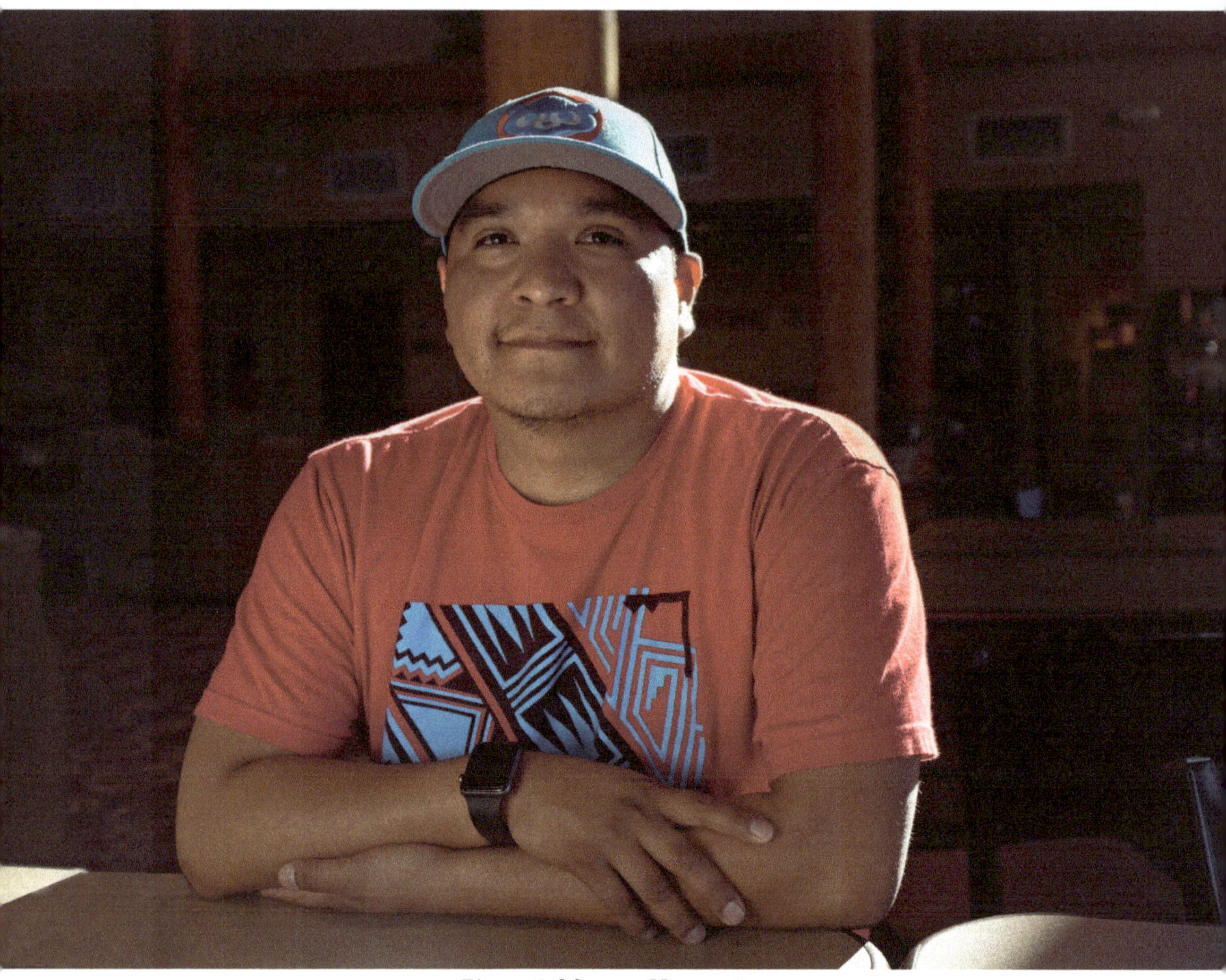

Figure 1. Mavasta Honyouti.

HONYOUTI FAMILY

Part II: Mavasta and Kevin

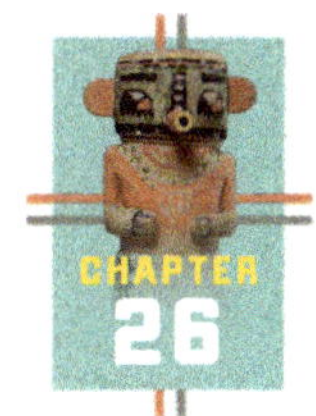

THIS CHAPTER WILL DISCUSS the third generation of Honyouti katsina carvers, first focusing on Mavasta, followed by Kevin. Mavasta is fifteen years older than Kevin. Please also read Chapter 12, which focused on the first two generations of Honyouti katsina artists.

Mavasta Honyouti

Mavasta Honyouti (Figure 1) was born in 1979 and grew up in Hotvela (Hotevilla). His mother, Carla, is Coyote Clan. Mavasta lives in Tuba City with his wife and four children, and teaches eighth grade in Hotvela. Remarkably, carving is a part-time endeavor for Mavasta even though he excels at it. He often works at his art in the evenings and weekends during the school year and full-time during his summers off.

During multiple conversations, Mavasta shared that he has never had any formal training in woodworking or carving; instead, he learned from his father, Ron, and uncle, Brian. (See Pearlstone, 2018, for a full-length volume on Brian Honyouti). This story echoes what Ron said in Chapter 12 about his father, Clyde.

Mavasta has a B.A. in Elementary Education from Arizona State University in Tempe. As he was graduating from college, he saw a flyer recruiting Native American teachers. He decided to apply so that he "could make a difference" and has been teaching Native students ever since. He enjoys his profession very much, saying he understands his role and how he can influence his fellow Hopi students. He teaches his classes about Native American peoples and world indigenous cultures, using content not found in textbooks. For example, one of his first lessons to start a school year focuses on the Pueblo Revolt of 1680. He stresses that all students are capable of success and he is clearly a model in two different realms.

Mavasta's reverence for culture also comes through in his artwork. He primarily makes two types of carvings: 1) multifigured katsina sculptures

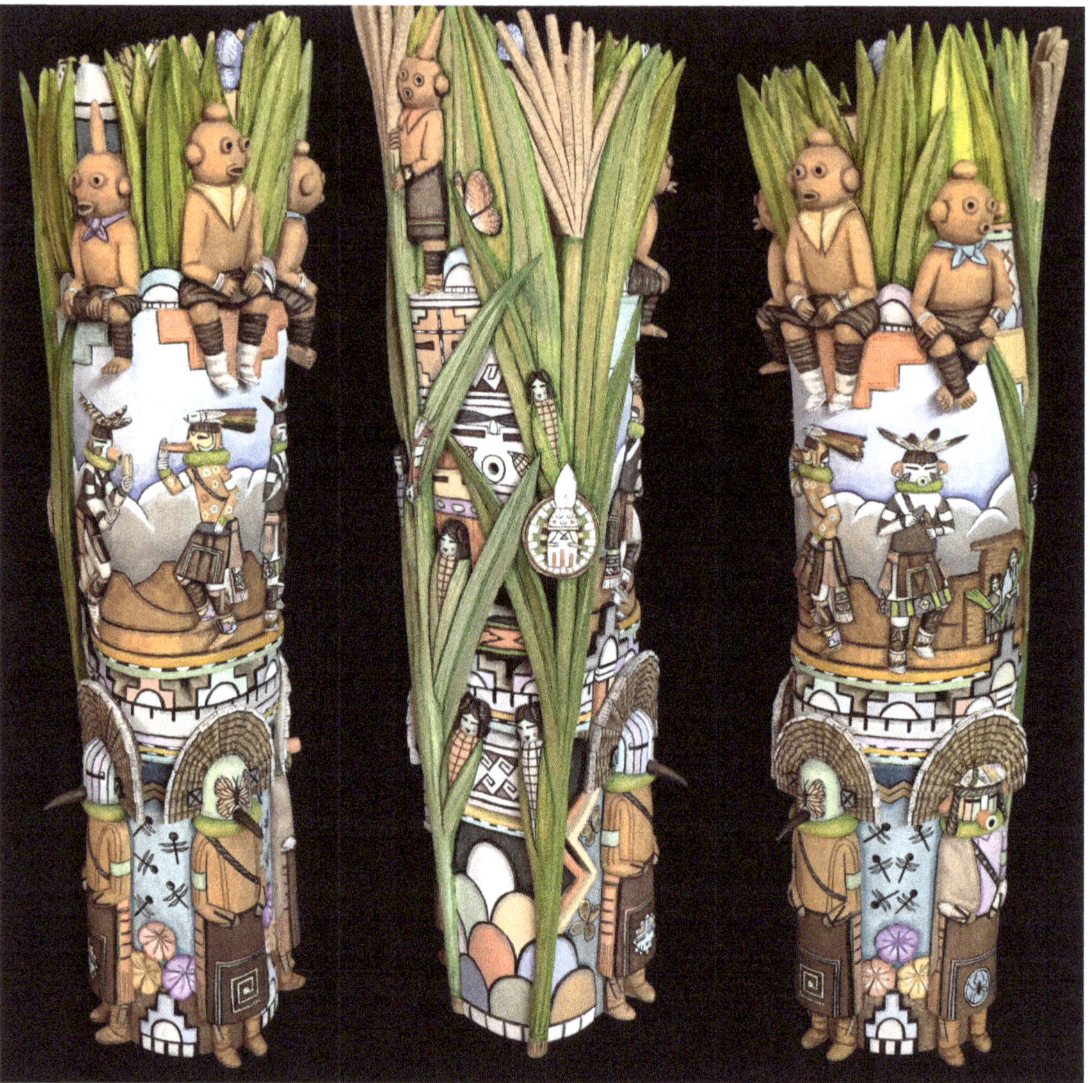

Figure 2. *Corn Dance,* a cylindrical, multifigured carving by Mavasta Honyouti.

portraying diverse aspects of a Katsina dance scene, and 2) flat, bas-relief plaques that often depict pop culture figures or portray multiple katsinam engaged in an activity. A superb example of a cylindrical, multifigured carving is shown in multiple angles in Figure 2. In my opinion, Mavasta has taken cylindrical carvings as done by his father, Ronald, (as shown in Chapter 12) and extended their range and complexity. Mavasta titled this work *Corn Dance.* It includes the dance itself, individual katsinam, baskets, katsina carvings, and more. This work won Best of Classification at SWAIA in 2015. He also received a First Place and

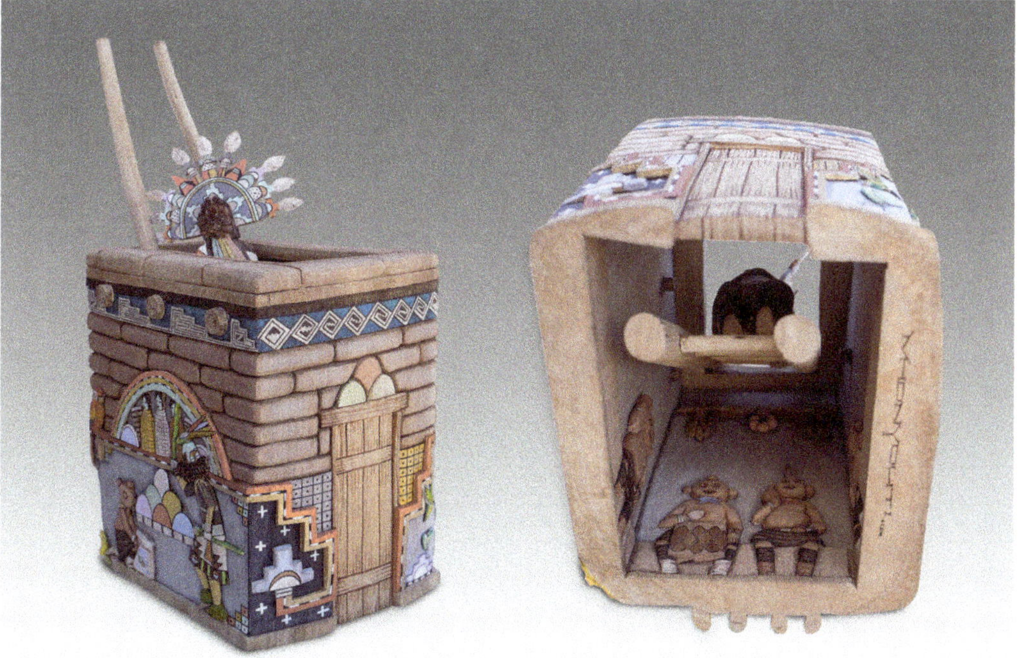

Figure 3. *Entering the Kiva* by Mavasta Honyouti.

the Judges Choice Award at the Heard Museum show in March, 2016.

Another exceptional piece is shown in Figure 3. Mavasta titled this work, *Entering the Kiva*. This unique carving won Best of Class and an Innovation Award at the Heard Show in 2018. It's no wonder this carving was cited for innovation as it has figures carved both inside and out—something I've not seen before. It is technically very difficult to carve such details on the tight interior of a cottonwood root object. Mavasta has a uniquely creative mind and the technical skill to execute whatever he aspires to.

A nice example of one of his bas-relief plaques is shown in Figure 4. This piece depicts a Masawkatsina and Masawkatsinmana in their germination roles. The bas-relief feature is multi-layered, with the blue sky carved deepest, followed by a mesa and dwellings, with katsinam in the foreground, along with dragonfly, corn, flower, and cloud symbols. For a relatively small artwork (7 inches square), there is a lot going on.

In Figure 5, Mavasta presents us with an updated version of The Beatles' *Abbey Road* with two Ho'es, a Kooyemsi, and a Kwikwilyaqa (a "striped nose," imitator katsina), standing in for the originals. Mavasta says he enjoys "fusing the two cultures," and his students enjoy these commentaries. Yet another

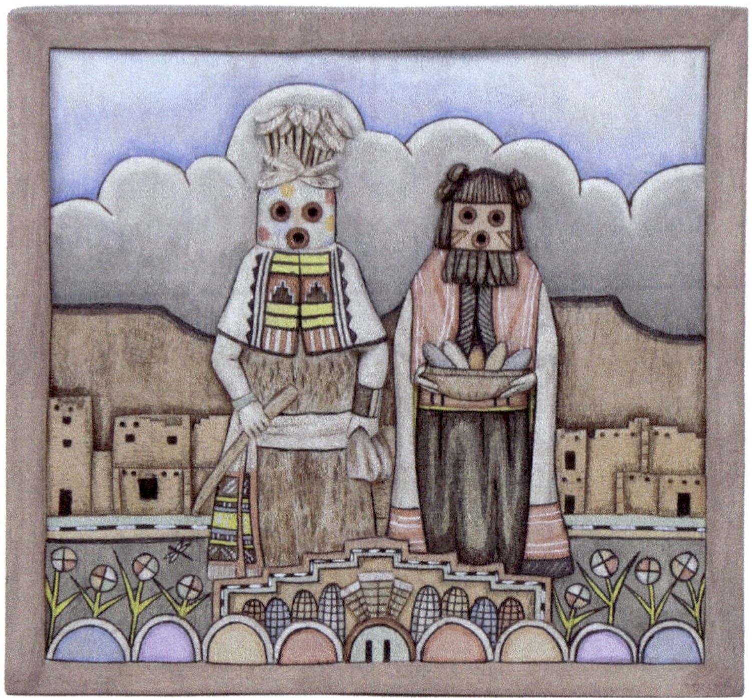

Figure 4. Masawkatsina and Masawkatsinmana by Mavasta Honyouti.

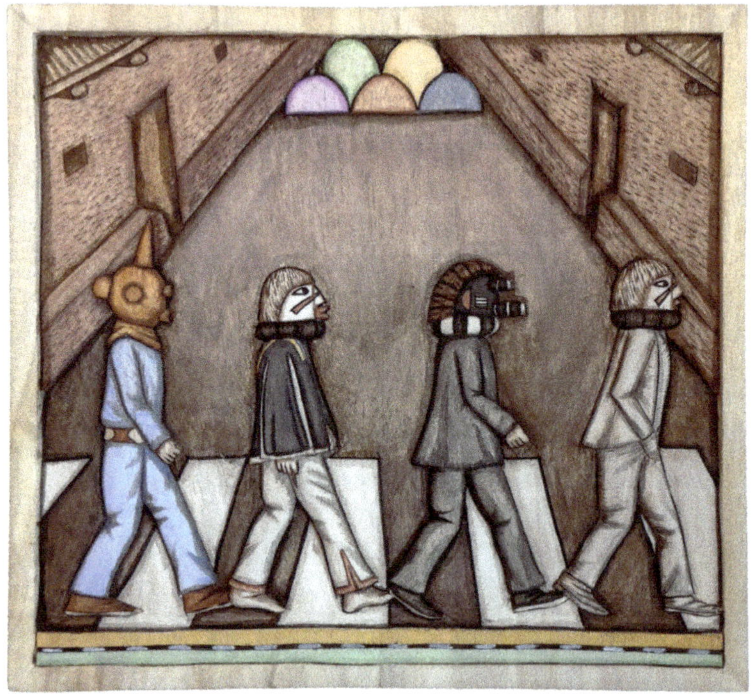

Figure 5. A version of The Beatles' *Abbey Road* with two Ho'es, a Kooyemsi, and a Kwikwilyaqa by Mavasta Honyouti.

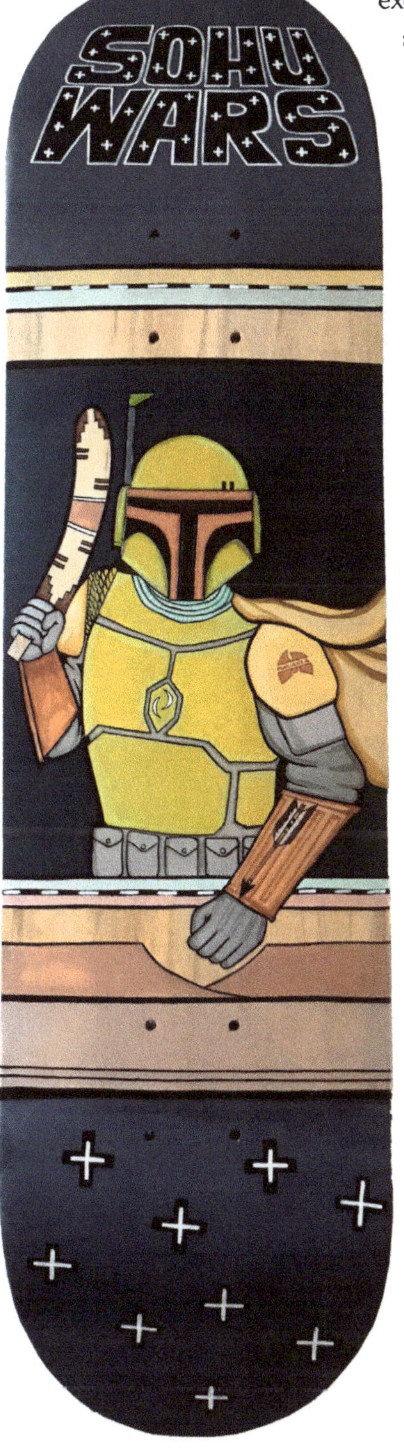

excursion into an unusual medium is Mavasta's skateboard deck depicting Boba Fett from what he calls *Sohu (Star) Wars* (Figure 6). Note that Boba Fett is fusing three cultures by carrying a traditional Hopi rabbit stick and bearing an arrow on his space gauntlets, while his logo is a spin on the logo of the hip-hop group, Wu-Tang Clan.

One remarkable aspect of Mavasta's prize-winning work is that he hasn't been carving that long. Although he started making katsinam at age fifteen, he eventually took a break for twelve years. He resumed carving around 2010–2011. He found working with wood came to him easily, probably because such talent is clearly "in the genes" of the Honyouti family. He divides his time fairly evenly between making cylindrical multi-figured carvings versus plaques. He said that with the cylindrical sculptures he sticks to traditional Hopi themes and portrayals. With the plaques, he has more freedom to experiment and go in unusual directions, as shown in Figure 5.

Mavasta shared that he would like to branch out beyond wood carvings. He has created a t-shirt design venture. He would also like to make sculptures in bronze and to experiment in home décor such as mantles, doors, and dividers. One can easily imagine his bas-relief carvings becoming full-sized mantles and doors.

Figure 6. *Sohu (Star) Wars,* depicting Boba Fett on a skateboard by Mavasta Honyouti.

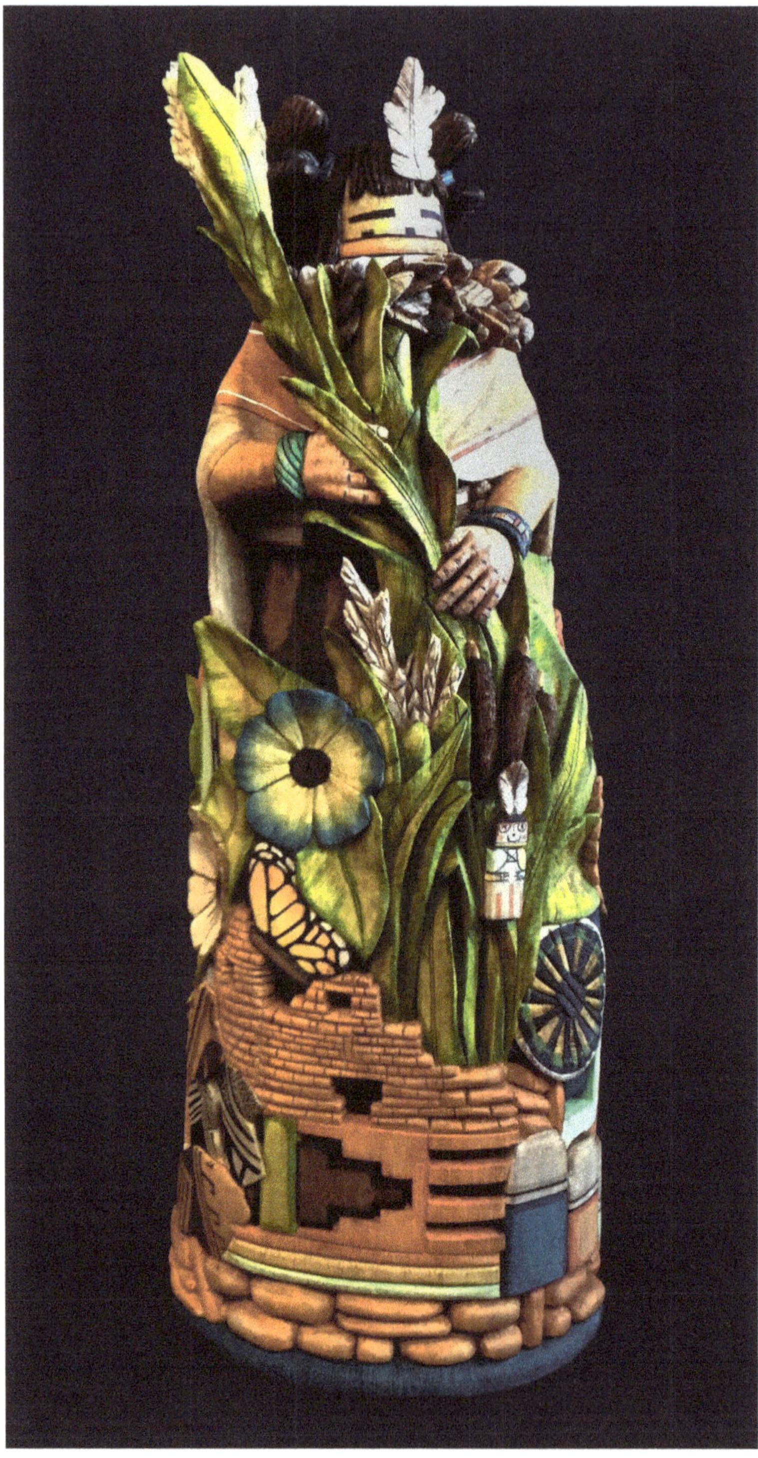

Figure 7.
Katsinmana sculpture by Kevin Honyouti.

Kevin Honyouti

The youngest of Ron's children, Kevin (born in November 1994) is also showing great promise as a carver. Kevin was born in Keams Canyon, and his mother is Coyote Clan. Kevin attended elementary school at the Hotvela/Paaqavi Community School and then went to Hopi Junior/Senior High School. In the previous chapter on the Honyouti family, which focused on Ron (Chapter 12), Ron noted that he essentially learned to carve katsinam from his father, Clyde. The same can be said for Kevin as to paternal influence. He never took art classes in school; instead, his father was his mentor and guide.

Kevin always thought he would become an artist. He told me, "It's been a clear direction since day one." He recalls being in his father's booth at shows as a child and "wanting to be just like him." Even now as an adult they do shows together and are comfortable in each other's company. Kevin added, "my parents are divorced so it's kind of always been me and him."

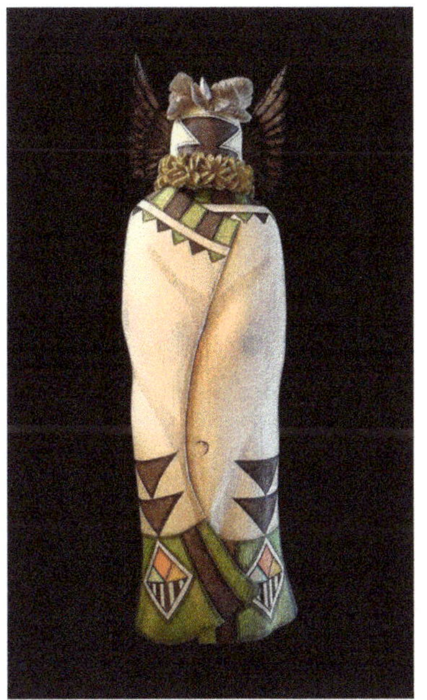

Figure 8. Angwusnasomtaqa (Crow Mother) by Kevin Honyouti.

An interesting aspect of Kevin's art is that unlike most other carvers in this book he carves in two "competing" styles. Sometimes he makes katsinam in the Sculptural Style such as shown in Figure 7. This elaborate cylindrical sculpture shows a Katsinmana in a complex vignette. She is surrounded by representations of full-grown corn plants, cradle katsinam, baskets, flowers, butterflies, pottery shards, Hopi buildings, and more. This sculpture is like a mini-lesson in Hopi history and culture. It is very fine and exceptionally detailed work.

Another example of a sculptural form by Kevin is the elegant carving of Angwusnasomtaqa (Crow Mother) shown in Figure 8. This carving has a simple, admirable grace. Now compare this work to the very same katsina that Kevin has rendered in the Traditional Style (Figure 9). On the traditional version, the use of feathers from a bird's wings makes the katsina appear eerie and haunting. Worth noting is that when Crow Mother, the Katsina, appears, she has bird (crow) wings attached to her head as well. In contrasting the two katsinam, we can say that the Sculptural Style version is graceful and minimalist, while the Traditional Style version is earthy, derived directly from nature. These are very different versions of the same katsina, indicating Kevin's artistic range.

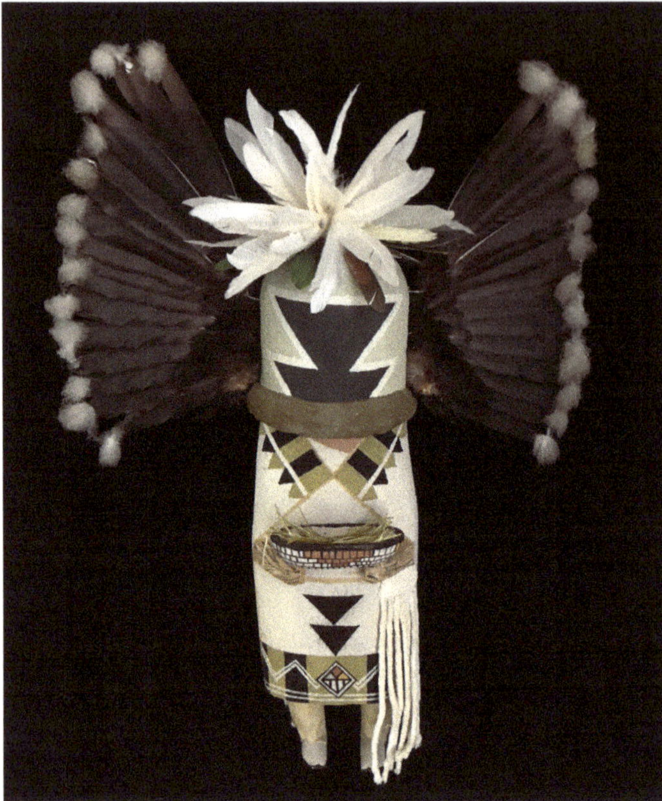

Figure 9. Angwusnasomtaqa (Crow Mother) by Kevin Honyouti.

Another remarkable carving in the Traditional Style is the Palhikwmana in Figure 10. Note the elaborate tablita, the tu'oynàanaqa earrings (composed of turquoise and abalone chips with a cottonwood frame), and hand-made rain sash.

For someone who is still in his twenties, Kevin has done very well in the marketplace. He has already won First Place ribbons at Tuhisma, the Hopi Show at the Museum of Northern Arizona, and the Gallup Inter-Tribal Indian Ceremonial, and a Second Place at Santa Fe's Indian Market. Despite his commitment to many shows, Kevin also finds time to tend to his traditional Hopi corn fields and is currently learning to weave Hopi belts. He is a traditional Hopi involved in village activities.

In Memoriam

The world of Hopi katsina carving is beholden to the Honyouti family for all its talent and innovations. In closing, I would like to dedicate this chapter and Chapter 12 to their patriarch, Brian Honyouti, who passed in 2016.

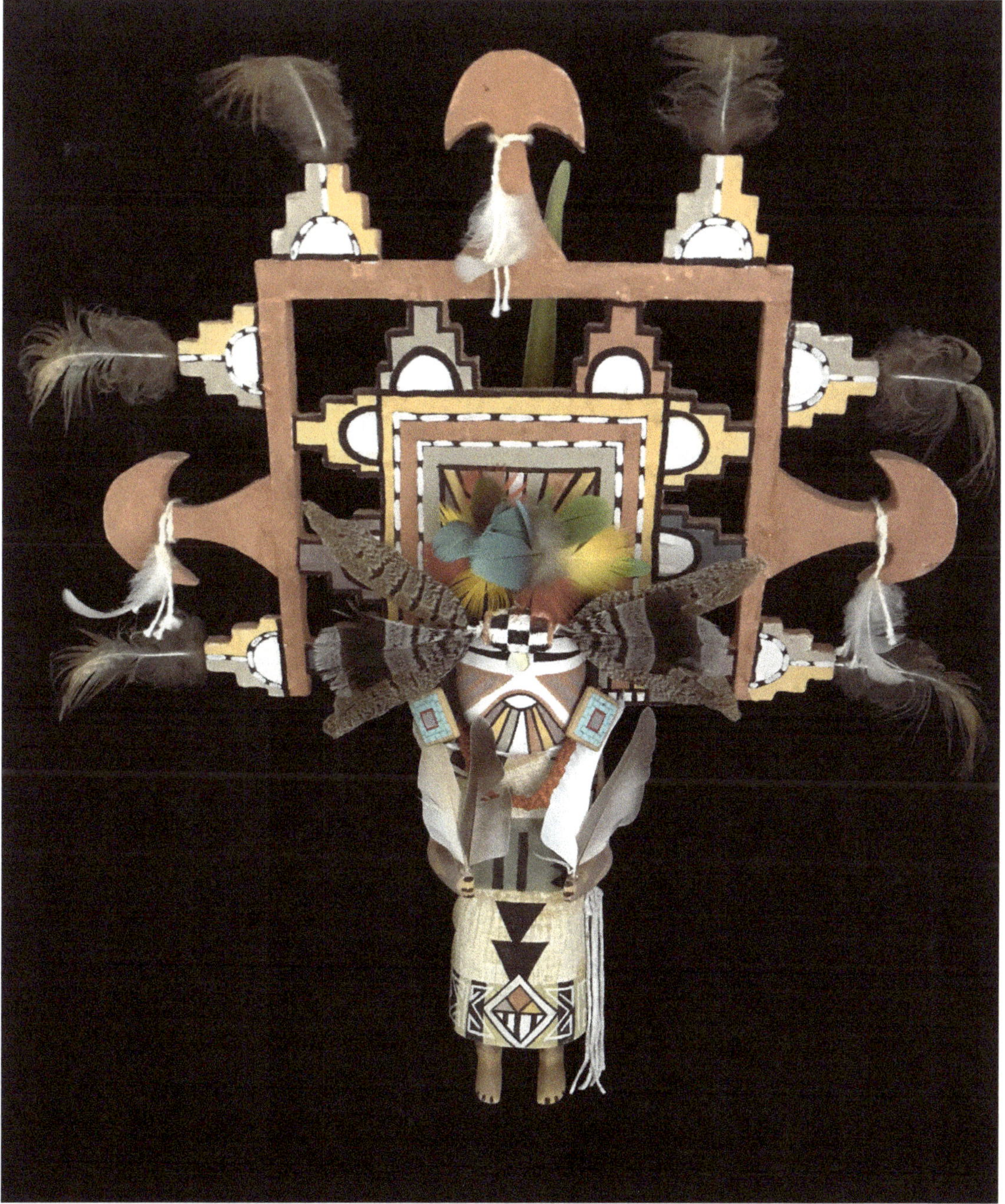

Figure 10. Palhikwmana (Water Drinking Maiden) by Kevin Honyouti.

CONCLUSION

In this book, I have attempted to feature some of the most outstanding katsina carvers in history, based on specific criteria given in the Introduction. At the heart of the book are the artist biographies and photos of their work. My method for conducting interviews—without exception—was to take handwritten notes during our conversations. Then I transcribed my notes and sent them to the carvers, or in the case of deceased artists, to their family members. They have reviewed my drafts, made changes, and approved final content. The only exceptions are chapters regarding deceased individuals for whom I was not able to locate family or friends. In those situations, I have relied on other published sources—which are fully cited.

A few common themes emerged for the artists in this book. Most spent time off the Hopi reservation. During the period of 1900 to the 1930s, this was often due to the forced removal of Hopi children by the United States government to Indian Residential Schools such as Sherman Institute in California, the Phoenix Indian School, or the Haskell Indian School in Kansas. These forced removals caused much pain and trauma, separating families from their children against their will. At these schools, the Native identities of the children were aggressively and punitively stripped away in terms of expunging their religions, tribal customs, languages, and changing their personal appearance. In addition, many of the Indian Residential Schools were known to have physically and sexually abused the children in their care (Giago & Giago 2006; Lajimodiere & Carmen 2014). This is a dark and troubling legacy in United States history.

Later on, Hopi families may have sent their children to schools off-reservation for economic reasons or because they thought there were educational advantages. Some Hopi youth lived off-reservation because a parent took a job elsewhere, such as in California, Utah, New Mexico, or southern Arizona. Other artists spent time off the reservation because they joined the United States military as young adults.

Many of the Hopi in this book who lived off-reservation cited some advantages to having had the experience. They noted that learning how to live in a Pahaana world assisted them in finding their way in the art marketplace controlled by Pahaanas. They learned how to be assertive, negotiate, and hold their own in competitive environments. They may have also at times been inspired by exposure to other Native and non-Native artists.

However, a key point that should be stressed is that almost all the carvers in this book eventually chose to return to the reservation to live and work. As Hattie Kabotie, daughter of Fred and Alice, told me, "they realize what they are missing and when they return, they especially value it."

Another complex theme for some in this book has been recovery from addiction. I was moved that some artists chose to share these trials with me and was inspired by their efforts at recovery. Many who have suffered from this challenge have overcome it, and their art and lives are the better for it. They serve as models and mentors to others in their communities who are still struggling with such demons.

Clark Tenakhongva commented during our conversations, "Art is a wonderful world, but a hard and cruel life." Supporting oneself and one's family as an artist is full of unpredictability, feasts and famines, defeats and celebrations. But many carvers shared that there can be a peace in the process of crafting representations of Spirit Beings.

ACKNOWLEDGMENTS

FIRST OF ALL, I would like to thank my collaborator on this project, my daughter, Anna Walsh. She took the large majority of photographs for this book. It was great to travel with her to Hopiland again as we had so many times when she was a child. As I've always said, "I don't take my kids to Disneyland. I take them somewhere real: Indian reservations." Anna and I had many adventures visiting and interviewing carvers and taking their pictures. Sharing such meaningful experiences at this phase in my life was profound. I also want to thank my ever-supportive wife, Valerie, for allowing me to travel to Hopiland so often to complete this project. She is the best!

I am very indebted to the Museum of Northern Arizona for their help with this project. Director and CEO Carrie Heinonen, former director Robert Breunig, collections director Elaine Hughes, and registrar Amber King, have been exceptionally generous with their expertise and in granting access to the world-class katsina collection of the Museum of Northern Arizona.

I owe a special debt to my teachers on Hopiland, Janice and Joseph Day. They have saved me from many mistakes, corrected and ridiculed me often (deservedly so), and fostered my knowledge of and respect for Hopi for more than thirty years. They have been my biggest mentors and guides on the reservation. Most important, Janice feeds me extremely well and they have the best trading post.

Joseph Day also assisted in consulting with Hopi experts to ensure my use of Hopi language regarding katsina names in this book has been as accurate and current as possible.

And their son, Jonathan, has been a great support, overall pest, mentor, mentee, and all-around great friend for almost as long as his parents. Thanks for letting me stay with you in Flagstaff repeatedly. I like sleeping with your lovable dogs. And thanks to Esther Aviles Garcia for all her hospitality including the best, most authentic Mexican food in Flagstaff!

I am indebted to Barton Wright (may he be resting in peace) for his support of my katsina publications over the years. He was always generous with information and reminiscences about several of the deceased carvers featured in this book. He was especially helpful regarding Jimmie Kewanwytewa, with whom he worked for many years at the Museum of Northern Arizona. His respect and affection for Jimmie K came through in every anecdote and insight he shared. He also assisted me with my work on Tawaquaptewa and Otto Pentewa.

Two others from the past I'd like to acknowledge are Jimmie K's spouse, Agnes, and son, Ross Joseysva. They provided biographical information regarding Jimmie K during an interview at Agnes's home in Songoopavi, Second Mesa, on February 18, 2001.

I have had many other mentors on my journey as an Indian art dealer and author. Fellow dealers I credit for their generosity of spirit and sharing knowledge include Al Anthony, Terry Dewald, Paul Elmore, Steve Elmore, Lyn Fox, Bob Gallegos, Barbara Goldeen, Toby Herbst, John C. Hill, Mark Humpal, Alan Kessler, Kim Martindale, Jim Mclellan, John Molloy, Deb and Alston Neal, Terry Schurmeier, John Selmer, Marti Struever (may the Grande Dame rest in peace), Mark Sublette, Susan Swift, and many more.

I am very grateful to call Chad Burkhardt a friend regarding Hopi matters. Since childhood, he has spent large amounts of time on the reservation and is by far the most knowledgeable Pahaana regarding Hopi culture that I know (competing with Joe Day). When I'm really stumped, I contact Chad and he either knows the answer or where to find it. He and his family know and love Hopiland. He and his mother also provided some examples of Neil David Sr.'s work for this volume.

My thanks to Mark Bahti for sharing firsthand knowledge regarding Otto Pentewa and Henry Shelton. Such information is simply invaluable.

I want to thank Marlinda Kooyoquaptewa for being my Walmart Auntie. Time and again she has provided me access to her husband, Manuel Denet Chavarria's marvelous work.

I'd like to thank *Native American Art Magazine* for their support in publishing some of my recent articles on katsina carvers and Mary Hamilton of *American Indian Art Magazine* for having published older pieces.

A number of people generously shared photos from their katsina collections. First and foremost, Suzy Golt arranged photos through Susannah B. Clark of Suzy's world-class collection. The book would have been far weaker without photos of Suzy's katsinam. Some of the best examples are hers. Also, Bob and Le Oehrli were very helpful in sharing photos of their Jimmie K katsinam. Peg DeMouthe provided excellent representations of work by Otto Pentewa and Makwesa from her collection, which were photographed by Peter ffoulkes. I'm indebted to Barbara Goldeen and John Selmer for sharing their exceptional examples by Tawaquaptewa and Makwesa, and thanks also goes to their photographer, Steven Lawrence. I make an appreciative bow to Richard Buckley for sharing his Jimmie Koots dolls for this book. And Steve Elmore provided a photo of a katsina by Neil David Sr.

Also, among the most generous spirits I've met are Pat and Kim Messier, who shared wonderful pictures of Jimmie K and great material from Neil David Sr.

My thanks to old friend, Barbara Rice, for providing examples from her impressive collection of Traditional Style dolls. I couldn't have done it without her.

The same goes for Phil Krotz and Randy Lazarus, who allowed me to share photos of katsinam I had sent their way. And appreciation to Janice Gonsalves who provided access to the best katsina I've seen by Charles Fredericks. Gracias to Howard Bowlin for his photo of a doll by Alvin James Makya.

I also want to thank my other photographer, Dan Vaillancourt of Patrick O'Connor Photography, who took and edited many photos in this book.

Lastly, I want to thank all the carvers and their families for letting me into their lives and sharing their stories. It was such a meaningful experience. I hope I listened well and have done you justice.

The styles of the Hopi artists portrayed here range from hard, flashing male rains to gentle, persistent female rains. Either way, the fields prosper and the spirit of Hopiland lives on strong and vibrant.

Barry Walsh
September, 2018

GLOSSARY OF HOPI KATSINA FIGURES AND DEITIES

The first word is the correct Hopi spelling for each katsina. All of the spellings are from the *Hopi Dictionary Project* (1998) or use the standard Hopi orthography. Words in quotations are the Hopi translations into English. Any additional text is explanatory commentary.

Aaloosaka: (no English translation). A deity, not a katsina.

Angaktsina: "Longhair katsina."

Angwusnasomtaqa: "one with raven wings attached as hair." The common English term is "Crow Mother" and refers to her role in the Powamuya ceremony.

Atosle: (no English translation). A female ogre.

Hahay'iwuuti: "Hahayi woman." A female katsina who represents the ideal characteristics of womanhood.

Hakto: (from the Zuni word, *yamahakto*). A katsina of Zuni origin. The word means "carrying wood on his head."

Hehey'a: (no English translation). Appears with the So'yoko katsinam and as an "uncle" with the Kuwan Hehey'a katsinam.

Hemiskatsina: "Jemez katsina." Only appears at Niman Tikeve, the Home Dance.

Hiilili: (no English translation). A guard katsina.

Ho'e katsina: (no English translation).

Honankatsina: "Badger katsina."

Honkatsina: "Bear katsina."

Hooli: (no English translation). Named for the sound he makes.

Hoot'e: (no English translation). Named for the sound he makes. Can appear as a group and also individually with a group of mixed katsinam.

Huuhuwa: (no English translation). Referred to in English as Cross-Legged katsina.

Katsinmana: "Katsina maiden."

Kawiikoli: (no English translation). A deity that may appear as a katsina.

Koo'aakatsina: (no English translation). Named for the sound he makes.

Kookopölö: (no English translation). A fertility katsina who has a humpback but does not carry seeds or a flute.

Kookyangwso'wuuti: "Spider Old Woman." Grandmother of the Pöqanghoyat.

Kooninkatsinmana: "Female Havasupai katsina."

Kooninkatsintaqa: "Male Havasupai katsina."

Kooyemsi: (no English translation). Name is derived from the Zuni word *koyemshi*. Often appears as a drummer for a group of katsinam or as a group of singers for the katsinam. Commonly referred to as a "Mudhead."

Koshare: "Pueblo clown."

Kowaakokatsina: "Chicken katsina."

Koyaala: the black and white striped clown of Tewa origin. Can also appear as the katsina aspect of that clown. Sometimes referred to as a "Hano" clown.

Kuwan Hehey'a: "Colorful Hehey'a."

Kwaakatsina: "Eagle katsina."

Kwasaytaqa: "One with a Dress."
Kwewu: "Wolf."
Kwikwilyaqa: "Striped Nose." A katsina who mirrors (imitates) those whom he encounters.
Kyarkatsina: "Parrot katsina."
Leenangwkatsina: "Flute katsina."
Lenwimkya: "Flute priest."
Maasaw: a deity not a katsina
Malatsveytaqa: "One with Handprint." A racer katsina.
Manangya: "Lizard."
Masawkatsina: "Maasaw katsina." The katsina aspect of the deity Maasaw.
Masawkatsinmana: "Female version of the Masawkatsina."
Mastopkatsina: (no English translation). A fertility katsina.
Matyawkatsina: "One with Handprint on his face."
Mongwu: "Great Horned Owl."
Morivosi: "Bean."
Mosayru: "Bison." Can appear as either a social dancer or a katsina.
Nalöq'ala: "Four Horn." Tewa version is called Pohaha.
Nata'aska: (no English translation). A black ogre.
Nuvakatsina: "Snow katsina."
Omawkatsina: "Cloud katsina."
Owak'katsina: "Coal katsina."
Owangaroro: "Stone eater."
Paakwa: "Frog."
Paakwa Wuya: "Frog ancestor."
Paalölöqangkatsina: "Water Serpent katsina." The katsina aspect of paalölöqang, the water serpent.
Pakiwkatsina: "Fish katsina."
Palhikwmana: "Water Drinking Maiden."
Palöngawhoya: the younger brother of Pöqangwhoya. Not a Katsina.
Palöngawkatsina: does not appear except in books.
Pangwkatsina: "Bighorn Sheep katsina."
Patro: "Sandpiper."
Pavatya or **pakwavi:** "Tadpole."
Poliimana: "Butterfly Maiden." The unmarried girls who dance in the late summer butterfly dance.
Poliitaqa: "Butterfly Man."
Poos'humkatsina: "Corn Seed katsina."
Pöqangwhoya: The older brother of Palöngawhoya. Not a Katsina.
Qöqlö: (no English translation).
Qötsahemiskatsina: "White Hemiskatsina."
Qötsahonaw: "White Bear."
Qötsamosayru: "White Bison." Appears as both a social dancer and a katsina.
Qötsatsuku: "White clown." Not a katsina; a descriptive term.
Saaviki: the katsina aspect of a clan Wuya or deity. At First Mesa it is called Tsaana'yo.
Sakwahote: "Blue hoot'e."
Sa'lako: (no English translation).
Sa'lakwmana: "Sa'lako Maiden."
Sa'lakwtaqa: "Male Sa'lako."
Sáyartasa: (no English translation). Zuni long-horn katsina.
Sikyatsuku: "Yellow clown." Not a katsina, a descriptive term for a yellow clown.
Siohemiskatsina: "Zuni Jemez katsina."
Siohote: "Zuni Hoot'e."
Siosakwahonankatsina: "Zuni Blue Badger katsina."
Sootangkwaakatsina: "Laguna Eagle Dancer."
Sootantaqa: "One that Pokes."
Sootukwnangw: katsina aspect of the Heart of the Cosmos deity.
So'yokmana: (no English translation). An Ogre Maiden.
So'yokwuuti: (no English translation). Ogre Woman.
Suyang'evu: "Left-handed one." Called "Suyang'ephoya" on Third Mesa.
Taatangaya: "Hornet."
Talavaykatsina: "Morning katsina."

Tasapkatsina: "Navajo katsina."
Tasapkatsinmana or Tasapmana: "Navajo maiden."
Tasapkatsinmuykwa'am: "Grandfather of the Navajo katsinam."
Tawakatsina: "Sun katsina."
Tiwenu: not a Hopi word; perhaps a Keres personage.
Tsaaveyo: (no English translation). An Ogre.
Tsöpkatsina: "Pronghorn katsina."
Tsukatsina: "Rattlesnake katsina."
Tsu'sona: "Snake dancer." Not a katsina; a denotative term to describe a member of the snake society.
Tuhavi: "Paralyzed katsina."
Umtoynaqa: "One Who Makes Thunder."
Wakaskatsina: "Cow katsina."
Wiharu: (no English translation). A white ogre.
Wiktsina: "Grease katsina." A racer katsina also known as Wiktsinhoya.
Wupamokatsina: "A Mong or Chief katsina and a Guard"
Wuyaktaywa: "Broadface katsina."
Wuyaqqötö: "Big Head." A descriptive term that refers to the Wupamo katsina who no longer appears at Third Mesa. Sometimes erroneously referred to as Wuyaktaywa, an entirely different katsina.
Yöngökatsina: "Prickly Pear Cactus katsina."
Yowe: "Priest Killer katsina." A figure related to the 1680 Pueblo revolt on Hopiland.

BIBLIOGRAPHY

Ahtone, Heather, et al. 2013. *Hopituy: Hopi Art from the Permanent Collections*. Norman: University of Oklahoma Press.

Antes, Horst, Wolfgang Haberland, and Badisches Landesmuseum Karlsruhe. 1981. *Kachina-Figuren der Pueblo-Indianer Nordamerikas aus der Studiensammlung Horst Antes*. Karlsruhe, Germany: Badisches Landesmuseum.

Arizona Archives Online, operated by Northern Arizona University (NAU). http:// www.azarchivesonline.org/xtf/view?docId=ead/nau/fredericks_white_bear.xml;query=;brand=default.

Bassman, Theda. 1997. *Treasures of the Hopi*. Flagstaff, AZ: Northland.

Bassman, Theda, and Gene Balzer. 1991. *Hopi Kachina Dolls and Their Carvers*. West Chester, PA: Schiffer.

Bassman, Theda, Cecil Calnimptewa, and Gene Balzer. 1994. *The Kachina Dolls of Cecil Calnimptewa: Their Power—Their Splendor.* Tucson, AZ: Treasure Chest Publications.

Branson, Oscar. 1992. *Hopi Indian Kachina Dolls*. Tucson, AZ: Treasure Chest Publications.

Breuning, Robert, and Michael Lomatuway'ma. 1983. "Kachina Dolls, Form and Function of Hopi Tithu." *Plateau* 54, no. 4. Flagstaff: Museum of Northern Arizona.

———. 1992. "Hopi Kachina Dolls." *Plateau* 63, no. 4. Flagstaff: Museum of Northern Arizona.

Bromberg, Erik. 1986. *The Hopi Approach to the Art of Kachina Doll Carving.* West Chester, PA: Schiffer.

Colton, Harold Sellers. 1959. *Hopi Kachina Dolls with a Key to Their Identification.* Albuquerque: University of New Mexico Press.

Crane, Leo. 1925. *Indians of the Enchanted Desert*. Boston: Little, Brown.

David, Neil, J. Brent Ricks, and Alexander E. Anthony. 1993. *Kachinas, Spirit Beings of the Hopi*. Albuquerque, NM: Avanyu.

Day, Jonathan. 2000. *Traditional Hopi Kachinas*. Flagstaff, AZ: Northland.

El-Habib, Beatrice, and Vincent Grille. 1999. *La Danse des Kachinas*. Paris, France: Paris Musees.

Erickson, Jon T. 1977. *Kachinas: An Evolving Hopi Art Form?* Phoenix, AZ: Heard Museum.

Fewkes, Jesse Walter, Smithsonian Institution, and Bureau of American Ethnology. 1903; reissue 1982. *Hopi Katcinas Drawn by Native Artists*. Glorieta, NM: Rio Grande.

Giago, Tim, and Denise Giago. 2006. *Children Left Behind: The Dark Legacy of Indian Mission Boarding Schools*. Santa Fe, NM: Clear Light.

Gilbert, Matthew Sakiestewa. 2010. *Education Beyond the Mesas: Hopi Students at Sherman Institute, 1902–1929*. Lincoln: University of Nebraska Press.

Gorg, Alan. 2009. DVD: *Autobiography of a Hopi*. Techquaikachi.wordpress.com

Hartmann, Horst. 1978. *Kachina-Figuren der Hopi-Indianer.* Berlin, Germany: Museum für Volkerkunde.

Hopi Dictionary Project. 1998. *Hopi Dictionary*. Tucson: University of Arizona Press.

Jacka, Jerry, and Lois Essary Jacka. 1998. *Art of the Hopi*. Flagstaff, AZ: Northland Press.

Kabotie, Michael. Artist Hopid reference. https://en.wikipedia.org/wiki/Michael_Kabotie

Keane, Maribeth, and Bonnie Monte. 2010. "Katsina or Kachina? Barry Walsh on the Spiritual Roots of Native American Dolls." *Collector's Weekly*. http://www.collectorsweekly.com/articles/katsina-or-kachina-barry-walsh-on-the-spiritual-roots-of-native-american-dolls/.

Kennard, Edward A., and Edwin Earle. 1971. *Hopi Kachinas*, 2nd Edition. New York: Museum of the American Indian, Heye Foundation.

Kessler, Alan. 1988. *Collecting Kachina Dolls*. Santa Fe, NM: Alan Kessler.

Kramer, Barbara. 1996. *Nampeyo and Her Pottery*. Albuquerque: University of New Mexico Press.

Kunze, Albert. 1988. *Hopi und Kachina: Indianische Kultur im Wandel*. Munich, Germany: Trickster.

Lajimodiere, Denise K., and Andrea Carmen. 2014. "The case of boarding schools in the United States of America." In *Indigenous Peoples' Access to Justice*, edited by Wilton Littlechild and Elsa Stamatopoulou. New York: Institute for the Study of Human Rights, Columbia University.

Loloma, Charles. https://en.wikipedia.org/wiki/Charles_Loloma

Loscher, Tricia. 2005. "The Volz Collection of Hopi Katsina Dolls at the Heard Museum." *American Indian Art Magazine* 30, no. 3. (Summer): 78–96.

McLeod, Roxie. 1994. "Dreams and Rumors: A History of *Book of the Hopi*." M.A. thesis, University of Colorado at Boulder.

Musee d'Arts. 1994. *Kachina*. Marseille, France: Musees de Marseille.

Nequatewa, Edmund. 1936/2008. *Truth of a Hopi*. London: Forgotten Books.

Nequatewa, Edmund, and Alfred Whiting. 1934/1992. *Born a Chief*. Tucson: University of Arizona Press.

Pearlstone, Zena. 2018. *Brian Honyouti: Hopi Carver*. Bloomington, IN: iUniverse.

Pecina, Ron, and Bob Pecina. 2011. *Neil David's Hopi World*. Atglen, PA: Schiffer.

———. 2013. *Hopi Kachinas: History, Legends, and Art*. Atglen, PA: Schiffer.

Schaaf, Gregory. 2008. *Hopi Katsina: 1600 Artist Biographies*. Sante Fe, NM: CIAC Press.

Secakuku, Alph. 1995. *Following the Sun and Moon*. Flagstaff, AZ: Northland.

Struever, Martha Hopkins. 2005. *Loloma: Beauty Is His Name*. Santa Fe, NM: Wheelwright Museum of the American Indian.

Talahongva, Patty. 2004. "Master Hopi Carver Ernest Moore." *Native Peoples*, (January/February): 58–60.

Tanner, Clara Lee, and Ray Manley. 1980. *Ray Manley's Hopi Kachinas*. Ray Manley Publishing.

Techqua Ikachi, accessed September 4, 2018. http://www.jnanadana.org/hopi/techqua_ikachi_i.html.

Teiwes, Helga. 1991. *Kachina Dolls: The Art of Hopi Carvers*. Tucson: University of Arizona Press.

Titiev, Mischa. 1992; originally published 1944. *Old Oraibi: A Study of the Hopi Indians of Third Mesa*. Albuquerque: University of New Mexico Press.

Walsh, Barry. 1993. "The Emerging Trend of Old Style Hopi Kachina Dolls." *Indian Trader*, (September).

———. 1994. "The Controversial Mass Production of Navajo 'Kachina' Dolls." *Indian Trader*, (March).

———. 1994. "The Controversial Mass Production of Navajo 'Kachina' Dolls." *Focus: Santa Fe*, (August/September).

———. 1998. "Kikmongwi as Artist, The Katsina Dolls of Wilson Tawaquaptewa." *American Indian Art Magazine* 24, no. 1 (Winter).

———. 2000. Foreword to *Traditional Hopi Kachinas* by Jonathan S. Day. Flagstaff, AZ: Northland.

———. 2001. "The Katsina Carvings of Otto Pentewa." *American Indian Art Magazine* 26, no. 3 (Summer).

———. 2010. "Katsinas, Wilson Tawaquaptewa, the Dick Jemison Collection." Catalogue for the Birmingham Museum of Art. Birmingham, AL: Birmingham Museum of Art.

———. 2016. "Mavasta Honyouti: Profile of an Innovative Hopi Artist." *ATADA News*. https://www.atada.org/atada-news.

———. 2016. "Wilson Tawaquaptewa, Hopi Katsina Carvings from the Don Redlich Collection." Catalogue for the Laird-Norton Center for Art & Design. Winona, MN: Winona State University.

———. 2017. "The Complex Genius of James Kootshongsie" (Jimmie Koots). *Native American Art Magazine* (February/March), 72–77.

———. 2018. "Dramatic Evolutions: The Transformations of Manuel Denet Chavarria." *Native American Art Magazine* (February/March), 78–83.

———. 2018. "Turning the Power: The Life and Katsinam of Wilson Tawaquaptewa." *Native American Art Magazine* (February/March), 74–77.

Walsh, Barry, and Valerie Wedge. 2003. "Jimmie Kewanwytewa—Carver and Cultural Emissary." *Plateau Journal* 7, no. 2 (Fall/Winter). Flagstaff: Museum of Northern Arizona.

Washburn, Dorothy, Ed. 1980. *Hopi Kachina*. San Francisco: California Academy of Sciences.

Waters, Frank. 1963. *Book of the Hopi*. New York: Penguin.

———. 1969. *Pumpkin Seed Point*. Athens: Ohio University Press.

Whiteley, Peter. 1988. *Deliberate Acts*. Tucson: University of Arizona Press.

Wright, Barton. 1973. *Kachinas*. Flagstaff, AZ: Northland.

———. 1975. *Kachinas*. Phoenix, AZ: Heard Museum.

———. 1977. *Hopi Kachinas: The Complete Guide to Collecting Kachina Dolls*. Flagstaff, AZ: Northland.

———. 1979. *Hopi Material Culture*. Flagstaff, AZ: Northland.

———. 1994. *Clowns of the Hopi*. Flagstaff, AZ: Northland.

———. 1997. Personal communication re: Tawaquaptewa and Jimmie K.

PHOTO CREDITS

Robert Stephen Albert: Pages 206, 207, 209, 210, 212, 213
Gene Balzer: Pages 80, 83, 106, 107, 108, 117
Susanna B. Clark: Pages, 8, 12, 13, 15, 22, 25, 26, 37, 39, 77, 78, 79 bottom
Paul Coze: Page 30
Steve Elmore: Page 125
Peter ffoulkes: Pages 48, 151, 152 bottom, 153, 168, 185
Ryan Gashweseoma: Page 190
John Hill: Page 45
Kevin Honyouti: Pages 228, 229, 230, 231
Mavasta Honyouti: Pages 224, 226
Ronald Honyouti: Page 109
Randy Lazarus Collection: Page 100
Survival International: Page 70
Steven Lawrence: Pages 38 bottom, 187
Manfred Susunkewa: Page 136
Dan Vaillancourt: Pages iv–v, vi, 10, 14, 20, 28, 29, 35, 36, 38 top, 43, 46–47, 63, 73, 74, 75, 76, 79 top, 132, 133, 134, 135, 138, 148, 150, 152 top, 155, 216, 217, 218
Anna Walsh: Pages iv, 4, 9, 11, 16, 17, 19, 23, 24, 40, 44, 54, 55, 60, 61 top and bottom, 62, 64, 66 top and bottom, 67, 68, 69, 84, 86, 88, 89, 90, 91, 92, 94, 96 top, 96 bottom, 97, 99, 101, 102, 104, 110, 112, 115, 116, 118, 129, 130, 142, 143 top and bottom, 144, 145, 146, 154, 156, 160, 166, 169, 170, 172, 173, 174, 176, 177, 178, 179, 180, 181, 182, 186, 188, 189, 196, 197, 198, 200, 201, 203, 204, 205, 214, 219, 220, 221, 222, 225, 226 top
Barry Walsh: Page 193

COLLECTION CREDITS

Jared Aragon collection: Page 218
Howard Bowlin Collection: Page 85
Michael Boxer Collection: Pages 68, 155, 179, 181
Burkhardt family collection: Page 121, 124
Jason Cohn Collection: Page 46-47
Janice and Joseph Day Collection: Pages 90, 141, 142, 145, 160
Peg DeMouthe: Pages 49, 151, 152 bottom, 153, 168, 170, 185,
Private collection: Page 6
Steve Fischer Collection: Pages 220, 221
Suzanne Golt Collection: Pages, 8, 12, 13, 15, 22, 25, 26, 37, 39, 76, 78, 79 bottom
Janice Gonsalves Collection: Page 63
John C. Hill/ Barry Walsh Collection: Page 45
Phil Krotz collection: Page 126, 173
Randy Lazarus Collection: Page 28, 100, 138
Pat and Kim Messier Collection: Pages 50, 52, 105, 122, 123, 128, 162
Museum of Northern Arizona: Pages 4: E5933; 11: E3748; 16: E3814m E3768, E3823; 17: E7371, E3785, E3771; 19: E4427; 58: E2508A-D; 59: E2450, E2394; 67: E7198; 80: IL 2011-73-42; 83: E6357; 91: E7545; 92: IL2015-81-1; 96: E8308, E10736; 97: E2996; 99: E8057, E8246; 102: EDU-ETH-248; 104: E5475, E5474; 106: IL 2009-35-79; 107: IL 2010-32-88; 108: IL 2010-32-71; 110: E11941; 112: E6376; 115: IL2010-32-128; 116: IL2010-32-171; 117: IL2011-73-129; 178: E11941
Bob & Le Oehrli Collection: Page 57 top and bottom
Paul Plener collection: Page 227
Barbara Rice Collection: Page 141, 158, 161,
Goldeen Selmer Collection: Page 38 bottom, 187

INDEX

Note: Page references in *italics* refer to illustrative matter.

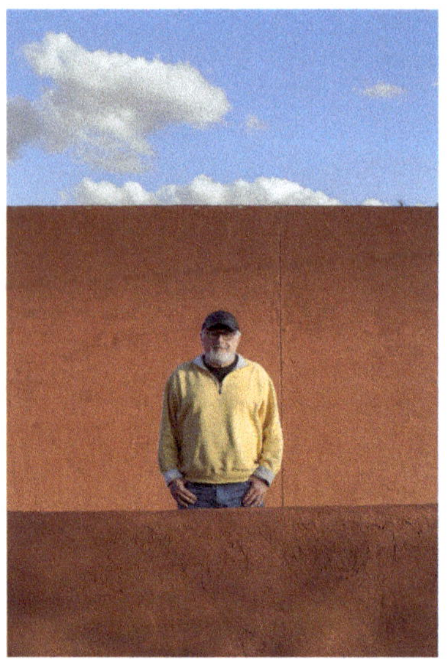

BARRY WALSH owns Buffalo Barry's Indian Art with his wife, Valerie Wedge. They specialize in Hopi material, especially antique and traditional-style katsina carvings. Barry has written extensively on Hopi katsina carvers from the past and present. In his other life, Barry is a PhD therapist who has specialized in treating people with self-injury and/or suicidality. He has presented internationally and written three books on these subjects.

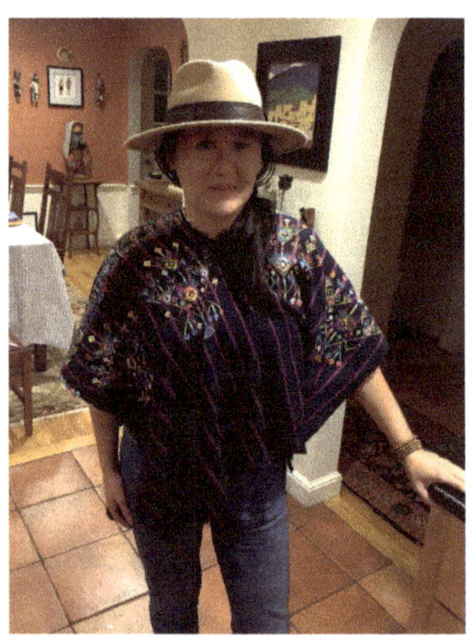

ANNA WALSH was born in Korea and raised in Massachusetts. She has been taking photographs most of her life. She studied photography and video at the Art Institute of Boston, New England School of Photography, and Massachusetts College of Art and Design. In addition to Native American art, Anna specializes in commercial, editorial, portraiture, and documentary photography.

www.ingramcontent.com/pod-product-compliance
Lightning Source LLC
LaVergne TN
LVHW070931160826
845679LV00018B/1775

9781940322353